CITY INVINCIBLE

I dream'd in a dream I saw a city invincible to the
   attacks of the whole of the rest of the earth,
I dream'd that was the new city of Friends.

WALT WHITMAN

The Symposium in Session in the Oriental Institute Museum

CITY INVINCIBLE

A Symposium on

URBANIZATION AND CULTURAL DEVELOPMENT IN THE ANCIENT NEAR EAST,

University of Chicago, 1958.

HELD AT THE ORIENTAL INSTITUTE
OF THE UNIVERSITY OF CHICAGO

DECEMBER 4–7, 1958

EDITED FOR THE PLANNING COMMITTEE

By

CARL H. KRAELING *and* ROBERT M. ADAMS

THE UNIVERSITY OF CHICAGO PRESS
CHICAGO · ILLINOIS

Oriental Institute Special Publication

Library of Congress Catalog Number: 60-13791

THE UNIVERSITY OF CHICAGO PRESS, CHICAGO 37
Cambridge University Press, London, N.W. 1, England
The University of Toronto Press, Toronto 5, Canada

Preface

On several occasions in the forty-odd years of its history the Oriental Institute of the University of Chicago has arranged conferences and symposia on stated topics, some compacted into successive days, others consisting of meetings held at regular weekly or monthly intervals, some participated in by members of other departments and universities, some held in the bosom of the family, so to speak. Such conferences fill a real need in the life of any group of scholars, counteracting the tendency of the individual to lose himself in the minutiae of his own work, furnishing opportunities for expressing and defending cherished convictions and, above all, providing occasions to systematize the subject matter of vast fields of knowledge in new ways. In the study of ancient Near Eastern civilization, where the guidelines that give coherence and meaning to masses of factual information are still only emerging, such effort to systematize is not only of the highest necessity but can also become a criterion of the effectiveness and leadership of any scholarly group.

The purpose of this symposium was to explore the circumstances under which in the Near East man for the first time in human history attained those higher levels of cultural life that we associate with the word "civilized." In Mesopotamia, at least, the great upward surge of the cultural process that continued the momentum gained in the technological revolution of the neolithic period coincided with the appearance of man's first great urban centers. What ecological and other factors led to the growth of cities? How does the life of the concentrated urban society affect culture? When the city-state gives way to empire is the culture pattern changed? These are some of the questions we had in mind.

The planning of the symposium was in the hands of a committee consisting of Professors R. J. Braidwood, Gustave Von Grunebaum (then a regular staff member of the Institute and now an Honorary Associate), Thorkild Jacobsen, John A. Wilson, and the undersigned. If the sessions as they actually transpired at the Institute on December 4–7, 1958, were a success, it was in large measure because of the careful preliminary work that spread over a period of several years and because of the co-operation of all of those who planned, prepared for, and participated in the event. To all of them the Institute owes and expresses its sincere thanks.

Two elements of the planning deserve special mention to explain certain features both of the event and of this report upon it. The first is the fact that the Planning Committee did not wish to have the time of the several sessions pre-empted by the presentation of long "set papers." What it wanted was an opportunity for free discussion. It was therefore decided that such "set papers" as might be desired should be prepared and distributed in advance of the meetings. This was done. As to the nature of the "background papers," it was decided that they should present primarily materials on topics germane to the discussion but drawn from other periods and from other areas than the ancient Near East. That is, they should set a wider frame of reference for the issues of immediate concern. This was of particular importance because the interaction between societal growth and cultural change, the way in which changes in environment, transportation, technology, and security tend to bring people together into even larger groups, and the continuous readaptation of culture to the complexities and the opportunities of expanded societies are, after all, phenomena typical of human life generally. The Near Eastern specialist needs to be able to see what happened in his sphere of interest in the light of developments elsewhere, just as the specialist in other disciplines can be expected to profit by observing how language, literature, legal and political institutions, social mores, art, and religion first came to flower when time was young and the urban matrix of culture emerged for the first time in history in the context of the ancient Near East. The papers pointing up the comparisons are therefore an essential part of both the symposium and this report and, properly used, should stimulate further thought upon the issues discussed. In this report they follow the record of the discussions, because this position seems more appropriate for documents that will provide occasion for further reflection.

The second aspect of the planning that deserves mention here is related in character to the first. Scholarship in a democratic society cannot move in a vacuum, and scholars have at all times to be conscious of their relation to the ongoing process of societal development. If the professional Orientalist needs to see the phenomena of cultural transformation in terms of the experiences of other societies, both he and the student of more recent periods need to apply their perspective to the interpretation of the contemporary scene. The city is not only still with us; it is perhaps the greatest single problem with which society has to cope as a matrix and menace of human civilization. Nowhere is this more evident than in the megalopolises of the United States, among them, of course, the city of Chicago, and at Chicago the problem is one in which the University of Chicago is currently taking a hand under the leadership of Chancellor Lawrence A. Kimpton, with the support of the University's Board of Trustees, the University's Citizens Board, and the appropriate agencies of the city, the state, and the federal government. Under these circumstances the Planning Committee decided to ask Lewis Mumford, who more than any other single individual has concerned himself with the city on the American scene, to participate in the discussions and to provide introductory and concluding remarks. The introductory remarks under the title "University City" were delivered at a luncheon meeting of the Citizens Board of the University held at the Chicago Club on the opening day of the sessions, with the members of the symposium attending as guests of the University. All other sessions were held in the Oriental Institute Museum.

We have chosen as the "short title" of this report two words from a poem of Walt Whitman because the adjective "invincible" describes so graphically the dominant, commanding role of the city in the development of culture and because we believe that without the vision of the "new city of Friends" the eternal struggle to make this powerful force serve its highest purposes must fail, especially now when under attack cities are the most vulnerable of all human institutions.

A few words will suffice for the more routine matters. The Planning Committee found itself in the usual embarrassment of wishing to invite more guests than those whose names appear in the list of members but adhered firmly to the principle that the number must not be so large as to make an effective exchange of ideas impossible. Our apologies are extended to those who should have been invited and were not. The work of reproducing what was said at the sessions proved much more complicated than we had calculated and fell on the shoulders largely of Robert M. Adams and myself. The discussions were taped, typed from the tapes, edited by Adams and myself, and submitted (like the papers) to the participants for their approval and correction. Footnotes were added, mostly by the participants but in some cases by the editors, for elucidation or documentation of certain remarks. We have compressed the record by omitting what was purely circumstantial but in all other respects have tried to preserve the spontaneity of the discussions. Naturally we have refrained from adding conclusions or syntheses where they did not in fact emerge. Participants in the discussions are referred to at the beginnings of their remarks by their last names only but can be identified further from the list of members (pp. xi–xiv).

CARL H. KRAELING, *Director*
The Oriental Institute

CHICAGO, ILLINOIS
February 1960

Table of Contents

The Members of the Symposium

PROTAGONISTS

ABBOT, NABIA. Professor of Islamic Studies, Oriental Institute, University of Chicago.

ADAMS, ROBERT M. Assistant Professor, Oriental Institute and Department of Anthropology, University of Chicago.

AL-ASIL, NAJI. Director General Emeritus, Department of Antiquities of Iraq.

ALBRIGHT, WILLIAM F. Spence Professor of Semitic Languages Emeritus, Johns Hopkins University.

BRAIDWOOD, ROBERT J. Oriental Institute Professor of Old World Prehistory and Professor of Anthropology, University of Chicago.

BRONEER, OSCAR T. Professor of Classical Archeology, University of Chicago.

BROWN, FRANK E. Dunham Professor of Latin, Yale University.

CAMERON, GEORGE G. Professor of Near Eastern Cultures, University of Michigan.

DELOUGAZ, PINHAS P. Associate Professor of Near Eastern Archeology, Oriental Institute, University of Chicago.

EDGERTON, WILLIAM F. Professor of Egyptology, Oriental Institute, University of Chicago.

ELIADE, MIRCEA. Professor of History of Religions, University of Chicago.

FERNEA, ROBERT. Danforth Fellow in Anthropology, University of Chicago.

GELB, IGNACE J. Professor of Assyriology, Oriental Institute, University of Chicago.

GIBB, HAMILTON A. R. Jewett Professor of Arabic, Harvard University.

GLUECK, NELSON. President and Professor of Bible and Biblical Archeology, Hebrew Union College—Jewish Institute of Religion.

GOETZE, ALBRECHT. Sterling Professor of Assyriology, Yale University.

GRENE, DAVID. Lecturer on Classical Civilization, University of Chicago.

GÜTERBOCK, HANS G. Professor of Hittitology, Oriental Institute, University of Chicago.

The Members of the Symposium

HARRIS, CHAUNCEY D. Professor of Geography, University of Chicago.

HAYEK, FRIEDRICH A. Professor on the Committee on Social Thought, University of Chicago.

HOSELITZ, BERT F. Professor of the Social Sciences, University of Chicago.

JACOBSEN, THORKILD. Professor of Social Institutions, Oriental Institute, University of Chicago.

KANTOR, HELENE J. Research Associate (Associate Professor), Oriental Institute, University of Chicago.

KLUCKHOHN,† CLYDE. Professor of Anthropology, Harvard University.

KNIGHT, FRANK H. Morton D. Hull Distinguished Service Professor of Social Sciences and Philosophy Emeritus, University of Chicago.

KRAELING, CARL H. Professor of Hellenistic Oriental Archeology, Oriental Institute, University of Chicago.

KRAMER, SAMUEL N. Clark Research Professor of Assyriology, University Museum, University of Pennsylvania.

LANDSBERGER, BENNO. Professor of Assyriology Emeritus, Oriental Institute, University of Chicago.

LARSEN, JAKOB A. O. Professor of Ancient History Emeritus, University of Chicago.

LOEHR, MAX. Professor of Far Eastern Art and Archeology, University of Michigan.

MCNEILL, WILLIAM H. Professor of History, University of Chicago.

MUMFORD, LEWIS. Visiting Bemis Professor in the School of Architecture and Planning, Massachusetts Institute of Technology.

OPPENHEIM, A. LEO. Professor of Assyriology, Oriental Institute, University of Chicago.

PARKER, RICHARD A. Wilbour Professor of Egyptology, Brown University.

PERKINS, ANN L. Research Associate in Classics, Yale University.

POLANYI, KARL. Professor of Economics Emeritus, Columbia University.

RHEINSTEIN, MAX. Max Pam Professor of Comparative Law, University of Chicago.

SEELE, KEITH C. Professor of Egyptology, Oriental Institute, University of Chicago.

SINGER, MILTON. Paul Klapper Professor of the Social Sciences, University of Chicago.

SMITH, GERTRUDE E. Edward Olson Professor of Greek, University of Chicago.

SPEISER, E. A. Ellis Professor of Hebrew and Semitic Languages and Literatures, University of Pennsylvania.

STRAUSS, LEO. Professor of Political Philosophy, University of Chicago.

TAX, SOL. Professor of Anthropology, University of Chicago.

THORNTHWAITE, C. WARREN. Director, Laboratory of Climatology, Centerton, New Jersey; Professorial Lecturer in Climatology, University of Chicago.

THRUPP, SYLVIA L. Associate Professor of the Social Sciences, University of Chicago.

VON GRUNEBAUM, GUSTAVE E. Director, Near Eastern Center, University of California.

WELLES, C. BRADFORD. Professor of Ancient History, Yale University.

WHITE, GILBERT F. Professor of Geography, University of Chicago.

WILLEY, GORDON R. Bowditch Professor of Archeology, Harvard University.

WILSON, JOHN A. Andrew MacLeish Distinguished Service Professor of Egyptology, Oriental Institute, University of Chicago.

OTHER MEMBERS

BOWMAN, RAYMOND A. Associate Professor of Oriental Languages, University of Chicago.

BRAIDWOOD, LINDA S. Associate, Oriental Institute, University of Chicago.

GEVIRTZ, STANLEY. Instructor in Palestinian History, University of Chicago.

HAINES, RICHARD C. Field Architect and Field Director, Nippur Expedition, Oriental Institute, University of Chicago.

HALLOCK, RICHARD T. Research Associate (Assistant Professor), Oriental Institute, University of Chicago.

HANSEN, DONALD P. Junior Prize Fellow of the Society of Fellows, Harvard University.

HODGSON, MARSHALL G. S. Assistant Professor on the Committee on Social Thought, University of Chicago.

HOWE, BRUCE. Research Fellow in Paleolithic Archeology, Peabody Museum, Harvard University.

The Members of the Symposium

HUGHES, GEORGE R. Associate Professor of Egyptology, Oriental Institute, University of Chicago.

JOHNSON, FRANKLIN P. Associate Professor of Art, University of Chicago.

KNUDSTAD, JAMES. Junior Field Architect, Oriental Institute, University of Chicago.

KRACKE, EDWARD A., JR. Associate Professor of Middle Chinese Literature and Institutions, University of Chicago.

MAHDI, MUHSIN. Assistant Professor of Arabic, University of Chicago.

MIKESELL, MARVIN W. Instructor in Geography, University of Chicago.

PITT-RIVERS, JULIAN A. Visiting Professor of Anthropology, University of Chicago.

REINER, ERICA. Research Associate (Assistant Professor), Oriental Institute, University of Chicago.

ROWTON, MICHAEL B. Research Associate (Instructor), Oriental Institute, University of Chicago.

SMITH, CYRIL S. Professor of Metallurgy, University of Chicago.

SWIFT, GUSTAVUS F., JR. Research Assistant, Oriental Institute, University of Chicago.

WAGNER, PHILIP L. Assistant Professor of Geography, University of Chicago.

WILLOUGHBY, HAROLD R. Professor of Christian Origins Emeritus, University of Chicago.

THE SESSIONS OF THE SYMPOSIUM

Introduction

The introductory session of the symposium, taking the form of a joint luncheon meeting of the participants and the Citizens Board of the University of Chicago at the Chicago Club, Chicago, Illinois, was called to order at 12:50 P.M., Mr. James Downs presiding.

DOWNS (*chairman*): All the meetings of the Citizens Board of the University of Chicago, it seems to me, are treats for those who are privileged to attend, but this one perhaps is augmented in that respect because the Citizens Board today is having an opportunity to hear the opening address of a conference on urbanization and cultural development in the ancient Near East.

The Oriental Institute of the University, under the direction of Professor Kraeling, has called this conference together, and it embraces some seventy scholars from universities all over the country, many of whom are in this audience today. The speech that we are to hear in a few moments is the opening address of that conference.

I would like to greet each of the scholars who are here, and particularly I would like to greet, and ask to rise and take a bow, Dr. Naji al-Asil of Baghdad, a Fellow of the Iraq Academy of Science and former Director General of Antiquities of Iraq.

I suppose that there are occasions when the man whom I am going to ask to talk to you for just a few moments before we introduce our main speaker would be entitled to be introduced as a distinguished scholar and educator. I, however, would like to introduce him to you as a man who has made a greater contribution to the long-term welfare of the city of Chicago than almost anyone I know and who has taken his job in the context of what it means to a great city and has done it excellently.

I mean, of course, Chancellor Kimpton.

KIMPTON: Mr. Downs, Professor Mumford, Dr. Al-Asil, members of the Citizens Board, and guests: I am pleased to welcome today not only the members of the Citizens Board but also the distinguished scholars who are participating in a symposium at the Oriental Institute of the University of Chicago. They will discuss a problem of great concern to all of us here—urbanization and cultural development.

It is both symbolic and significant that academicians from all over the country have assembled in the city of Chicago at this time for this purpose. Their coming is a manifestation of the increasing desire for a more critical and profound understanding of a fundamental problem of modern civilization. They will spend a great deal of time on the origins and evolution of the city and will raise—and answer—questions which might seldom occur to the rest of us. But their discussions will have a bearing, as basic scholarship always has, on the day-to-day concerns of Chicago.

This gathering of scholars to treat a fundamental problem in a fundamental way is one of the things that a university is best equipped to stage. But a university's responsibility cannot end here. A university, because it is a strong and important institution of the city, has a responsibility to share in an active program to make it a better place in which to work and live.

I cannot truthfully say that we have always clearly recognized this obligation; for years we were content merely to analyze and study our city. Until our own neighborhood was threatened, we were as little disposed as anyone else to bring our resources to bear on our common urban problem of blight and slum. I hope I can say honestly at this point that we have helped develop a program of urban renewal which goes far beyond our own concern for survival and contains valuable lessons for Chicago and for the nation. I hasten to add that whatever has been accomplished has been possible only because of the active interest of the Mayor and his executive departments, the City Council, federal and state officials, and many, many private citizens.

What are the lessons to be learned from the last six years? I cannot yet fully answer this question, since there is still much to be learned, but let me touch on a couple of points.

The first lesson is that a community can pull itself up by its bootstraps. Perhaps this is the most important outcome of the Hyde Park–Kenwood program; it is now dramatically clear that slum and blight are not inexorable processes.

Second, it is also clear that a renewal program can be accomplished on a partnership basis, that all elements of the community have something to contribute. As essential as governmental participation was and is, urban renewal need not sit back and wait for a fully organized and financed government program; there must be a partnership of public agencies and private initiative to do the job.

We have come very far in a few years. We have a long way still to go. We are better equipped than we have ever been, thanks to all the people I have mentioned, including the scholars present, who provide us with inspiration through fundamental and original ideas about urban life.

There is no longer doubt in my mind that we will meet our goals and that we will show the way to a university city which will provide a model for our city of Chicago and our nation.

Downs: Thank you, Chancellor Kimpton.

I see in this room many distinguished citizens who have made a great contribution to the trend of our society in the form of economics, politics, building construction—every phase of city development.

Our speaker today is a philosopher and a man of letters who, during the thirties, began to take a profound interest in the impact of modern technology on the environment in which we live.

From that period came his well-known books—*Technics in Civilization* and *The Culture of Cities.*

From 1952 to 1956 he was Professor of City and Regional Planning at the University of Pennsylvania, and, at present, he is serving as visiting Bemis Professor in the School of Architecture and Planning at the Massachusetts Institute of Technology.

His concern with the place of universities in contemporary culture is shown by his contribution to the volume on *The University and the Future of America.*

Today we are to hear a talk on the subject "University City."

It is a great pleasure to present to this audience our speaker, Professor Lewis Mumford.

UNIVERSITY CITY

Mumford: Mr. Chairman, learned colleagues, distinguished guests: I regret to say that the talk that you are going to hear this afternoon is an inferior version of the one which I gave sometime around three o'clock this morning, between Buffalo, New York, and South Bend, Indiana.

I will do my best to remember some of the excellent points I made in that talk, but then I cannot guarantee, after a night on the train, that they will all be there.[1]

This is a very exciting occasion because the real theme of what I am going to say today is the relation between power and culture—the relation between La Salle Street and Ellis Avenue—and this is something that goes back to the very origin of society.

I myself have already learned a great deal from the distinguished archeologists who have been working here at the University of Chicago and in other sister institutions. While you may perhaps be interested in the new projects for space travel, shooting rockets to the moon or to some other planet, I assure you that the work that these gentlemen have done in exploring time is infinitely more interesting.

Nothing is really more boring than fast navigation in space. The faster you go, the less you see; and, the less you see, the more the place you get to resembles the place you have just left. Explorations in time, however, are explorations in human depth, and, when you follow the work of these scholars, you will understand that there is far more to learn from an Egyptian mummy than from what is left of life in a space-man today. The person who will travel to the moon will probably be in a comatose state most of the journey and will have very little to reveal except how the apparatus worked when he finally gets back. Therefore, this is rather a time when we can listen with profit to what the archeologists have been finding about the beginnings of our urban life. In the very beginnings of the ancient city we shall find more than one clue to the processes that are now bringing the city, in its overgrown historic form, to an end.

I myself got a great illumination a few years ago when I was giving a course dealing with the religions of the ancient world. Face to face with the gods of Mesopotamia and Egypt, I suddenly realized that the deities of those days, with their exorbitant claims of power, with their push-button commands and their methods of remote control, with their obvious pleasure in demolishing a whole city if it suited their purposes, were all, in fact, expressing a new ideology of power, which contrasted with the preoccupation with fertility, reproduction, and nurture that characterized the old village culture, with its necessarily modest and limited ambitions. What struck me was that the powers reserved to cosmic deities in the late Stone and Bronze Ages have become the workaday realities of our own period. And we can

[1] In revising the stenotypist's copy, I have taken the liberty to recall and restore some of these forgotten points.

realize the danger we are in today if we examine the behavior of those ancient gods, who wielded unlimited power, like us, before they had learned the ways of understanding and love or practiced the life-conserving restrictions of morality.

Mind you, what I say about the city and the university today I must say with my fingers crossed, for here are my superiors in every department listening to me. I must try to interpret some of their diggings in the ancient cities to you, putting together and interpreting the scattered fragments, and yet I cannot hope to do it to their satisfaction. As one of the notable scholars here remarked to me just before lunch: "During the last nine years my views about Egypt have very considerably changed." Though digging and translating old documents seem to go on slowly, it is hard to keep up with fresh discoveries that keep pouring in. Therefore, how can I go further without uttering in advance an uneasy prayer for their scholarly forgiveness?

If I read the record right, the first beginning of urban life, the first time the city proper becomes visible, was marked by a sudden increase in power in every department and by a magnification of the role of power itself in the affairs of men. A variety of institutions had hitherto existed separately, bringing their members together in a common meeting place, at seasonable intervals: the hunter's camp, the sacred monument or shrine, the paleolithic ritual cave, the neolithic agricultural village—all these coalesced in a bigger meeting place, the city. What caused this to take place is open to divergent interpretations. My own best guess comes from the finding, in the heart of so many ancient cities, of a formidable walled inclosure, a citadel, a sacred precinct dominated by the temple and the palace. At some point in human development, somewhere perhaps between the establishment of the Egyptian solar calendar and the organization of the Sumerian phalanx, there was a sudden fusion of sacred power and secular power, which produced the nucleus of the city. With this came a new kind of container, more complex than the village, which brought together relatively large numbers of men and held them together in a new pattern of relations. All this enormously increased their scope and their working efficiency. The original form of this container lasted for some six thousand years; only a few centuries ago did it begin to break up. At the center was the civic nucleus, where the organs of both power and culture were concentrated; around it were the houses and footways of the old village, now united in a larger unity, firmly bounded by a wall that inclosed the whole city.

This union of secular and sacred power greatly simplified the art of centralized government, for the palace, the temple, and the granary not merely monopolized the main agents of political and economic power but, by their architectural magnificence, expressed in symbolic language that even the illiterate could easily understand, imposed respect and obedience upon the mass of the population. By these means a whole region, finally a whole river valley, might be transformed into a single co-operative unit. The city itself was conceived as an image of the universe, an example of cosmic order in the midst of confusion and insecurity. You came to the city because there—and only there—the universe was fully represented. All the makings of a significant life could be found within this walled urban container, where men met each other face to face and came close to their common god in the area where his power was greatest.

The city, as it first appears in history, then, did not come about through a mere growth of population or an extension of the market. It was one aspect of the same great expolsion of power, the same widening of human ambitions and human possibilities, that came in with technical improvements like the plow and the potter's wheel, with decisive inventions like writing and permanent record and systematic astronomical observation. And the city played a special part, not merely in bringing together a mixed population and giving them a common meeting place, but in stepping up power itself, accumulating it and storing it in symbolic forms, and transmitting it from generation to generation.

Now there are two forms of power. There is physical power—the power to coerce and command. The rulers of the palace, armed with improved weapons like the Bronze Age chariot and full of audacious confidence, exerted physical power to the limit and often succeeded in bringing large populations, large at least for their days, within the scope of their regime. Then there is an even greater power, which can never be successfully dispensed with—the power of mind. That power was represented originally by the temple, sometimes unified in a pharaoh, who was both a king and a god, a great ruler and a cosmic deity, sometimes, as in Mesopotamia, separated. In the long run, this power of mind is an even more potent one. And there lies the beginning of the university. Of course it was not called a university at first; the functions of the university were mixed up with other sacred powers, of myth, ritual, and magic, carried on by the temple.

But one of the university's main pursuits, the extension of orderly knowledge, based on accurate observation, goes back to the very beginnings of the city.

Neither the city nor the university would have been possible without a great surplus of physical resources and man power: free energy and free time. This surplus derived originally from the great neolithic revolution in agriculture and cattle-breeding. But it was stepped up further because the rulers of the citadel had not merely produced a new urban container for concentrating and storing human energy; they had also invented the first complex machines for applying power at a distance, machines long unrecognized as such because the standardized, uniform, moving parts were composed, not of metal, but of human flesh and bone. These new machines, the military machine and the bureaucratic machine, maximized the power of the new urban centers. By means of the military machine and the bureaucratic machine, large populations of men were systematically regimented and governed as they had never been regimented and governed before. With this new machinery, tens of thousands of men could be marshaled into work armies, capable of building structures like the pyramids of Egypt or the great irrigation systems of Mesopotamia or even turning the course of turbulent rivers.

But physical power alone is ineffective, even as an agent of government. You can use just so much of it, and then your victim dies. Power, to be really effective, has to be transformed and made over into forms that everyone can, in some degree, understand and participate in. That great old Chicago scholar, James Henry Breasted, whose name deservedly stands over the portals of the Oriental Institute, pointed out long ago an interesting fact. Around 3000 B.C. command and understanding both became attributes of Atum, the sun-god. The fact that understanding came to the aid of naked military and political power in general is what made it durable, made it tolerable, because it made power more meaningful. In a measure, understanding has been trying to catch up with power ever since, to give it goals and purposes large enough to include the whole community, to unite the values of the past with the possibilities of the future. For power by itself is meaningless; left to itself, indeed, it tends to be wasteful and destructive. The virtue of the urban container was that up to a point it kept power within bounds and directed it to a common purpose, by creating within the city a life more dynamic and significant, more rich in meaning and value, than was possible in a small, undifferentiated community.

Now one important side of the new urban life was a process of division and differentiation that took place within the human personality itself. When a villager came to the city, he ceased to be a man among men; he became a specialist among specialists. The old neighborly life, of give and take, of share and share alike, following the traditional rules, could not be transported into the city. In coming within the sacred inclosure, the villager left part of himself behind; under the new regime, it might take twenty different kinds of craftsmen and vocational specialists to make a single man. The old Egyptian "Satire on the Trades" seems to be less a satire than a factual description of the disabilities of having to devote a whole lifetime to a single occupation, under the pressures of urban life. The joke is on the scribe who wrote it as well as on the people he felt so much above. To offset this, the city created a sort of super-personality, visible in the city's god or its ruler, who brought all the parts together and, in return for their sacrifice of wholeness and the simple forms of village democracy, gave them a share in vast public works no village could even have dreamed of, much less carried out.

But this inner division of the personality, into vocational specialists, into economic classes and social castes, also had an immensely stimulating function; for within the city it promoted an intermixture of occupations, technological practices, and local customs and local dialects which brought about an intermixture and cross-fertilization. If the neolithic culture produced new strains and crosses in plants, the new urban container promoted cultural hybridization. Hybrid vigor perhaps accounts for some the exuberance of urban culture. With this division, two other things happen. Life itself becomes a drama, and everybody has a part in the drama, gets involved in the plot, and has a role to play. In the city, people escape some of the conformity, the routine, the deadly sameness of the village. Life now becomes a drama; it has a place for the accidental and the unexpected; and it goes forward to something beyond the accustomed and the anticipated. In short, static ritual turns into a dynamic plot.

For the scholars who are here I must note the source of this interpretation of the mission of the city. I learned to understand this passage from Jane Harrison's work on *Ancient Art and Ritual*. There she showed how the spring and harvest festivals of the village, mainly magical invocations of fertility, became transformed almost overnight in the city into drama, with all the old forms and gestures heightened by the tensions and conflicts that urban life promotes. Thus the city itself becomes a theater, and all its inhabitants are included in the cast of characters, in a plot that keeps on knitting and unraveling through successive generations. Before the dramatic stage itself, the audience becomes a participating chorus and comes face to face with its own existence, detached and transformed.

The other function fostered by the city is the dialogue. Within the city you meet face to face people you might have spent all your life looking for if you wandered up and down the great river valleys. Here they are concentrated, and a meaningful exchange takes place. Plenty of literary examples of the dialogue are preserved from the earliest times in Egypt and Mesopotamia; they witness the differentiation and self-consciousness that take place in the city. The verbal dialogue is of course a sort of barter, and it probably preceded the meeting of buyer and seller in the market place; or, rather, the economic function is a by-product of the social opportunity provided by a festival or a funeral. I see Mr. Polanyi sitting here. He has been reinterpreting the principles governing exchange and marketing in the early civilizations before the market itself had an independent existence. Since the early distribution of goods was in the hands of the temple, the modern notion that the market was the chief reason for the city's existence, at least at first, seems to have no foundation. The drama and the dialogue are the central activities: in the city, power and culture meet face to face and influence each other, as they are meeting once again in this room—let us hope to our common benefit.

Now, then, this is where the university comes in. The university is essentially an age-old institution that has taken many forms; but it exists in principle wherever two or three are gathered together in the name of truth. Through the growing force of a body of people dedicated to truth, preserving old truths and searching out new ones, scanning the heavens or searching the hearts of men, the monologue of power was partly replaced, in the city, by the open dialogue of the intellectual life, the inner dialogue of moral understanding. Though the city, from the moment of its origins, exhibited many serious limitations—for war itself, as an institution, seems one of the institutions it brought into existence and magnified—the great achievement of the city was to keep power and understanding within speaking distance of each other. Urban concentration and control increased communication by extending its transmission lines and multiplying the facilities for interchange. That made it possible for both sides of life to develop together. This was a brilliant achievement that compensated for many miseries, repressions, and restraints. How many other inventions have remained practically unaltered for five or six thousand years?

Obviously, the city performed a unique service, or the pattern that first took shape there would not have been transmitted, with only the smallest alterations, to a whole series of different cultures, spreading to every region on earth, or growing up afresh wherever there was the same juncture of forces. But the original form of the city had a serious defect: both the nucleus and the city were walled in. Just because the city was a world in itself, a replica of the cosmos, it remained self-contained; it was easier to destroy the whole city than to create a new pattern of unification and co-operation on a give-and-take basis. What is worse, the social walls within the city, between classes and castes, slowed up the passage of goods and values from the citadel to the whole community. Originally, only the pharaoh had all the attributes of personality; only he was immortal. Some of the mechanical improvements one finds in the earliest palaces—like water closets and tiled drains—did not become general municipal conveniences for thousands of years, and only with the coming of the prophetic religions in Persia, Greece, Palestine, and Arabia did the attributes of personality spread, at least theoretically, to every member of the community.

But the city was both a closed corporation and a closed container. While the citadel retained a virtual monopoly of power and culture, it might transmit a large part of the social inheritance, but only a small part of its potential man power and potential creativity could be employed. Because of the original nature of the city, then, two problems were never quite solved. One was the problem of distributing all the advantages monopolized by the citadel to the rest of the community. Though there is an old Egyptian text in praise of the city Ramses that boasts that in the city the small are like the great, it is doubtful that this was quite true even under the so-called democracies of Greece or the Middle Ages. The other problem that was never solved was how to expand and multiply the functions of the city, in all their increasing complexity, without destroying the form and bursting through the urban container. Even Rome did not solve that, nor any other empire. Rome itself became a vast formless

mass, worse than New York or Chicago, at the very height of its imperial glory. There was something fatally constricted in the very
nature of the original container which balked all attempts to divide
the nucleus and to remove the walls, in order to create a more federated order, circulating power and culture to small and great, to
near and distant.

This brings us to the world that we live in today. If some phantom
archeologists a thousand years from now went peering around over
the face of the earth, seeking amid the still radioactive cinders and
debris for some faint traces of our civilization, and if down deep in
some mine in the Alleghenies he found a cache of documents, hidden
by some provident scholar, he would see that what we proudly called
the rocket age, the space age, or the nuclear age might better be
summed up in a more comprehensive term "The Age of Explosions."
He would point out that our astronomers were talking about an
exploding universe, that our population experts were talking about
an explosion of population, that our city planners were talking about
metropolitan explosions, which were scattering urban dust and rub-
bish all over the landscape; that our immense gains in technology
had come to a climax in a nuclear explosion, or rather a whole series
of blasts, which had brought the whole process to an end, because
we lacked the power to command the physical forces we could produce and lacked the understanding to humanize our specialized
automatons, each working in his isolated cell, even more remote from
face-to-face contact with other human beings than any early rule of
the citadel. Whatever the nature of the explosion, the final result is
the same: to release the particles once held together in the atom,
the chemical molecule, the bomb, or the city, in a fashion that both
disintegrates their own form and destroys all the other srtuctures
within the radius of the container.

Though the contrasts between the earliest form of the city and
our own exploding metropolises are many and obvious, there are
many points of resemblance, too. Like that early age, we live in an
economy of abundance, and one of our most serious problems, in
every department, is the problem of quantity, of distributing and
reapportioning for human purposes the vast quantities of food and
machines we can turn out annually. Unfortunately, ours is just as
one-sided an economy of abundance as that of the early pharaohs—
perhaps more so. We have too many flatulent motor cars and too
few schools; too many salesmen and too few teachers; we have too

many hydrogen bombs and too few people who understand that we cannot go on living indefinitely in a world of overdeveloped weapons and underdeveloped men. Like the early rulers, we have tried to deal with the problem of surpluses, of unassimilable quantities, by developing our own special forms of pyramid-building, not so different from that of the pharaohs as we would like to think.

I realize that Mr. John Wilson has challenged the suggestion that the original Egyptian pyramid-builders were trying to cope with their economy of abundance by oversized public works projects. But, whatever their religious purpose, they were utilizing unemployed labor, apparently not needed in agriculture. Our own form of Keynesian pyramid-building does not work out very differently. Even apart from our short-lived space rockets, those spectacular multi-million-dollar pyramids, there are our six-lane highways spreading across the country, wiping out one city after another, reducing entire urban areas to one low-grade smear, merely in order to give more employment to our oversized and overpowered chariots, in preference to more useful forms of mass locomotion.

In the old days the mark of a city was a temple, a man-made mountain that rose in a green agricultural sea. Now the mark of the city is a spreading mass of debris, a layer of human slag, with a little green island of still unoccupied real estate, sinking in its midst, soon to be submerged and buried. That is the ultimate transformation that we are now threatened with: a transformation which would level away all human variety and distinction, all beautiful form and coherent purpose, as a bulldozer levels the contours of the land and uproots the trees and fills in the brooks to make room for an assembly line of uniform houses, occupied by increasingly uniform people, living uniform lives, laughing at uniform jokes, thinking at a uniformly low intellectual level, and getting their chief recreation by traveling at high speeds to places just as uniform as those they have left. The individuality of city and region, an individuality that gave each collective entity a positive personality, now yields a depersonalized and de-individualized urban mass. The old form of the city has disappeared or is fast disappearing. And the new formlessness is not a city; indeed, it is almost an anti-city, which threatens, like anti-matter, to destroy all the forms and individualities it encounters.

This uncontrolled explosion of power, which has been distributing power in the wrong places or expending it for trivial and harmful purposes, naturally affects the congested cores of the old cities that still survive. But we can no more put the power and culture we now have at our disposal back into the old urban container than we can put the contents of a volcano back into the old crater after it has erupted. Our complex society needs to have its activities sorted out, its essential needs distinguished from its subordinate or insignificant activities, in order to bring about an orderly simplification of the whole day's routine. But we cannot and should not return to the old, isolated container; and we must and should face the problem of creating a new kind of urban organization capable of holding large populations and finding a place, within a new pattern of order, for all their activities.

Those who think that this can be done simply by congesting in a seemingly more orderly way the original overpopulated centers have not, I suggest, yet come to grips with the real problem. The image of the container holds for only one aspect of the city today. To do full justice to our own age, we must think of urbanization in terms of a telephone system or electric power grid, in which the whole system distributes high-tension power or a multitude of messages to local stations—and in turn receives and transmits the power or the messages that they produce. This last part is very important; for one of the worst things about the metropolitan explosion is that it nevertheless has preserved the old monopolistic hold of the citadel and is thereby rapidly creating, even in our own country, a totalitarian order.

Let us look into the implications of this new organization of the city, conceived as a big cultural distribution grid with a multiplication of local urban transformers. How would such an urban reorganization affect the university? Fifty years ago a university with five thousand students was a very big university. Today a university with fifty thousand students cannot accommodate half the students who could profit by its facilities. And though the university has not, like the city, exploded, it is dangerously near the bursting point. Even by purely local changes, it is possible, to a degree, to create a much better organization of these established centers by bringing the too widely scattered university community, particularly its teachers, back within the orbit of the university campus, so that the dialogue that begins in the classroom or the laboratory shall not be abruptly brought to an end by lack of further opportunities for face-to-face contact and communication.

From this standpoint, I am filled with admiration over the plans now being made for the rehabilitation of the whole area around the University of Chicago, so that it shall be a place of residence at least partly for those who work there. The wider and more complex the communications grid becomes, the more abstract the messages, the more necessary it is to recover the old advantages of the village, as an easy meeting place, with everyone within walking distance, more or less, of his neighbors. That is a step in the right direction: the building of a true University City. It will give to the University of Chicago precisely those human advantages that Thomas Jefferson, in his great wisdom, sought long ago to provide for the University of Virginia. Such differentiated communities, limited in population and size, coherent in purpose, are necessary components of the larger urban pattern.

But there is a limit to what can be done in urban improvement on a merely local scale. The next step must lead beyond this into an effective redistribution of the university's services, so that it may extend its advantages to even larger numbers, now drawn to the present center by its well-justified eminence in scholarship. Our further problem is to reapportion some of the administrative load that now falls on the center and to distribute it through a whole network of partly self-governing units, perhaps widely scattered in space, able to accept many of the responsibilities for themselves, while utilizing more fully and constantly the resources of the central institution. The new urban pattern cannot be superimposed on a whole mass of institutions still clinging to the old form they had in the ancient city. There is not a single transformation that is necessary in the city that does not have its counterpart in the organization of the university and likewise in the organization of a great hospital, of a central library, or of a great industrial or business organization. Some of our large industrial corporations, like General Electric, have assimilated this lesson and have instituted a large-scale decentralization of their plants; and, once we throw off the image of the overgrown, overcongested metropolitan container, a new pattern of decentralized organization and federated control will probably define itself, if only because there seems to be no other way of avoiding the grim alternatives of totalitarian coercion or anarchic disorder.

Our problem now, therefore, is to define a new human method of attacking the problem. Do not think that there is any purely mechanical solution open to us: there is only a human way to handle it. I know that there are many people who dream of solving the difficulties of handling large populations by increasing the means of mass communication, doing by one-way television sets what can only be done through a two-day dialogue. Mass communication, so far from being a solution, is actually one of our problems, one of the activities we must find a way of reducing to more human terms, if only by encouraging countermeasures of give and take and do-it-by-yourself. If we are going to reorganize the city in a way that will retain its historic advantages, we have to create a form which will permit people to answer back.

I understand that there was a considerable amount of answering back in the course of putting through the project for the urban renewal district around the University. But I was informed that this improved the early plans that had been made and that the whole project was in much better shape as a result of the struggle, the drama, and the confronting of opposing forces face to face than it would have been if it had been possible to shove the original project through, without evoking criticism or dissent. This willingness to listen to the opposition was in the best spirit of the University; and I am not at all surprised over the happy result. This demonstrates, in fact, the real function of the city. The kind of power that used to be exercised by the pharaoh in Egypt, by the *lugal* or "big man" in Mesopotamia—habits of command not unknown among the old railroad kings and magnates of Chicago, as some here will remember—is as obsolete as the walled city that once enhanced that power. The days of the "big men" are over. We are all little men, and we realize that in a complicated and delicately balanced organization we cannot give orders except in a persuasive and considerate way, with all the resources of understanding behind us. The monologue of power must be replaced by the dialogue of understanding. Habits of mutual aid and co-operation are essential. It takes two sides to settle every question.

That, is of course, where the university comes in. In order to create a new urban pattern, we must think of using all the university's functions on a greater scale than ever before; no part of the community can afford to remain untouched by its spirit, unaffected by its method of transmitting values and arriving at truth. Modern society has to think in terms of an open world, one that can never have a wall around it, not even a national frontier. The university is an essential nucleus for holding such a society together. National frontiers disappeared in practice, from a military standpoint, just about a hundred years after the last stone walls disappeared as city fortifications. We live in an open world and in every essential respect a united one—united in death if not in life. We have to find ways and means of uniting it in life, unless all mankind's achievements are to be reduced to radioactive rubble and dust.

Fortunately, the university has a special role in preserving the human inheritance and in maintaining continuity between the past and the future. For this institution has a long memory. You may not like the fact that scholars often do not live very successfully in the day-to-day world. There are some gentlemen here who, I am sure, know better how to entertain a schoolmaster in Sumer in the year 3000 B.C. than how to get a vote through the P.T.A. today. This memory is helpful because some of the undigested problems of the ancient city, as I have suggested, have now at last to be faced on the principle not of monopolizing and concentrating power but of diffusing and democratically distributing it, giving every member of the community the opportunity to ·develop his abilities and his interests and his potentialities to their natural limits.

As our machines become more automatic, our men and women must become more deeply human. It would be fatal to our whole civilization if people became more automatic, too, and knew no other life than the instructions fed to them by remote control from the tape. When the university takes its full part in the whole community, it cannot be content to leave its potential student or fellow worker isolated in some distant suburban cottage, alone before a television set, courting sleep, after a tedious journey from work, by the simplest means possible. He and his local community will be part of a wide-spreading grid, distributing power and culture, without loss, from the biggest center to the smallest.

Then there is also one other fact that makes the university's function very important in the development of modern society. We live in a world that in many respects has become as small as a village. Mr. Buckminster Fuller illustrated this the other day in a striking figure that shows how our space and time have shrunk as our energy and technological resources have increased. Think of a planet twenty feet in diameter. Let that represent the world in terms of walking distance. The world of the railroad train is the size of a baseball in comparison; the world of the jet plane is the size of a marble; while the world of 1968 may be the size of a pea. That is the sort of shrunken world we are now living in. We are all treading on the toes of our neighbors, before we have quite learned how to be neighborly.

Here is one of the great contributions that the university can make, through its very constitution, to the understanding of our civilization and the better use of the magnificent resources mankind as a whole—but only if it can remain whole!—now commands. From the beginning, probably, the university must have had some of the international character it now has. We know that it was an international institution in the Middle Ages; but I suspect it also was so constituted even earlier—certainly in Greece but seemingly in Mesopotamia, too. There is record of Plato's chartering a boatload of olive oil to get the traveler's checks he needed to visit Egypt, where he consulted the priests in their temples and absorbed their ancient lore. The university's international role is an old one. This willingness to receive as equals scholars and students from other nations and cultures gives the university a special function today. Anyone who is a member of the university community, no matter what land he comes from, is a brother; he is welcome.

This is one of the greatest gifts of the university to the modern world—a gift we have not yet sufficiently made use of. When we do, we shall be ready to think of the next step in urban development, the development of a container, or rather an inclusive network of containers and transformers, for a much more complex society—a network capable of transforming power into culture, transmuting one-way commands into two-way understandings, creating a larger stage where significant drama and dialogue can again take place. Above all, we must conceive of a new urban form, with a multitude of attractive cultural centers, true university cities, where each smaller part of the community will be able to use all the resources of the whole and contribute, in its turn, to developing those resources.

When we begin to tackle this task, we shall find form coming back into our civilization. We shall find that the urban explosion can be contained. We shall find, too, that power and culture, command and understanding, are both necessary to our lives as never before—power to be put at man's service, and understanding to present him with life-enhancing goals far beyond those of space travel to another planet.

DOWNS: Professor Mumford, we thank you for an exciting and stimulating experience. Gentlemen, the meeting is now adjourned.

I

The Background for the Expansion of Society in the Ancient Near East

KRAELING (*spokesman*): Ladies and gentlemen: You have already been welcomed by Chancellor Kimpton on behalf of the University of Chicago at the opening of the first (luncheon) session of this symposium in the Chicago Club. As we gather here now at the Oriental Institute for the second session and move from the introductory address to the discussion of the first topic listed on our program, let me add also the welcome of the Oriental Institute and of all its members. We are sensitive of the high honor you have done us by coming and we hope you will enjoy the days of your visit with us.

The theme of our symposium is urbanization and cultural development, or, in broader terms, the expansion of society and its cultural implications, with particular reference to the ancient Near East. Let me try to set the stage by explaining in a few words, first, how a strongly humanistic institution like the Oriental Institute comes to pose a problem in such broad terms for interdisciplinary discussion and, second, how the problem poses itself to the Institute at the various levels of Near Eastern cultural development.

In describing the purpose for which the Oriental Institute was organized, its founder, James Henry Breasted, said that it was to concern itself with the question of how man became what he is. He meant, I take it, that as a group and individually we should seek with the scholars of other institutions at home and abroad to discover and interpret the materials bearing on the origin and growth of human culture in the ancient Near East, where civilized man first emerged. To this purpose the Institute has adhered faithfully throughout the years. But as time has moved along some of the emphases have changed, as indeed they should. If in the earlier years the emphasis was on "Man," that is, on the hypostasized, idealized Man with a capital *M,* on man the responsible, moral, and ethical being, the emphasis in later years has turned rather to "men" in the plural, that is, to the descriptions of societies at different levels and to the appearance of culture patterns in which such institutions as government, law, religion, the arts, letters are seen as instruments of the interactions and the welfare of the society that sanctions them.

The change is in accord with the experiences of our generation and with the demands of the material we are studying. The hypostasized Man died on the battle fields of Ypres and Verdun, though we did not quite realize it at the time, and the period that has followed has been dominated by a succession of societal movements marked by strongly intrenched forms of group ideology and group behavior. It is therefore quite natural for us today to see and understand the history of our race in the societal form. More than that, as exploration and research in the history of Near Eastern civilization have moved back in time, from the historical to the protoliterate and prehistoric periods, it has become necessary to use the methods and procedures developed by the sociologist, the anthropologist, and the ethnologist to describe and interpret what we find. Finally, the more we have realized that the complex culture patterns in the more advanced societies are both analogous to and not to be dissociated genetically from the simpler culture patterns of primitive societies, the more it has become necessary to use the culture-historical approach to the interpretations of the material. While this approach cannot be said to exhaust the interpretative possibilities for the historian, it does require the participation of specialists in many different fields if description and interpretation are to be full and competent, and thus analogies and parallels from other periods and areas begin to take on even for the Orientalist additional meaning. Over the years we of the Oriental Institute have found ourselves working in ever closer co-operation with representatives of other faculties on the campus here. It is therefore not only a special privilege but a real necessity for us to create an occasion such as this symposium, at which we can exchange views also with scholars from other campuses and parts of the world on an interdisciplinary level. We believe we shall be accomplishing the purposes set for us the better if we erect not fences against but lines of communication with colleagues in all related fields.

The theme of our symposium derives from the general observations that typologically as well as historically human societies increase in size and that the change from the smaller to the larger coincides with a change also from thinness and simplicity of culture equipment to relative depth and complexity. As the transition from the camp site to the open agricultural village coincides with the technological revolution that permitted food-production to supersede food-collecting and with the rise of clan and tribal organization and institutions, so the appearance of the market towns, the large urban establishments, and the metropolises coincides with the appearance of the high and multiform cultures. What, we would ask, can a typological and comparative study of the larger urban communities, their opportunities and potentialities, their problems and hazards, tell us about the culture equipment that appeared in them? Or, vice versa, how do the cultural instruments and institutions of the most developed ancient Near Eastern societies respond to or function with respect to the urban matrices in which they appear? Can we describe and understand the relationship?

In entering upon a discussion of these questions we will do well to inquire at the outset whether most recent investigations into the cultural use of the Near Eastern alluvium and upland have given any new perspectives upon the natural, ecological, social, and technological factors that contributed to the rise of urban centers. This is the subject of the present session. Since the question we are raising states itself at a variety of levels and in various aspects of the cultural history of the Near East, further subdivision is necessary to give order and coherence to our discussion. First we propose to explore the relation of societal expansion and cultural institutions at the level of the national states. Here our attention will be directed successively to Mesopotamia, where urban centers played an outstanding role, and to Egypt, where seemingly they are less prominent. This will provide the subject matter for the third, fourth, and fifth sessions. In the sixth and seventh sessions we propose to explore our problem at the level of the great empires, when the urban centers were comprehended in supernational political entities, to see what are some of the changes which the required reorientation produced in culture equipment and its function. At this level we must give separate consideration to the empires whose cultural history was largely the further development of traditional indigenous patterns and, finally, briefly consider societal expansion and cultural development in the Near East in the Greek and Roman periods, when the area was forced to reconcile itself with fully developed and differently oriented culture patterns brought in from the outside. That we will gain a total picture at any one of the several levels or in any one of the several areas of cultural development is naturally too much to

22

expect. But some facets we can hope to clarify, and, if we pay due attention to analogies from other periods and other areas of cultural development, the approach may reveal its fruitfulness and helpfulness not only to the specialists in the ancient Near East but also to those in other fields who may wish to make use of the vast treasures of information about its cultural achievement.

So far as procedure is concerned, we propose to begin each session with an oral presentation by a person well versed in the particular subject. It will be his function to raise specific questions or to point up promising lines of approach. Each session will also have its own chairman, who will keep the discussion within the proper limits of time and subject. Before Professor Tax takes charge as chairman of this second session I wish to say a particular word of welcome to Dr. Naji al-Asil, distinguished emeritus Director General of the Department of Antiquities of Iraq. He has come farthest to honor us with his presence, and, through his understanding of the issues and through his forceful leadership on the scene, has done more than any of us to advance the study of ancient Mesopotamian civilization. A word from him at this time would be most appropriate.

AL-ASIL: Mr. Spokesman, ladies and gentlemen: I should like to take this first opportunity to say how deeply gratified I am to have the privilege of participating with you in this very important symposium. My special thanks are due to Chancellor Kimpton and to Professor Kraeling for having made it possible for me to be in the United States at this time. I have read the papers prepared in advance for this occasion and feel that many of them deal with a problem with which we have been confronted in Iraq during the past ten years or so—the problem of the emergence of a new urban culture.

As historians and archeologists we of the Department of Antiquities had long been familiar with the Ubaid, the Sumerian, and the Assyrian cultures, but, when we began our excavations at the ancient city of Hatra, we were confronted by something new—an Aramaic culture. Those of us who were at the excavations found many inscriptions in the Aramaic script, and none of the staff was really versed in it, although Sayyid Fuad Safar had some knowledge of the Aramaic language, acquired while he was studying at Chicago. Both he and Sayyid Muhammad Ali Mustafa spent their nights trying to establish the forms of the different letters used in the script of Hatra for recording the words of the Aramaic language. I think it took them something like eighteen days to arrive at a point where they thought they had the written alphabet defined. Then all of a sudden in one of the temples we found the whole alphabet inscribed on a wall. The conclusions reached inductively by hard work were verified, and the problems we had faced were resolved by one single item of new information. This is typical of the nature of the process by which we move forward in scholarly research. While reading the papers prepared for the symposium I felt that many of the problems that have long occupied our attention in the cultural history of Iraq and about which there have been obscurities and uncertainties were dealt with in masterful fashion and elucidated with the help of fresh new insights. I look forward to further enlightenment during the several sessions. To the entire subject of the symposium the address of Professor Mumford delivered at the luncheon this noon was a wonderful introduction.

The second point about which I would like to say a few words is that of the necessity of co-operation among various institutions in dealing with archeological matters. I see here representatives of many academic institutions, with many different fields of interest, who are familiar to me from their archeological work in Iraq. This really justifies the policies which Iraq has been following, and I am sure will continue to follow, in giving the greatest possible assistance to scholars from abroad who wish to come and excavate. Only in proportion as opportunity is afforded for pooling the knowledge gained by scholars working in different periods and on different subjects can we hope to fill the gaps that still exist in the historical picture. In proportion, moreover, as the maximum assistance is given to the scholars from many lands there is provided the possibility of developing a spirit of cordiality and comprehension among representatives of various nations, the kind of spirit we need if the problems we face together today are to be understood and resolved.

TAX (*chairman*): Dr. Robert M. Adams will now set the stage for the first part of our discussion.

FACTORS INFLUENCING THE RISE OF CIVILIZATION IN THE ALLUVIUM: ILLUSTRATED BY MESOPOTAMIA

ADAMS: My task is to introduce the first of a series of discussions which it is hoped will pool the insights and experience of the many disciplines represented here. This requires steering a difficult course between, on the one hand, detailed analyses which perhaps might carry conviction to the specialized Orientalist and, on the other hand, a series of broad (and correspondingly less well-supported) generalizations which might initiate a fuller exchange of views. The first alternative is rendered impossible by shortage of time, while the more generalizing approach is more difficult to apply in an introduction than in a summation. All that I can attempt, then, is to outline—but neither to examine adequately nor to defend—a series of major problems and hypotheses dealing with the rise of a civilized social order in the Mesopotamian plain.

The bulk of this symposium is concerned with the culminating, or at least the most stylized and distinctive, achievements of the civilizations of the ancient Orient: their expanding political institutions, the changing character of their religious thought, art, and literature, and the growing *oikumene* which they brought about. But for prehistoric and protohistoric periods, as the preponderantly archeological record gradually gives way to the vastly fuller picture that can be drawn only from large and well-understood bodies of texts, the more the imprecise and impersonal character of the available data forces us to begin by concentrating on ecological and subsistence patterns, which, while indispensable, were no more than a very remote and indirect background for the culminating achievements of civilizations. Only as a second, necessarily more speculative, step can we attempt to reconstruct the changing patterns of social and economic organization which largely mediated the relationship of subsistence and technology with political and religious institutions.

This symposium takes the established village-farming community as its point of departure and asks how and why the tide toward civilization rolled on from there. We know that cultivation began earlier in the zone of rainfall farming that extends across the hilly uplands of northern Iraq,[1] but our beginning in the alluvium nonetheless is not an arbitrary one. In many respects the introduction of irrigation agriculture on the semiarid alluvial plain represented a separate and radically different development. Direct evidence on early stages of settlement still is lacking, but indirect evidence is beginning to accumulate suggesting that the origins of lowland agricultural occupation are not to be found in a simple expansion of upland patterns into new areas. Instead of a cautious fingering-down from north to south along the major rivers, it appears that we have to deal with a more rapid process of adaptation in which the con-

[1] R. J. Braidwood, "Near Eastern prehistory," *Science* CXXVII (1958) 1428–29.

version of indigenous food-collectors may even have played some part.[2]

As with the origins of the agriculturalists in the alluvium, the preliminary steps by which suitable irrigation techniques were evolved still remain largely conjectural. It can be said only that by the late fifth millennium B.C. numerous Ubaid villages and small towns were scattered along the alternately bifurcating and rejoining channels of the major rivers. The size and distribution of Ubaid settlements, together with the changing settlement patterns of later times, imply that these early communities relied on short canals taking off from river channels in their immediate vicinity, and perhaps also on even simpler irrigation techniques involving uncontrolled flooding. Both occupation and cultivation were limited, in other words, to linear enclaves along natural watercourses. Expanses of permanent swamps along these watercourses formed a more uniform and prominent feature of the landscape than they do at present (when they are virtually absent in the northern, or Akkadian, part of the plain). Interspersed between the channels were depressions subject to occasional flooding, where catch-crop cultivation sometimes was possible. Slightly elevated areas also occurred sporadically between the braided stream channels; receiving less runoff, they were suitable only for

2 "Husking trays" at early Eridu in the extreme south (Seton Lloyd and Fuad Safar, "Eridu," *Sumer* IV [1948] 125) may date the beginnings of that site as far back as the early village horizon in the north, while the collateral rather than derivative character of the Hajji Muhammad and early Eridu pottery with respect to Halaf, Samarran, and early Iranian styles (L. le Breton, "The early periods at Susa, Mesopotamian relations," *Iraq* XIX [1957] 86–88; cf. C. Ziegler, *Die Keramik von der Qal'a des Ḥaǧǧi Moḥammed* ["Ausgrabungen der Deutschen Forschungsgemeinschaft in Uruk-Warka" V (Berlin, 1953)] pp. 54–57) argues for the same point. The known occurrences of Eridu-type pottery are limited to the lower course of the Euphrates, while recent surveys have shown that settlements of the subsequent Ubaid period dwindle in number and perhaps begin later as one moves northward through Akkad. Moreover, surface finds confirm earlier excavation reports (R. C. Thompson, *The British Museum Excavations at Abu Shahrain in Mesopotamia in 1918* [London, 1920] p. 119 and Pls. 6, 9; L. C. Watelin, *Excavations at Kish* IV [1934] 2) in disclosing a fairly extensive industry of microlithic blade tools in flint and obsidian; this industry apparently persisted in the south into Early Dynastic times. Since microliths, and indeed all skilled flintwork, entirely disappeared from the northern piedmont by the Hassunah period, it is difficult to explain their survival in the south unless a coeval southern tradition—with or without agriculture—is postulated. In sum, several independent lines of distributional evidence argue for a separate, admittedly somewhat tarriant, agricultural adaptation in the heart of the alluvium rather than for the adoption of the new pattern by degrees as colonists moved cautiously down from the uplands. Although recent work casts some doubt on the similarity of modern ecological conditions to those of the remote past, Sir William Willcocks ("Mesopotamia: Past, present, and future," *Annual Report of the Smithsonian Institution*, 1909, pp. 401–16) long ago noted the apparent advantages the lower Euphrates offered for initial attempts at irrigation.

spring grazing. Although a marked growth in community size took place during later prehistoric and the protohistoric periods, the essentials of this pattern continued unchanged for a very long time. Large-scale, integrated irrigation systems apparently were not introduced even in the most urbanized (i.e., Sumerian) part of the area until after the process of political integration into territorial states was well under way. For Akkad and the adjoining basin of the lower Diyala River, the onset of large-scale irrigation occurred even later.[3] But if, on the basis of this reconstruction, we now discount the requirements of irrigation for a powerful, centralized bureaucracy as having precipitated and largely shaped the political systems of the early city-states, this only underlines how little is known of the substantive effects of irrigation on an increasingly complex and stratified social order. I hope we may hear from Robert Fernea later today about the operation of even a moderately large modern irrigation system by a markedly segmentary and acephalous tribal Arab society.

While agriculture began later in the alluvium than in the uplands, the relative balance of social and cultural development was rapidly reversed in the sequel. At least as seen in such indices as community size and scale of public building, the southern plains had forged ahead even before the end of the Ubaid period. During the subsequent Warka, Protoliterate, and Early Dynastic periods the precocious expansion of society on the alluvial plain continued, establishing there by the early third millennium B.C. a literate, urban civilization which lacked even a pale contemporary reflection on the northern piedmont. This striking differential in rates of growth poses a basic problem for us here. To what extent was it rooted in the difference between rainfall agriculture in the uplands and irrigation in the alluvium? What was the nature and magnitude of irrigation agriculture's superiority? In what ways may features of the new subsistence pattern have influenced the long-term trends of institutional growth which characterized Sumerian society?

A possible source for part of the difference in growth rates may be differences in productivity between irrigated and rain-watered lands; V. Gordon Childe, for example, attributes the growing population and capacity for "nonproductive" works and trade to the "social sur-

[3] T. Jacobsen and R. M. Adams, "Salt and silt in ancient Mesopotamian agriculture," *Science* CXXVIII (1958) 1251–58; Adams, "Survey of ancient watercourses and settlements in central Iraq," *Sumer* XIV (1958) 101–4.

plus" which irrigation made possible.[4] Certainly the fertility that attended cereal cultivation in the south was very respectable until the effects of soil salinization first began to be felt seriously late in the third millennium B.C.;[5] comparable and contemporary figures unfortunately are unobtainable for the illiterate northern uplands to quantify the extent of the difference. But in any case the full explanation is certainly less clear cut, for fertility is only one element in agricultural productivity. The labor input of the southern farmer, for example, included land leveling and diking, canal construction and maintenance, and practically annual provisions against minor but destructive changes in river channels. None of these activities occupied the piedmont farmer, so that it is highly debatable whether a comparison of the ancient productivities would favor the irrigation zone if based on grain production in relation to labor input. Finally, it may be observed that the concept of "social surplus" is itself a misleading one when divorced from the institutional complex which alone made possible the concentration and employment of a surplus as an instrument for societal expansion. In short, important differences in agricultural productivity consequent upon the introduction of irrigation are difficult to isolate from more general differences in subsistence patterns and socio-economic institutions, and in any case they are virtually impossible to demonstrate at present.

Several other features of the alluvial subsistence pattern may have contributed more to the pace and direction of institutional growth than a putative increase in productive efficiency. Since their roles are described more fully in an accompanying paper (pp. 269–92), a brief summary will be sufficient here. In the first place, the reliance on widely different food resources must have been a factor in maintaining continuity of settlement and in providing a material basis for further expansion by limiting the consequences of the failure of a particular crop. Thus, although cereals continued as the major staple they had been in the north, in the irrigation zone the date harvest provided a crucial supplementary source of subsistence;[6] in addition fish were a new and very prominent source of protein and fat, while

[4] Childe, *New Light on the Most Ancient East* (London, 1952) p. 115; *Social Evolution* (London, 1951) p. 163 and *passim*.

[5] Jacobsen and Adams, *op. cit.* p. 1252.

[6] Grown along the banks of watercourses, the date crop was less subject to fluctuation with the size of the annual flood than were crops from most irrigated fields; moreover, the nice periodicity of spring cereals and fall dates reduced the hardship if one or the other failed.

smaller contributions were made by dairy products. Secondly, the complementarity of these resources and the occupational specialization which they engendered lent support to the establishment of redistributive institutions like the temple, the manor, or the palace (at least in their economic-organizing aspect), which in turn helped to give the area its distinctively civilized character as contrasted with the northern uplands. Third, the adoption of irrigation (even on an alternate-fallow system) substituted relatively permanent fields and ownership by smaller family units for shifting plots allocated by extended kin groups, introducing (or at least greatly strengthening a trend toward) social stratification based on unequal access to the strategic agricultural resources.

Behind these generalized features just enumerated, however, lie complexities which the thinness of our data can mask but not entirely hide. The kind of complex interrelationships existing between subsistence pursuits and wider cultural patterns can be illustrated briefly with the case of animal husbandry. If pastoralists at times were a disruptive external influence whose successive appearances were followed by ethnic shifts (the only aspect of husbandry which has received close historical scrutiny), pastoralism nonetheless was always an integral part of the agricultural regime. To begin with, the grazing of sheep and goats on stubble in the fields after the harvest apparently was the only fertilizing agency employed by the ancient Mesopotamians. As much as the periodic political difficulties between settled cultivators and incoming pastoralists, this may account for the stress laid by early mythology on peaceful symbiosis between the herdsman and the farmer. Again, it can be argued that the ox- or donkey-drawn plow was essential for widespread irrigation agriculture under alluvial conditions. But the larger ruminants were not so well adapted as sheep and goats to the available natural forage, particularly during the blistering Mesopotamian summer. Perhaps their greater dependence on supplemental feeding[7] helps to explain the concentration of cattle in large herds by the centralized and integrated little economic systems which also collected and dispersed much of the agricultural produce and even took direct charge of the

7 Given the high contemporary crop yields and the stated daily ration, barley from fields covering approximately 80 hectares was consumed annually by the 394 cattle and donkeys listed in an enumeration for the Baba temple (one of twenty) in Girsu under Urakagina (A. Deimel, "Die Viehzucht der Sumerer zur Zeit Urakaginas," *Orientalia* XX [1926] 13–15). For a month during the worst of the summer even the sheep received a ration of barley (A. Schneider, *Die sumerische Templestadt* [Essen, 1920] p. 55).

plowing.[8] Some of the largest, although by no means all, of these relatively self-contained economic units were temples, and it is not unreasonable to trace part of the key social role played by temples in late prehistoric and protohistoric times to the necessary control they exercised over the herds. Partial confirmation for this view is to be found in the important place occupied by herdsmen in early administrative hierarchies and in the stress on herds in contemporary symbolism and ritual associated with the temples. In short, animal husbandry not only influenced closely related subsistence and economic patterns but also ramified widely into such seemingly remote fields as political relations, administrative elites, religious institutions, and even mythopoeic thought. Although our data are inadequate to document the point, there is little reason to doubt that the reverse process also occurred: that pre-existing suprasubsistence activities and attitudes exercised an influence over the organization of husbandry.

Turning from the relatively stable subsistence patterns which sustained the rise of Mesopotamian civilization, we also need to consider the developing social and economic order which was a central feature of civilization itself. Because the content of most social and economic relationships lies beyond the normal reach of archeological inference and because extrapolations backward from the more adequate cuneiform accounts of later times have inherent limitations of their own, we are limited to the description of fairly gross and concrete changes whose wider functional contexts remain hypothetical. For purposes of this discussion, I believe there are three ongoing processes of change which are most critical and best documented.

Perhaps the single most significant development of the late prehistoric and the protohistoric periods was the emergence of a stratified society. The results of this process are seen most unequivocally in the appearance by the end of Early Dynastic times of a class of powerful landowners, able to acquire and alienate estates with no more than token payments to communities whose occupants worked the land but had sunk into a dependent client status.[9] A different aspect of the same process probably can be identified in the gradual

8 Deimel, "Das Betriebpersonal der Tempelacker zur Zeit Urukaginas," *Orientalia* VI (1923) 24–26, and *Sumerische Tempelwirtschaft zur Zeit Urukaginas und seiner Vorgänger* ("Analecta orientalia" II [1931]) p. 81.

9 I. M. Diakonoff, *Sale of Land in Pre-Sargonic Sumer* (Moscow, 1954) pp. 19–29; L. Matouš, "Zu den Ausdrucken für 'Zubagen' in den vorsargonischen Grundstuckkaufurkunden," *Archiv orientální* XXII (1954) 434–43; I. J. Gelb, *Sargonic Texts from the Diyala Region* ("Materials for the Assyrian Dictionary," No. 1 [Chicago, 1952]) p. xiii.

differentiation of a contemporary class of burials in which costly *Beigaben* were included and in the differentiation of living accommodations, although the reflection of class differences in domestic architecture is little known until the final phase of the Early Dynastic period because of the prevailing archeological predisposition to excavate mainly in ceremonial precincts.[10] To be sure, this picture suffers seriously from imprecision. For the attitudinal and behavioral correlates of wealth or for an appreciation of the extent to which the pattern of stratification was modified by social mobility, one is forced to depend almost entirely on royal inscriptions which may not accurately reflect the general circumstances of nonroyal upper-class families. The impersonality and fragmentary character of the data also makes it difficult convincingly to trace the interconnections of social stratification with other important contemporary trends. It is only reasonable to assume that the expansion of political institutions along superordinate-subordinate lines, the intensification of militarism, and the increase in private demand for craft products all were functionally interrelated with the formation of stratified society, but the evolution and actual workings of these relationships still escape us.

The greatly increased importance of specialized craftsmanship represents a second crucial feature of the attainment of civilization. While the development of different branches of the crafts naturally proceeded at different rates and in response to different stimuli, at least a few generalizations apply fairly uniformly. To begin with, rapid technological progress and greatly increased consumption of craft products seem to have occurred successively rather than contemporaneously. The earlier phase, consisting mainly of very small-scale production of cult objects within and largely for the temple establishments, apparently coincided roughly with the Protoliterate period. The Early Dynastic phase, on the other hand, is correlated with a burgeoning military demand for vehicles and weapons and with the growth of a private market economy alongside the normal redistributive mechanisms of the temple and palace. As best illustrated by metallurgy, the latter development produced little further technological advance but, instead, involved an important extension of administrative procedures (originally introduced by the temples for control of subsistence products) to provide for greatly expanded

10 R. M. Adams, "Level and Trend in Early Sumerian Civilization." Unpublished Ph.D. dissertation, University of Chicago, 1956.

capitalization, training, production, and distribution of commodities not directly associated with primary subsistence. Tool and weapon designs were somewhat improved and bronze made its appearance during the Early Dynastic period, but the tremendously increased volume of available metal during the same period implies a whole series of far more striking organizational changes.[11] Probably it is justifiable to conclude from this sequence that the expansion of craft production and the market, and the simultaneous appearance of craftsmen and merchants as important (although still numerically small) social groups, occurred too late to be regarded as major precipitating factors behind the growth of cities, class stratification, and the emergence of dynastic authory. Nevertheless, once set in motion the demands for raw materials, weapons, and markets may have stimulated further stratification, increasing administrative complexity, and greater emphasis on military expansionism as a conscious state policy.

The third and final feature of societal expansion to be considered concerns the changing character and function of the population centers themselves. Here, even more than with the other aspects of change that have been reviewed, we are at the mercy of fragmentary and unrepresentative evidence. The confinement of excavations in the main to ceremonial precincts provides us with a number of fine sequences of changing temple forms reaching back to the very beginning of the occupation of Eridu, but it discloses only isolated or incomplete private houses and not a single reconstructible town plan earlier than the Early Dynastic structures exposed by the Oriental Institute in the Diyala basin. As a result, the observed regularities in architecture and settlement from which wider interpretation must proceed are at once very gross, very tentative, and very few in number.

The more important of these trends may be briefly summarized.[12]

11 For example, metal objects occur in only one-sixth of the late "Jamdat Nasr" Early Dynastic I graves at Ur but in four-fifths of those of Early Dynastic III date. Moreover, the average quantity of metal in the later graves increases substantially (C. Leonard Woolley, *Ur Excavations* [London and Philadelphia]. II. *The Royal Cemetery* [1934]. IV. *The Early Periods* [1956]). In order to obtain these greatly increased supplies, a concomitant expansion was necessary in other industries whose products could be transported and exchanged for copper at its distant sources beyond the Persian Gulf and in Anatolia. The large labor force engaged in production of exportable textiles that is accounted for by the Baba temple archive (Deimel, *Sumerische Tempelwirtschaft* . . . , p. 108) thus may be a reflection of the increasing demand for metals.

12 Cf. Jacobsen, "Early political development in Mesopotamia," *Zeitschrift für Assyriologie* LII (1957) 97–99.

There is a striking increase in size between the largest known Ubaid settlements (e.g. Tell ʿUqair, occupying perhaps 7 hectares) and the great political centers of the Early Dynastic period (e.g. Uruk, with 435 hectares within its wall) which justified describing only the latter as cities. The Ubaid, Warkan, and Protoliterate towns are dominated by temples of increasing size, and until almost the end of this long time span other forms of monumental architecture are virtually unknown. During the succeeding Early Dynastic period, however, city walls and palaces also became prominent features; both were intimately associated with the rise of new patterns of dynastic authority.[13] Beyond these limited observations it is difficult to generalize with any confidence. They raise doubts and invite speculation better than they invoke an orderly sequence.

One might ask at the outset, for example, whether the village-town-city transition which pervades our thinking is a valid historical construct or only a typological one. Alternatively, it might be agreed that village and city are distinguishable organizational forms but argued that between these polar types lay only a fluid transition without separate characteristics of its own. If towns are meaningfully to be distinguished from villages, at what historical point do they appear and what new organizational features do they embody?

Again, there is still much obscurity over the role of the temples in Protoliterate communities. In the full light of Early Dynastic archives it appears that they engaged in many economic activities, but can we properly invoke their later activities as compelling utilitarian functions which somehow explain their precocious early development? At what point in the long course of their development were temple hierarchies formally constituted, and when did they assume a central role in organizing economic activity?[14] There is an instructive parallel for these problems in the great temple centers of the Maya lowlands in the New World. I hope Professor Willey will speculate a bit during the discussion on the role of the Maya temples and on the degree to which their suggested "utilitarian" functions (like astronomic calculation of the proper time for planting) help him to explain the heavy emphasis which the religious centers received.

13 *Ibid.* p. 114.

14 Possibly the appearance of formally arranged, architecturally specialized complexes consisting of several temples and related buildings during the Protoliterate period, first noted by H. J. Lenzen (*Die Entwicklung der Zikurrat von ihren Anfangen bus zur Zeit der III. Dynastie von Ur* ["Ausgrabungen der Deutschen Forschungsgemeinschaft in Uruk-Warka" IV (Berlin, 1941)] p. 15), signifies the acquisition of these new functions.

Another important question concerns the appearance of the walled city-states after the end of the Protoliterate period. There are suggestions that the amalgamation of several small neighboring centers frequently was involved,[15] and the general practice of circumvallation confirms the emphasis in the epics on militarism and growing dynastic power. But does the formation of the city-state signify that a qualitative change already had occurred in the organization of the populace? Alternatively, one might imagine that the institution of kingship at first had little effect on the ordinary social bonds. If so, the initial appearance of the city involved no immediate organic change but only the massing-together of traditional population groups primarily for defense. In time, of course, new and more complex organizational ties would tend to replace the older ones in the new, larger, and more stratified settlement as it came increasingly under the influence of royal authority. Perhaps these possibilities never can be confirmed with the Sumerian evidence alone, but insights into our material also may come from comparable sequences elsewhere. The interrelated growth of African urbanism and militarism during the early centuries of European contact, at least partly in response to the slave trade, may be a case in point.

The speculative character of many of the foregoing points is uncomfortably clear. Shortage of time and paucity of data have forced me to deal not with the detailed processes by which social stratification, craft specialization, and urbanism emerged but, instead, with a macroscopic view of those processes which may only impose the regularities it seeks to elicit. In a sense, this is an inherent limitation of prehistory and protohistory, one which underlines our dependence on other specialists present at this symposium for a full understanding of the material.

TAX: Thank you, Dr. Adams. To answer the questions you have raised might not take us long if the answers were known, but to discuss them all without being able to answer them would require far more time than the symposium affords. There are many people around this table who should have a lot to say on these questions, and our problem obviously is one of trying to get the most out of a very brief period of discussion. I suggest that the only way we can do this is to pursue a few points more thoroughly.

By agreement with Dr. Adams, I propose that we consider espe-

[15] A. Falkenstein, "La cité-temple sumérienne," *Journal of World History* I (1954) 784–814.

cially the three major features of the developing socio-economic order to which he drew attention: the emergence of a stratified society, the way in which specialized craftsmanship developed, and the changing form and functions of the population centers. But in the beginning, we might call on two individuals mentioned by name from whom particular information was sought. One was Mr. Robert Fernea, who has recently returned from a modern Iraqi irrigation village. I think the question here was whether a rather complicated irrigation regime required a great society or whether it could be handled by a little village society. Perhaps, as briefly as possible, you can tell us something about that.

FERNEA: The society that I worked in was not just a village society but rather a tribe which had in its midst a village, so that questions about irrigation will have to be answered within the larger context of a tribal community. Mr. Adams mentioned several characteristics of such a society. The fact that it is typically segmentary in its political organization presents an interesting problem when we ask how it manages problems of irrigation which to us might seem to demand central controls for solution. I observed that in the society in which I worked an endogamous lineage is strong and cohesive as an individual social grouping but relates to other lineages only for limited purposes, among which are certain problems of irrigation, such as sharing the work necessary to maintain access canals or cleaning out the canals irrigating the land belonging to the tribal sheikh and supporting the tribal guesthouse. The coming-together of otherwise competing social groups under a sheikh for limited purposes is familiar to students of Bedouin life, and many of the agriculturalists whom I studied were recent descendants of nomadic Arabs. To consider the social organization and practices of the desert nomad is altogether pertinent to our understanding of the southern Euphrates agriculturalist of the present. The Bedouins gathered together for raids or war and co-operated under the direction of their sheikhs, but much of the time lineages acted independently of one another. Actually, the terms *sa'ada* and *'una*, which are now used to refer to the jointly under-taken activities of canal construction and cleaning, are apparently the same terms that once meant mutual help for purposes of war. Of course, I am talking about a society which is not directly responsible for the operation of dams, sluice gates, and the like. These raise a different range of problems. Nevertheless, the southern Euphrates tribes, without hierarchical organizations of centralized authority, handle quite a range of irrigation problems, and there is probably no reason to feel that the capacity of a segmentary political organization to handle such problems is fully explored in the example of southern Iraq.

There is another matter Mr. Adams mentioned that I might comment about now. That is the role of the irrigation expert, in this case the irrigation engineer appointed by and responsible to Baghdad but resident in the village where I worked. I was interested to observe how lineage groups sharing an irrigation system tended to carry problems which had nothing to do with a section of the irrigation system under government control to the engineer. In other words, traditional problems which earlier had been resolved by consensus and public opinion processes, or by the invited intervention of third parties, now are being carried to the irrigation expert in increasing numbers. Testimony from British and Iraqi officials as well as a sample of the records confirmed my impression in this regard. This seems to present a way in which we could imagine an urban center, which has risen by some means, or is in the process of formation, developing its control over a rural population so that this control is not only military and coercive but rather becomes freely acknowledged by the society. For instance, imagine a situation in which an urban center has managed to increase control over a water system through monumental creations like dams, constructed by forced labor. We might find the officials appointed to look after the state's interests called by the indigenous communities to solve problems which they had once handled themselves. This might have been part of the process by which rural areas became integrated with urban centers, one way in which the power of the urban ruler became legitimate authority in the eyes of the subject rural peoples.

ADAMS: As I understand you, then, you are agreeing that the initial managerial requirements for irrigation systems of small to moderate size need not have precipitated the formation of the early city-states or the trend toward political integration in general. But where such political integration does appear, and where it enters into the economic activity of the region, you are pointing out that irrigation control provides an avenue whereby political authority may find sanction and increasing support.

TAX: In other words, the irrigation needs themselves would not be the cause, or at least not the sufficient cause, for the growth of the state.

36

FERNEA: Yes. Even though we cannot rely too much on the evidence from one study, at least in this instance I looked particularly for practices tending to shift the balance from a segmentary to a more centralized political system. And within the context of the traditional culture I could find no indications of such a shift.

MUMFORD: Does not a large-scale irrigation system differ from a smaller-scale one that a village culture could handle in that the former is really multipurpose? That is, it is not just for agriculture but also for transportation and communication. A multipurpose system is a necessity for big states but not for small communities.

TAX: Who can tell us of the nature of a large-scale irrigation system in which transportation all along it is an important feature? What is the picture of its operations as contrasted with a little village watering its gardens?

ADAMS: We may hear more on this from Professor Jacobsen and others later in the symposium, but my point is that we have no evidence for large-scale systems during the period I am concerned with here. They apparently did not antecede the formation of the urban centers and thus cannot be invoked as having brought about that formation. Certainly there were the other functions for canal construction which Professor Mumford has pointed out; in fact, it is my understanding that the role of canals in promoting commerce and communication between cities is stressed in the early historical accounts. But all of this comes as a consequence, not a cause, of the establishment of city-states and dynastic authority.

JACOBSEN: I have just a very few points. First, I should like to concur with Dr. Adams in his remark that we are not justified in assuming that large and fully developed irrigation systems were a primary and original force. The evidence, a large part of which Dr. Adams has put together and interpreted, clearly indicates a series of stages. Irrigation systems begin as a number of small, separate, simple units; the large irrigation systems that we know from history are a later development. For our purposes today, it is the small beginnings that particularly occupy us.

The second point that struck me was the one made by Mr. Fernea when he called attention to the extention of the authority of the government expert. Here I must ask indulgence for drawing a parallel from the inscriptional material of the later periods. It seems to me that the process he describes may help us to explain many of the historically known titles of rulers and organizers. To take just one example, I believe that the common term for the head of the later city-state, the *ensik*,[16] originally denoted the administrator who was in charge of the plowed land. In view of what Mr. Fernea says of the irrigation engineer, it seems at least possible that the *ensik's* later political influence may have gone back originally to a position of technical competence. The man who organized members of the small community for their plowing activities gradually may have achieved a larger role in the organization of the community as a whole. I only mention this as possibly a fruitful way in which we can look at some of the questions which confront us.

PARKER: I also was drawn to the remark by Mr. Fernea that people in the small community he observed took problems which had once been settled locally to the government agent for solution. I wonder whether this shifting of responsibility, if projected far enough into the past, could account for a growing-together. He implied that it is a desirable thing. If it is desirable now, could it not also have been desirable in the past? Communities coming into conflict, perhaps over water rights or disputed border claims, might have sought adjudication of their disputes by someone else. And as that someone became a recognized authority in such matters there could have been a tendency toward development, in a small way, of such power as Professor Mumford told us of at luncheon.

TAX: Mr. Fernea, do you want to respond before we go on?

FERNEA: Just one remark. It is interesting to look at the records of the administrative officers in Iraq during the period of the British mandate. If you consider what they have to say about tribal or even intratribal conflict and its causes, you find that disputes over water often were at the root of the problems. And, while at first these officers had to assert actively their right to make and enforce judgments in such matters, it seems that later they were besieged at times by contesting groups with requests for judgments. In going through this material I gained the impression that everyone agreed it was a good idea to remove the responsibility for decision-making from anyone having a direct connection with the groups in question. Seeking an informed and impartial judge is a traditional Near Eastern practice, and I found that tribesmen very often do not consider their sheikh, or tribal leader, to be such a person. Certainly this substantiates your observation, Professor Parker.

RHEINSTEIN: I would like to ask a few questions, primarily of Pro-

16 Jacobsen, "Early political development in Mesopotamia," *Zeitschrift für Assyriologie* LII 123, n. 71.

fessor Jacobsen. One frequently hears the statement that the transition from a society which functions on a basis of customs and habits to a society which keeps order through a staff of governmental officers and the organized use of governmental powers was sparked by the needs of irrigation, especially large-scale irrigation. It would be interesting to learn what evidence there is in the sources for the existence of officials endowed with formal power to take care of the peculiar tasks which arise in connection with irrigation: the maintenance of canals, the regulation of the use of water, etc. In addition, I would like to know whether in Mesopotamia there were not only irrigation canals but also levees as protection against floods. And if the presence of levees can be shown, is there evidence from Mesopotamia that someone with clearly defined governmental power and a staff of subordinates was formally charged with the responsibility for their maintenance? Or, on the other hand, does it appear that such tasks were performed as a result of informal social pressures such as still may be seen at work today in the maintenance of little irrigation systems in the villages of the southern Tyrol?

JACOBSEN: Professor Rheinstein very clearly states the central problem of the relation of irrigation to the rise of a stratified society. In answering as far as I am able in a limited time, I should first like to make a clear distinction between the prehistoric range, about which there is no written evidence, and the historic periods, for which there is at least some material. Now for prehistoric times all that we know is the picture emerging from recent surveys, a picture of irrigation beginning in small and isolated areas typically organized around villages and perhaps economically unable to sustain larger groupings which might be called towns. For these early periods, when small and relatively isolated irrigation systems were being maintained by a relatively unstratified society, I think it is of great importance to be able to use contemporary observations like those of Mr. Fernea for purposes of reconstruction. In time, the originally isolated irrigation areas began to join and grow larger; with the larger groupings of people that were then possible we come to the appearance of the city. From then onward, there is considerable evidence in the earlier texts that the major canal lines were a general responsibility of the ruler, by whatever name he might be called. From Sumerian times onward, moreover, we know of a governmental officer called the *gugal*,[17] who was specifically in charge of the maintenance of canals and the dis-

[17] *The Assyrian Dictionary of the Oriental Institute of the University of Chicago* **V** (1956) 121 f., s.v. *gugallu*.

tribution of water. What interests me is that this later situation still continues in Iraq; apparently the cleaning of the large canals in a developed system is and must be a government task.

In other words, once we get the development of the society of the city going we also get indications of the presence of authorized officials exercising control over irrigation on behalf of the state. But for the long previous range I believe we must think seriously in terms of such societies as the one Mr. Fernea has described.

WILLEY: Some data from pre-Spanish Peru may be of interest in the matter of irrigation. I certainly would concur with Dr. Adams that there is evidence, at least in the sequence of settlement patterns, for the emergence of a complex society including temple centers as well as scattered hamlets five hundred to a thousand years before the rise of the irrigation networks. However, the subsequent development of settlements which certainly could be called cities, numbering as many as thirty thousand rooms clustered around a temple, seems to march right along with the rise of overall valley irrigation systems. Earlier irrigation was tucked away in little corners of the valley, but coincident with the appearance of the great population centers we find full, complicated canal networks covering the valley floors. Now I take it that this is appreciably earlier, in an analogous or homotaxial sense, than your Near Eastern picture. Is that right?

ADAMS: Partly so, but in part also I suspect that this difference is an artificial construct arising out of the separation between two academic traditions. Specialists in the Near East begin with a consideration of the really great systems like the Nahrwan Canal, which ran for 200 miles and watered perhaps 2,000 square miles. Viewed in this light, your Viru Valley example (5 or 10 miles long) seems quite small, and only the later construction of canal systems integrating two or more such valleys on the Peruvian north coast introduces something remotely resembling in extent or purpose the Orientalist's picture of a great canal system. However, viewed in relation to the still smaller beginnings of irrigation in both the Near East and Peru, the valley networks you describe may represent an important new level in size and complexity. We are left with the problem of ascertaining the limits within which a simple society structured mainly by kinship can be effective.

ALBRIGHT: There is in South Arabia an instructive intervening stage, if we may call it that, between the Peruvian and Mesopotamian irrigation regimes. During the early first millennium B.C. the kingdom of Qataban was built up there on the basis of wealth brought in by an extensive caravan trade. In the Wadi Beihan, the central valley of the kingdom, an earlier situation in which there were as yet no elaborate irrigation and no large cities contrasts with the later situation in which, after the caravan trade had developed, there were a prosperous capital and a network of elaborate deflector dams, canals, and sluices. After a long subsequent decline the present level of population and subsistence in the area is not very different from that of the second millennium B.C., before the expansion began. We can see that the cause of the growth of this irrigation system was the wealth obtained from commerce; in fact, irrigation was developed primarily in order to sustain the home base of this commerce. At the same time, there is impressive evidence that only a rich and well-organized state could have built and maintained this system. The accumulation of silt, for example, led to the gradual enlargement of dikes until they attained a height of as much as 20 meters above the plain and required the construction of massive supporting walls painstakingly hewn out of granite. If these works were once allowed to fall into decay, flash floods could do terrible damage to them, virtually requiring that they be reconstructed completely.[18]

SINGER: While Mr. Fernea's observations are interesting in their own right, I would like to raise a question about drawing inferences from them in relation to the historical-archeological problem at hand. I believe it has been suggested that, because the small segmentary society he observed was able to maintain a small irrigation system, ancient irrigation systems need not have transformed the societies which operated them. There are two major obstacles to this line of reasoning. In the first place, the situation Mr. Fernea has described differs importantly from the early historical situation. The modern example deals with a local group in the context of an already developed national state, urban centers, and irrigation technology, while in the ancient case we are seeking to discover how these social and technical features developed in relation to one another. Secondly, I think the failure of his segmentary tribal society to transform itself in the process of maintaining an irrigation system may be partially explained by the fact that it does coexist with a larger society; in fact, the intervention of the larger society is illustrated by the example of the irrigation engineer to whom disputes are taken. The situation might be

[18] Richard Bowen, Jr., and F. P. Albright, *Archaeological Discoveries in South Arabia* (Baltimore, 1958).

quite different if Mr. Fernea's society were truly isolated. For these two reasons I think that the interdisciplinary inferences drawn here are quite illegitimate and highly dubious.

TAX: Do you suppose, Dr. Singer, that if this were an isolated little society we would find it tending to become a large organized society as a result of irrigation, or are you simply denying that this case can be used in the way it has been used?

SINGER: Certainly the latter is my main point. What would happen under other conditions I do not know.

BRAIDWOOD: Mr. Fernea's first point was that it was possible to maintain an irrigation system in a segmentary unstratified society. Whether or not we accept the historical inferences this is valid, is it not?

SINGER: I wonder whether we do not need always to include a description of the larger context within which the simple tribal society is operating.

TAX: This case is particularly useful because it occurs in the ancient zone and approximately the ancient environment, but we may need to seek examples of more isolated villages which have maintained irrigation systems for several generations but which have not become large stratified societies.

SINGER: But of course any case of a so-called isolated society in modern times is hardly isolated completely. The technologies and forms of political organization that civilization has produced over the years surely must have influenced almost all tribal societies that we know in one way or another.

ADAMS: I concur wholeheartedly with Professor Singer's strictures against drawing historical parallels between like institutions or processes in basically unlike contexts, but I think the differences in broad social context between the modern and ancient examples are less striking than he suggests. While the pattern Mr. Fernea describes exists today within the framework of a well-established central government controlling all the appurtenances of state power, the same general pattern can be shown to have prevailed seventy or eighty years ago at a time when there was little intervention on the local scene by any greater society than conflicting tribal groups. Although undoubtedly influenced by Islam and by the presence of a predatory but remote Ottoman power, these conditions are not too dissimilar from what might have occurred during the beginnings of urban life five thousand years earlier. Moreover it is worth noting that, except for the large state-maintained canals and works, the modern irrigation regime does not depend on an elaborate technology which has evolved far beyond its prehistoric level. In this respect, too, I find the similarities of Mr. Fernea's example to the late prehistoric events we are concerned with more striking than the dissimilarities.

HOSELITZ: It has been suggested here that seeking an impartial judgment from someone outside a local society is a traditional Near Eastern practice. I think the practice has a wider distribution than that. In India, for example, what I have read of the settlement of disputes in contemporary socially stratified villages suggests that there is an increasing tendency to go to outsiders. Intercaste disputes, in other words, are being settled increasingly by members of the dominant caste, and it is interesting to note that much of the recently developed theory of dominant castes revolves particularly around the role of the dominant caste in the settlement of disputes. I believe a number of examples could be found to show that even if a stratified society is relatively isolated at the village level, outsiders who are members of higher castes frequently are sought out and appealed to for judgments. In many cases, other intercaste institutions for the settlement of disputes have tended to wither away, leaving the dominant caste as the sole mediator. While I am not sure to what extent this is a generalizable process, at least it can be observed widely in societies in which stratification already is present.

A second point concerns the relation of social stratification to adaptability in meeting changed conditions. I urge consideration of the Maori of New Zealand as an example of a group quite as susceptible to change as the ancient Mesopotamians, although they pursued an apparently divergent course with respect to stratification. Starting from a collecting or food-gathering level aboriginally, the Maori during the first thirty or forty years of the nineteenth century not only adopted agriculture but introduced some very considerable increases in agricultural productivity. While not based on irrigation, their agricultural technology increasingly came to rest on the application of modern (in so far as the 19th century is concerned) agricultural tools. This was achieved (to judge from the available evidence, consisting mainly of missionary reports) essentially without the interference of white settlers, within their own tribal framework, and without a simultaneous process of social stratification. I would conclude that essentially unstratified societies also are capable of making very considerable adjustments in their livelihood patterns or technology.

TAX: While it may be frustrating not to continue with the inter-relationships of irrigation and social stratification, I think we must turn now to some of the other themes on which discussion was invited. One of these dealt with the growth, form, and function of population centers, and it was suggested that Professor Willey might contribute to our comparative understanding from his knowledge of the role of Maya temples in the lowland rain forests of aboriginal Mesoamerica.

WILLEY: While the suggested typological sequence of village, town, and city may apply to nuclear America in a general way, there are suggestions of some significant formal differences from this pattern. To be sure, the spottiness of the archeological record may distort our perceptions and limit our understanding in the New World as much as in Mesopotamia, so that these differences can only be suggested tentatively.

Unlike the situation described for Mesopotamia, from the very threshold of full dependence upon agriculture in Middle America and Peru there existed communities that were differentiated in a physical sense. One finds villages of a few hundred inhabitants containing a temple center or other specialized public buildings in addition to scattered hamlets. In the semiarid, semitropical Peruvian coastal valleys this kind of pattern began around 1000 B.C. and persisted for five hundred years or so with little change except for an increase in the number of such little nucleated centers. Later there was a gradual coalescence of more and more dwellings around some of the temple centers to produce something comparable to the Mesopotamian town or even city.

On the other hand, in certain nuclear American environments like the Maya lowlands the nucleated dwelling center never came into being. Recent surveys in the northeastern Peten, near the heart of Maya civilization, seem to indicate that all through the Classic Period there (i.e., down to *ca.* A.D. 900) the bulk of settlement was segmented into small hamlets including from five to a dozen or so houses. Occasionally within a hamlet of this kind there was a little mound or separate structure larger than the others, suggesting a special building or shrine occupied by a local elder or priest. Up to a dozen hamlets occurred within an area about a kilometer in diameter, which generally also included a minor ceremonial center consisting of two or three small plazas surrounded by ceremonial mounds.

A number of these minor ceremonial centers in turn would be found grouped at a distance from a major center, where a monumental ball court, carved stelae, hieroglyphic writing, and evidences of the great arts point unequivocally to the definition offered by Childe for the city in civilization.[19] Yet even the greatest of these centers was primarily ceremonial in character; they cannot be described as large dwelling clusters. In a sense the Maya offer a sequence of development toward civilization without cities, to borrow Professor Wilson's term for Egypt.[20] Perhaps the interim processes were entirely different, but there was a similarity in the end result.

GIBB: In trying to trace the development from preliterate villages to towns and cities, I wonder whether we have not neglected altogether the possibility that this may not have been a direct line of development at all. In other words, did the Sumerians derive from the earlier village societies on the Mesopotamian plain or did they enter Iraq subsequently from overseas to the south? Does a cultural break appear in the archeological record, after which new technological ideas and practices indicate an infusion from outside?

ADAMS: The archeological picture to me at least still seems to show important elements of continuity from the beginning of the occupation of the alluvium into the historic periods. On the other hand, the bulk of the evidence derives from ceremonial contexts, where there may have been unusual stress on the maintenance of unbroken traditions. Moreover, there are of course clear limits to the use of archeological evidence for the confirmation or denial of ethnic continuity. Sir Mortimer Wheeler,[21] for example, recently has described how the tremendous political, religious, and ethnic shift produced in India by the Moghul invasion was accompanied by a surprising retention of the older architectural forms. To be sure, they were invested with new meanings and functions, but the identification of function in archeological material is, to say the least, hazardous.

SPEISER: I know time is pressing, but I feel that among the questions raised so far there is one fundamental omission. If all of the questions were answered successfully, we would have only a blueprint for sameness. None of the questions that have been asked can give us the slightest understanding of why the prehistoric civilizations of

19 V. Gordon Childe, "The urban revolution," *Town Planning Review* XXI (1950) 3–17.

20 John A. Wilson, *The Burden of Egypt* (Chicago, 1951).

21 "Archaeology and the transmission of ideas," *Antiquity* XXVI (1952) 180–92.

Egypt differed from those in Palestine, Anatolia, and Mesopotamia, why those within Mesopotamia differed from one another, nor why the prehistoric phase in Mesopotamia differed so radically from the succeeding urban phase. Even if we answered the questions fully we would not, in short, have any understanding of what caused that great revolution at the beginning of civilization which was not only quantitative but qualitative as well. We would not understand why one day mankind realized with delight and trepidation that it could ride a bicycle and turned as if to say, "Look, Mom, no hands!"

ADAMS: I am sure we all are conscious of the limitation you have just expressed. It is the plan of this symposium to begin with features of the economy and environment which inevitably are the most similar as we move from one area of civilization to another. There is no need for us to continue to be preoccupied with these same features as we move tomorrow into historic realms for which new and vastly superior kinds of documentation are available. I share your impatience with the generality of the questions we have asked and with the spurious similarity of the answers we have sought to give to them. But I fail to see any alternatives that would serve us better.

TAX: I think perhaps we now should leave the alluvium for a time and take up our second major topic, which will be introduced by Professor Glueck.

FACTORS INFLUENCING THE RISE OF CIVILIZATION IN THE UPLAND: ILLUSTRATED BY THE NEGEV

GLUECK: May I commence with some questions? Are the essential factors influencing the rise of civilization in the upland basically different from those affecting its development in the lowland? Does the juxtaposition of the two themes indicate the priority of one over the other—of the latter over the former—as might be thought possible? Is there an inference that civilization first developed in the alluvium and then moved to the less fertile and less watered highland? Could it not be that it developed simultaneously in both areas, or that the lag between them, if there is such a lag, is of no consequence? May it not be that factors not primarily related to water and soil, such as trade and trade routes, are of decisive importance in the establishment of civilization in particular areas?

The character of these questions indicates my own feeling that while the factors influencing the rise of civilization in the alluvium

and in the upland, respectively, may be at times radically different, although frequently of closely related nature, they must first of all
methodologically be considered on an equal basis as an *x* quantity,
without any a priori prejudice as to the time sequence of their development in relationship to one another.

I have for some years been tracing the development of civilization
in the broken upland country of the Negev. An advanced type of
civilization existed there in the late Chalcolithic period of the fourth
millennium B.C. The brilliant excavations of Jean Perrot at Tell
Abu Matar, outside Beersheba, have revealed the presence of a sophisticated community that smelted and worked copper into various
tools and possibly dishes, carved delicate figures of ivory and bone,
wove baskets, built underground dwellings and aboveground houses,
and produced fired pottery, among other things.

This was no isolated community. I have discovered pottery remains of other Chalcolithic sites in the southern part of the Beersheba
basin of the northern Negev, and it is quite possible that still others
will be found farther south in the central Negev and in various places
in Sinai. These pottery remains have the closest affinity with those
of related sites in the rich irrigated lowlands of the Jordan Valley
and the northeast end of the Dead Sea and of sites in adjacent lands.
There was thus a discernible cultural interconnection between all
these sites in this early period, which for all practical purposes marks
the first, or for the present the first known, advanced civilization in
the Negev. There was no previous relationship to earlier Chalcolithic
phases and certainly none to the still earlier Neolithic period, which
is so magnificently represented by the highly advanced civilization
of Neolithic Jericho. The point that I am trying to make is that the
Chalcolithic civilization which established itself in the Negev was
contemporaneous with that of surrounding areas but was conditioned
by factors essentially different from those which influenced the rise
of Chalcolithic Tulailat Ghassul in the Plains of Moab at the northeastern corner of the Dead Sea, where there was plentiful water and
rich soil. In a word, the question to be asked, it seems to me, must
involve the objective factors determining the rise of a civilization,
be it in the lowlands or the highlands. We must assume, it seems to
me, that a civilization could develop contemporaneously in both
places.

Indeed, in the history of civilization, as in the history of ideas, the
proper procedure is to go on the premise that there is no *Ding an*

sich, no isolated civilization, no isolated site, unrelated to others of the same period; indeed, all sites are bound to others by all sorts of connections. It is only in completely isolated islands, separated from other lands by great bodies of water, that in very ancient times isolated or unique developments or arrested forms of life could occur which did not keep pace with growth and change elsewhere. Such phenomena could occur also, until recently at any rate, in isolated areas of virgin Africa, where a Stone Age civilization, almost completely unaffected by the modern world, could preserve itself, much as if it had been located in aboriginal Australia or Tasmania.

What is true with regard to the corelationship of the Chalcolithic civilization in the upland of the Negev and the lowland of the Jordan Valley is equally applicable to the Middle Bronze I civilization, which existed throughout the ancient Near East in low and lush lands, in fertile uplands, and in marginal lands such as the broken uplands of the Negev and Sinai. We have discovered dozens of Middle Bronze I sites in the Negev, dating between the twenty-first and nineteenth centuries B.C., marked by building remains and above all by clearly datable pottery remains. The pottery of this period in the Negev is in no wise distinguishable from that of contemporaneous sites anywhere in Palestine, Transjordan, or Syria. I doubt whether much of a time lag, if any appreciable number of years at all, existed between the establishment of Middle Bronze I sites in the lushest parts of the Near East and in the comparatively poor lands of the Negev, where the practice of agriculture was incomparably more difficult. The fact remains that, for many reasons, during this period as in earlier ones, people settled permanently in the Negev as well as in more clement regions of the Near East. The reasons for settlement may not have been the same, but the results may be included within the same pattern of a single and easily recognizable civilization which endured for approximately three centuries.

The location of the Negev, as part of the bridgehead between great continental masses, made it inevitable that from earliest historical times settlements would be located in it. Travel and trade routes led through the Negev between Egypt and Arabia, on the one hand, and between Palestine-Syria and Mesopotamia beyond, on the other, probably from the dawn of history. Each land mass exercised forces of attraction upon the other. Bedouins and merchants, messengers and mendicants, armies and refugees passed through the Negev, some staying permanently as peasants or soldiers or pilgrims or miners,

striking roots in the soil, and together with their families and kins-
folk building up civilizations, which maintained relationships with
the places and cultures of their origins. This was true of every period
of civilization in the Negev, which showed particular parallels with
the periods of early civilization in Transjordan. By the same token,
the same gaps in the history of sedentary civilization manifested
themselves at the same times in these two lands.

It becomes apparent, therefore, that the factors causing the rise
and fall of civilization in Transjordan and the Negev, each of which
comprised both fertile and marginal as well as completely inhospitable and incultivable desert stretches, were attributable not primarily to the nature of the soil and the quantity of water available
but to additional and often even more compelling factors chargeable
to the vagaries of trade and the fortunes or misfortunes of war. We
are compelled to conclude that in much of the Near East some of the
major factors causing the development of civilization in both upland
and lowland, in both lush and irrigated lands and marginal lands
oppressed by a scarcity of water, were essentially the same.

Perhaps the question dealing with the factors causing the rise and
development of civilization that is implied by the title given to this
session should be more specifically formulated than it has been. Perhaps it was intended that we should try to ascertain just when and
where civilization as such first commenced, although we are increasingly inclined to believe that that question is unanswerable. Damascus was one supposed to be the oldest city on the face of the earth,
but I know of none at the moment that is older than Natufian and
Neolithic Jericho, although it is highly possible that a still older one
or contemporary ones may be discovered elsewhere in the Near East
or in China or in some other area of the earth. So many variable
factors have to be considered that it is difficult, and I believe un-
scientific, to venture a definite conclusion, at least on the basis of
present knowledge.

Not only the factors of soil and water and exploitable mineral
riches need to be considered, but also those of ambition and exploitation and those involved in the seeking of new dwelling places and
the escape from intolerable persecution, all of which have to do with
the will and whims and the loves and hates of human beings. Certain
lands might never have been occupied and settled but for the potent
factor of religion. The very intensive occupation of the Negev during
the Byzantine period, when this marginal area of greater Palestine

contained hundreds of settlements graced by many magnificent churches and synagogues, may be attributed in considerable measure to the efflorescence of Byzantine civilization and particularly to the rise and expansion of the constructive forces of early Christianity.

It was natural for the early Christians to seek out the austerity of the desert of the Negev, in accordance with the living tradition of the presence of God's spirit there, which the Essenes and the Rechabites before them had transmitted from generation to generation and from century to century. Monks built cells in lonely places in the Negev. Monasteries were established in increasing numbers throughout the centuries of the Byzantine period. And gradually the settlements increased in number, and public security was re-established throughout the Negev. As the entire Byzantine Empire expanded in strength and wealth and as commercial relationships were renewed between lands stretching from and beyond Constantinople and Arabia and Egypt, the Negev knew a period of civilized settlement which was more intensive than any that had ever preceded it. Goods and emporia to contain them, hostels to provide lodging for travelers, whole cities to house those who dwelt permanently in the Negev, and an impressive renewal of the intensive and highly skilled practices of water and soil conservation and of agriculture that had been developed by the earlier Nabateans and Judeans all made their appearance. Some of the Byzantine cities, such as Abda and Isbaita, in the Negev could be compared favorably with others in more fertile parts of Palestine.

All of this efflorescence of civilization disappeared shortly after the advent of Islam in the seventh century after Christ. Trade routes were diverted, repressive economic measures were undertaken by the new authorities, but, above all, the economy and the religious attractiveness of the Negev were not of primary importance to the new rulers of the Near East. And soon the permanent population dwindled and drifted away, the terraces that preserved the soil and absorbed the rainwater were neglected (although many remain intact to this day), the cities crumbled and became the haunts of Bedouins, and civilized life disappeared from the Negev and Sinai.

In a word, I am convinced that the most important factor that affected the rise of civilization, in upland or lowland, in irrigation areas or areas with 4 to 8 inches of annual rainfall, is the human factor. I should like to point in this connection to Abraham, who may or may not be historical. (I think he was, but that is beside the point at the moment.) We are told in the Bible that when Abraham was in the Negev and Sinai and was about to sacrifice his son, a revelation came to him and he desisted. You may recall from excavations at Tulailat Ghassul and elsewhere that in Chalcolithic Palestine there was the practice of stuffing the bodies of infants into jars and burying them under the foundations of houses. Suddenly an idea comes to an individual and he is convinced—or a revelation comes to him, if one uses the language of religious experience—that this is not what the gods want or what God wants and therefore he desists. So a new order develops, and so in the religions of Judaism and Christianity and Islam we are told that what God wants is the sacrifice of the heart and not the sacrifice of the first-born.

TAX: The meeting is open for discussion, and perhaps initially we should seek agreement on whatever the important factors may be which influence the rise of civilization either in the upland alone or in the upland and the lowland together. Since the contrast and juxtaposition of upland and alluvium is a major geographical problem, we might turn first to Professor White for information about promising lines of approach to an understanding of these factors which have been developed by geographers.

WHITE: I think there is one concept in particular which comes out of the geographic analysis of decisions involved in resource management in various societies that may throw some light on certain of the questions that were raised. Reference was made to contemporary development of water resources in this region which we are considering. Some of us have been making a rough kind of appraisal of current uses of water resources. We find, tentatively, that even when we take into account all the new works which are being constructed with outside capital or with locally accumulated capital the probability is that for the southwestern Asian area the net change in arable acreage each year at the present time is a decrease, and we are not quite certain of its magnitude. That is, more land is going out of cultivation than is being brought in. The reasons for the decrease seem to be the standard explanations for the deterioration of irrigated land: salinization, silting, waterlogging, and occasional flood destruction, but primarily salinization. In trying to discover why there is an apparently very rapid loss of land through salinization in modern times, in the face of large-scale outlays for engineering works, agricultural extension activities, and education, we are driven to analyze the different elements in the decisions that are made by the operators of irrigated land. One of the significant elements seems to be the perception which the irrigator, as an individual or as a community, has of the resources involved. For example, in the Indus Valley land is going out of cultivation at a rate perhaps of 40 to 70 thousand acres a year through waterlogging. To a considerable degree this can be traced to the inability of the irrigator to perceive the effects in the long run, both downstream and in his immediate locality, of the water-management practices he follows. To generalize from this case, one may ask whether the distinctions that we were trying to make between different environments or areas may not be stated more accurately in terms of the relationship between the perception which the individual or society has of the environment at any given time and the environment itself. Put in this fashion, we can characterize the perception of the ancient Negev farmer as extremely clear. Similarly, there are certain irrigation situations, particularly the more simple ones of the kind which Dr. Adams referred to for the earlier periods of antiquity, where an accurate understanding of the major problems by the farmer was fairly easy. But, on the other hand, there are irrigation situations which are extremely difficult to recognize and deal with even in contemporary times with a very complex society and elaborate provisions for both research and education. I wonder whether this accuracy-of-perception factor may not explain some of the features which have been cited as not deriving readily from differences between the upland and the alluvium but rather as reflecting an indeterminate human factor.

GLUECK: I think that that is a very interesting point. I have noticed that large parts of the Near East are being rapidly denuded of trees, which are being cut down to make charcoal. The trees are frequently on hillsides, and, when intact, serve to hold the soil in place. Once the trees are cut down, the area laid bare is often plowed and planted to some crop or other. This, however, can be done only for several years, because the rains wash away the soil, which is no longer anchored by the tree roots, and soon the jagged rock ribs of the hill appear, and its fertility has been destroyed. If the modern inhabitants of the land would construct terraces on the hillsides which they have deforested, then their children and their children's children for generations would be able to till the soil which would be held in place by such terraces. Much of the land is terraced, but the terraces were for the most part anciently constructed. Where the terraces are intact, or where they have been kept in repair, the soil is still in place and is cultivated or is cultivable down to this very day.

JACOBSEN: I would like to speak to the question of what the factors are which give rise to civilization. This involves a number of suppositions, which I will state in so far as possible as questions rather than as assertions. First, does it seem in the light of all our historical and anthropological experience that what we call a high civilization is dependent on large concentrations of human individuals? Such concentration may take the form of cities, as it did in Mesopotamia when civilization there first arose, or it may take other forms not conditioned by the city pattern. But I think the record does show fairly uniformly a concentration of population in small areas. If this is a likely presupposition for the rise of a high civilization, is it not then incumbent upon us to inquire into what the possibilities are under which such a concentration can take place? Many factors may combine to influence the achievement of a high population density, but at least one is clear and difficult to avoid: the economic factor in its simplest form. In order to have a large concentration of individuals in a small area there must be the means to sustain these people economically. This in turn leads to a question relating more directly to our theme, the differences between the upland and the lowland. Were the conditions for creating economic surpluses that could sustain large populations the same in each? To deal with materials I know best, I shall compare the northern, upland part of Iraq and the alluvium. In the northern part there was no irrigation agriculture, and for all the prehistoric periods the pattern of settlement remained at a village level. For the earliest of our archeological periods in the upland we also have some conception of agricultural techniques, and one of the things which so far seems to be absent is the plow. In the alluvial lowland, through use of irrigation agriculture, it was possible to cultivate a very large area with perhaps greater ease than elsewhere because the stoneless soil could be worked with a wooden plow. I think it is very likely that the plow developed out of the adaptation of the hoe, which had been known previously in the upland, to being dragged along as the use of animal traction became better understood. It should be mentioned that, as far as we know, metal or stone were not utilized in the construction of the ancient plow until fairly late, a fact that points to its development in an alluvial area where even a wooden tip would not seriously limit its usefulness. In short, I think we can identify two features of lowland agriculture that greatly increased at least its initial productivity as compared with the upland: animal traction and the use of the plow. And productivity, I think, is closely related to the production of economic surpluses which alone could sustain large urban populations.

GLUECK: I am of the opinion, Dr. Jacobsen, that cultivation of the soil in the uplands in large parts of the Near East is relatively as easy and productive as in parts of the lowlands, particularly in those parts of the lowlands which require irrigation. Large parts of the east side of the Jordan Valley, which are dotted with ancient tells, are abandoned or lie fallow today because of the difficulties encountered by the moderns in irrigating them, as their ancient predecessors were wont to do. Irrigation could be reintroduced with beneficent results, but it is beyond the economic capacity of the present inhabitants without considerable governmental assistance. In the Jordan Valley crops are dependent largely upon irrigation. However, in the uplands on both sides of the Jordan Valley, where the climate is more temperate and where the rainfall is greater, it is possible to raise crops more easily. From this point of view, one might—although I am not attempting to do so—make a case to show that civilization developed first in the uplands and then, when more sophisticated means of agriculture had been developed through irrigation, descended to the lowlands, where agriculture was dependent upon irrigation.

ALBRIGHT: Perhaps it should be observed that, after all, most of the upland areas that have been mentioned consist of alluvial soils also. The alluvial deposits may be much more ancient, or they may have been laid down recently in narrow upland valleys by sheet erosion and flashfloods, but nonetheless they are as alluvial as the southern Mesopotamian plain. This is true of the Beersheba area, of most of the northern Mesopotamian uplands, and of all of the South Arabian valleys whatever their elevation.

WHITE: Beyond noting that both frequently are of an alluvial character, I feel that there is a more important fallacy in being satisfied with the contrast between *the* uplands and *the* alluvium. Within each of these great categories there is tremendous diversity in soil types and texture, in position of the ground-water table, in amount of organic matter in the soil. In fact, it is extremely difficult to generalize even between several small wadies or stream beds in the uplands or between successive hydrological regimes occurring along a great river like the Tigris or the Euphrates in its lowland course. I merely want to express a caution against lumping radically different environments too lightheartedly into great contrastive categories.

GELB: The contrast we are undertaking to define between upland and lowland civilizations raises the more general problem of how justifiable it is to make comparisons when there are apparently great differences in complexity. I have been particularly concerned for some years with the central role that writing played in the Mesopotamian and Egyptian civilizations. Writing was the basis of the whole economic life, the vehicle for the dissemination of myth and theology, the medium for the recording of what may be called history. Indeed, I have reached the conclusion that writing is of such importance that civilization cannot exist without it, and, conversely, that writing cannot exist except in a civilization.[22]

Yet in areas of the New World, which also have been called "civilized" here, I note that indigenous systems of writing were poorly developed or absent. The Inca of Peru, for example, relied on a mnemonic device of knotted strings called the "quipu," suitable only for rudimentary accounting purposes. Maya writing is more baffling, but even if the recent news of its purported decipherment[23] proves to be correct, it still was used only within very narrow religious and calendrical contexts. Aztec writing, while used to a limited degree for more secular purposes, such as the recording of tribute lists, never developed beyond a fairly crude pictographic level. This contrast between Old and New World civilizations can be extended to other important cultural features, for the pre-Columbian cultures in America are characterized by scarcity of metals, poverty of tools and weapons, limited agriculture and almost no domestication of animals, lack of the wheel and consequently of carts and wheel-made pottery, extensive human sacrifice, and cannibalism.

In short, I wonder whether we do not need to identify certain factors which are crucial for civilization and then to distinguish different kinds of civilization according to the degree to which these factors are present. And just as this approach leads me to see basic differences between the Old and the New World, so also it suggests tremendous differences between the riverine civilizations of Egypt

---

[22] Gelb, *A Study of Writing* (Chicago, 1952) pp. 221 f.

[23] See Y. V. Knorozov, " 'Drevnjaja pis'mennost' Centralnoj Ameriki," *Sovetskaja Etnografija*, 1952, part 3, pp. 100–118; "Pis'mennost, drevnich Majja. Opyt rasšifrovki," *Sovetskaja Etnografija*, 1955, part 1, pp. 94–125; "New Data on the Maya written language," *Proceedings of the Thirty-second Congress of Americanists, Copenhagen, 1956* (Copenhagen, 1958) pp. 467–75; "The problem of the study of the Maya hieroglyphic writing," *American Antiquity* XXIII (1957/58) 284–91.

and Mesopotamia, on the one hand, and upland civilizations like those of the Negev and Transjordan, on the other.

TAX: All at once we have not only the lowlands *versus* the uplands but also the New World *versus* the Old World. Perhaps the scope of our inquiry now has expanded beyond the limits of time that are available.

AL-ASIL: While listening to Dr. Glueck discuss the origins of civilization in the uplands, my mind turned to Hatra in the uplands of northern Iraq. While this great city-state came late onto the historical scene, the very important part it played during the centuries of rivalry between the Parthians and the Romans is well known. The point which emerges most strikingly is that its importance is in no way related to a favorable local basis for subsistence. With only a single small stream near by, water for agricultural and even domestic uses had to be provided through an elaborate chain of cisterns. Instead, the power and prosperity of Hatra was tied almost exclusively to its command of trade.

GLUECK: One could cite important parallels to that. Palmyra was a trade emporium which depended largely upon the riches of trade between Mesopotamia and Arabia, on the one hand, and Syria-Palestine and Egypt, on the other. Petra in Transjordan was a great trade center in the midst of a fertile agricultural area; it was occupied in early Biblical times, when it was known as Sela, and later became the capital of the Nabatean kingdom. In the Negev, proper, however, there are large cities, such as Abda, Khalasah, Isbaita, Ruhaibah, which were founded mainly in Nabatean times and flourished particularly in the Byzantine period, that were dependent upon trade and commerce and whose inhabitants cultivated the soil in the carefully terraced beds of innumerable wadies. They also constructed imposing systems of channels and cisterns and dams and covered whole hilltops with rows of so-called grapevine hills, *tuluilat al-anab,* to direct every possible trickle of the occasional rain water from the barren slopes to the terraced dry stream beds below, where the water was absorbed into the sponge of the earth and retained to nourish the crops planted in the terraced plots. The ancients knew all about water-spreading devices. I have seen a stretch of a terraced wadi bed, about a mile long and a quarter of a mile wide, whose water supply was derived from a catchment area of approximately 16 square miles on the slopes and tops of the hills on either side of it. The terracing of wadi beds was carried up to the very beginnings of the stream beds. Whenever the rains came, instead of being permitted to roar in unrestrained fury down the normally dry stream beds and tear up the good soil with their tremendous torrents, they were forced by the terraces to yield some of their flood to every terraced plot. Other parts of these floods were channeled to innumerable cisterns and sometimes caught behind dams, such as the one at Kurnub, and thus, in the aggregate, a tremendous amount of water was made available for drinking, for watering cattle, sheep, goats, and camels, and for storing sufficient moisture in the soil to nurture the crops. Fortresses and caravansaries marked the settlements which existed in the Negev from early historical times on. Soldiers became farmers and raised crops for themselves and their families and for the caravans that followed the roads they protected. Traders and merchants settled in villages, as early as the Iron II times of the Judean kingdom, which were guarded by hilltop fortresses above them. The terracing of stream beds in the Negev was extensively practiced in the time of the Judean kings, and, as I have said, was probably practiced as early as the time of Abraham in the Middle Bronze I period.

The Negev, which was supposed to be uninhabited and uninhabitable, turns out to have been occupied by a whole series of sedentary or semisedentary agricultural civilizations, with gaps of centuries between them. The history of sedentary settlement, based on agriculture, animal husbandry, and pottery-making, to speak of some of the main accomplishments, goes back to the Chalcolithic period; it continued in the Middle Bronze I period (21st–19th centuries B.C.), was renewed in the Iron II period (10th–6th centuries B.C.), and flourished particularly from the Nabatean to the end of the Byzantine period (i.e., from the 2d century B.C. to the 7th century after Christ), with a decline setting in for about a century after the conquest of the Nabatean kingdom and the diversion of the trade routes by the Romans in the second century after Christ.

KRAELING: I was very much interested in Dr. Glueck's account of the civilizations that developed locally in such places as Petra, connected with the Nabatean kingdom, and in the Negev and Palmyra. But all these local units, although involving the development of urban centers, presuppose a larger matrix of established civilization elsewhere. They arose from the establishment of military strongholds in the interstices between the great settled areas for protection of the main trade routes. As I understand it, we have been trying to establish during the first part of this symposium the original process of settlement, the earliest urbanization. Hence I wonder whether Dr. Glueck would also tell us something of how the earliest urban units became established in this part of the world, in order to provide a pendant to Dr. Adams' discussion of the earliest large social agglomerations in the alluvium.

Now we start, I believe, with traces of settled human habitation mainly along the littoral and in the great Jordan rift. Urbanization, at least according to Miss Kenyon, appeared first in the area of the great Jericho spring. What were the environmental factors that contributed to the growth of this first city? Although problems of water distribution enter the picture both at Jericho and along the Mediterranean shore, clearly there never was irrigation depending on the control of great streams like those in Mesopotamia. Other factors obviously must be considered. What animals were available for transport in the regions? What were the wild plant and animal sources of subsistence? What special natural resources were available to support an urban economy? In this connection, it is worth noting that a large income was still obtained in Roman times from the export of balsam from this region. If we knew more of the answers to these and similar questions, I think we would have a clearer picture of how urban aggregates first arose in at least a limited part of the Near Eastern uplands.

DELOUGAZ: I should like to emphasize a point just made by Dr. Kraeling. To my mind there is an essential difference between the situation presented to us by Dr. Adams and that given by Dr. Glueck. This difference involves primarily the contrast between primary and secondary development in distinction to the contrast between alluvium and upland. In other words, I think we must distinguish two separate sets of processes: those which brought about the first rise of civilization anywhere on this globe and those which led to the extension of civilization in later periods into areas where it had not been present previously. The second set of processes, I believe, derive from a substantially wider area of historical interaction, for they relate to geographic, climatic, political, and economic conditions of the preexisting civilized centers as well as to the local and derivative conditions civilization meets in areas into which it spreads.

One sees this difference very strikingly in the case of Mesopotamia. In the south one can trace the appearance of civilization through its several phases of development. The increase in average size and numbers of settlements during the Protoliterate period became apparent to us from the Oriental Institute's work in the Diyala region during the thirties. Another chapter is being added with current studies of the layout of the ancient irrigation systems. In these and many other respects, one can trace with considerable historical continuity many interdependent facets of the growth of a complex civilization. By contrast, in the north, where agriculture apparently began earlier than in the south, typical Mesopotamian civilization appeared only many centuries later as an importation from the alluvium. Clearly, in at least this case the processes of derivation and spread have nothing in common with the processes of primary origin.

TAX: I regret that there is time only for Dr. Glueck to have a last word in response to these comments.

GLUECK: Thank you. I think perhaps a brief word of caution is necessary with regard to using the relatively inhospitable Negev as an illustration of upland civilization in general. Since I freely confess that it is a marginal land and since civilization nonetheless developed there as early as the Chalcolithic period, the environmental potentiality for the growth of upland civilization in more clement regions such as central Palestine or central Transjordan stands out all the more clearly.

Particularly in relation to Dr. Gelb's assertion that civilization can be defined virtually in terms of writing, I should like to remind this body of the substantial chronological priority of Neolithic Jericho as what must be considered a civilized urban center in the broadly defined upland zone as contrasted with the Mesopotamian alluvium. Although lacking writing, Jericho is qualified by its excellent art and architecture for description as a civilized urban center as early as the eighth millennium B.C. In other words, the concept of civilization being dependent on writing needs to be re-examined.

In conclusion, I am as convinced after this discussion as I was before it that the factors contributing to the growth of civilization cannot be divided into upland and lowland categories. Aside from the question of the priority of upland or lowland civilization, which seems to me insoluble at the present time, the factors which produced civilization seem to have been the same for both.

BRAIDWOOD: Knowing that I have different views on the subject, Dr. Kraeling, who loves to tease the animals, has used the word "city" for Jericho. Dr. Glueck's comments suggest that he also believes in

Miss Kenyon's phrase "urban pre-pottery Jericho."[24] Professor Zeuner, who is studying the botanical and zoölogical specimens from Jericho, suggests in a recent paper[25] that the pre-pottery inhabitants of Jericho may not have practiced agriculture in the strict sense of the word, that is, including reaping, storage, tilling the soil, and the deliberate sowing of grain. In other words, if pre-pottery Jericho was a city, it may have been a city without agriculture.

[24] R. J. Braidwood, "Jericho and its setting in Near Eastern history," *Antiquity* XXXI (1957) 73–81; K. M. Kenyon, "Reply to Professor Braidwood," *Antiquity* XXXI 82–84.

[25] F. E. Zeuner, "Dog and cat in the Neolithic of Jericho," *Palestine Exploration Quarterly*, 1958, pp. 52–55.

II

The Development of Culture in the National States

MESOPOTAMIA UP TO THE ASSYRIAN PERIOD

Political Institutions, Literature, and Religion

WILSON (*chairman*): I would like to start this third session with a historical footnote. On December 5, 1931, twenty-seven years ago today, this building was dedicated with speeches by Raymond Fosdick of the Rockefeller Foundation, John H. Finley of the *New York Times,* and James H. Breasted; on that occasion John Finley recalled that Alcinoüs, King of the Phaeacians, had been called *ptoliporthos,* the "sacker of cities," and went on to say: "We hail you, Dr. Breasted, for whom the Orient flames again with a new day, . . . as Ptolisoter, the 'saver of ancient cities.'" It is interesting that on an anniversary we are talking again about the saving of cities or whether cities can be saved, and I thought it was an amusing coincidence.

I want to give our setting here. Yesterday we dealt in terms of background and, to a very considerable extent, material background: the problems of location, of utility, of resources, and some reference to technology at the beginnings. Although we come into a zone of human activity which we loosely refer to as "civilization," we never have succeeded in defining that or in being sure whether it *is* valid in each of the geographic areas in which we are interested. But we have to take it for granted, despite the open questions which are left, that this is a factor with which we are to deal, and we now move ahead with it into different areas. Today we are concerned with Mesopotamia, with the process which went on from that uncertain point in time at which civilization began, and with the uncertainty as to what happened at that point in time. We are engaged in a discussion which, inevitably, with all the talents that are here present, is an uneasy discussion. Some factors of uneasiness were present yesterday.

I am happy that to start off our discussion today we have one whom I regard as a great humanist and one who has successfully worked with social scientists, has engaged in projects which are essentially of the social sciences, and yet has retained, as you will see, the values which are of interest to humanists. Thus he may successfully, I think, engage in this difficult discussion which crosses disciplinary lines.

JACOBSEN: Mr. Chairman, ladies and gentlemen: I wish first to thank Dr. Wilson for the grave responsibility that he puts on my shoulders, a responsibility that I am not at all sure I can live up to.

This morning we move into the second day of our symposium and into a new and complex set of problems. Yesterday we discussed the ecological, economic, and technical factors which played roles in the expansion of the basic human unit from the small roving band of hunters and food-gatherers to the village, and from the village to the town and city. Our time range was that of prehistory, and our concern with culture was mercifully limited by the nature of the archeological materials to those aspects which serve man's bodily needs for food and shelter: economy and technical achievement. Today our time range takes us down into early history and our concern with culture correspondingly widens to include aspects which serve man's broader and more subtle security needs: government and law, religion, art and literature. But our basic focus remains. We are inquiring into the expansion of the human unit, into its scope, its nature, and its effects.

To keep this focus sharp and to avoid losing ourselves in the blur of variety and complexity of our large subject I would suggest that we concentrate our discussion as far as possible around four points central to our theme of expansion, and, since discussion proceeds most easily from a concrete thesis, I shall try not only to state these points but to commit myself positively on all of them.

The first point which, it seems to me, must necessarily demand consideration is the fact or nonfact of the expansion itself. Was there, in the time range and place which we are to consider, an expansion of the human unit? If there was, what were its nature and its terms?

To answer let us borrow the wings of archeology and history—not yet, I am afraid, an altogether safe means of transportation—and soar down the centuries and millenniums allotted to us. What do we see?

At first undoubtedly only caves, small roving bands, camps. Then, with the advent of the Jarmo and Hassunah age, small villages begin to dot the landscape of northern Iraq. This picture stays uniform for quite a while, and it is not until the Ubaid period that we spot our first cities. These cities are clustered in a tiny area, a narrow band along the edge of the swamps that border the Persian Gulf. A line east-west through Eridu and a similar line through Uruk delimit them approximately. Here the cities stay confined through all of the Ubaid and the following Warka period and part of the Protoliterate. Only at the middle or end of this last period is there movement, and the new larger form of settlement, the city, begins to spread northward toward Shuruppak and Nippur, into what was later Akkad, and into the Diyala region and so forth. As we move on to the following Early Dynastic period we begin to notice beyond the cities and their immediately surrounding territories the beginnings of rather shadowy units of larger scope: leagues of cities with a common meeting place, as for instance the Kingir League with a meeting place at Nippur; one-city hegemonies, arising when one city subdues other cities by force. The earliest of these is the kingdom of Kish; the climax of the form comes with the hegemony of Agade, which has empire proportions, reaching from the shores of the Mediterranean far into the Iranian highlands. As we continue our flight down the centuries we see the Agade empire shrink to a rather more firm and stable core: the territorial state of Kingir Uri or Sumer and Akkad, ruled by the Third Dynasty of Ur. But when this first territorial state breaks up under the impact of economic catastrophe we return to the smaller unit of the city-state, which dominates the scene through the Isin-Larsa to the Old Babylonian period. The Old Babylonian period, however, forms the beginning point for the creation of two new relatively weak but coherent territorial states, Babylonia or Akkad in the south and Assyria in the north, and these two remain in mutual rivalry through the Kassite and Middle Babylonian periods until a new powerful drive for expansion, centered in Assyria, takes us beyond the national state into empire and the problems that will face us tomorrow.

We have thus something to discuss. There was expansion of the human unit in our time range: from city and city-state to a grouping of city-states to territorial or national state. What, specifically, were these units? They were, rather clearly, political units, held together by common rule—"nations," to use Professor Gelb's termi-

63

nology—for we know of them primarily from statements of rulers telling us what they ruled. When the territory was so small that a single city entirely dominated the unit, we call it a city-state; when the capital has other cities, villages, and open land to balance it in the unit, we speak of a territorial or national state. There is thus relative clarity of outline. Do we also have a firm grasp of substance? Unfortunately not. We are as yet pitifully uninformed as to what went on inside these units: number and distribution of individuals, degrees of interaction. As to kinds of interaction, the material is somewhat better but still very spotty and treacherous. On the fairly central question of loyalties to the unit, in-group feeling, we can say that expressions of in-group feelings are exclusively in terms of city until shortly before the territorial state of the Third Dynasty of Ur, when Utuhegal resents the ravages of Gusium in terms of Sumer (Kingir) as a whole rather than in terms of any individual city or group of cities.

This, I think, is what can be safely said about our units. However, the question might be raised—and is raised by Professor Gelb in his paper (pp. 315–28)—whether we should not, besides or instead of these political groups, reckon with ethnic groups, peoples, cohering through shared cultural features such as custom, religion, language, etc. I tend to think that the answer for early Mesopotamian history should be a clear "no!" And by that I mean that, while groupings of individuals by common language, religion, custom, and so forth undoubtedly existed, such affinities do not seem to have found expression in conscious common aspirations or to have formed the basis for concerted action on the political scene. Rather these features existed as cultural distinctions between individuals on a purely private level inside the political unit, competing with and adjusting to one another peacefully. They did not become political issues. There are in our data no religious wars such as once plagued Europe, no wars about language such as now threaten India, and—though such would be new and refreshing to the historian—no wars based on preferences in artistic style. In fact the very thing which makes the concept of a people useful to the historian, that it gives him a constellation of cultural features which remain together as a unit and find articulate expression in political aspiration and action, is absent in ancient Mesopotamia. The cultural features do not form bundles but can only be followed separately in separate histories. Thus, after the Akkadian-speaking and Sumerian-speaking individuals come under common rule in the Agade period we see Akkadian religion swallowed almost completely by Sumerian religion, and all that remains is a handful of Akkadian names for Sumerian gods. Conversely, in art the elegant style favored in the city of Agade conquers the south completely, but—curiously enough—in calligraphy the much less attractive southern style persists. The Akkadian language does not conquer in the south. The south goes on speaking Sumerian, which enjoys political supremacy under the Third Dynasty of Ur and through a long period of independent city-states; then, late in the Isin-Larsa period, for reasons which are quite obscure to us, the Akkadian language takes over in the south also. The cultural features are seen to move singly and mysteriously, not in bundles which we can label "people" or *ethnos.*

Since our units are thus essentially political, it is natural to ask what kind of political structure they had and what happened to that structure as the units grew in size. This we may pose as the second point for discussion. The oldest type of political organization which our sources reveal is of a primitive democratic cast. Ultimate political authority is vested in a general assembly called into session in emergencies only. The assembly agrees on what should be done and elects a temporary officer to carry out its decision. Among such officers we may note especially the young leader in war, the king. This type of pattern is well known elsewhere in the world and can be found over and over again on tribal and village level. It relies for its efficiency on mutual agreement and works relatively well in a small area such as a village, where people know one another well. If it is extended over a large area, difficulties tend to arise. People find the long road to assembly irksome or dangerous; they are relative strangers to one another and find it more difficult to agree. Such difficulties arose in Mesopotamia as the human unit grew from village to city and then to leagues of cities such as the Kingir League. As a consequence the pattern was felt as more and more cumbersome on the top administrative and political level. The assembly was called more and more rarely, and the originally temporary officer, the king, tended to take over, to make himself permanent, and to run things on his own. This development was undoubtedly aided by the growing frequency and seriousness of war in Early Dynastic times, which made a permanent war leader a necessity. Thus the expansion had the effect of overextending and breaking the pattern of primitive democracy on the top political level and replacing it with a new type of pattern: monarchy. For a broader perspective on this development we may turn to Professor Rheinstein's paper, in which he points out that societies as high in the scale as agricultural societies may cohere and maintain order on the basis of custom and mutual agreement alone without force, without law, and without government to enforce laws. "These forces," he says, referring to customs, "can suffice to hold a society together for a long time, but they are insufficient when a society finds itself confronted with major tasks which require the long-term, disciplined, and organized co-operation of large groups. Such tasks are typically induced by war . . ." (p. 408).

Monarchy, the new political form to which the expansion of society gave rise, was based not on agreement but on force. The king relied on a standing army of retainers set apart from society as a whole and standing to him in an almost serflike relationship, and with this array he garrisoned the major cities of his domain. Through further historical development the monarch came to embody in his person a variety of functions, some old and some new. Economically, he became responsible for fertility through maintaining proper relations to the gods and through administrative tasks and responsibility for major irrigation works. Internally, he became the keeper of the peace by assuring his subjects access to legal relief, by establishing relatively early a "monopoly of force," and by his power to adjust and ameliorate common law through legislation. The earliest codes are all royal reform decrees. Externally, too, the king's aim was peace, usually, of course, to be achieved through victory and extension of his rule. Generally speaking this was as far as development carried in Mesopotamia during our time range. Adequate formal safeguards and checks on tyranny were only imperfectly developed.

These momentous developments on the political scene, in which expansion of the human unit overextended and broke a primitive democratic system based on agreement and replaced it with a monarchic system based on force, must be kept in mind as we turn to our third point, the implications of the expansion for religion.

Professor Eliade in his background paper (pp. 351–66) calls attention to a central characteristic of the religion of agriculturalists which he very finely terms "solidarity between man and plant life." It can hardly escape even a casual observer of ancient Mesopotamian religion that solidarity with vegetal and animal life is the very essence of its oldest layer, its base which gives it its pulsating life. If we travel northward through the changing landscape of Mesopotamia, paying attention as we go to the character of the chief deities of the oldest cities, we find in the south solidarity with the life of the swamps and marshes in the water god Enki at Eridu, Nanshe at Nina, Ninmar at Guabba. Next we come to a belt of herdsmen in solidarity with bovine life in Nir-esen-lal at Ki-abrik, Nanna at Ur, Ninsun and Lugalbanda at Kullab. As we approach the pastures of the Edin in central Sumer we find a circle of deities connected with the flocks: Inanna and Dumuzi in Uruk, Bad-Tibira, Umma, and Zabalam. And, lastly, on the northern edge of the Edin we find the cereal deities, Ninlil in Nippur, Sud in Shuruppak, Nisaba in Eresh, Ningirsu in Girsu.

Superimposed over this basic religious stratum lies, however, a later and quite different one. The major Mesopotamian gods, including those just mentioned, are not only forces in nature with which man is solidaric. They have at some point become rulers, with rulers' powers and responsibilities. They govern cities, have administrative and political tasks, meet in political assembly, choose political officers. Very clearly we touch here on religious concepts which have their roots in the process of social differentiation and the new political powers and responsibilities which were a consequence of the growth of the human unit beyond the village. And as we study in myth, hymns, and prayers the implications of these new concepts we see that they are no mere externals but rather that the social and political development has created experience and formed concepts which allow deeper understanding and more profound approach to the nature of the numinous itself. The social differentiation—and perhaps only social differentiation—first makes possible some grasp of the distance, the *majestas,* of the divine. The application of concepts such as "lord" and "ruler" carries implications of a new basis of trust and expectation, that of the retainer to his lord. With the image of lord and king, finally, expectations of justice are fixed upon the divine and the concept of a moral world order—such as Mr. Grene has dealt with for Greece (pp. 367–89)—rises into awareness in Mesopotamia. It is not too much to say that a new dimension of understanding, namely the nature of the divine, is opened up in the expansion of the social unit.

Our last point for discussion this morning concerns the implications of the expansion for art and literature. And, though I have

promised to commit myself, I must ask indulgence for moving somewhat cautiously on the periphery of the subject. The reason is doubt
about our ability for any real appreciation of ancient art and literature. I fear that a major part and perhaps all of the appreciation we
do have may be spurious. This said, and approaching obliquely, I
would submit as a valid axiom that the major art of any culture
avoids the trite and trivial and concerns itself with celebrating cultural essentials and that consequently pointers may be found in the
major motifs, since these will show the cultural areas instinctively
selected as proving grounds by the artists in the various periods.

I therefore first call your attention to our earliest known Mesopotamian art, that of the Protoliterate period. Its major theme is the
sacred marriage (*hieros gamos*), shown on the Uruk vase and on
numerous cylinder seals. The artist here celebrates the solidarity
with plant life, that solidarity which Professor Eliade mentions. The
literary counterpart may be found in the Dumuzi literature, which
celebrates this marriage and also the death of the life-giving powers
in vegetal and animal life. We find expressed here, in deeply moving
and often very beautiful form, emotions of joy shared with the god
and of sorrow at this death as sung by wife, sister, and mother. But
as one works with these materials they curiously begin to close in
on one, to suffocate the spirit almost. They are, so to speak, too personal in their values. The god is beloved but not for any special
virtue of his. Goodness, courage, character are all absent. He is, one
might say, "beloved" for no virtue but "for his own sake." Values
are immediate, unreflected, embodied in persons as is the love of a
mother for her son whatever he may be, whatever he may do. They
are not measured—and indeed are not measurable—against any external scale.

The major theme of Mesopotamian art in the Agade period is exemplified in Naramsin's stela of victory. Here we breathe a very
different air. Instead of a recurrent cultic event the artist celebrates
an individual historical moment in time. Central to the composition
is the triumphant king on a mountain top; toward him, as leader,
are turned the eyes of his warriors. The literary counterpart is the
epic, which also celebrates the human hero. And in the manner of
celebration we notice important and distinctive features. In the story
of Gilgamesh and Agga, for instance, Gilgamesh's drive to leadership
cannot be realized except in conflict with his moral debt to Agga,
who has helped and befriended him. The tale shows how he resolves

the dilemma in terms of nobility. In the story of Gilgamesh and Huwawa the human impulse to spare the conquered foe finds expression in the hero Gilgamesh but succumbs to the lower morality of the slave Enkidu. In the Gilgamesh epic the limits to all human endeavor set by death are explored. Thus in the figure of the hero, the warrior king, a new morality, more explicit and more abstract, arises from the expanded scene. Moral duties to oneself, nobility of action, moral claims of strangers or even enemies have come into consciousness. With the expansion of the human unit, in Professor Kluckhohn's words (p. 403), "the moral order becomes more explicit and self-conscious, more abstract, more codified, more rationalized."

The last major theme in Mesopotamian art to which I would call your attention is the presentation scene, immensely popular from the Third Dynasty of Ur onward. It is best known perhaps from the stela which bears the law code of Hammurabi, where the ruler stands attentive before the god and awaits his orders. Here the artist celebrates perhaps an even greater vision: the moral order grounded in divine will carried out by the human ruler permeating the harmonious universe. As literary counterpart I suggest the Creation epic with its grandiose vision of world order as a political order achieved by Marduk, who was chosen to be war leader of the gods and later administrator and who assigned to the gods their official tasks and created man to serve them.

Comparing the atmosphere surrounding the first of these three major themes with that of the two later ones, we can perhaps make a good case for assuming that the expansion of the human unit gave to the Mesopotamian artist for the first time "the great theme"; and this we can perhaps follow up with Schiller's lines "Im engen Kreis verängert sich der Sinn / Es wächst der Mensch mit seinen höhern Zwecken." In a sense these lines may be applied to all the cultural implications that I have dealt with. The expansion set greater goals, with which man grew to greater stature in statecraft, in religion, in art and literature.

In conclusion may I say that the presentation of these points in such heartening and optimistic light was, of course, not achieved without rather considerable sacrifice of sophistication. I have implied that the development of culture toward greater profundity and richness is a supreme value. That does not mean that I consider such a development *the* supreme value; I consider it only *a* supreme value. It should be kept in mind also that we are dealing with a degree of expansion which never threatened the unity of culture. It affected culture, but there was never any danger that culture would be broken. To the great national state corresponds a great, coherent, and consistent national culture. Tomorrow, when we deal with expansion in terms of empire, we shall face a degree of expansion where, within the same political unit, great national cultures must challenge each other on levels so basic that their very identity is at stake and the possibility of arriving at a valid higher unit necessarily becomes problematical.

WILSON: Thank you very much, Dr. Jacobsen. To start off, perhaps a little arbitrarily, I will ask Professor Speiser to comment on this presentation.

SPEISER: After listening to the masterful summary of an experience involving a large sector of mankind and extending over centuries of prehistory as well as twenty-five hundred years of recorded history and, in spite of its necessary brevity, expressed in terms of philosophical thought rather than as merely an accumulation of facts, I find the task of commenting just a bit short of impossible. Perhaps this is fortunate, because as a result it can be done in a very few words.

The emphasis throughout has been on expansion. This, I suppose, is another term for continuity, a continuity, moreover, through diversity. In spite of a series of ethnic elements, a number of languages, including at least two dominant ones, and a number of different political phases, there remains, when all is said and done, a unity which we know as a cultural manifestation. That culture is not Sumerian or pre-Sumerian; it is not Akkadian; it is not Babylonian; it is not Assyrian. It *is* Mesopotamian;[1] it is a conglomerate of them all. In some way that remains mysterious, integration did take place. The process of the Tower of Babel was reversed, and a unity was achieved that is significant in modern terms, for otherwise we would not be talking about it here. It was unpredictable. We cannot gather up the facts of prehistory as we have them and arrive at that juncture which we know as the beginnings of history, or the urban revolution, and say, given these things, "Out comes Mesopotamian civilization." There is that quantum element in it which will always mystify. And while we collect the facts—and as specialists that is all we are allowed to do—we must also, as humanists, ask ourselves "why?" and hope that the social scientists will not scold us for asking this question. But that "why?" is important.

[1] E. A. Speiser, "Ancient Mesopotamia," *The Idea of History in the Ancient Near East* ("American Oriental Series" XXXVIII [New Haven, 1955]) pp. 42–43.

Egypt and Mesopotamia grew up side by side. Each gave us important experiences of mankind, yet each was very different. And the differences did not consist just of material things, or language, or literature, or architecture. There was not merely the difference between the pyramids and the zigurrats; there were also the differences in thought that lay behind these, in the way of life reflected by the pyramid and the way of life expressed in the zigurrat. The source of these differences is elusive, but a problem that we have to consider. Henri Frankfort, in his inimitable way, spoke of a difference in underlying mentality,[2] for which he was scolded by the ever vigilant social scientists. Today the social scientists themselves have developed a subdiscipline devoted to the study of "national character." In other words, perhaps it is becoming respectable again to talk in such terms. The source of the differences is, in any case, a central problem in spite of its elusiveness. I urge that we consider in the discussion to follow just how these mutations, these sports that somehow mark our yesterdays, came about.

ALBRIGHT: Mr. Chairman, I agree entirely with my distinguished colleague, Professor Speiser, that it is next to impossible to comment briefly on Professor Jacobsen's presentation. In fact, I should say that it is impossible. I learned something about Professor Jacobsen's way of going at research in 1946, when I sat at his feet for three months. After we had discussed various questions until long past the appointed hour, he would go home and spend the next night or weekend sitting up and solving the problems which had been brought up. I then learned to admire his extraordinary gift for analysis and classification.

And now for Mesopotamian civilization! In analyzing the origins of civilization we must remember that the literate period was extremely brief, going back only to about 3000 B.C., and that it was preceded by some two hundred thousand years of tool-making and, presumably, speaking man. (I follow here the latest estimates of man's antiquity based on enriched radiocarbon counts and their correlation with the evidence of oxygen isotopes.) In other words, literacy represents only a thin veneer over a tremendous accumulation of preliterate drives and experiences. From the first beginnings of an incipient agriculture somewhere around 10,000 B.C., at the beginning of the Mesolithic period in western Asia, to the effective introduction of writing we have some seven thousand years. From

[2] E.g. *The Birth of Civilization in the Near East* (Bloomington, Indiana, 1951) p. 42.

the introduction of fixed towns and villages, often surrounded by walls, about 7000 B.C., to the introduction of writing we have some four thousand years. During some two thousand years of prepottery Neolithic (*ca.* 7000–5000 B.C.) hundreds, if not thousands, of such installations were constructed, from Pakistan to Thessaly. There can be no doubt that Jarmo and Jericho, Shimsharah and Khirokitia are only isolated examples belonging to a vastly greater number. I do not mean that they all arose at the same time, of course. We must expect to find deposits of pre-agricultural, agricultural, and even town culture underlying the literate civilization of the third millennium. (Note that I agree with Professor Braidwood in objecting to the use of "urban" and "urbanization" at this remote time.)

After recognizing the long prehistory of Mesopotamian civilization, we must reckon with the centrality of Mesopotamia and with the fact that it was exposed from all directions to invasions, including attacks from Syria, Anatolia, Armenia, and Iran, to say nothing of unending raids from the exterior and interior deserts. In other words, we have here a civilization which had to fight for its very existence, a vivid illustration of Toynbee's principles of "the stimulus of blows" and "challenge and response." Moreover, since the Mesopotamians had to develop a civilization at the same time that they were resisting aggression, they were forced to find means of building up this resistance and thus had to develop agriculture and commerce. Commerce inevitably brought with its expansion the development of a strong economy at home, which meant enlargement of irrigation. Without commerce there could be no irrigation of importance, but without irrigation there could be no commerce of significance. This is the old story of the chicken and the egg. The chick needed food in its egg, so we have irrigation; the chick needed protection in its egg, so we have empire—whatever the original order of stimulation may have been.

Mesopotamian higher culture developed much farther than Egyptian in some directions, although certainly not in all. For example, Babylonian higher culture attained a capacity for abstract thinking and classification which Egypt never reached. I think that Professor Neugebauer hit on the true explanation years ago, when he pointed out that the place zero in Babylonian mathematics could only arise in an ideographic system of writing.

If for the moment we forget the ordinary Mesopotamian, who presumably spoke only one language in most periods, we must recognize that all educated scribes during the thousand years between the late third and the late second millennium were bilingual. Of course, there was earlier and later bilingualism, but during the period in question virtually all higher culture had to be bilingual. This situation, which has many parallels, directly contradicts those philosophers, anthropologists, and linguists who insist that a radically different linguistic structure entails different logical approach to thought. Thanks to the practical bilingualism of higher culture in the formative period of Mesopotamian civilization, it became possible for the Babylonians to free themselves from the tyranny of words for the first time in history. In some ways they were actually ahead of all known peoples before recent times. (It is no accident that in Mesopotamian literature we find surprisingly few plays on words, paronomasia, especially when contrasted with Egypt, where plays on words were basic to much religious and other thinking.) It was this bilingualism which made Mesopotamian writing ideographic rather than almost purely logographic like Egyptian. (Though I do not deny the importance of the logographic element in cuneiform, the numerous instances in which many different Sumerian and Akkadian words are all represented by the same sign cannot be called "logographic" but must be termed "ideographic.") By freeing themselves to some extent from the tyranny of words and by being forced to contrast radically different linguistic structures, the Babylonians were able to create, for the first time in history, a primitive linguistic science emphasizing structure. On the other hand, Egyptian philological efforts remained incredibly naïve; the Egyptians never even learned to arrange their onomastica according to any systematic order.

Particularly instructive is a comparison between Egyptian and Babylonian mathematics. The Egyptians did reach respectable heights in empirical geometry because they had to redistribute their fields after inundations, plan the construction of mathematically exact pyramids, and so on. Thus they developed fine practical skill in surveying and architecture. But, on the other hand, they did nothing in such fields as algebra, where a certain amount of abstraction and a place zero are essential. Here the Babylonians anticipated Diophantine algebra by some two thousand years.

This is a good illustration of the importance of human geography, as well as of basic physical geography, without which it would be impossible to understand the fundamental difference between static

Egyptian and dynamic Mesopotamian cultural tendencies. There is no substitute for infinitely painstaking collection of physical and archeological data in order to understand the background of any civilization. Arbitrary assumptions, whether drawn from idealistic philosophy, as in the case of Collingwood, or from some other source, are doomed to failure. I do not deny for a moment that philosophical idealism is an indispensable ingredient of modern Western higher culture or that we owe a great deal to it for increasing our stock of ideas and widening our mental horizons, but no form of it has any value for the interpretation of history prior to the impact of philosophical systems on history itself. The career of R. G. Collingwood, who combined active archeological work with neo-Hegelian thinking, is perhaps the best illustration of the impossibility of effecting the synthesis at which he aimed. To be sure, his failure was itself a rather brilliant *tour de force*.[3] The fact remains that we cannot use any form of idealistic speculation to complement archeological and documentary fact when we try to reconstruct the development of Mesopotamian civilization. The attempt to do this has, for example, vitiated much of the late Henri Frankfort's brilliant work.

WILSON: Thank you, Professor Albright. Continuing to be arbitrary, I am going to call upon two more speakers before asking Professor Jacobsen to reply.

GELB: I welcome the challenge thrown my way by Professor Jacobsen, and I might add that I have never enjoyed anything more than a good debate with him all through the years that I have known him. I shall speak to the topic of *ethnos* and *demos*. In order to explain the situation, I must go back about twenty years, to the time of Dr. Jacobsen's article on "The assumed conflict between Sumerians and Semites in early Mesopotamian history."[4] The main point of this article was that the conflict between the different human groupings in ancient Mesopotamian history was based not on racial but on purely political and territorial factors. It maintained that the conflicts which can be attested in texts were not between Sumerians and Semites as representing two different racial groupings but between one city and another or between one city-state and another, whether they were occupied by Sumerians or Akkadians. Without attempting to define what he meant by the terms "race"

3 Cf. Professor Speiser's running dialogue with Collingwood in notes to his article on "Ancient Mesopotamia" in *The Idea of History in the Ancient Near East.*

4 *Journal of the American Oriental Society* LIX (1939) 485–95.

and "racial," Professor Jacobsen expressed himself rather strongly against the Nazi racial theories prevalent at the time and specifically attacked four historians of the ancient Orient, namely Eduard Meyer, James H. Breasted, L. W. King, and H. R. Hall, for their misuse of racial terminology.

Even at the time of publication I had the feeling that his attack on the four historians was not quite justified. Upon recently going again through my edition of Meyer's history, I find that, while the German historian used terminology which may not be acceptable today, he was quite clear on the matter of race. He did not believe in the purity of races; he assumed that from the very earliest historical times both the Indo-Europeans and the Semites showed marked racial admixtures coming from all directions, and he never attempted to explain historical processes in terms of the superiority or inferiority of certain races.

While it is true that the expression "race" appears frequently in the publications of Breasted, King, and Hall, here again it seems to me that Dr. Jacobsen's attack was not quite justified, for he might equally well have attacked the English language, where the word "race" is used in many bewildering senses. Cases in point are the uses of the terms "race" or "racial" in the works of, let us say, Rudyard Kipling or Winston Churchill. With his great historical insight it seems to me that Breasted in particular, in spite of his occasional misuse of terminology, could not have failed to perceive that not the slightest trace of what we would call racial conflict can be attested anywhere in ancient times.

In fact, the very concept of racial conflict is quite recent. It seems to me that it does not go farther back than the nineteenth century, to the theories propounded by Count Gobineau, Madison Grant, and Houston Chamberlain. We find nothing of the kind in the Orient. The Mesopotamians, who call themselves "black-headed people," seem to show a certain preference for light-skinned slave girls; a "ruddy" David is found among the presumably darker Hebrews; and in more modern times we find people of Negroid descent playing an important role among the Arabs.

What Dr. Jacobsen accomplished in his article at the time was to purge the atmosphere of Nazi racial theories and to persuade scholars in the Oriental field to avoid loose usage of the term "race." While I fully agree with him, of course, on the elimination of racial considerations, I wonder whether the territorial-political factor he introduces instead is as important as he makes it out to be. The astonishing thing, it seems to me, is that Jacobsen does not even mention the word "people" or *ethnos* in this article.[5] For many years I have thought that Jacobsen refused to consider the ethnic factor because of the old-fashioned belief that a people or *ethnos* forms merely a subdivision of a race in the sequence race-people-clan-family. Today it has become clear that at least he recognizes the existence of ethnic differences founded on the basis of common language, religion, customs, and so forth, but he treats them as "distinctions between individuals on a purely private level," which do not form a basis for concerted action on the political scene.

Now, what is an *ethnos?* An *ethnos* to me is a unit, a group of individuals, linked together by all kinds of different characteristics, such as a community of traditions, especially tradition as to common descent, common customs, common religion and mythology, a definable continuity of geographic position, and, above all, a common language. All these elements need not be present in the same force in all cases, and some of them may even be completely absent. For instance, the element of religion at one time must have played a very important role in linking certain groups of individuals in an *ethnos,* while today it may play a less important role. My conclusion about the paramount role of language as a factor in ethnic groupings of ancient times grew out of observation of the history of such diverse peoples as the Sumerians, the Amorites, the Kassites, the Babylonians, and the Assyrians. I find that whenever a linguistic attestation for a certain people disappears, at the same time the very ethnic entity disappears. Thus when Sumerian stopped being used as a spoken language, the Sumerians disappeared as a separate people. (The problem of bilingualism raised by Professor Albright is not pertinent here, since Sumerian was continued, after it died out as a spoken language, only as a second, literary or religious, language of the learned classes.) Of course the Sumerian-speaking peoples were not killed off by the Akkadian-speaking peoples. The Sumerians were simply assimilated to the next milieu and gradually gave up their own language, and, once the process of the linguistic change-over was completed, they lost their identity as the Sumerian people

[5] As pointed out by D. O. Edzard, *Die zweite Zwischenzeit Babyloniens* (Wiesbaden, 1957) p. 4, n. 17, and, indirectly, by A. Falkenstein, "La cité-temple sumérienne," *Journal of World History* I 808.

and became Akkadians. The same process of assimilation took place with the other peoples mentioned above.

The problem of Greece is more difficult. However, even the Greeks gradually realized that they too represented a rather homogeneous linguistic community. They called themselves Hellenes, and they called all other people Barbaroi, which means the same thing as Barbarophonoi, that is, people who speak foreign or barbarian languages. Basically they thought of themselves as speaking different languages. Of course in their conception of the extent of their own, Greek, language they were not always correct, as shown by their inclination to reject the Macedonians as a Greek people, but we find parallels to such possibly chauvinistic attitudes in chapter 10 of Genesis, which places the Phoenicians (very closely related to the Hebrews) among the Hamites and not among the Semites. In referring to the Greeks it is noteworthy that Herodotus talks about the common language that unified them, about common blood and religion, and about their way of life. To be sure, the unification of all the Greek-speaking peoples was not easy; there was always a struggle between the polis-centered attitude, on the one hand, and the tendency toward a single *ethnos*. But when that union was finally achieved in the Hellenistic period, it manifested itself chiefly in the use of one common language, the *koine*.

In pleading the importance of language in the consideration of ethnic entities in ancient times, I am fully aware that this may not apply with the same force to modern times, colored as they may be by new ideas about peoples and nations which came out of the Age of Enlightenment. But the Arabic situation at the present time is very enlightening. We find today Arabic-speaking peoples living in a wide area stretching from the Atlantic to the Indian Ocean. We find a striving there to achieve a kind of political unity. What is it based on? It is not based any longer on common religion, for Christians (in Lebanon, Syria, and North Africa) are playing an increasingly great role; it is not based on common customs, for customs are probably as varied in that vast area as anywhere in the world; and it certainly cannot be based on any tradition as to common descent, since obviously the peoples living in that area are of many and varied origins. What we do find is a geographic continuity and, above all, Arabic as a common language or, at least, as a common literary language.

Thus we have all kinds of problems to consider: first of all the

linguistic situation, then the paramount role of language as the unifying force of an *ethnos,* and now the relationships of *ethnos* to
demos. Somewhat arbitrarily, I use the term *demos* to denote a body
of people linked together by a state or by a common will to achieve
a state. Is there such a thing as a striving of a folk society, called
ethnos or people, to achieve a political form, *demos?* According to
Dr. Jacobsen, there is not. However, if we observe the political units
in Mesopotamia as they grow from smaller to larger bodies, from
city to city-state, from city-state to national state, and then to empire,
we can note in each case the importance of ethnic considerations. On
the city-state level we note that the city-state does not represent a haphazard agglomeration of different individuals but has a certain type
of population that speaks a certain type of language. The ethnic organization of the population became clear to me only a few years
ago, when I discovered that the expression *šu,* "of," attached to personal names (cf. O' in O'Callaghan, O'Reiley) designates not pater-
nity but clan affiliation. Now "clan" is an ethnic term. When we
pass from the city-state to the larger state, we meet again with units
based on ethnic ties, as shown by the evidence of the terms Kingir
and Uri, Sumer and Akkad, which denote two national states, each
composed of a number of what were originally city-states of markedly
uniform ethnic background, either Sumerian or Akkadian. As the
national states grow we find states composed not of one but of several ethnic groups. And here again an observation can be made.
There is always one and only one dominant *ethnos.* The importance
of language in the new setup can perhaps be illustrated by the expression *ana pî išten turrum,* which is found frequently in Assyrian
inscriptions. Word by word it means "to turn (a certain people) to
one mouth"; its real meaning is "to subjugate." If my interpretation
of "to turn to one mouth" as "to turn to one language" is correct,
then we have here important evidence that "to subjugate peoples"
originally meant to the Assyrians "to impose on them their own
(Assyrian) language."

Robert Redfield, quoted by Milton Singer, expressed himself in
the following way: "The unit of political life tends to become identified with a people who share a common moral order." It is this
moral order, or community of interests, as I would rather call it, that
is of the greatest importance in our evaluation of ethnic groupings.
What is it based on? Did the political bodies of the ancient Near
East arise and grow in a completely haphazard way on the basis of

some nebulous interests artificially acquired within some territorial boundaries—something like the Monacans of our day—or did they have as their basis a community of interests deeply rooted in a certain ethnic background?

OPPENHEIM: By way of reacting to the very stimulating talk of Dr. Jacobsen, I would like to tie in what he has said with what was the center of interest yesterday and eventually with what is, in some way, the purpose of our being here, that is, the concept of the city. Dr. Jacobsen has traced in a persuasive and poetic way the development from village to city to empire, whereas I would like to stress the aspect of that development for which we have actual philological evidence. Since I am a philologist, I will stick to that evidence and make the best of it, attempting to describe it for my colleagues and for other scholars here from across disciplinary borderlines.

To put it in a nutshell, it may be said that the city is the institutionalization of the desire for continuity in Mesopotamia. We have quite a bit of material which illustrates this. We may know very little about how these people felt, how they considered themselves, since they were not Greeks who looked at themselves critically and found it essential to describe their own place in their world. However, there are some indications, very often indirect but occasionally quite direct.

I shall begin with a small unpublished tablet in the Babylonian Collection of Yale University. It is an Old Babylonian legal text in which a city sells an ownerless plot of land within its walls. While this is a unique text, it shows that the city, whatever that meant, is to be considered as a legal personality which had the right to dispose of territory within it to a private person.

A possible parallel to this collective attitude can be found in the way the city's inhabitants thought about themselves in relation to royal authority. There was at all times a definite contrast, a clash of interest, between the king and the city. This attitude shows as early as the time of Ishme-Dagan (1953–1935 B.C.), who found it important to mention in a state formula that he relieved the city of Nippur of paying taxes and that he released its citizens from certain services and from military obligations. From this point we have to skip nearly a millennium to find a parallel statement, the document that is known as the "charter of Assur," in which the Assyrian king Sargon (721–705 B.C.) grants the same liberties and privileges to his capital city. There is, furthermore, a passage in Ezra (4:13) which revealingly says: "Be it known now unto the king, that, if this city is builded, and the walls set up again, then will they not pay toll, tribute, and custom, and so thou shalt endamage the revenue of the kings." And this Bible passage describes exactly the attitude of the Mesopotamian city from the earliest period on. What the original relation was between palace and city I do not know and can offer only a number of suggestions. But the stress placed on civic liberty, the pride in being a citizen of a city, is very characteristic of Mesopotamia. In about the middle of the second millennium B.C. a special term was used for it, an Akkadian term (*kidinnūtu*) that refers to the rights of the inhabitants of the city, and it seems that every king, in Assyria in the first millennium B.C. at least, had to confirm these rights if he was not in position to enforce his will upon the city. That the city and its representatives write letters to the king and that the king writes letters to the city are already attested in a much earlier period.

Apart from the pride and the self-sufficient attitude of the city-dwellers, there also existed in Mesopotamia throughout its history an anti-urbanization trend. There was definite resistance against urbanization in large regions, the very regions where no cities grew naturally, where there always have been villages only. There may have been ecological reasons for this, as was pointed out yesterday, but at the same time it is worth noting that in some sections of Mesopotamia people had to be forced to live in cities. A policy of forced urbanization was tried time and again by the Babylonian and Assyrian kings and was continued by the Persian kings. Moreover, the Greeks and Romans, whenever they ruled the region, had likewise to compel or lure people into cities. Thus we see that the phenomenal urbanization in Mesopotamia was in fact restricted with regard to location. It was natural only in the south, in the small region of which Dr. Jacobsen spoke earlier. That region is quite narrow, and I have always liked to recall that from the tower of the temple in Eridu one can see as far as Ur and from Ur one can see Larsa and Uruk. Outside that region there are no city clusters. Assur may originally have been a sacred city, like Jerusalem, rather than the royal city of an empire, like Boğazköy and other cities in the ancient Near East. Genuine urbanization, in my opinion, was restricted to central and southern Mesopotamia. It developed there together with a concept of the city which is quite unique, and both perhaps should be compared with the concept of the Greek polis, which also is unique. The polis seems to have been a typical product of the Greek social experience exactly as the Sumerian *uru*, the Akkadian *ālu*, was the expression of Mesopotamian social experience. Of course the kings tried to build new cities and were often quite successful; in fact, the building of new cities characterized Mesopotamian history from the time of Sargon of Agade to the disappearance of the Assyrian empire. The kings had to build new cities because the old cities opposed them; they could not tax the old cities, they could not use them for services, they could not run them as they wished.

In spite of the forced-urbanization policy of the kings, there was never in Mesopotamia an articulate opposition against the city as we have it in the Old Testament and in the classical Greek and Roman periods. The city was always accepted as the basic institution for civilized living.

WILSON: Dr. Jacobsen, do you want to comment before we go on?

JACOBSEN: Dr. Speiser raised a very important point, to which Dr. Albright returned, with respect to the mysterious entity that gave unity and, figuratively speaking, personality to the large cultural units. One of the fascinating problems in our field is the contrast between Mesopotamian civilization and Egyptian civilization, and the comparison can be very rewarding if one tries to regard these as persons, that is, to respect their separate identities. Dr. Albright mentioned some possible clues as to why these two civilizations show different characters, and I think we will all agree with him that the fact of a bilingual situation in Mesopotamia had interesting and important consequences. Among them certainly was the rise of interest in language and the advanced state of Mesopotamian study of language.

In this connection one might think of another factor that presumably played a part in the development of separate identities: the very distinct differences in inner security that are immediately apparent when one compares the Mesopotamian and Egyptian scenes. There was in Egypt an inner security that led to what one might call a polished society. As one looks over world history he finds few societies that are distinguished by this quality. To some extent it may be found in the history of Rome, where there was an ease, an elegance of manner in living together which was almost a climax of what human beings are able to attain. More definitely, that feeling of grace and ease of manner can be perceived in Egyptian art. I think it is justifiable to mention this point at a symposium that deals with civilization because you will notice that terms for civilization—civilized, urban, etc.—all aim at an ideal of the ease and gracefulness of humans living together. It would be wrong, I think, to forget that this lies very close to the concept of civilization and civilized.

As to Dr. Albright's kind remarks about sitting at my feet, I believe you will all realize what a terrible experience it was to have a student who was so far ahead of me that I could only try to keep up with him. His remarks on the necessity for an objective approach to ancient culture prompt me to say "yes." However, in another sense I think that this is one of the curious cases where both sides are right. Unless we try with all sincerity to project ourselves as far as we can into the forms and the lives of the civilizations we study, even though that never may be entirely possible, we shall distort rather than clarify our subject.

As has Dr. Gelb, I have always enjoyed our airing of our differences. We always have agreed in fact far more than in words. The difference in our views on the question of *ethnos* is not really so deep as one might think. My own chief concern is that we provide ourselves with the sharpest and the most useful intellectual tools available as we approach our subject. And for this purpose I find it more useful to view the ancient scene in political terms than in ethnic terms. This is because the sources from which our knowledge comes speak in political terms, so that any transfer of an early political term into an ethnic framework is a reconstruction on our part; until we have more definite evidence, I think that excessive reconstruction will tend to be misleading.

I feel this so much the more because we now are witnessing a period of history in which national movements are among the strongest forces at work. It is certainly very tempting to draw parallels, to say that because national feeling and national self-expression are so dominant on the political scene today they must have been so also in antiquity. But I think we have no right to do that. We have to say it may have been so, but until we have proof of the parallel we cannot operate truthfully and effectively as scholars with such conceptions. For the ethnic distinction to be a useful tool it must correspond to the data. It must represent a bundle of cultural features, including language, which stay together through time and can be recognized in political actions. So far this is not the case with older Mesopotamian history, and I limit myself to that field. It is possible that ethnic concepts may be useful when we consider the Babylonian and Assyrian cities and states. But there again, as far as I know, we have no concrete evidence to show that unity of ethnic aspirations found a distinct and clear-cut form in political aspirations and political actions.

I would like to express my gratitude to Dr. Oppenheim for bringing out so clearly a feature that is of great importance for our subject. In the time allotted me I cannot touch upon the continuation of the city into later Mesopotamian history as a separate entity in unspoken conflict with the royal power. Yet, even in tracing developments on higher political levels, one cannot escape the fact that the city continued to be a very important and effective organism. In fact, while saying in general that Mesopotamian civilization did not develop organized checks on tyranny, one must mention the city as a form of organization which was able effectively to challenge the king many times in Mesopotamian history. As to why this conflict developed one can only speculate, but I think it is pertinent to note that in our oldest materials the title "king" always represents an authority that extended over more than one city. Similarly, the royal power was based on an army which stood apart from the local citizenry. As early as the Third Dynasty of Ur three extremely interesting cases are known in which the army authority and the civil authority went to court to settle issues between them in an orderly manner. In short, I should like to thank Dr. Oppenheim again and to underline his conclusion that in the Mesopotamian city we have a major institution which in many ways embodied the lives of people in that civilization better than any other.

WILSON: Thank you. Since time is short, and since a number of individuals already have requested an opportunity to comment, I can only urge speakers to be as brief as possible.

CAMERON: In our discussions thus far there has been one apparent omission, an attempt to deal with the economic situation. It is generally assumed that the temple and state institutions played a vital part in the collection and the redistribution of the agricultural resources. But when we remember that our earliest written records come almost exclusively from temples, how valid are these judgments as to the over-all importance of temple and state institutions? Possibly to invoke some comparative insight into the question, one might ask if it really can be proved for Egypt that the state was the exclusive center for the distribution of the resources before perhaps the Third Dynasty? Possible cross-cultural evidence may be provided by a reference in Dr. Adams' paper to the fact that in Peru llama bones were ceremonially buried in a community shrine and that in another case the only llama bones found were with the *Beigaben* of a possible priest's grave (see p. 277). Can Professor Willey tell us whether this really implies that only temples and the states distributed the agricultural resources?

ADAMS: Gladly leaving the llama bones for Dr. Willey, I want only to raise two relatively minor points. What Dr. Jacobsen very persuasively has invited us to do is to stand off far enough from the details of early Mesopotamian history to see beyond the cyclical character of its successive political integrations certain accumulative elements. There are two such elements which I hope we may hear a little more about. One is the development from the city-state to the territorial state. What does this transition really involve beyond a presumed increase in the area controlled by the city? It seems to me that it should involve an expansion in the size of the administrative elite, a qualitative increase in the complexity of the administrative organization, and this perhaps not only at a time like the Third Dynasty of Ur, when conditions were well integrated and relatively peaceful, but even in times when the controls were less well established. The second question is one, I recognize, which can be answered only in impressionistic terms. With reference to our theme of an expanding society, it was said that the social order established new moral and artistic goals and that in the literature man can be seen growing with these goals. Can this expansion in self-consciousness and moral stature be traced during the range of time with which we are concerned this morning for any individual except the king and, ordinarily, for the king in any capacity other than as war leader?

WILLEY: In reference to llama bones in the Peruvian temples I would say that surely this small bit of evidence does not in itself indicate redistribution of produce and goods by the temple hierarchy. However, I would like to add that in the context of Peruvian civilization as we can trace it through many thousands of years up to the Inca horizon there is a growing feeling of centralized control by the state and government, although it is only on the Inca time level that we have the actual ethnohistorical documentation to indicate that this was indeed the case. Quite contrary to the situation in Middle America, the open market played very little or no role and goods were distributed by the temple-palace hierarchy.

I would like to refer again for a moment, in a broader context, to the dichotomy between Middle American or Mayan civilization, on the one hand, and that of Peru, on the other. It is comparable in a way to the feelings that Orientalists seem to have about the differences in total cultural configuration between Egypt and Mesopotamia. I was impressed by, and even envious of, the presentation by Dr. Jacobsen, not only on my part but on the part of my Americanist colleagues. So far at least, we cannot attain this level of synthesis; I am not sure whether the explanation lies in our data, our personnel, or in a bit of both. But I would like to pose this question particularly to Dr. Speiser, for his earlier comment touched on it: Do you feel that the attempt to understand the mental state of man in the past by inferences drawn from artifacts, settlements, art, temples (inferences which are all we have, lacking texts) is an essentially antihumanistic approach? As an American archeologist I have never faced up to the question whether I am a humanist or a social scientist. What do you think, sir?

SPEISER: Well, as you yourself have indicated and perhaps as Dr. Jacobsen also has implied, I believe that after you have your data under the most rigid control possible you are not only free but in fact compelled to call intuition into play. If it is not well done, of course, you will find that instead of dealing with pottery you have gone off into the somewhat dangerous field we might call "psychoceramics." But without using the leads to which your intuition points I agree that you are not going to make much progress.

GELB: Returning to Dr. Cameron's question as to the role of the temple in the economy, I want to say that the traditional view on this important problem is based wholly upon Anton Deimel's single reconstruction from texts found at a single site.[6] This group of texts happened to be a temple archive, and because at the time it was found it probably was the only substantial body of information that we had for the period, his reconstruction has become widely known and has been quoted over and over again in primary as well as secondary evaluations. In more recent years, however, we have learned about a number of other archives and many more sources. I first thought that these new sources showed the predominance of a private economy based on individual ownership of land. The Rus-

[6] Deimel, *Sumerische Tempelwirtschaft zur Zeit Urukaginas und seiner Vorgänger* ("Analecta Orientalia" II [1931]).

sians have corrected me, showing that many of the lands and manors were owned not by individual persons but by families or clans.[7]

SINGER: At the risk of putting an end to some of the pleasures Professors Gelb and Jacobsen find in their controversies, I want to suggest that their differences are not very great when they are slightly restated, as Jacobsen himself has pointed out already. They agree that ethnic groupings are not racial or genetic but historical and cultural, and I think it follows that an ethnic group is something in process which can be made and unmade in historical periods; surely in that case it must have some relationship to political grouping. We often find a noncoincidence of political with ethnic or cultural grouping. There are many cases where peoples of similar cultures, language, customs, and religion extend more widely than the political groupings among them. We can also see cases of another, more usual, kind, where the political grouping is wider than any single cultural grouping. I would like to suggest that perhaps the frequent noncoincidence of ethnic with political grouping is itself an unsettling and dynamic factor in the historical processes we are concerned with. If so, one might slightly reinterpret Dr. Jacobsen's account to mean that in the very earliest periods cultural groupings did not have or seek political expression, while in later periods when we deal with national states there were national cultures more or less coinciding with national political groupings. Dr. Jacobsen also raised the question whether, when one goes on still farther in time to imperial levels of organization, it may not be that this unity and continuity of cultural groupings again was threatened. In those terms one sees perhaps that the process of societal expansion itself at certain points tends to bring about a coincidence of political and cultural grouping.

VON GRUNEBAUM: I would like to return first for a moment to Dr. Gelb's somewhat too positive equation of national identity with linguistic identity. There are numerous examples to illustrate that linguistic identity does not necessarily lead to a sense of unqualified ethnic or national identity, for example the German-speaking Austrians in the Austrian monarchy and the many Spanish-speaking states in Latin America which do not for this reason crave political unification. With regard to the example of the North African Arabs which he introduced, the complexity of the situation there is such that I do not think it should be allowed, so to speak, to burst the temporal and spatial frame of this symposium.

[7] I. M. Diakonoff, *Sale of Land in Pre-Sargonic Sumer* (Moscow, 1954).

This touches on a more basic point in the context of the symposium at large. Our meeting is predicated on the basically correct assumption that an expansion in the size of political organisms is apt to lead to, or even to be the essential precondition for, the expansion of cultural organisms. But, while this is true to a certain extent, one also must bear in mind that there were periods when the finest flowering of a specific culture, in terms of both its inner complexity and its geographic range, coincided with conditions of political fragmentation. There is not time to introduce many examples, but the tenth century in Eastern Islam and the eleventh century in Spanish Islam are two with which I am particularly familiar. Hence I would plead for a slight modification of what seems to emerge as the basic thesis of this symposium. Political expansion, the ability to rule larger geographic areas, is not necessarily and always accompanied by cultural expansion, nor is cultural expansion necessarily predicated on the continued holding-together of large political groupings.

KRAMER: I should like to touch first upon the point raised by Dr. Speiser concerning the psychological factors responsible for the rise and growth of Mesopotamian civilization, limiting myself, of course, to the Sumerians. This is a question about which I have been thinking a good deal recently, and perhaps some of these thoughts will help to tie up our earlier discussion of factors in the background of civilization with what is being said today.

It looks to me as though the psychological factor responsible to no little extent for both the material and the cultural achievements of the Sumerians was an all-pervading and deeply ingrained drive for pre-eminence and prestige, for victory and success. This view first came to me while I was trying to translate and understand the contents of a number of Sumerian compositions which the ancient scribes themselves categorized as "contests" or "disputations," in which such pairs of rivals as "Summer" and "Winter," "Cattle" and "Grain," "Copper" and "Silver," "Farmer" and "Shepherd" argue about who is superior, who has done more for civilization, who is more useful to man, whom do the gods like better, etc. At first glance, these texts might not appear to be very significant; literary arguments of this type are found in many cultures. But, on further study, it did seem rather unusual that this particular literary genre was a high favorite among Sumerian men of letters; of some thirty-five extant mythological and epic poems, at least eight belong to the "disputation" genre. This fact led me to analyze more closely the "tone" of these texts, and I noted that the two protagonists are not at all "nice'" and "gentlemanly"; they do not hesitate to hurl insults at each other; they constantly boast of their own importance and belittle that of their opponent. This, too, seemed rather remarkable and not insignificant.

Then I looked into the Sumerian essays revolving about their schools—their *edubba*'s, "tablet-houses"—and found these, too, full of acrimonious, ill-tempered argumentation. In one of these, recently published in part by C. J. Gadd,[8] two students belabor each other with such insulting and vituperative names as "dolt," "numskull," "pest," "illiterate," "sophomore," "bungler," and "windbag." But even the essays in which the arguments are more subdued and those which are not "disputations" at all but deal with school life or the value and importance of education stress constantly the competitive drive for superiority and prestige.

I next turned to the Sumerian political scene and observed the same kind of thing. As you all know, the kings and cities of Sumer were constantly striving with one another for superiority. With regard to the kings, it is not only the historical documents which show this to be true. There is a large group of royal hymns whose tone and temper long had troubled me: self-laudatory panegyrics in which such kings as Ur-Nammu, Shulgi, Ishbi-Irra sing of their own virtues in extravagant, hyperbolic, and uninhibited language. Evidently the Sumerians found this tone to their taste; it fitted well with their passion for glory and prestige.

In short, wherever I turned I found that the Sumerians (not unlike Americans, for example) placed an extraordinarily high value on rivalry and competition, on victory and success, and it seems not unreasonable to regard this as the psychological drive which sparked and sustained some of their more significant material and cultural advances.

Before we leave this point, it might be well to consider this suggestion briefly in the light of the well-known Mesopotamian priority in written laws and law codes. There is a general tendency to think of written law as somehow indicative of high moral virtue and lofty spirit on the part of its originators. But in the case of the Sumerians indications are that what drove them to originate legal documents and law codes was the aggressive, cantankerous, and quarrelsome pattern of behavior which dominated their culture; they did not

---

[8] *Teachers and Students in the Oldest Schools* (London, 1956).

trust one another enough to be content with verbal promises and agreements. I was led to this rather unpalatable conclusion by the school essay mentioned earlier, in which two students hurl vituperative insults at each other. The text ends with this sentence: "In the dispute between Enki-Mansi and Girni-ishag the teacher gives the verdict." The Sumerian word here used for "verdict" is the same as that designating the verdicts of court trials, which would indicate that the Sumerians themselves thought of their legal procedures in terms of the disputations and argumentations which characterized their conduct in general.[9]

My second point has to do with the Sumerian god Dumuzi, the biblical Tammuz, about whom numerous far-reaching but erroneous statements appear in works concerned with the history of religious ideas. For example, it is often said that Dumuzi is a god of vegetation, that his death is due to physical violence of one kind or another, that as the god of vegetation he is resurrected annually in the spring. I recently examined the Dumuzi mythological themes rather carefully in the course of preparing an article.[10] I was particularly interested, naturally, in finding as many parallels as I could between the Bible and Sumerian literature, and the Dumuzi-Tammuz theme seemed to offer a striking "resurrection" parallel. But as I went back to the Sumerian sources I realized that none of these claims are correct. Especially important is the fact that Dumuzi was never resurrected at all; in fact, according to the Sumerian mythographers, he could not possibly be permitted to leave the nether world. He was the surrogate for his wife, the goddess Inanna, who was allowed to depart from the nether world for the world above only after she had promised to obtain a god to take her place. For this reason the Sumerian literature includes many laments for the death of Dumuzi but no songs of rejoicing for his return to life.

LOEHR: I am not sure to what extent this symposium will consider testimony from the Far East relevant to the subject treated here, but the dramatic points made in both Dr. Jacobsen's introduction and Dr. Speiser's commentary remind me strongly of some of the things that went on in the Far East at a later period.

9 For a fuller and more amply annotated treatment of this subject see Kramer, "Rivalry and superiority: Two dominant features of the Sumerian culture pattern," Anthony F. C. Wallace (ed.), *Men and Culture* (selected papers of the Fifth International Congress of Anthropological and Ethnological Sciences, Philadelphia, September 1–9, 1956 [Philadelphia, 1960]) pp. 287–91.

10 "Sumerian literature and the Bible," *Studia biblica et orientalia*. III. *Oriens antiquus* ("Analecta biblica," No. 12 [Roma, 1959]) pp. 185–204 (cf. esp. n. 21).

I believe that what might be termed a manifestation of China's cultural genius cannot be dated earlier than the Shang dynasty (traditionally 1766–1122 B.C.). This is a comparatively late appearance for full-blown culture as compared with Mesopotamia, but the Shang dynasty was preceded only by the semilegendary Hsia dynasty (which I do not doubt did exist), headed by a man who is still widely remembered in China as the emperor Yü, Tamer of the Floods and the first man in history who was able to dam the Yellow River. This late building of flood dikes along the Yellow River no doubt might be regarded as a major factor in the formation of orderly government and political unity. The Shang dynasty in any case was the first to stand out as a government supported by organized military power, represented by a standing army of three to five thousand men, as contemporary tortoise-shell and bone oracle inscriptions testify. In addition it was the first to have a script, and on the whole it seems to me that it was Chinese writing that made the Chinese civilization. Of course at that time there was already a developed system of city-states; in the testimony of the *Bamboo Annals,* eighteen hundred states did homage to the first ruler of the Shang dynasty. Thus I think it is clear that the date of the rise of what in China can be termed civilization occurs, relative at least to Mesopotamia, at an astonishingly late point in its historical development.

GÜTERBOCK: As all our philological colleagues know, of course, there is no distinction in either the Sumerian or the Akkadian language between what in English we call "city," "town," "village," and "hamlet." Even if we ignore the difference in English between city and town, perhaps substituting the German *Stadt* and *Dorf,* there is no early Mesopotamian parallel for such distinctions. *Uru* and *ālu* are all these things. This is not to deny the existence of different kinds of settlements, since we find them. But I think it is a little disturbing not to find a word for "city," as distinguished from words used for other kinds of settlements. I wonder whether Dr. Jacobsen, or anyone who feels in a position to do so, can explain this point.

JACOBSEN: This is a difficult and interesting problem. I can think of only two distinctions that bear on it, and they both are in Sumerian. In Sumerian, the large city that would correspond to an English city or town rather than to a village usually carries the so-called "city determinative" with its name. The small villages that surround the large cities, as for example the villages surrounding

Ur, are often referred to in the texts as *uru barra.* This problem warrants further investigation.

OPPENHEIM: There is an Old Babylonian term referring to villages, *kapru,* which I believe occurs in Aramaic and other Semitic languages also. It is found in such phrases as "in my village." One text clearly says that "in the village where I live there is no diviner," so that it was necessary for the writer to go to the city to get a diviner. But, of course, the term is applied only for reference rather than address; such a phrase as "the *kapru* of so-and-so" never occurs.

KRAMER: Speaking only of Sumerian, I question whether we have the right to deduce from our evidence that the Sumerians did not have an idea or word for village. I think rather that we may question the nature of our evidence. It is not likely, for example, that the word "village" would occur in hymns or literary texts.

GELB: It seems to me that Professor Güterbock is completely right. While other expressions occur in the course of time, the main distinction that I know of in the oldest period is that between a manor and an estate, *é* (Akkadian *bītu*), on the one side, and a city-like settlement, *uru* (Akkadian *ālu*), on the other.

SPEISER: We have been coming back again and again to a disagreement that is not completely resolved between Dr. Jacobsen and Dr. Gelb, and it seems to me that those of us who have dealt with this question for a number of years also should stand up and be counted. Dr. Gelb has continued over the years to produce results which have placed us all in his debt, but in this case I could not disagree with him more emphatically. I cannot see how we can possibly make sense of Mesopotamia and the contribution of Mesopotamia through its long history if we are limited to terms of *ethnos* or even to the narrow contrast of *ethnos* and *demos.* It is the very genius of the culture of Mesopotamia that in some mysterious way it managed to make use of numerous quite disparate elements and themes, blending them together into a unit that was cosmopolitan, assimilatory, and infectious.

WILSON: I am sorry, but the chair must recognize a final speaker.

DELOUGAZ: Both Professor Jacobsen, in his lucid presentation, and Professor Albright, in his subsequent remarks, seem to have passed over a problem which is important to me and apparently also to Professor Speiser and others around this table. Professor Speiser referred just now to the genius of Mesopotamian culture that managed to blend numerous disparate elements into a single civilization. My question is this: "At what moment may we first recognize Mesopotamian civilization as an individual and distinct entity?" Since both Dr. Jacobsen and Dr. Albright were preoccupied in tracing man's past in broad strokes from very remote times, somehow this moment of recognition was lost. Yet I would claim that there *is* such a moment. And, in keeping with Dr. Von Grunebaum's remarks about expansion not always being unilateral and continuous, I would add that this moment occurs during a process not of expansion but rather of contraction. To be brief, in Mesopotamia the Ubaid culture covered a very large area. It was based on agriculture and was presumably adequate or even "prosperous" from the point of view of basic human needs. But the genius of Mesopotamian culture is not recognizable in it. This distinctive quality emerges somewhat later, during the phase of civilization which I call "Protoliterate," and is geographically confined at first to a much smaller area, that of southern Mesopotamia. Were there time, I could dwell a bit longer on the process of emergence of the earliest phase of a complex yet cohesive and articulate civilization which is so distinctly Mesopotamian. However, it is to the rise of this earliest civilization in a contracting, not an expanding, society to which I would like to draw your attention.

WILSON: I am sorry; this is a theme we could explore further with profit if time were available. But our remaining few minutes are Dr. Jacobsen's to round off this session with any comments he may have.

JACOBSEN: It is very difficult to comment on a discussion which has maintained such a uniformly high level and which has brought out so many important and profoundly difficult problems. So you will forgive me if I do not always in these brief answers get to the bottom of the issues that were raised.

I concur generally with Dr. Gelb in his reply to Dr. Cameron's question about the economic situation, but I should like to add that the Sumerian economy was far more complex than the present handbooks indicate. We certainly must reckon with a variety of types of large agencies of distribution, including not only the temple but also the large and unified economy of the palace, the private estates in the country, and perhaps still other types we cannot get at.

This brings me to the point raised by Dr. Adams on what can actually be said about the transition from city-state to territorial state.

In all honesty we must admit that the material is still so sparse and incompletely analyzed that we do not yet have very much that is concrete to offer, but it seems essential to me that in the coming work in our field this point be given close attention. As to his second question, about the breadth of the group, apart from the king, which participated in the king's reaction to the expanding political and social scene, I can only think of what one loosely would call "the upper classes." The king must have had a group of active and intelligent administrative helpers around him, who shared his ideas and worked on the same large goals. I think also should be included in that group the royal singers or bards, who were responsible for maintaining the literary tradition and giving form to these aspirations.

To Dr. Willey I just express my thanks for what he told us of the situation in Peru and particularly for eliciting from Dr. Speiser the wonderful term "psychoceramics."

With Dr. Singer I agree. I think he stated the case very well. This connects up with subsequent remarks by Dr. Von Grunebaum along similar lines, attempting to define the aim of the symposium. I think that all who had the privilege of planning this symposium were of one mind, that the theme of expansion in no way could provide a single key to our understanding of an enormously complex subject. Rather, it was a means of imposing some sort of order, an initial way of looking at things. Considering the whole of our geographic and temporal range of cultures in relation to the theme of expansion, I think it is apparent that we have all been seeking a viewpoint and in no way trying to find a cause or an explanation.

On Dr. Kramer's delight in scrapping the Sumerians, I would like to comment with the Danish saying that the seen depends on the eyes that see. My own interpretation of the very same texts is slightly different. In all of them I get a clear impression that both participants contribute very significantly to the fields that they are dealing with, even though each can see only his own values; when I listen to them I see that both are necessary. This comes out very clearly, of course, in a text such as the one that deals with the farmer and the shepherd, where in the end they recognize that they are both needed for the good of society. This is an extremely interesting group of texts because in many ways the less privileged members of society get a voice through them. Consider, for instance, the dispute of the plow with the hoe; the latter is a cheap instrument which anyone can have. There is no doubt in my mind that the victory of the hoe, which is able to show that it is useful in civilization in so many more

93

respects, is a symbol to the little Sumerian who sees that his contribution is necessary and useful. As for the remark on Dumuzi, I am afraid that I shall have to shock Dr. Kramer and say that I agree entirely and have agreed for years. There is no resurrection of Dumuzi.

To Professors Loehr, Speiser, and Delougaz I would like to express my gratitude for the introduction of the question: When does a culture become recognizable as a unit, when does every one of its products immediately tell us that it derives from this particular civilization? How that crystallization takes place is something that we would certainly like to know more about. The point made by Mr. Delougaz, that when Mesopotamian culture crystallized it tended to be in contraction, calls to mind an informal observation by Professor Mumford. He spoke very aptly of the city as a container. One of its important functions is that it contains a group of different individuals in one small place and forces them to interact and to get along with one another. I think perhaps some of the answers to these questions lie in this factor of containment.

Scribal Concepts of Education

JACOBSEN (*chairman*): This afternoon's (fourth) session has a special character. When we were discussing the plans for the symposium, realizing that we were going to deal with the great civilizations, we felt that somewhere in the program there should be time to consider at least one aspect of a civilization in somewhat more detail; therefore we asked Professor Landsberger to speak on the scribal concepts of education. I do not think I need to introduce Professor Landsberger to you. I will just say that you are going to hear a man who, in my opinion, for the last twenty years has set not only the course but also the manner of approach for Assyriology.

LANDSBERGER: In 1949, Samuel N. Kramer recovered, almost completely, a Sumerian composition of 90 lines which he called "Schooldays." Texts of this genre, consisting mostly of dialogues between teacher and student or between two students, provide a detailed and vivid description of the techniques of schooling in the Old Babylonian period. In an intimate way, they reveal the spirit and the morals of a very respected institution of this golden age (called by Professor Oppenheim the "Mesopotamian Miracle," which it really appears to have been, as far as we can judge, in that it was far ahead of both previous and subsequent historical periods in its wealth of conceptions and institutions). They further reveal the self-image of the scribes, one that reflects a sense of humor. The institution in question is the *edubba,* "tablet-house," whose members, old and young, called themselves to the outside world its "sons" but addressed one another as "colleagues" (Sumerian *gi.me.a.as,* Akkadian *kinātu*) within the *edubba;* the master was called "the father" and the preceptors, the "older brothers." The tablet-house formed both the school and the parliament of the scribal guild; "son" was the honorary title of this caste.

Certainly this newly discovered literary genre uses the dialogue motif primarily for the purpose of forming a conversation in Sumerian, couched in an amusing framework, in order to instruct the student in this difficult language. Professor Kramer's achievement has already inspired three learned lectures (see bibliography on pp. 101–2), but there are five or six other compositions of the same genre which are still virgin territory. Moreover, the historical or social aspects of our subject have hardly been touched; opinions concerning the historical role and status of this important class are quite divergent. Assyriology suffers, and profits at the same time, from an almost indigestible afflux of new material. This, of course, has to be paralleled by a deeper penetration into the culture, necessitating, in subjects like the present one, a complete and continuing re-evaluation of almost every item. More nilly than willy, we are forced to become amateur sociologists. Thus my remarks today fall into the genre of "programmatical essay" (which I feel guilty of having introduced into Assyriology in 1926), for there is no other escape from being completely lost in details. A superficial, even distorted, position is better than no position; the latter is chaos, the former at least begs correction and improvement. In following this approach I shall try to free my presentation from subjectivity by letting the scribes speak for themselves.

No other institution contributed as much to the preservation of the past as the tablet-house; it did so by transmitting a spiritual inheritance from one generation to another. For example, among the school texts of Fara (*ca.* 2400 B.C.) Professor Jacobsen has discovered a so-called "wisdom text"—a not well-studied subject—which was preserved and transmitted until the Old Babylonian 1 period (*ca.* 1720 B.C.).

For as long as the script existed, its complexity was such that years of professional training were required for any mastery of it. In neighboring Assyria in the Old Babylonian 1 period there was an attempt to simplify and reduce the script to about one hundred signs; the simplified script, however, did not survive.

In spite of its conservative character, the institution as a whole underwent radical changes. Accordingly, the subject can only be presented by distinguishing several main periods, as outlined in the accompanying chart (p. 101). Since the entire achievement of what we may call, provisionally, the higher civilization of Mesopotamia and her cultural provinces was due to the successful crossbreeding of Sumerian and Akkadian elements, the main differences between these periods must lie in the preponderance of either Sumerian or Akkadian elements.

The way in which these two languages supplemented each other has often been described. Sumerian, because of its transparent and unambiguous structure, was suited for classifying the world, and Akkadian, with its plasticity and richness in verbal aspects, for the exact description of all phenomena. Sumerian, by its *Sprachgeist*, gave birth to some 30,000 lines of so-called "lexical" texts, which the Old Babylonian student had to memorize, while Akkadian produced uncounted lines of omina, which stemmed from the Old Babylonian 2 period and which belonged partly to the *dubsar* profession—the scribal profession—and partly to that of the liver experts, the diagnosticians and the physicians. We know now—but this discovery is not more than a few weeks old—that the Sumerians (as attested first in Ur III) considered themselves the elite of the people, including the connotation of an "intellectual elite" (Sumerian *dumu.gir*). I quote from one of the *edubba* texts of Old Babylonian 1, where two students are quarreling; both bear common Sumerian names.

A: I am of Sumerian descent, the son of so and so. You are the son of a dirty rowdy, you cannot even write your name.

B: I am a Sumerian as well as you are!

In another quarrel we read: "Your mouth is not fit for Sumerian!" (The scribes still bore Sumerian names in the Babylonian Middle Age, even in the cultural provinces of Babylonia.)

I will not commit myself to any judgment as to how long in the periods before Old Babylonian 1 Sumerian was still spoken in the ordinary households of Nippur or Lagash. Since it was taught in the schools by a specialist called a "professor of Sumerian," we may surmise that the conscious struggle for preserving a noble heritage was only partly successful. The decisive change came with Old Babylonian 2, when the university shifted from Nippur to Babylon. In the new capital the greater part of Sumerian literature was doomed to oblivion, the only major exception being the lexical lists, which still were being expanded. Some selected texts, however, were transmitted and provided with Akkadian translations. The professor of Sumerian disappeared, but composition of poetry in a highly artificial Sumerian continued. The maintenance and vitality of Sumerian cannot justifiably be compared with school Latin. Sumerian was a kind of mental superstructure, a system of notions. The names of things, each of them visualized by the script sign, comprised a primitive "realism," in the medieval sense, wherein the names had more reality than the things. This difficult concept can best be illustrated by the fifty names of Marduk in the Creation epic, which was composed in Old Babylonian 2. (I support this dating in spite of recent attempts at a dating of 1000 B.C. or later.) Only by, so to speak, *feeling* the impact of these Sumerian compounds could the essence of the omnipotent god be conceived.

The difference in attitude toward Sumerian was, however, not the only difference between the old and the new scribes. After Old Babylonian 2, the tablet-house disappeared, and scribal education, paralleling the change from a kind of democracy to feudalism, fell into the hands of individual families, a kind of nobility who traced their ancestry back ten or twelve generations.

Because of shortness of time, the following remarks must be made rather summarily. The lexical lists distinguish, according to the degree of erudition and specialization, fifteen varieties of *dubsar* or scribe; but most significant for us is the fact that the poet and the teacher are not distinguished. All these varieties disappeared after Old Babylonian 2. Subsequently, but only in the latest period, the astrologer branched off as a specialist. At the same time, the incantation priest, still illiterate in the Old Babylonian period, but now a high scholar, took away the greater part of the influence of the scribes.

The scribal profession combined a highly introverted scholar with an active and indispensable helper of the two great powers, god and king. The self-picture idealizes the "scribal craft" as a kind of abstract spirit; it also reveres another abstract numen, a kind of primitive conception of substance in the philosophical sense, basically "raw form"; when the Greeks came into contact with Babylonian culture, they rendered this concept by *kosmos noetos,* the intelligible world order. The scribes also boasted of their ability to give the rulers advice, called *nadiga* (Akkadian *māšartu*).

One must castigate as false romanticism the conception of the so-called *Priesterweisheit,* still to be found in secondary handbooks. The scribes, although the greater number of them were deeply religious, were completely a lay group. The priests as well as the kings (not counting some exceptions among the latter), and the governors, and the judges were illiterate.

In their capacity as poets, or as secretaries of state, the scribes could create gods by intellectual revolutions; the aforementioned Creation epic was, so to speak, the magna charta by which the supreme god, Marduk, attained his constitutional rights. As a kind of reward, in Old Babylonian 2, the scribes instituted and popularized their own patron and prototype, the divine scribe Nabu, as Marduk's secretary, thus projecting their self-image into the cosmos. The scribes could depose gods as well, such as the old set of gods—Enlil, Belit-ili, and Ishtar—in the Gilgamesh epic, where they were ridiculed and despised for their more than human attitudes and whims. Only the sun-god and his father, the moon, who, so to speak, borrowed his light from the sun, were intangible and uncontested and did not need any propaganda; it was to this pair that the poor and the wronged man prayed.

In using the word "popularized" I have already touched upon a most crucial, yet poorly documented and uninvestigated, subject, namely, whether there were any arteries through which the simple, folkloristic education of the people drew upon the learning of schools. If not, we are in danger of applying the term "Babylonian culture" to what was only the privilege of a small elite and, in doing so, ignoring the real Babylonian culture. For this problem, I call upon three examples, the most famous products of the Babylonian school.

The law code of Hammurabi, falling within our Old Babylonian 1 period, was destined, according to its epilogue, to be read to any wronged man so that he could discover his rights. We have strong proof that this concept was a dream that was never realized. The illiterate judges continued to judge according to their customary law. The magnificent code was relegated to the schools and the *dubsar*'s, whence—this is true—it influenced later legislation. As to the Creation epic, sometimes called *"The* Book" or the "Bible of the Babylonians," it is from its last lines that conclusions have been drawn concerning its use for general education or *paidea;* the mention of a shepherd in line 148 has been interpreted as the wish of the visionary, prompted by the god Ea, that this poem penetrate even to the lowest level of the population. Not only does this particular poet generally give the impression of an ingenious, though rather confused personality, but this particular line seems to have been confused by transmission. It can be proved that "shepherd" in this line means the king, the person to whom most contemporary poems allude at the end. As far as we know, this famous poem was edited only in schools, and the same is true of the Gilgamesh epic, which, justly or unjustly, has been claimed to be the Babylonian national epic, comparable to the *Iliad.*

Let us dismiss these classics and go deeper into our problem. In the Sumerian period, no doubt, a broad stream of folklore penetrated the schools. This can be proved quantitatively by the hundreds of Sumerian proverbs transmitted by the scribes, whereas hardly five Babylonian-Assyrian proverbs have come down to us, and those at random. Popular songs were likewise well preserved by the schools in the Sumerian period. From the text which I shall excerpt at the end of these remarks, we learn that the well-trained scribe had to be acquainted with the art of the *nar,* the musician, and with all the different genres of this highly developed Sumerian specialty.

But the natural communication between school and folk ceased with the Old Babylonian 2 period. We may justly assume that leisure time was filled with all sorts of songs, with theatrical games, with riddles and jokes. But of the more than three hundred *incipit's* or first lines which an Assyrian singer of the Middle Age must have known, comprising love, war, and work songs and hymns in honor of gods or kings, not a single line has been preserved. The arteries connecting the *tupšarrūtu* (the scribal craft) and the *narūtu* (the art of a singer and musician) had been cut.

A word about the social status of the scribe: Except during the Ur III period, when the *dubsar* could climb to the highest administrative posts, he was generally a secretary. Street scribes, to whom the poor man or woman could, for a little money, dictate a letter or an application, existed only in the Old Babylonian period. The class, as a whole, can be described as poor aristocracy.

I would like to present one of the most difficult bilingual texts, labeled "Examination Text A" and stemming from the Old Babylonian 2 period. The name is not quite justifiable, since examinations did not exist. What is involved is rather a general testing not meant to be formally passed or failed. I translate, as the scribe, in the courtyard of the tablet-house, tests his son before the assembly of the masters.

A: Come, my son, sit at my feet. I will talk to you, and you will give me information! From your childhood to your adult age you have been staying in the tablet-house. Do you know the scribal art that you have learned?

B: What would I not know? Ask me, and I will give you the answer.

A: You will not.

B: Why should I not answer?

Here follow 16 or more questions. First question:

A: The element of the scribal craft is the simple wedge; it has six teeth, and, as a matter of fact, it is sixty. Do you know its name?

This question applies to six different directions in which a wedge could be impressed in the clay, but it must be admitted that some of these directions are quite unusual; the equation $1 = 60$ stems from the sexagesimal system, where the numbers 1 and 60 are denoted by the same single wedge.

I excerpt the following questions, which are difficult for modern *dubsar*'s to understand.

2. Secret meaning of Sumerian words.
3. Translation and explanation from Sumerian to Akkadian and vice versa.
4. The three Sumerian equivalents of each Akkadian word (the second and third belonging to an occult language).
5. Sumerian grammatical terms (intelligible to us: perfect, punctual, and durative).
6. Sumerian conjugation: I, you, he, etc.
7. Another trick of translation of Sumerian into Akkadian (not clear to me).
8. Different kinds of calligraphy and occult script.
9. Writing of phonetic Sumerian.
10. To understand the occult language of all classes of priests and members of other professions.
11. How to draw up, cover, and seal a document.
12. All categories of songs and how to conduct a choir.
13. The technical jargon of silversmiths and jewelers.
14. Other complicated and intentionally distorted languages of professional groups like the shepherds and scribes.

15. Mathematics, division of fields, allotting of rations.
16. The use and technique of various musical instruments.

At this point, the candidate gives in and charges the master that he had not been taught these matters, neither by the master nor by the big brother. Then he receives the following reprimand:

> What have you done, what good came of your sitting here? You are already a ripe man and close to being aged! Like an old ass you are not teachable any more. Like withered grain you have passed the season. How long will you play around? But, it is still not too late! If you study night and day and work all the time modestly and without arrogance, if you listen to your colleagues and teachers, you still can become a scribe! Then you can share the scribal craft which is good fortune for its owner, a good angel leading you, a bright eye, possessed by you, and it is what the palace needs.

CHRONOLOGICAL TABLE[11]

Fara	2400 B.C.
Early Dynastic III and Dynasty of Agade	2150
Gudea, Ur III	2020
Old Babylonian 1, ends with Samsu-iluna's 29th year	1720
Old Babylonian 2, ends with Samsu-ditana	1600
Dark Age	1400
Kassite period of scholarship (canonization)	1200
End of cuneiform writing	0

BIBLIOGRAPHY[12]

WOLFRAM VON SODEN, "Leistung und Grenze sumerischer und babylonischer Wissenschaft," *Die Welt als Geschichte* II (1936) 411 (outdated but comprehensive).

*ADAM FALKENSTEIN, "Der 'Sohn des Tafelhauses,' " *Die Welt des Orients* I (1948) 172.

*S. N. KRAMER, "Schooldays: A Sumerian composition relating to the education of a scribe," *Journal of the American Oriental Society* LXIX (1949) 199.

J. J. VAN DIJK, *La sagesse suméro-accadienne* (Leiden, 1953) p. 21.

*BENNO LANDSBERGER, "Babylonian scribal craft and its terminology." Abstract in *Proceedings of the 23rd International Congress of Orientalists* (Cambridge, 1954) p. 123.

F. R. KRAUS, *Wandel und Kontinuität in der sumerisch-babylonischen Kultur* (Leiden, 1954).

E. A. SPEISER, "Ancient Mesopotamia," *The Idea of History in the Ancient*

[11] Dates denote the ends of the periods, according to the chronology of Sidney Smith.

[12] All titles except those marked with asterisks are for non-Assyriologists.

Near East ("American Oriental Series" XXXVIII [New Haven, 1955]) p. 37.

ADAM FALKENSTEIN, "Die babylonische Schule," *Saeculum* IV (1955) 125.

C. J. GADD, *Teachers and Students in the Oldest Schools* (London, 1956).

*W. G. LAMBERT, "Ancestors, authors, and canonicity," *Journal of Cuneiform Studies* XI (1957) 1.

JACOBSEN: I shall follow the pattern set by Dr. Wilson this morning and ask four members of the symposium whether they have any comments on Dr. Landsberger's brilliant statement. But I shall reverse Dr. Wilson's procedure—I feel that charity begins at home—and ask John Wilson for comments.

WILSON: Mr. Chairman, it is quite impossible for me to comment on Professor Landsberger's statement except with a loud shout of admiration. As our sessions proceed into tomorrow, we shall discover that within this symposium we see the Mesopotamian picture a little hazily, as though through a morning mist. Into that mist Egypt is going to throw dust, so that the clarity will be less than it might have been had Egypt been left out. And this, I regret to say, is particularly the case with education, because we cannot present a strictly analogous picture.

There is a theoretical presumption that education in Egypt was very responsive to or was controlled by the priests. I think this is a good theoretical presumption because of the preservation of the sacred language against the inroads of time and secularization after a thousand years or so, but we cannot put our finger upon priestly schools. Thus we present the theoretical presumption that there was at the beginning a very considerable control of the transmission of lore by the priests.

What we know may be briefly summarized. We know that a term applied to the sacred writing was the "word of god" or the "divine words," or something like that, and that this applied not simply to the pictorial hieroglyphic writing but also to its derivatives in script. Furthermore, we know that there were priestly depositories of writings—the Egyptian term is "House of Life"—containing the revered old manuscripts and that these manuscripts were used over successive periods. However, they were never inviolate as to their selection, their words, and so on. A text might appear in early times and then again in later times in changed form, so that a body of material (of which the classic examples are the Pyramid Texts, the Coffin Texts, and the Book of the Dead) continued with a certain kind of content but was never absolutely inviolate. Such texts came, one assumes, out of the House of Life, the scriptorium where the religious records were kept and periodically rewritten. But, while this seems almost certain, it cannot be validated by any known description of priestly transmission of lore or priestly teaching.

A second phenomenon is the wisdom or teaching text. The Egyptian word *sebayet* means "teaching" and even sometimes "discipline" or "punishment," but the Coptic and Greek evidence shows that the word implies both "wisdom" and "teaching." Of this genre we have many texts, and, although the extant copies may not go back earlier than 1900 B.C., they project back into the Old Kingdom—let us say to about 2300 B.C.—in their pretense to antiquity. The mechanism of fathers giving teaching or wisdom to sons is universal, so that we may treat it as though it went back into the earliest large body of literature. This *sebayet,* this teaching, is almost always from father to son, and we might just as well say that this is its normal setting even though occasional texts have a superior giving instruction to an inferior, or a king to his subjects. There normally is an introduction, in which the father, feeling that his son should follow in his profession, gives him advice, or the father, feeling that his son should have *a* profession, gives him advice. Then come a series of discrete maxims, without clear logic, form, and content, about obeying a superior in a profession, about marrying and setting up a household, about conduct in law court, even in some cases about behavior in crossing a river in a ferry. These are just transmitted advice on a series of situations in either professional or social life. They normally are found on papyrus, but they may be carved on stelae with very specific setting in the reign of a certain pharaoh and in relation to that pharaoh.

The third phenomenon is the government school, which we know relatively late—let us say 1300 B.C.—but in theoretical terms can project back to about 1900 B.C. This school was demanded for the training of the personnel required by a large government: secretaries, letter-writers for important officials, paymasters on government jobs to keep the daily journal, clerks to record attendance and receipts for pay from the government, and so on. This was a distinctly secular enterprise; it was designed to train people to be in the "white-kilt" class, people who would not need to soil their hands or garments with work. Instead, they could sit elegantly holding a piece of papyrus or a scrap of pottery and check off what other people were doing. A major persuasion was: "If you want to rise high and to have a nonmanual job, stick to your classes in school and you will get ahead." I regret to say that in Egypt there were not the nice relations between professor and student which Professor Landsberger has described. The teacher says rather definitely that the ear of the boy is on his back so that when he is beaten he will hear. I said previously that the same word was used for "teaching" and "discipline." And this word goes over into law cases, where it refers to punishment of someone who has been condemned. Thus there was a rather considerable element of unpleasant control, and certainly there was no close or happy relationship, as far as we know, between teacher and student. We know the literature used in these secular schools of 1300 B.C. particularly from a series of documents: the "Story of Sinuhe," the "Teaching of Amenemhet I," the "Hymn to the Nile," and the so-called "Satire on the Trades." The last is a persuasion in favor of a secretarial or white-kilt job, arguing that all other trades are difficult except being a secretary. These documents were copied over and over again by poor schoolboys, who mangled them grossly; it is questionable whether even the teachers knew the texts very well, since the corrections seem not to have been very effective as time went on.

To this brief summary of what is known of education in ancient Egypt must be added that from about 1100 B.C. there is the classic document which has come to have the name "onomasticon," the list of phenomena. This is called a "teaching," a *sebayet*, so that the individual writer may have his manuscript control of what he sees and does. It simply has classes of things: god, goddess, spirit, king, etc.; sun, moon, star, the big dipper (to use its modern name), the dog star, etc.; professions such as vizier, treasurer, etc.; a series of places within Egypt, starting from the south and going north, and a series of places abroad. This is a late manifestation, probably an adaptation by ignorant Egyptians of what they thought to be lexicography over in Asia. They thought that just memorizing the writings of these things in categories had something to do with knowing and classifying phenomena.

I have described three educational categories: the religious, about which I know almost nothing, the teaching from father to son, and the later government school. This is the picture from Egypt and, as I have said, it has very little relation to the picture which Dr. Landsberger has given from Mesopotamia. Two factors are involved in the difference. One is real and absolute difference, while the other results from the chance character of survival which has left us without comparable material. Thank you.

ALBRIGHT: It is naturally quite impossible for me to discuss Professor Landsberger's brilliant statement without a profound sense of *hubris*. To me Professor Landsberger will always be what the Germans call *eine Naturerscheinung*. I was surprised to hear Professor Jacobsen make an error in arithmetic, since he is usually so meticulous. He said that Landsberger—forgive me for dropping the handle to his name, in accordance with universal practice among Assyriologists—had been the guiding light of Assyriologists for the past twenty years. Actually, he was already the recognized leader of cuneiformists more than thirty years ago.

I was so fortunate as to hear Landsberger's paper on scribal terminology at Cambridge in 1954. Unfortunately it has not yet been published. From it, together with the statement we have just heard, we gain a most extraordinary impression of the relative importance of the Sumero-Babylonian school system. In fact, I venture to say that the school system with which we can best compare it would be the Latin schools of the late Middle Ages, and perhaps the Chinese schools in their heyday. I venture also to suggest that, but for the Sumero-Akkadian schools, the influence of Mesopotamian civilization on surrounding lands would have been far less than it was. When a school system is developed so intensively and men are trained so thoroughly, the impact on less advanced countries becomes correspondingly greater. To a certain extent the Mesopotamian scribe learned to think for himself, since cuneiform spelling was seldom, if ever, so hard and fast as Egyptian, and scribes were usually able to choose their own orthography in copying from dictation as well as in writing letters. The march of empire and especially the growth of trade carried cuneiform writing, and with it some imitation of Mesopotamian scribal schooling, to Iran and Armenia, Asia Minor, Syria, Palestine, and even Egypt, at least during the New Kingdom. We now have a considerable body of school texts, especially lexical tablets and exercise texts, from all these countries. To a certain extent it appears that Babylonian terminology was adopted elsewhere. For instance, the Sumerian word *ummea*, "master," in its Akkadian form *ummānu*, was borrowed by the Phoenicians and Hebrews as *omman, ammun*, "master," "master craftsman," "tutor." We now have tablets, graffiti, and local seal cylinders from Syria and

Palestine which carry the date of the oldest known cuneiform in the west to about 2000 B.C. Just recently, within the past few weeks, word has come that Yigael Yadin has discovered a liver model with a cuneiform inscription on it at Hazor in northern Palestine. I don't know whether it was imported from Babylonia or made in the west.

OPPENHEIM: Definitely made in the west.

ALBRIGHT: Good. Thus there were schools in the west, probably beginning about the eighteenth or seventeenth century B.C. (low chronology). On a minor issue I should like to rebel against Landsberger's authority and to differ with his interpretation of a cuneiform tablet found by a German expedition at Shechem in central Palestine. I interpret[13] the text as written by a schoolmaster or schoolmistress complaining that the boy's tuition had not been paid, while Landsberger[14] thinks that it refers to pederasty. However this may be, we agree in recognizing the tremendous impact of Mesopotamian education on the west. There native scribes taught Akkadian century after century, while the original Akkadian of the First Dynasty of Babylon became more and more corrupt. After centuries much of the "Babylonian" had been replaced by Canaanite words, phrases, and syntax thinly covered by a barbaric Akkadian. The measure of the success of the scribal schools is shown by the fact that they perpetuated this barbaric Akkadian for generations. I do not think that we can overestimate the importance of the Sumero-Akkadian school system for the development not only of Akkadian higher culture but also of higher culture in the surrounding countries, especially in Syria and Palestine, where linguistic differences were comparatively minor.

JACOBSEN: Thank you. I accept with great pleasure the correction of Professor Albright that Professor Landsberger has been a leading force in Assyriology for more than thirty years; my only plea is that this is not in the realm of arithmetic but in chronology, a field which I gave up long ago as completely impossible. May I call next on Professor Speiser?

SPEISER: By now we have all had a speed-up course on Mesopotamia, and I can assume that everybody here is fully acquainted with every work of Mesopotamian literature. So, of course, you all know the Babylonian Creation epic and will easily recall the concluding lines of Tablet III (vss. 130–38): An important decision had to be

13 *Bulletin of the American Schools of Oriental Research*, No. 86 (1942) pp. 30 f.

14 *Journal of Cuneiform Studies* VIII (1954) 59.

made in heaven, but, because the Babylonians were incurably democratic, even in heaven, the decision of the gods had to have popular
approval. Thus when it came to selecting as new head of the pantheon an upstart by the name of Marduk, the thing had to be done,
but of course the old fuddy-duddies must agree. And in order to
make sure that they would agree, all the gods were brought together
and given plenty to eat and more than plenty to drink, after which
there was no difficulty in getting their signatures on the dotted line.[15]

When you have heard a talk by Dr. Landsberger, you are in much
the same position, not because you have imbibed an excess of spirits,
but because of the intellectual and spiritual content of what you
have heard. You simply say "yes." There is little to comment upon
or to oppose in the substance of what he has said. At most you can
move about on the peripheries. In addition to those already heard,
I want to make some further comments that are peripheral to his
presentation.

First, of course, it is clear why Babylonians and Mesopotamians in
general should have been people of the book, why the local *edubba*
should survive as the word for school in Hebrew *beit-hassefer,* why
appreciation of learning should have been so great among all the
societies influenced by Babylonia, and why—much later—it is in
Babylonia that we witness the *floruit* of both postbiblical and Islamic law. It is a national, old, and honorable tradition. The scribes
were honored and appreciated. It was considered respectable to be
an "egghead" and even to undergo some of the privations that led
to that classification.

But, while the scribal profession was important, some of its practitioners occasionally discredited it; it went to their heads. One case
that comes to mind is that of the scribe who inscribed the statue
of Idrimi.[16] He knew how to write. He left us tablets that are quite
passable. But when he inscribed that statue, he insisted on showing
off what he knew. Following the principle of not being simple when
he could be complicated, he scarcely ever wrote the same sign twice in
the same form; as you may imagine, this principle adds considerably
to the headaches of Assyriologists.

Another one who followed a similar policy was King Ashurbani-

15 Cf. Jacobsen in *Journal of Near Eastern Studies* II (1943) 167.

16 Cf. S. Smith, *The Statue of Idri-mi* (1949) Pls. 9–13, with D. J. Wiseman, *The
Alalakh Tablets* (1953) Nos. 17, 47, 72, etc., which were written by the same scribe
(Sharruwa).

pal. He tells—and I would like Dr. Landsberger to say whether he believes it—how much he studied, how he accomplished he became, how many of the old types of texts he could read. The very fact, however, that Ashurbanipal boasted about these things proves that it was considered respectable to be a scholar, that it was not necessary to apologize for being one, and that royalty was happy to claim the honor. However, because Ashurbanipal was overimpressed with his own learning, he composed some of his inscriptions in a way that, if they are not altogether obscure, they cannot be considered as being in the best literary taste. Nevertheless, because of his love of learning he sent agents all over the country with instructions to procure by hook or by crook every tablet or text that was lacking in his library. And it is to that feverish collector's activity that we owe the famous library in the first instance; and it is to that library, in turn, that we owe our insight into so much of Mesopotamia's culture, an insight which, to some extent, is responsible for the title and much of the content of this symposium.

JACOBSEN: I would like next to call on Professor Grene, perhaps a little unfairly. Would you be willing to comment?

GRENE: I am afraid it would be very unfair. I really have nothing to add to what has been said beyond expressing my appreciation of Professor Landsberger's address. However, I might reveal my ignorance of the subject matter by inquiring further about the series of questions that the student was supposed to answer. Since they are mostly grammatical and literary in the simpler sense of the words, it would be interesting to know whether this is an exhaustive list of subjects. Were there other questions that would have partaken more of what the Romans called rhetoric: how to express certain kinds of subject matter, what kinds of arguments would or would not be used? Or was such a concept entirely alien?

JACOBSEN: The last person that I shall call upon is the discoverer of the Sumerian school text, Professor Kramer.

KRAMER: Let me first say something about Dr. Wilson's comments. I was happy to learn that while there are many differences between the Egyptian and Mesopotamian cultures, there are also quite a number of similarities. For instance, the wisdom genre he described, consisting of a father's instructions to his son, is found in Sumer as well. In Sumer it contains similar expressions, the same kind of introduction, and, in one case at least, it is even attributed to the ancient historical figure of Shuruppak, the father of the Sumerian "flood"-hero Ziusudra. An Egyptian essay also was mentioned in which a father is urging his son to follow in his footsteps. In a Sumerian *edubba* essay which I have recently translated we find a scribe deeply embittered at his son's refusal to follow in his footsteps and become a scribe.[17]

Turning to Professor Landsberger's introduction, I shall begin by listing the five extant Sumerian *edubba* texts for the benefit of noncuneiformists; this purely factual bit of information is not otherwise readily available. First there is the "Schooldays" essay, mentioned at the very outset of this session. Then there is the one about the unhappy father-scribe to which I have just referred. Third is a brief composition of some 75 lines consisting of a disputation between an *ugula* (some kind of supervisor) and a scribe. Somewhat surprisingly, the arguments in this case are kept within gentlemanly limits, and one gets the impression that the disputants are forcing themselves to be relatively sweet tempered. Then there is a text, which both Professor Landsberger and I have already mentioned, consisting of a most vituperative and abusive debate between two students who presumably were "seniors" and about to graduate as full-fledged scribes. Finally, there is a composition of 96 lines revolving about a quarrel between two younger schoolboys, which is "judged" by the *ugula*.

So much for some of the factual data about the extant *edubba* essays. Now let us turn to several specific questions which long have troubled me. First, the matter of an "audience" for the literary tablets in general. I have never been able to decide for whom the Sumerian literary works were intended. Certainly not for the ordinary Sumerian; he was undoubtedly illiterate. Did the Sumerian men of letters, the "sons of the *edubba*," write for one another? Such works as hymns may well have been used in the temple services, especially those containing liturgical rubrics. But who read the proverbs, or the essays, or the "disputations"? Did some of the ancient scribes actually have personal libraries? Of course, the teachers must have had collections of tablets which they used for pedagogical purposes, as "textbooks." But were there also "reading" libraries, where a man sat down and read for entertainment as well as for instruction?

Another and related problem is just what the Sumerian *edubba* designated. Was the word used, like our words "university" and "academy," with both general and specific meanings? Could the

[17] S. N. Kramer, *History Begins at Sumer* (London, 1958) pp. 12–16.

Sumerian say, for example: "I attend the *edubba* of Nippur, or the *edubba* of Ur, or the *edubba* of Kish"? And what was the relationship between the various Sumerian *edubba*'s? Were they all on the same level, with identical curricula and faculties of equal standing? Or was the *edubba* of Nippur perhaps the academy par excellence, with the others being merely branches of it? These and related questions about the *edubba* have puzzled me not a little, and I hope that Professor Landsberger or others will have an opportunity to discuss some of them in the course of the afternoon.

LANDSBERGER: First, I leave it undecided whether I have led or misled Assyriologists during the last three decades; perhaps the truth is somewhere in the middle.

Secondly, we must deal further with the question I raised as to the character of schooling, whether it was narrowly professional or regarded as general education. I left this undecided because I do not feel able to decide it, and Dr. Kramer very justly presses the question: For whom was all this intended? Was this *l'art pour l'art* or did it penetrate wider circles? As the general trend of my survey showed, I believe that almost beyond any doubt it was *l'art pour l'art*. Perhaps also the scholars declined to make it simpler in order to retain their own importance as a closed corporation. But, on the other hand, how could such a thing survive without the understanding and support of the kings and administrators? If this was an absolutely closed corporation, Dr. Kramer asks where were the windows? And I cannot provide a satisfactory answer. I only can refer to what I have already said about the drive to preserve Sumerian by the bringing of folklore into the school. But it cannot be shown that the Gilgamesh epic was read somewhere in the street or that it was sung in the palace.

Bearing on this problem are Ashurbanipal's claims to literacy; if true, they suggest that the king was familiar with the learning of the scribes. But we know he boasted of everything; his claim that he was able to read and write, to decipher tablets written before the flood, comes at the end of a list of other improbable accomplishments. There is even evidence that this particular claim was unfounded, because tablets have been preserved that were written by the court scribes for Ashurbanipal and they explain simple Sumerian logograms which can be read today by any student in his second semester. For example, a scribe provided the signs *ur-ku* with the gloss *kalbu* so that the king could read them. So there was nothing behind his boasting, although perhaps this is less important than his conception for the first time of the idea of a man trained in all the arts. Darius, who later boasted of the same achievement, dropped the conception of being a scribe, although it was very much easier for Darius to learn writing than it was for Ashurbanipal. It is worth noting that Ashurbanipal had boastful predecessors. King Shulgir, who claimed to be a god, also boasted that he knew how to write. Typical of his attitude is the highly improbable claim that he ran from Nippur to Ur, for which achievement he then, adding insult to injury, named a year; the following year he named for his running back from Ur to Nippur. Similar doubts surround the claims to literacy of Lipit Ishtar, another predecessor of Ashurbanipal. And in the long history of Mesopotamia only these three kings even claimed to know how to read and write. This emphasizes, I believe, both the closed character of the scribal corporation and the dependence of the palace on the specialized services that the scribes provided. While I do not know how it was managed, I can only suppose that the dependence of the king—or better, the symbiosis between the political power of the palace and the intellectual power of the scribes—is what led to the elevation of the scribal prototype to a position in the pantheon second only to that of Marduk.

Turning now to Professor Grene's question about the possibility of training in rhetoric, as in the classical world, this also I cannot answer. All the numerous dialogues may suggest some sort of training for speaking before a court, but unfortunately there is no proof that anyone ever pleaded his case before a court. The assemblies would have furnished another possible stage for rhetoricians, but I agree with Dr. Speiser that they were convoked to grant approval, not to listen to discussion. I can only conclude that, from the evidence available, formal training in rhetoric played little or no role; the king or administrator stammered out his order or concept verbally and left the written niceties to the scribes.

From what I have said here and on other occasions, it may be charged that I maintain an antagonistic bias toward the temples and priests. If so, I have been provoked into it at least in part by having to read too frequently of all this *Priesterweisheit* which is supposed to have been carefully preserved in the texts. But I do not think any of the scholars here will undertake to defend this romanticized old notion of "priestly wisdom," which in large part consists of no more than a heavy, didactic moralism; personally, I am a

Nietzschean, holding that *das Moralische versteht sich von selbst.* The so-called "wisdom texts," in any case, play a very, very small part in the literature. They clearly have to be distinguished from the body of proverbs, which were derived from folklore.

Now as to some of the concrete questions raised by Professor Kramer. The centralization of the scribal school, first in Nippur in the Old Babylonian 1 period and then in Babylon, clearly poses a problem. Perhaps my earlier formulation of this transition was a little too brief and positive; it should be stressed that, in spite of the shift, Nippur continued to exist as a center. We read that some texts in Nippur, for example, were copied from an original in Babylon, while others in Babylon were copied from an original in Nippur. But between the earlier dominance of Nippur and the later dominance of Babylon there is nevertheless an important contrast. In the Old Babylonian 1 dialogues Sumerian is still considered a living language, while in the Old Babylonian 2 schools it has disappeared. Moreover, the whole character of the dialogues changes. The master becomes more boastful, and the examinee assumes the merely secondary role of giving the master an opportunity to display his knowledge.

Finally, I want to emphasize that my account has necessarily ignored many important aspects of the scribal schools. For example, there are hints of a kind of examination marking the transfer from the lower school to the university, which was located only in Babylon and was called the *edubba gula.* Again, I have not had time to touch on later developments in the scribal arts, such as the revival of the old tradition in Nippur under its Kassite governor and the attempt to bring together singers and scribes as in the education of Arabian princesses in the arts of singing in Nippur. These features all are later than the periods I have dealt with, but they contribute to our understanding of the integration of scribal culture into the general culture.

JACOBSEN: The session is now open for general discussion.

PARKER: I merely wish to ask a question about the texts which Professor Kramer listed and whose purpose seems to be unknown. Can they conceivably be simply school models for the scribes? We have any number of Egyptian school exercises which, as Dr. Wilson pointed out, generally are pretty badly written, but there are also fairly good examples of the prototypes. If there are school exercises in Babylonia that include excerpts from these texts, then this possibility may be worth considering.

KRAMER: Mr. Chairman, may I retort to that with further questions? Granted that they are models, what would be the reason for making them the way they are? Why were these particular kinds of texts used as models? Just as excerpts were made from the Gilgamesh epic and from the hymns, so also excerpts were made from these; but this still does not tell us of the original purpose and audience. Would you imply, then, that nobody read your Egyptian equivalents except the chap who copied them and the professor who prepared them?

PARKER: I think so. I think that, in a sense, they were "McGuffy's Readers"; they taught. That is, they inculcated in the pupil moral principles or good behavior while he was learning to write.

KRAMER: And how about the Egyptian hymns? You would say that there was no outside audience?

PARKER: I would not think that there was.

LANDSBERGER: I only want to say that while there was no concept of general education or *paidea,* this does not mean that the average citizen was not guided by a conscious morality. For example, *awīlutu* means "to be a gentleman" and *tašimtu* means "to have good judgment." These and similar terms suggest that there were ideals of citizenship and that higher moral qualities were honored. One might mention in this connection the conception of a specifically Sumerian character.

JACOBSEN: In a line from the story of Gilgamesh and Huwawa, usually called "Gilgamesh and the Land of the Living," Gilgamesh is said to have taken pity on Huwawa after subduing him. The phrasing is, "Gilgamesh the Sumerian took pity on him."

LANDSBERGER: Yes. And there were not only ideals of Sumerian national character but also ideals held in common by the sons of a particular city; in addition, there were general conceptions of what the Turks might call a *chelebī,* or a gentleman.

WILSON: A possible lead to Professor Kramer's problem is provided in a very interesting article by Georges Posener, "Littérature et politique." He makes the origin of many of these texts a little too neat: that they were first established as didactic texts for the purposes of the state and especially for the purposes of the king, inculcating love of country, obedience to the king, willingness to serve the state, and so on. This is *an* argument. I doubt that it can be the whole argument, although Posener tries to bring several of the most-used texts under this general rubric.

With regard to Professor Grene's questions about rhetoric, it could be argued that there is a stress on persuasiveness that tends toward eloquence in some of the Egyptian texts. In one, for example, which I will continue to call a "wisdom text" even though it is wisdom only within an Egyptian definition, a father asks the king if he may instruct his son. The king replies: "Yes, instruct him first in good speaking." In addition, several of the common maxims provide advice on conduct in situations of debate, such as: "When debating with a superior you must be cautious, when debating with an inferior you may mow him down." Another very interesting suggestion that has been made is that a text copied for a certain length of time, and having the most bombastic phrases, provided a model of the proper kind of flattery for use in pleading before a magistrate. While this last suggestion may or may not be true, I think we can conclude that there is some relation of teaching to eloquent presentation in the Egyptian setting.

ALBRIGHT: For some reason, the participants in this discussion have not referred to the fact that eventually all literature is transmitted orally. As you know, Babylonian literature and belles-lettres were all poetic. These poems were all composed to be sung. In other words, the *nar* must have had the duty of reciting them. Since I do not believe that it was a precondition of the Babylonian scribe's profession that he be myopic, I doubt that scribes read their tablets to any extent for mere pleasure. As Professor Landsberger pointed out long ago, the texts were put into canonical form and then remained virtually unchanged for centuries. Since they were composed to be sung or chanted and since almost the only practical means of communication was oral, it would follow that these texts were intended to transmit the canonical form and to serve as school tablets and in repositories or reference libraries.

LANDSBERGER: As to the character of the Mesopotamian scribal tradition, in my opinion it was preserved without libraries until the time of Ashurbanipal. Hence the tradition, was, so to speak, fluid; it was copied from one *Vorlage* to another, with the originals being thrown away. While at times there may have been something of an accumulation in the temples, what we know to date at least comes only from school tablets. Moreover, it is known that the process of canonization did not hinder the gradual introduction of new compositions. In addition, there was a related body of noncanonical texts, the so-called *ša pī ummāni*, that which comes from the mouth of the teacher. In other words, the whole corpus reflects a continuing fluidity in spite of its canonization.

SEELE: In considering the Egyptian school texts one must not forget that a principal purpose of a good many of the school texts was not to educate students but to teach them to become scribes. By that I mean that they were not necessarily given any general education at all but were merely taught to write hieratic writing. The texts were dictated to them; they wrote down what they heard; the teacher corrected their handwriting. Many such texts are quite difficult to understand because they were so badly written, but I think for the most part that there was no intention of instructing students in the content of the lectures.

At the same time, I would say that there certainly was the concept of teaching rhetoric. After all, one of the most famous compositions that has come down to us from ancient Egypt is the story usually called "The Eloquent Peasant." It tells of a peasant who was unjustly treated and cheated out of some of his possessions, of how he went to the court and was finally brought into the presence of the king to make his complaints, and of how the king, enjoying the eloquent high-flown language, gave orders that he should be fed and taken care of so long as he continued. Eventually, we are led to suppose, he was given justice, but unquestionably the very existence of this composition proves how much the Egyptian enjoyed talking and appreciated the command of rhetoric. We have another composition in which the writer says "would that I had language such as has never been expressed before." He was fishing for a new, more vivid, vocabulary.

As to the purpose behind education of the scribes, further light may be thrown on this problem by examination of different copies of some of the manuscripts which have come down to us. It is not uncommon to find in a copy of a manuscript the words which mean "found lacking." The scribe, copying an old book written in hieratic on papyrus, was content to skip over a passage that had disintegrated with age or been eaten by worms, sometimes even omitting the expression "found wanting." He did not, so far as I know, ever attempt to fill a gap by any kind of creative thinking; instead, he slavishly copied what he had before him and was content to leave it just as it was. Likewise, there are frequent errors in the manuscripts that have come through with copying from dictation. Grotesque errors in understanding what the speaker intended sometimes occur, while others reflect pure ignorance of the language which the scribe was supposed to master as far as the calligraphy was concerned but about which he did not need to have a very precise knowledge from the point of view of meaning and content.

In connection with Egyptian school writings, attention should be called to the fact that we possess perhaps a hundred-thousandth or even less of what once existed in Egyptian hieratic manuscripts. The Mesopotamian clay tablets, of course, are almost imperishable, and hundreds of thousands of fragments of them have been found. However, there are far fewer fragments of hieratic papyri; in general, when hieratic papyrus goes to pieces it perishes utterly. Moreover, the early travelers in Egypt, in burning mummies by the hundreds in order to keep themselves warm, destroyed an immense number of old manuscripts that had been included in the wrappings. In short, while one does not like to admit that because of the perishing of the sources we do not know very much about ancient Egypt, this is nonetheless literally true. Our picture is terribly incomplete as compared with that of Mesopotamia, where the writing materials have been preserved to a much greater extent.

PARKER: I am afraid I cannot quite agree with Professor Seele that the material dictated in the Egyptian scribal schools was completely irrelevant as to content and was only intended to provide training in calligraphy. Apart from the purely didactic literature we have any number of examples of model letters which were dictated to and copied by the students, and through them it appears that the student learned how best to phrase typical communication necessary in his later life as an acting scribe. Moreover, it is difficult to think of some of the material not being taken to heart by the students as they wrote it down. For example, there is a composition phrased as a letter from a father to his son in school, scolding the boy in very vigorous terms for cutting class, spending time in the tavern drinking quantities of beer, falling into the dirt, and generally engaging in behavior that was unacceptable for any good student.

LANDSBERGER: In the Mesopotamian schools the conception of dictation was absent. Instead the common practice was that the "older brother" or preceptor would write down 25 lines or so on a clay tablet. Then, on the reverse of the same tablet, the student was required to write from memory the whole section of the literary series from which the particular composition had been chosen. Finally, the student's work was cut off but the preceptor's text was saved for further use. The practice of exact replication was introduced only in the late schools, where we know of a distinction between *liginna-qabû,* "to dictate," and *liginna-šatāru,* "to take dictation."

GELB: Before raising several specific questions I would like to comment a little on the *nar*'s, who apparently were not only singers but also musicians. They appear in very large numbers in the early Sumerian and Akkadian texts, and the most interesting thing about them is that either the majority of them or all of them were blind. Thus it is obvious that they were not scribes; evidently they were a part of the population which could not easily serve any other useful purpose but that of singing and playing musical instruments.

My first question has to do with the problem of bilingualism. In your opinion, Professor Landsberger, roughly what proportion of people actually used Sumerian as a learned language and were there any actual speakers of Sumerian after the end of the Old Babylonian period?

Secondly, I should like to hear more about the secret languages to which you alluded very briefly. This is completely new to me, that four out of sixteen questions in an examination might pertain to secret languages. Does this mean secret languages or only secret writings?

Finally, I should like to raise the very general and difficult question as to the extent of literacy in its relation to the different types of writing and the difficulty of learning them. All things considered, cuneiform writing is perhaps the most difficult writing I know of, and I cannot quarrel with your conclusion that no one except the scribes knew how to read and write in Mesopotamia. But I think there are suggestions of a greater extent of literacy in neighboring areas. I vaguely recall an incident, perhaps in the Book of Kings, suggesting that even shepherds knew how to read and write in Palestine. Can some biblical scholar here confirm this?

LANDSBERGER: I have a certain reserve as to when Sumerian died out as a spoken language. Certainly it was at an early date, well before the periods I have been discussing here. On the other hand, the artificial Sumerian of the scribes persisted for a long time afterward; as Falkenstein first pointed out, it even underwent a sort of rejuvenation after the time of Samsuditana. This inexplicable revitalization is indicated not only by the reappearance of Sumerian names (frequently of types not previously known) but also by compositions such as the famous "Exaltation of Ishtar," composed at a very late time in a rather artificial Sumerian and provided from the beginning with Akkadian translation. I want to make it absolutely clear, however, that this artificial Sumerian was not a spoken language. With Samsuditana, if not earlier, such Sumerian as had continued to be taught in the schools died out completely and was replaced by its rather artificial successor.

As to secret writing and the cabala, this is relatively late. While I do not like to rely on an *argumentum ex silentio,* we might provisionally assign the beginning of a division between a public and a secret science to the Kassite period. The only known documents come from the time of Ammizaduga and are distinguished by over-complicated logograms and signs. We might speak of them as concerned with occult subjects, except that the objective seems to have been merely to conceal the meaning by distortion rather than to deal with special metaphysical insights.

I am afraid I have little to offer on the question of the extent of literacy. Perhaps, as in Professor Kramer's "Schooldays" text, there were limited periods like the Third Dynasty of Ur and the Old Babylonian period when the upper class and the principal administrators sent their sons to schools. But this was a very isolated phenomenon, and I suspect that those who were sent to school under these circumstances generally did not learn very much. They belong in the category of the *dubsar ḫurrum,* the scribe who could only read a little and take down a letter with many inaccuracies, from which we, in reading their letters, now have to suffer. Incidentally, the description of this class as the *dubsar ḫurrum* is no compliment to your Hurrians.

GELB: What does *ḫurrum* mean in that context? Something like *barbaros?*

LANDSBERGER: Or mountaineers, hillbillies. And derived, of course, from the Hurrians.

GELB: That is very good.

LANDSBERGER: The *dubsar ḫurrum,* by the way, is not known in later periods. Scribes in the later periods again exhibited a nearly perfect command of the script and language.

HOSELITZ: This discussion compels me to ask what was the job of these scribes? After they had learned to write, they went out into the ordinary life of Babylon and wrote for businessmen, for temples, for the government, and for various other purposes. Now is it possible to interpret these secret languages that they were supposed to understand as merely meaning that they had to learn the professional slang of the people with whom they had to deal? A scribe who wrote business documents presumably had to know something of the technical terms of banking. If he worked for a temple and did land surveying, presumably he was required to talk to shepherds and peasants and thus had to know the nonliterary, common, ordinary language, the professional slang, the technical terms of these people. Does the reference to various types of nonliterary or secret languages imply essentially that the scribes took a variety of jobs in many places and had to know special technical vocabularies in order to function?

LANDSBERGER: The greater number of scribes had administrative positions; private use of scribes was quite limited. The only exception was the Assyrian colonies, where all the merchants had scribes. Otherwise, scribes were limited to positions connected with administration or with substantial accumulations of private capital. Perhaps, also, they filled out contracts and legal documents at the gate of the city. If I were to make an intuitive sweeping estimate, I would say that perhaps seventy per cent of the scribes had administrative positions, twenty per cent were privately employed, and the remainder became specialists in the diagnosis of illness, charms, magic, and other activities calling for some knowledge of writing.

SPEISER: Returning to the subject of literacy, I hope Professor Gelb's question about biblical evidence can be answered by reference to a passage in Judges. Gideon, in his campaign across the Jordan, was not treated very well by the city of Succoth. Having no time to settle accounts with the elders, he just managed to pick up an urchin on the street, "a boy" the text calls him, almost suggesting that he was a juvenile delinquent, and that boy managed to write down the names of all the elders in Succoth. Now, do with it what you want, but it does suggest that literacy was not limited to the privileged alone.

Coming back to the perplexing question as to the extent of literacy in Babylonia, we find some straws in the wind even though conclusive evidence is lacking. Take the epic of Gilgamesh. There was a legendary hero about whom later on a number of Sumerian compositions were written. These compositions still later were used as a theme by some nameless genius who made of them a completely new creative synthesis, an epic that became one of the great works of

world literature, a "Great Book," even if the Great Books Foundation does not seem to have heard about it. Now, knowledge of this
epic was not limited to a small group, it was not even limited to
Babylonia. This is proved not only by the number of tablets on
which that epic appears but by the places where fragments of it have
been found. Boğazköy, the Hittite capital in Anatolia, has yielded a
number of them, and I understand more have been found and will
be published. Recently a fragment was found in Palestine, at the
site of Megiddo. Surely someone had to read them, and not merely
scribes. What is more important, these texts were not only read in
the original over a wide area but they were translated. We have a
sample of a Hurrian translation and fragments of a Hittite translation, the best possible proof that the epic received wide circulation
because of its universal values and universal appeal.

And this finally brings up the point about the Hurrians, in whom
I share a slight vested interest with Professor Gelb. I think it was
someone by the name of Landsberger who at one time interpreted
the word *ḫurrum* as *aḫurrum,* having nothing to do with Hurrians
as an ethnic group but meaning a backward fellow. I do not know
whether he still holds to that, but even if the Hurrians should have
been thought of as being just as naïve and rustic as the Kurds are
thought of by some Arabs today—people who, if asked which is their
right ear, invariably point to their left ear with their right hand—
this might just be one of those amiable, joshing references and no
more. At any rate, whether or not the Hurrians were as advanced as
the Babylonians, they transmitted a good many literary works to the
Hittites, some directly and some with their own additions. And
many of these works, as Güterbock has shown so conclusively, went
on to become the heritage of the Greeks; much of the theogony of
Hesiod was influenced by them. In short, there was a great deal of
intellectual ferment transmitted through literary channels, and it
was not simply the work of a few benighted scribes who had nothing
better to do and therefore studied.

LANDSBERGER: No doubt Professor Speiser, who has been concerned for many years with the poetic feeling of Mesopotamian poetry, is somewhat provoked by my consideration of only the more
mundane question of its popularity. But I must insist on making a
clear distinction between the so-called national heritage and the
scribal traditions. About the former we know very little. At one time
I myself thought of the Gilgamesh epic as a "national epic." Now,

having grown older, I have also grown more cautious; I do not know that it was not widely popular among the ordinary people, but neither can I prove that it was. That the epic spread to adjoining areas no one can deny. But it can be argued that in every place from which fragments have been reported scribal schools also were present. Hence its spread is not an argument for its wide popular acceptance, at least in its Mesopotamian homeland.

I have also grown skeptical of the too-convenient concepts which attach basic importance to differences in the complexity of writing systems. Perhaps the difference between a narrow, highly specialized scribal class in Mesopotamia and a Palestinian population which provided schooling even for its street urchins can be explained in this fashion, but I should first like to ascertain whether the contrast was really as great as the story from Judges would suggest. Might we call upon Professor Güterbock to say a word about the character of schooling and the extent of literacy in the Hittite empire? And might Professor Albright deal with the same questions for Palestine?

GÜTERBOCK: The most striking thing about the so-called archives or libraries, or at any rate the collections of tablets that have been found in the Hittite capital, is that they all seem more or less concerned with the government, the royal family, and especially the royal person. To cite just one example, there is hardly any Hittite prayer that is worded as the prayer of a private person to the gods; almost every prayer was pronounced by King Mursilis or by King Hattusilis or by his wife on some certain occasion and taken down by a scribe. How far literacy went is very hard to say. Certainly the king himself could neither write nor read, for once or twice in a colophon, that is, a scribal subscript to a tablet, it is said that a certain ritual text was taken down "from the mouth of his majesty."

As to Hittite schools, we have very little evidence. There are the famous Sumero-Akkadian vocabularies, about which we have already spoken in another connection, that were copied by the Hittites and provided with a Hittite translation. Other genres of Babylonian literature also entered into the Hittite textbooks, including omens, medical texts, and I would even add the epics. But what use was made of this borrowed literature is not clear. There are just one or two tablets from Boğazköy which appear to have been pupils' copies, and even these are doubtful. The *edubba* is mentioned in just one text, and this, interestingly enough, is a private letter. Professor Otten recently has demonstrated that all the known private letters (i.e., those exchanged between private persons rather than between officials) were exchanged between members of the scribal class or caste.

In short, my own feeling has always been very similar to what Professor Landsberger has just said, namely that the presence in Boğazköy of the Gilgamesh epic in Akkadian, in a Hurrian translation, and in a Hittite translation is somehow to be understood as connected with the schools. Why was it translated? Why did the Hittites produce Hittite versions of, let us say, the Kumarbi epic or all the epics that found later reflection in Hesiod? For whose benefit? Is it possible that it was merely for the amusement of the king, the royal family, and the nobility that was admitted to the court? I do not know.

The problem of literacy among the Hittites is complicated by the existence of a second system of writing, called "Hittite hieroglyphs," which always has baffled us. It is slowly becoming evident that the language which was written in this system was not Hittite but Luwian and that it came in, or at least increased in popularity, relatively late in the Hittite New Kingdom. Perhaps this had something to do with an increase in the Luwian-speaking element of the administrative elite, of the scribal group, or even of the population at large, but there is no evidence at present.

Finally, I should like to illustrate concretely Professor Landsberger's suggestion that scribes might be found sitting at the city gate. Two years ago a gate was excavated in a wall separating sections of Boğazköy, and built into it was a stone with the scratched-in hieroglyphs of a name followed by the hieroglyphic logogram for scribe. One would imagine a man sitting at the gate under the sign of his profession, ready to take down dictation in either of the two writing systems.

ALBRIGHT: I will only mention the Byblian enigmatic or syllabic script of the early Middle Bronze period and the Ugaritic alphabet of the Late Bronze period but will say a few words about the Akkadian diplomatic script and language and the linear alphabet from which our own is derived. The Akkadian diplomatic script was understood only by a limited number of Canaanite, Egyptian, Hurrian, and other scribes, whose Babylonian always shows clear traces of having originated in a scribal school. We have, for instance, a number of letters written in very crude Babylonian characters with the same words and in the same hand but written from different cities, obviously the work of one scribe who traveled from city to city and wrote letters for the local chieftains. In other words, Babylonian writing was possibly known only to a few score scribes in the whole of Palestine. As for the linear alphabet whose development we can now trace century after century from the seventeenth century down to the first millennium B.C., we can say that virtually all texts so far found are inscriptions written by unlettered turquoise-miners in Sinai. They are full of mistakes and very badly executed, just as badly executed as the drawings and carvings in Egyptianizing style which accompanied them. Among the other texts are some in the nature of amulets, while still others are graffiti. So far we do not know of a single formal document in our own ancestral alphabet before the tenth century B.C. However, it is perfectly clear, as Professor Speiser has pointed out, that after the 28-letter alphabet had been replaced by the 22-letter alphabet somewhere between 1250 and 1100 B.C., the use of the script spread very rapidly. We now have documents in this script from the twelfth, eleventh, and tenth centuries in Palestine proper. Since the forms of the letters are very simple, the 22-letter alphabet could be learned in a day or two by a bright student and in a week or two by the dullest; hence it could spread with great rapidity. I do not doubt for a moment that there were many urchins in various parts of Palestine who could read and write as early as the time of the Judges, although I do not believe that the script was used for formal literature until later.

LANDSBERGER: Do you think the Bible would have been possible without writing?

ALBRIGHT: No. Most of the early parts of the Hebrew Bible were probably transmitted orally, but I think that they could have been put into writing long before they were.

LANDSBERGER: So the greater part was orally transmitted before it was taken down?

ALBRIGHT: Perhaps so. But this oral transmsision was controlled and supported by the fact that writing was known and that there were some formal documents which could be consulted.

LANDSBERGER: Our time having been exhausted, I only want to thank all of you very much. I hope I have fulfilled my duty to initiate and provoke this discussion, and I only can say how much I have enjoyed your participation.

JACOBSEN: This brings our discussion for this afternoon to an end. I suppose, in view of our subject, the proper formula is "school dismissed."

EGYPT THROUGH THE NEW KINGDOM
Civilization without Cities

GÜTERBOCK (*chairman*): Ladies and gentlemen: This morning at our fifth session we are continuing our discussion of the development of culture in the national states but turning our attention from Mesopotamia to Egypt. Professor Wilson, who has made a special trip back from Egypt to attend this symposium, will introduce the subject, using as his *Leitmotif* "civilization without cities."

WILSON: I want to begin with the Gospel according to Saint Matthew, the second chapter and the fifteenth verse: "That it might be fulfilled that which is spoken through the prophet, out of Egypt have I called my son." The question is what is going to be fulfilled this morning? Since airplane luggage is limited, I have brought back to you only two of the plagues of Egypt, the last two in fact. You remember that the next to the last one was the thick darkness. The thick darkness results from the fact that Egypt just is "ornery" in our context. Egypt refuses to conform to the terms which have been agreed upon for this symposium. And this leads to the last plague: the slumber of the first boredom. Instead of taking twenty minutes as I was instructed, I am going to take forty minutes to say over and over again "I can't do it, I can't do it, I can't do it."

It is customary to think of the development of culture in the national states as a generally similar process in the two great river valleys of Mesopotamia and Egypt. For the broad purposes of universal history this generalization is of course true. The major phenomena of the organization of society, the interplay of the individual and the community, technology, the arts, the controlling sanctions set up by government and religion are broadly a single process illustrated by these two cultures. The general psychology of two cultures which relied upon the myth as explanatory of the phenomena and processes in the world was basically a single psychology.

When, however, we come to describe the two cultures with clear and specific illustrations, we become increasingly aware of differences in experiences and in expressions between the Mesopotamian and the Egyptian scene. A well-known example lies in the dogma of rule. In Mesopotamia the ruler was a deputy for the gods, without divinity in himself. In Egypt he was a god in his own person. The reasons for this differential can only be matters of speculation; it may be related to an African scene in the Egyptian case and more of an Asiatic scene in the Mesopotamian case, but this possibility is in itself no explanation.

Another factor which has been in view over the past twenty-five years is the alleged "Mesopotamian stimulation of predynastic Egypt." I say "alleged," even though I personally believe in it, because it has not been universally accepted in its particular manifestations or even in its general description. According to this hypothesis, the final predynastic period in Egypt (the Gerzean) started off with fresh vigor but slowly ran out of initiative and became undistinguished and sterile. In contrast, in Mesopotamia there seems to have been progressive development of the forms of cultural expression, without any loss of initiative and with enrichment of form. Then, just before the First Dynasty, Mesopotamian elements entered into the Egyptian context as striking novelties and survived for several centuries. Synchronous with this Mesopotamian incursion of forms and techniques was the Egyptian leap into history, into that thing which we apologetically call civilization. The theory would then claim that the Mesopotamian stimulation was the catalyst for the change in Egypt from relatively simple forms and congeries of forms to that developed complexity or maturity which we call civilization. If this theory is true, the specific factors of expression were not important in themselves; the important thing was the fact of a stimulation.

This is confirmed by the observation that some of the borrowed art motifs disappeared rapidly, while other factors eventually became vestigial. The one really major contribution which Mesopotamia may have made to Egypt was the idea of writing, with the principle of ideograms being borrowed for phonograms on the rebus method. However, some Egyptologists are reluctant to admit that the idea of writing was borrowed by Egypt from Mesopotamia, and they point out essential differences between the two systems and the truly native character of the Egyptian pictures. Even if we do not include writing, the Mesopotamian stimulation seems a potent factor.

When the Egyptian culture finally in dynastic times did express its Egyptianness, that expression was radically different from the Mesopotamian expression. Visibly the abundant stone of Egypt produced a different monument and different complexes of monuments from those in Mesopotamia. In religion the dogma asserted that the authority of the state was innately invested in the king, because the king was a god. Rule was thus highly personal, so that Egypt was extraordinarily slow in developing the instrument of rule by an impersonal written law. Written law appeared early in Mesopotamia, but it is possible that it did not effectively come into Egypt for twenty-five hundred years. Until impersonal and codified law finally gained ascendancy, there ruled customary law, interpreted as the divine word of the god-king. In religion the emphasis was on eternity, and the supreme energies of state and individual went into an investment for eternity in pyramids and tombs, in the psychology of the mortuary religion which also pervaded the religion of the day. This was not morbid; this was rather a confident commitment to everlasting life. It was part of the security of Egypt, perhaps a geographic security, that the Egyptians felt that life could not end but must go on eternally.

Further, at the beginning of her history Egypt developed a nation, without the visible preliminary stage of city-states. The word "nation" is used here in no modern political sense but simply because of the size of the unit. At this jump into historic times all of arable Egypt, whether one reckons it from the First Cataract to the Mediterranean or only from the Hierakonpolis region to the southern apex of the Delta, was a single organism under a single rule. A state 500 to 600 miles long is functionally different from a state focused upon a single city. The Egyptian nation appeared centuries before Mesopotamia had passed through its series of city-states and reached a kind of imperial (or national) age under Agade.

Yet Egypt the nation had nothing which can be recognized as a city in modern terms, to serve as the firm and fixed heart of a large political organism. Egypt was an agricultural land, crowded with agricultural villages, some of which waxed into temporary importance and then waned again. To be sure, Egypt had its important capitals such as Memphis from about 3000 B.C. and Thebes from about 2000 B.C. To be sure, there were important focal towns such as Sais, Heliopolis, Hermopolis, and Abydos. It is also true that we do not know definitely the size and complexity of these towns, because exploration and excavation in Egypt cannot achieve the same results as they do in Mesopotamia. The old towns lie too deep under the alluvium or under modern life. However, what little we do know from excavation does not suggest any large and continuing size for such places as Memphis, Heliopolis, and Thebes.

There is another factor. Professor Oppenheim spoke yesterday of the city in Mesopotamia as a legal personality. The texts provide evidence on this. We have no similar evidence of "cities" as legal personalities in Egypt. And the only time "cities" seem to have an independent activity is in those periods when the state breaks down and a "city" may temporarily assert itself against other "cities" or against other provincial areas. But when the state is secure the "city" has no visible legal existence or independence.

In practice the smallness and impermanence of the town made it easy to shift the capital from place to place. There arose in Egypt no early metropolis of such centripetal force that it could survive political changes and remain a great city in later days. In pharaonic Egypt there was no Alexandria, no Athens, no Rome to serve as the continuing heart of a culture. There was nothing of an acreage to compare with Nippur or Babylon.

Another contrast between the geographical history of Mesopotamia and that of Egypt should be stated. The earliest Mesopotamian civilized weight lay in the moist area at the south, in such places as Ur, Eridu, and Erech. Gradually the focus moved northward in Mesopotamia. This is now explained to us partly in terms of the gradual salting-up of the southern area and the necessity of finding new productive lands for the focus of the national interest and activity. There was a kind of substractive or substitutive process at work.

In Egypt, on the contrary, the process was additive. Most of Upper Egypt was viable from the beginning and at least by the Third Dynasty was divided into its administrative provinces, the nomes. The Delta, however, Lower Egypt, was more slowly conquered and rescued from the swamps in its south and the salt marshes in its north. The growth of a viable Delta, the development of its administrative provinces, was a prolonged process, and most of that process took place, I think, in historical times. In antiquity the process was not completed, and the Delta reached its widest extension only under the Ptolemies.

In essentially rainless Egypt the water is from the flooding of the Nile; the alluvial mud dries out in deep natural bricks. In this process much of the salt remains deep in the fissures between the bricks and does not rise near to the surface of the land. A second factor in the problem of salinization is that the Nile floods the fields and when the flood subsides there is a flushing-out, a drainage back into the Nile; the natural drainage is away from the fields. In Mesopotamia, with the increasing height of the canals and the banks of the canals, the source of water was often above the level of the fields, so that the natural drainage was onto the fields; the water did not drain away but sank into the soil. The abandonment of land because of saliniza- tion was no problem in Egypt. Egypt was able to add agricultural land whenever a strong government wanted to make the effort. That was true under the Old Kingdom in the Delta and the very extreme south; it was true under the Twelfth Dynasty and under the Ptole- mies in the Fayyum district.

Ancient Egypt used a principle of irrigation different from that of Mesopotamia. In the earliest time, when the Delta was very little usable, trunk canals were probably extremely rare. For the long trough of Upper Egypt the flood waters were utilized through indi- vidual catch basins rather than through a system of canal arteries. At the time of the inundation the water was let into rectangular earthen basins, was held there to permeate the soil, and there it de- posited its refreshing load of silt. In Mesopotamia the canal system might be likened to a tree, with the river as the trunk and the canals as strong branches thrusting out from the trunk. Thus the fruits— the urban settlements—are found growing along the courses of these arteries, and they had some organic relation to one another at any time when one of these canals was strong and usable. Hence city- states might develop axially, or the problems of competitions of cit- ies might be axial. In Egypt the Nile River might be likened to a stalk of grass or bamboo, from which the basins grew out as leaves. Clearly the Egyptian system was decentralized; the maintenance of local basins did not require a large community effort. Each small lo- cality probably had its own basin. This decentralization may have some relation to the failure to develop large organisms which might be called "cities," since there were myriads of villages within sight and shouting distance of one another.

On the other hand, in Egypt the trunk—the main artery—was much more important because everything was close to the Nile River. This was both the means of communication and the great ar- tery of refreshing water. This artery may be related to the develop- ment of a single nation in Egypt without that visible prior stage of a series of city-states building up as a kind of brickwork into the na- tion.

After these speculative generalities, I shall outline the develop- ment of the Egyptian organism from prehistoric times to the end of

the New Kingdom about 1100 B.C. Even such a brief outline must
continue to be interpretative rather than factual, because the terms
with which we are dealing today are not easily supported by solid
data.

It is particularly in dealing with the prehistoric periods of Egypt
that we are baffled by the sparseness of evidence for the living community in contrast to the plentiful evidence for the community of
the dead. The rise of the alluvium in the Nile Valley has wiped out
evidence for towns and villages, for houses and palaces, for harbors
and market places. Because the dead were laid out in the desert, we
are left with a generous profusion of cemeteries and the problem of
how much the dead can tell us about the living. The few villages that
we may examine, such as Marimdah Beni Salamah on the edge of
the Delta and Hammamiyah in Upper Egypt, may be marginal and
atypical. We cannot offer an honest comparison with the Mesopotamian sites of Jarmo, Hassunah, Tepe Gawra, Eridu, Warka, and
so on. For Mesopotamia the evidence starts on the watered hillsides
and later is visible within a valley where the silt piled up either in
the beds of canals or along the canal banks. Ancient mounds can still
rise out of the plain. For rainless Egypt there is no comparable evidence from hillside or plain. Its villages were marginal to the Nile
River and surrounded at the inundation, so that the accumulating
alluvium deeply buried most of the oldest habitations.

Thus we can only speculate on the economic, communal, and political structures of Egypt before the dynasties. Conceivably the oldest scene in Upper Egypt showed a Nile fringed with a thicket of
tangled vegetation, covering the best soil, so that man made his first
approach to this thicket rather than to the river itself. It is likely that
the first economy involved herds rather than cereals until there
could be penetration into this extraordinarily fertile soil along the
river. Man had first to convert the thicket into arable fields; only
later did he carry water over to the desert edge by means of catch
basins. For Lower Egypt, similar reclamation of swamp or desert in
predynastic times must have been confined to the southern apex of
the Delta, the western and eastern margins, and isolated spots within the jungle, but along arms of the river, as at Sais, Buto, or Mendes,
the situation must have been very much like that in the swamp area
of southern Iraq at the present time. It seems likely that the vast
proportion of the Delta was not reclaimed from the jungle until historic times. The Ptolemies finally pushed farthest to the north, but

even today brackish swamps near the Mediterranean await reclamation.

The earliest sedentary economy, with its conversion of riverine thicket into fields, presumably demanded only the work of the immediate village. Even the first catch basins required no more than a limited understanding between a few villages. It is difficult, then, to relate prehistoric rule, predynastic "kingship," to the control of water rights. The earliest kings did not gain recognized power by conferring or withholding water. Broad territorial water rights, which would imply wider control by a political unity, do not appear to be essential to the picture. About the only area where they might have developed in predynastic times is in Middle Egypt. There the agricultural land is not restricted to a 3-kilometer strip along the river bank but may extend a dozen kilometers inland. Wider use of water in this area may have required some short regional canaling toward the more remote basins, and this could have produced limited territorial control and rule of a city-state pattern. But I cannot see any possibility in this hypothesis of accommodating a network of irrigation canals as the geographic foundation for a predynastic administrative district or nome.

The abrupt emergence of the Egyptian nation at about 3000 B.C. is a terrible embarrassment. How could it have come into being if we deny some of the formative factors? At any rate, there is now a king, claiming to rule a vast territory from some point north of the First Cataract to some point within the Delta. I do not think this claim for Menes—the alleged first king of the First Dynasty—could have rested on fully accomplished fact, but the claim was made. Probably this claim had to be validated by continual spread, by power and acceptance, by recognition of community of interest through the first two dynasties—covering a minimum of two centuries and perhaps as much as four centuries—in order to secure consolidation of this new organism, the nation.

If hydraulic engineering and the consequent highly productive agriculture were limited at the beginning of the First Dynasty, they presumably made their great advances after there was a state. A control slowly extended through conquest could have received the supporting sanction of slowly extended prosperity, coming from a more effective irrigation system and from the spreading use of a new mechanism, the plow. If so, more efficient irrigation and agriculture followed the Egyptian dynastic union and thus were not the factors which made that union possible. Indeed, there is little evidence that the state as a political agent was concerned with irrigation works or, better, with agriculture. Such a concern emerges in the Twelfth Dynasty but cannot be documented earlier.

Nearly two years ago Dr. Adams asked me a series of questions about ancient Egyptian kings, waterworks, and agriculture. These questions put the Egyptian scene into a new light or, shall we say, into different shadows. I no longer think that the king was the water magician and that this role was a factor in his acceptance in Egypt. Two points in Dr. Adams' paper (pp. 269–92) are that the earliest kings and nobles were administratively unconcerned with problems of water and food and that large-scale irrigation works were a consequence, rather than a cause, of the appearance of a dynastic state. The state of course benefited tremendously by such works, but the works were not, so to speak, the purpose of the state at the beginning.

So, we have two dynasties of consolidation, and Egypt appears as Egypt in expressing culture in architecture, art, literature, governmental organization, the statement which religion makes, and so on from the Third Dynasty on. We credit Djoser, first king of the Third Dynasty, not only with the beginning of monumental architecture in stone in Egypt but also with the setting-up of a new monster, the bureaucracy. The bureaucracy which he started ultimately came to be the great counterweight to the god-king. Gradually the absolute centralization around the person of the king, with members of the royal family used as the highest servants of the state, was to give way to a dependence upon skilled civil servants who could assume a degree of independent responsibility. This was the familiar process within which the tight centralization of the state in the Third and Fourth Dynasties relaxed progressively into decentralization in the Fifth and Sixth Dynasties. The official dogma that the god-king *is* the state and effects everything by divine understanding and divine command was formulated in the period of tight centralization. It was to be asserted throughout pharaonic history, even though the later periods might show a superior control of the king by other gods, might show the power of priests or civil servants behind the throne, or might be interims of feudalism or of competing dynasties.

We go into an age of decentralization which may be called "feudal," if you will permit feudalism to be defined to fit the Egyptian scene, with a decentralizing process against which a new organism, the Middle Kingdom, had to try to force its way. The kings of the end of the Eleventh Dynasty and of the Twelfth Dynasty were able to arrest this decentralizing process and to establish centripetalism in two ways.

First, the unchanged dogma that the god-king is the state was asserted more in terms of divine function and responsibility than in terms of innate right and privilege. The Old Kingdom had only had to assert the power and majesty of the king; the Middle Kingdom had to argue his benevolent efficacy for the state. I mentioned yesterday an article by Georges Posener, "Littérature et politique," which perhaps exaggerates the factor of the state arguing its case, or the king arguing his case, to the people, but which I think is basically a correct analysis. Second, a new factor I believe, the state showed an immediate and functional concern for agricultural prosperity in the Twelfth Dynasty. There was a new alertness to the expected volume of the Nile inundation, so that there might be more efficient use of the flood waters. And there were extensive reclamation projects, notably in the Fayyum.

Egypt had maintained isolation and it had security. The only early exception to this generalization was the development of the mines in the Sinai Peninsula. But the Middle Kingdom experimented with empire-building, expanding south into Nubia with a series of frontier posts set up there, a blockade trading post established at the Third Cataract, and so on. And this was a breakdown of the attitude that Egypt was the only country that counted, that its prosperity was sufficient unto itself, that it need not bother about the impoverished lands which were its neighbors. I cannot explain this change; Nubia in itself was lightly populated and not important for security purposes. Perhaps the answer lay in gold mines there, but this suggestion is speculation.

After the Middle Kingdom came that sharp shock to the Egyptian sense of self-satisfaction and security, the Hyksos "invasion" and rule. The shock of this humiliating foreign rule led to an enlargement of empire-building, with frontiers pushed deeper into Africa and now, for the first time, far into Asia. The Fourth Cataract to the south and the Euphrates River to the north were claimed as frontiers of Egypt, no matter whether the claim was administratively valid in all parts or not.

Security, then, broke down, along with the sense of a superiority so self-assured that nothing need be done to maintain it. And in a sense the underlying psychology of Egypt was reversed. The previous self-assured emphasis on immortal life was replaced by a sense of insecurity and peril, and it was necessary to have a more disciplined organization of the state to meet both the larger problems of empire and the constant peril of contacts with outside peoples. The dogma of the state, which had had a saving element of tolerance and flexibility, now had to limit these qualities and demand disciplined unity. Differences between Egyptian expression and Asiatic expression became less. Men had to be more obedient; the role of the legal ordinance became stronger and was added as an impersonal element to the personal word of the god-king.

In art the earlier preoccupation with eternity was not abandoned, but there came into being side by side with it a narrative expression —storytelling—of the immediate experience. In architecture there developed an emphasis on the colossal, expressed not so massively as in the pyramids but rather in high-standing colossal architectural elements. In literature we begin to find an invasion of secularism; and the documents may be purely literature of entertainment, of love poetry, and quite innocent of any interest in religion.

This large complex organism, the Empire or New Kingdom, was also a very wealthy organism, in which the control of power was far more important. Its size and complexity meant a new professionalism, leading to cleavages between the laity and the clergy, between priests and officials, between officials and the newly specialized army —all of them competing with the king for power.

The civil service, headed by the vizier, gained specifically stated areas of immediate control by royal patent. The priesthood won a power over the king by forcing him to seek oracular guidance from the gods before embarking on any enterprise. Among the three forces, palace, priesthood, and civil service, there might have been a restless balance of power. But the newly professional army wielded the only effective police power and thus was able to seize rule at any time of crisis and confusion.

The pharaoh lost authority in all directions. This was a major factor in Egypt's chronic weakness after the New Kingdom. When the dogma continued to drone on that the only source of rule was the king and the king was visibly a captive of these other forces, Egypt just crumbled. She became that vacillating and fragmented force which she was during the first millennium B.C.

After this brief outline of the development of the Egyptian organism, let us consider what may be called the "plasticity" of Egypt.

Dr. Jacobsen spoke of Egypt as being highly civilized, highly sophisticated, and I agree that this is true in both the complimentary and the disparaging sense. There was a kind of elegance, but in a way a surface elegance. The ancient Egyptian was urbane even though he had no *urbs*. He had a politesse even though there was no polis. He was civilized without being in the Latin sense a *civis*. Art and literature attained a high level of subtlety; technology accomplished extraordinarily well the highest demands of the culture, as in the superb architecture of the pyramid age. The range was limited, when one compares Babylonia or Greece, but the range seems to have been adequate for the demand made on it by Egyptian culture in its earliest time.

When one studies the religion, one is impressed with the great amount of tolerance and flexibility possible within a culture so religion-saturated. There were certain broad and stable features, like the ever-immanent activity of the gods, the centrality of the king as a god, and the confidence of immortality; but within these fixed limits there was a remarkable tolerance of varying ideas and interactions. Because the factors are so fluid, no two modern scholars agree in their interpretations of ancient Egyptian religion. For example, in a milieu which is commonly accepted as polytheistic, some authorities write about "primitive monotheism" and others about "essential monotheism." Some insist upon the basic uniformity of religion over three thousand years, while others are impressed by the extraordinary changes which took place over the course of time. This is confusing, but it may perhaps be referred back to the word "sophistication."

As a community, Egypt had both unity and disparity. If one considers the desert area of northeastern Africa, Egypt was a single oasis more than 600 miles long. In its sharp contrast to its immediate neighbors, it had a unified and markedly distinct culture. Yet within Egypt there was sharp variety. The broad fields of the Delta opened out to Libya, to the Mediterranean, and to Asia, whereas the long trough of Upper Egypt was hemmed in by blighted deserts. The agricultural richness of Middle Egypt contrasted sharply with the poverty of southernmost Egypt. The two factors of insulation from strong outside influence and of wide internal variety help to explain the tolerant flexibility and genial sophistication. Certainly the flexibility, the self-assurance, and the active sense of gaiety stood in contrast to an austerity which marked the Asiatic cultures. Only after a millennium and a half, after Egypt had suffered the foreign domination by the Hyksos, and after Egypt had tried to hold foreign lands within an empire and had come to final failure in that effort, did the Egyptian expression harden into something like the Asiatic austerity.

As a biological organism, Egypt was primitive. The arable land was packed tight with living protoplasm: hundreds of agricultural and commercial villages within sight of one another. Yet the total organism did not develop a central nervous system which we should consider adequate. It had no fixed heart, no fixed brain. At a certain time the chromatin gathered together to form a temporary nucleus at one point; at another time the nucleus appeared elsewhere. Successively the capital shifted from Memphis to Herakleopolis, to Thebes, to Lisht, to Avaris, to Thebes, to Ramses. There was no eternal city, no Rome, which could exhibit such strong polarity that it became the inevitable center of government, religion, commerce, art, and science. The temporary capitals seem never to have gained any remarkable size. Memphis-Sakkarah, Abydos, and Thebes had extensive temples and cemeteries, but there is no evidence that any of them was and continued to be a large and active metropolis of commercial and intellectual life. Ancient Egypt carried on her life through dozens of moderate-sized towns and myriads of agricultural villages. It is legitimate to say that for nearly three thousand years, until the founding of Alexandria, ancient Egypt was a major civilization without a single major city.

The organism was also capable of mitosis or fission at times when the central government broke down, with the chromatin centers drawing apart into separate, opposed nuclei at Thebes and Herakleopolis, at Avaris and Thebes, or at Tanis and Thebes. Where the throne was, there was the capital; if there were rival claimants to the throne, there were rival capitals. Certainly Memphis would seem to have been ideally located to serve as the continuing capital of Upper and Lower Egypt. Thebes was poorly located for that purpose. Ramses was a capital facing outward toward the Asiatic empire, rather than inward toward Egypt. Yet all these cities were temporary nuclei. Ultimately, in the first millennium B.C., when external forces had broken down the former sense of isolated unity, the fission of the nation into two or more organisms became the rule. Thereafter, only an outside empire penetrating Egypt was able to enforce some temporary unity.

The tragedy of ancient Egypt was that she had worked out a satisfactory national expression in her earlier days of insulated security. Religion provided a tough cell wall, within which the protoplasm had remarkably free movement. But the cell wall of religion was so tough that the whole organism could not change easily. When the organism was free-floating, without major contact, it was vigorous and healthy. When the change from insulated security to perilous involvement in a larger world occurred, when the organism came into opposition with other organisms, all that happened was that the cell wall hardened and the inner protoplasm ceased to have free play. Then the Egyptian system became introverted and tried to encyst itself in ritualism and otherworldliness. Drawn to the protecting shelter of religious form, it succeeded in ignoring the new world of the Greeks for a few centuries. Even when Alexander the Great forced that world upon it by conquest, the change was superficial, confined to Alexandria and those intellectual elite who lived inland. Only a sharp knife could pierce the Egyptian shell, and that sharp knife was the brutal Roman taxation which finally killed the ancient Egyptian system. There had already been a trend toward pietism and otherworldliness, so that, with pagan Egypt dead, the Christian message was highly acceptable and the Egyptian expression became formally different.

GÜTERBOCK: Thank you, Professor Wilson. The pattern which worked so well yesterday will be repeated again at this session. I shall call on four or five of those who, I know, will want to comment. Afterward there will be general discussion.

PARKER: Twenty-five years ago I took my first steps in Egyptology under the guidance of John Wilson. I have learned a great deal from him in the years that have passed; I have learned from him today; I expect to learn a good deal more in the future. I count it a genuine privilege to follow him in this symposium.

The difference between Egypt and Mesopotamia has been very lucidly portrayed for us. Previously it has occupied the attention of other speakers. Perhaps some of the difference is to be accounted for by geography, and I want to elaborate on a hint to this end which was given by Dr. Wilson.

I would concur with Dr. Albright's observation that we must begin, not as we have done here with the village-farming community and the introduction of agriculture, but some two hundred thousand years before that time. Man was growing all through that tremendously long interval, and he must have been developing gradually some of the distinctive traits and ways of facing life that he exhibited in later, literate times.

Having raised the subject of beginnings, I should also like to call attention to an article recently published by A. J. Arkell in which he takes my friend Professor Braidwood somewhat to task for combining two distinct processes into a single constellation of events and period.[18] Do the domestication of plants and the domestication of animals have to be bracketed together? Arkell says "no." He suggests that plants are domesticated where plants are native, and if plants such as wheat and barley are native in Asia then that must be the center for their domestication. But animals can be domesticated anywhere. Arkell gives a number of examples from his own field work, where very timid animals attached themselves to his expedition through the pressure of hunger and stayed as long as they were fed. Through the course of history animals must have sold themselves into dependence on man over and over again through hunger. Arkell suggests that the goat was perhaps the earliest domesticated animal simply because it was the bravest animal and was willing to go to extremes to satisfy its hunger.

My basic thesis, although clearly overstated for purposes of presentation here, is that Egypt was the eventual outcome of a people who in earlier times depended primarily upon animals, while Mesopotamian civilization was the eventual product of people who in earlier times depended upon plants. Obviously, when we get down to historic times, there is little or no real difference; both Egypt and Mesopotamia had animal husbandry and plant husbandry together. But I suggest that their distinctive attitudes, ways of looking at the earth and life and the forces that are invisible to man, developed through the many millenniums when one or the other source of subsistence prevailed.

One of the earliest settled communities of which we have any record is Khartum, near the Egyptian end of the Fertile Crescent, which Arkell would date to somewhere around 7000 B.C. He regards it as a settlement for the convenience of fishermen and hunters and absolutely without agriculture. Thus it appears that a village settlement does not necessarily involve domestication of plants, and this is the pattern that I believe was followed in Egypt. Hunting would, of course, have been the first stage. But, with the beginning of post-

[18] "Khartoum's part in the development of the Neolithic," *Kush* V (1957) 8–12.

Pleistocene desiccation throughout northern Africa there must have been pressure upon the animal population to group together in those areas where food continued to be available. It seems to me that we might visualize the Nile Valley itself as a sort of game preserve, where animals driven from the former Sahara steppeland could easily be hunted. Primitive man would have been induced to camp around its margins, in time domesticating its fauna and settling down himself.

Professor Wilson has already discussed the alleged stimulus of Egypt by Mesopotamia just before the dynastic period; I should think it very likely that there was interchange between these two areas much earlier. Can it be that the idea of domestication of plants came to Egypt from Asia and, vice versa, that the idea of domestication of animals came to Asia from Egypt? It is just this sort of cross-fertilization that might have set a progressive trend toward civilization into motion in both areas. Perhaps survivals of an early nomadic pastoral existence might be recognizable in historic Egypt. I have not attempted to ferret out evidence, since this is still a relatively new idea to me and one on which I would welcome criticism. But a few things do occur to me, which I shall mention briefly.

Dating in early Egypt, for example, was based on a formula: "the year of such and such an occurrence of the numbering of all large and small cattle in the north and south." One entry on the Palermo stone for a year of King Snefru says: "He hacked up the land of the Negro and he brought back seven thousand prisoners and two hundred thousand large and small cattle." Cattle seems to have been the primary booty in that area of the world. The donations to the gods of the temples as listed on the Palermo stone consisted for the most part of large parcels of land in the Delta, and I suggest that the Delta was the pasture-land of Egypt. A narration on the war of King Kamose against the Hyksos states that he determined to wage war upon the Asiatics, whereupon his councilors replied: "Why should we? We are all quiet where we are; our oxen are in the Delta." Thus it appears that even when Egypt was under foreign domination pasturage rights were accorded to southerners in the Delta. Again, one of the earliest feasts in Egypt was the "Running of the Apis." We know the animals that were so significantly honored: the bull of Montu, the ram of Amon, the Kamutef, the Hathor cow. And I suspect there are many other instances of this sort of thing which I cannot recall. On the other hand, Osiris as a god of vegetation came in late in the Old Kingdom; he was not one of the earliest deities. The pharaoh himself was frequently depicted, very fittingly, as a herdsman, as the shepherd of his people. "To rule" in Egypt was written with the sign of a shepherd's crook. And men were conceptualized as the cattle of the gods.

I can say very little about Mesopotamia, but I should like to hear from my colleagues as to whether there is any indication that in the very earliest times there was more dependence upon plants than upon animal husbandry. One small bit of evidence came to my attention last night: the myth of the "Wooing of Inanna." This is a "disputation" text, of the type described yesterday by Professor Kramer, in which two people argue with each other as to the value of their respective professions. The divine farmer Enkidu and the divine shepherd Dumuzi are competing for the hand of Inanna, and in the end of course they are shown to be equally desirable. But Inanna chooses the farmer. I think that in Egypt the shepherd might have gotten her.

Finally, I want to make a quite unrelated point that possibly has some small bearing on a different aspect of the contrast between Egypt and Mesopotamia. This thought came to me as I was reading a recent article by Jaroslav Černy[19] on the terms for family relationships in Egypt, of which there were surprisingly few. There were words for "husband," "wife," "father," "mother," "son," "daughter," "brother," "sister," and nothing else. All other terms had to be built up: "uncle" would be the "brother of my father," for instance, since there was no simple word for "uncle." Černy points out that this system of nomenclature is in strict contrast to the Indo-European system, where there is a tremendous vocabulary, even including separate words for "husband's brother's wife" and other such relationships. The Indo-European vocabulary is based on the idea that when a woman marries she leaves her own family and enters into her husband's family, so that the latter remains intact through a male line. In ancient Egypt, on the other hand, when a man marries he leaves his own family and *grg pr,* "founds a house," for himself. Does this have anything to do with the absence of a tendency to cohere, to build up into larger units and so perhaps into cities?

OPPENHEIM: I would like first to say that, as always, I was impressed very much by Professor Wilson's introduction. Whenever I

[19] "A note on the ancient Egyptian family," *Studi in onore di Aristide Calderini e Roberto Paribeni* II (Milano, 1957) 51–55.

hear him talk on Egypt I am conscious that his views change, that he continually seeks a new synthesis, that he grapples openly with his problem. I feel here a kindred soul, because very frequently I catch myself presenting Mesopotamia in different lights. This, I think, is what we should try to do: to assimilate what we have learned and then to change and enlarge our pictures. Nothing is more dangerous than to remain in a pattern.

It is, of course, very difficult to make comparisons. While the task is necessary, I doubt that very much can be achieved by comparison for comparison's sake. Differences are always, in my eyes, more revealing than similarities; the latter tend to be superficial. Moreover, there are tremendous differences in the nature and amount of the philological source material from Egypt and Mesopotamia. Hence it is the underlying differences that I should like to stress.

Professor Wilson touched on differences in irrigation and topography, and he also referred to the fact that in Egypt fertilizing mud remains on the fields. There is an additional feature of this kind which I should like to bring out: the difference in timing with regard to the agricultural cycle, especially for cereals. Egypt is an ideal country for growing cereals, but Mesopotamia has difficulty in getting water at the right time and place.

Then there is a basic difference in the concept of royalty. As far as I have been able to ascertain, the concept of royalty remained static in Egypt. In Mesopotamia it did not. I venture to say that the concept of the role of the king in the Sumerian period, in the period before the First Dynasty of Babylon, in Assyria, and again in the Neo-Babylonian period varied considerably. Thus it is difficult to compare the concept in the two lands.

And then, as always, we must turn to consider the city. When the Assyrians came to Egypt, they spoke of hundreds of cities—for them the Egyptian towns were cities—and I remain unconvinced as to the extent to which Egypt was a "civilization without cities." Even if there were no metropolitan centers, there may have been specialized urban settlements: the capital with its royal court and retainers, garrison centers, and the like.

There is one important difference, to my mind, between the Egyptian world view and the Mesopotamian, that is, the attitude toward the outside world. In Mesopotamia outside influences and relations with surrounding countries were not looked down upon; in Egypt they were. A very revealing document for this point concerns Sargon's conquest of what is today Armenia. He speaks with admiration of the technical achievements and intelligence of his enemies. And when the Assyrians came to Egypt they found everything wonderful and they took as booty what was better than they could produce at home. A further reflection of this cosmopolitan attitude is seen in the fact that everybody who lived in cities was considered civilized by the Mesopotamians; only those who did not bury their dead or who disregarded any authority or had certain eating habits, like the Bedouins, were really despised.

Another difference, already pointed out by Dr. Wilson, is the stress that in Egypt was put on life after death. It was a clear expression of inner security, to borrow Dr. Wilson's very happy formulation. In Mesopotamia the concept assumed a very different form: a belief in the continuous presence of the gods and their continuous care for the individual which was expressed by omens. Everything that happened within the human ken reflected divine intervention. There was somebody who cared, there was somebody who urged "Do this, it is good." And this attitude enveloped the individual's entire life from birth to death.

The early influence of Mesopotamia on Egypt has been mentioned, as deduced from cylinder seals, writing, and monumental architecture. There was also a much later influence, around the beginning of the first millennium B.C. It is reflected in the onomastica that Dr. Wilson mentioned yesterday, in certain types of Coptic omen texts which must go back to Mesopotamian prototypes, and especially in astronomy. In connection with the sciences, I would like to return to something that was touched on yesterday in relation to mathematics. Egyptian mathematics was much more primitive than that of Mesopotamia, but, on the other hand, Egyptian medicine was far more refined and "modern" than that of Babylonia; the latter, in fact, was very primitive and crude.

ADAMS: Having learned what very little I know of Egypt from Professor Wilson himself, I do not have the temerity to comment directly on what he said. Rather, I regard the opportunity to participate in this discussion as a poacher might, as a chance to come in and scatter a few shots in the form of rhetorical questions and then, hopefully, get away unscathed.

My first question has to do with the reality, even at the height of the Old Kingdom, behind the picture which we have been given of stately and statelike political control. Superficially, there seems no doubt of its all-pervasiveness, and yet, perhaps simply because the contrast is so great with what went before, I am moved to ask whether the superficial uniformity of inscriptions (which, of course, were designed to maintain the existence of the state) is really sufficient evidence that the myth closely approximated the fact. I have in mind such apparent lapses, lapses at least to the eye of an outsider looking at the Egyptian material, as tomb-robberies, the robbery of Hetep-heres' grave for instance. This kind of activity at a time when political conditions ought to have been as firmly under control as at any time in the Old Kingdom somehow leads an outsider to wonder whether there was not a marked discrepancy between the accounts of the strength of the state and its actual capabilities. Perhaps this doubt is made somewhat more reasonable by the known mendacity of some of the historical inscriptions; this at least makes it seem not unreasonable that the writers of inscriptions were not overly concerned with reporting what we would regard as "objective" reality. In seeking further information on a question like this, I suggest that probably it is less useful to look at the scale of a few monumental works such as the pyramids than to look at the level of continuing organization maintained by the state throughout the year. To the degree that monumental works could have been constructed by masses of *corvée* labor during fairly brief periods of the year, they may be a somewhat exaggerated source of information on what the Egyptian government really was.

To phrase this point somewhat differently, I am seeking to find chinks in the panoply of the Old Kingdom as it has been described today in order to see some kind of cumulative advance in later Egyptian history, just as I would like to find it for Mesopotamia. Reference has been made to a breakdown in security and the growth of imperial pretensions. How were these trends paralleled internally? Is there evidence for a significant increase in the size and complexity of the bureaucracy, or royal court, or craft organization at the same time?

Related to this question, perhaps, is a question as to what the real benefits or effects of the centralization of pharaonic power were upon Egypt at large. Some years ago, very superficially, I looked into the accounts of excavations in some of the provincial cemeteries and came away with the rather subjective impression that the quality of the *Beigaben* in the provincial cemeteries improved markedly during times of decentralization. If this is more than a subjective impression, the traditional glories of the Old, Middle, and New Kingdoms have to be tempered in our thinking by the recognition that they depended on the siphoning-off of wealth which was otherwise available throughout the country into a royal court and capital. Admittedly, it was only when concentrated in a capital that this wealth could produce works whose remains we still admire today, but perhaps these are not simply to be equated with the general prosperity of the country.

Finally, and this is not even a rhetorical question but simply a question, what puzzles me most when I read and hear of Old Kingdom Egypt is the backgound for the precocious and relatively sudden appearance of a unified state. In what Professor Wilson has told us, and in what I gather of the available material, there is no hint of an underlying economic unit, such as the private manor or temple in Mesopotamia, where the bureaucracies might have been trained, where the administrative practices might have been developed, which subsequently were used by the new state to conduct its business. Is there something in what is known of the character of Egyptian villages, made up of simple nuclear families as has been described, which had this economic-organizing aspect and which thus might have provided the background and training for the subsequent expansion of a bureaucracy?

EDGERTON: I have been listening with very lively interest to all the presentations at this symposium, and that is especially true of what has been said this morning, which falls within my own field of labor. I particularly admired Professor Wilson's extremely lucid and well-considered introduction, and that applies also only in lesser degree to the comments of my three predecessors on what he said. I should add that any seeming disagreement between me and them this morning should probably be regarded merely as a difference of emphasis; I scarcely disagree at all with any firm statement that has been offered this morning. Of course much of what was said was frankly speculation. That is a different matter; we speculate in different ways.

I think one fact which it is especially important for Egyptologists to make clear to non-Egyptologists is that we really know very little about pharaonic Egypt, owing to the extreme scarcity and the chance character of the evidence that has come down to us. As you all know, the Egyptians unfortunately did not write on clay; they wrote on paper. And paper can be burned, paper can rot when it gets damp,

paper can be eaten by termites, and so forth. Our friends in Mesopotamia are embarrassed by an opposite difficulty; they have scores
of thousands of tablets which they do not have time to read. Almost
everything that we know about pharaonic Egypt has come out of
either the temple or the cemetery. Practically nothing has come out
of the city except in so far as the temple may be associated with the
city, and the temple is quite likely to be remote from the city.

There is a nice illustration of the difficulties which we face with
inadequate evidence. Up to about twenty-five years ago, I suppose
everybody believed that the Twentieth Dynasty, the Ramessid dynasty, was brought to an end by the growing power of the high
priests of Amon of Karnak, which finally reached such a point that
the high-priesthood became supreme and was able to displace the
weak pharaoh Ramses XI. About twenty-five years ago Hermann
Kees, in Göttingen, published a short and very interesting paper in
which, for me and as far as I know for all my friends, he simply
reversed that view. Herihor, the high priest of Amon who superseded
Ramses XI, was fundamentally not a priest at all. He was an army
officer who had been viceroy of Nubia, and from his position in
Nubia he was able to lead his military forces into Egypt and, it is
true, overthrow the pharaoh. But in this process he first overthrew
the high priest of Amon. Herihor's rise to the throne was in no sense
a triumph for the priesthood, but quite the contrary.

I believe this new account, but I have tried to examine the evidence on which it rests, and, to be quite frank, I cannot regard it as
by any means certain. I think it is possible that we may have a whole
series of reversals on this one very specific phenomenon. And unfortunately this is not unusual in our study of pharaonic Egypt. We
try, of course, to present as clear and as broad a picture as we can.
But, while certainly some things can be said with confidence, much
of what we say must, I fear, be taken with a good deal of salt. The
"thick darkness" which John Wilson mentioned is certainly a reality.

Mesopotamian influence just at or just before the beginning of
the dynastic period in Egypt I regard as fact, and I suppose everybody does. It would not occur to me to say that the Gerzean period
had settled into a kind of stagnation, but it seems to me as firmly
established as any fact in early Egyptian history that important influence of many kinds reached Egypt from Mesopotamia just before
the beginning of the First Dynasty.

The question of a written code of laws is a nice illustration of how much we do not know. We do not possess a written code of laws nor even any fragment of a written code of laws from Egypt antedating Alexander. But that lack is a far cry, I think, from saying that the Egyptians did not have a written code of laws before Alexander. Personally, I think they did; I admit that it cannot be proved, and there we are. I do not think it would be useful for me to discuss this point any further.

Similarly, it has already been brought out that when Professor Wilson speaks of "civilization without cities" he means civilization without cities that are known to us. I think the reason why the cities are not known to us has been made sufficiently clear this morning. I cannot take quite the same attitude as Professor Wilson does particularly toward the question of cities in the Delta. It seems to me that there are strong reasons for believing that there were important cities in the Delta at a much earlier period than John apparently believes. This again is speculation, if you like, based on very slight evidence.

Again, the interpretation of the relation of irrigation to the state of life in general in Egypt is a matter on which our views are necessarily tentative and changing. The basic factors involved I think need further elucidation by experts in irrigation engineering before we can feel sure again, as we did some decades ago, about the real significance of the phenomena of irrigation in Egypt.

John Wilson and Leo Oppenheim have referred to the steps which the Egyptian took to secure a blessed hereafter as reflecting a sense of security. I do not feel quite that way about it. The Egyptian, I think we will all agree, loved life, and he was determined to carry on a life after death as nearly as possible identical with the life he had lived or would have liked to have lived on earth. I do not see his efforts to achieve that good end as expressions of security; I see them rather as expressions of desperation. The Egyptian I think must have realized, as we all do, that people do in fact die, and I think he was throughout his known history desperately trying to overcome this obvious and inevitable fact. Even the Great Pyramid, that immense concentration of the resources of the state on a tomb for a single individual, the king, seems to me to reflect not so much the king's confidence that he could achieve a desirable hereafter as a desperate determination to achieve it in the face of the fact of certain death. The long history, the very complex history, of the elaborate devices that Egyptians kept using and kept changing with the passing centuries to achieve a good life after death seems to me throughout a history of successively defeated attempts to achieve a blessed hereafter. Certainly by the Twelfth Dynasty it was notorious that many tombs of earlier pharaohs had been robbed, as well as a much larger percentage of tombs of ordinary people. To cut the matter short, the Egyptian eventually was led to give up almost all purely physical means of getting a blessed hereafter in favor of very inexpensive and essentially magical methods, because gradually the Egyptian learned that the physical methods were not effective.

As to Bob Adams' question about the reality behind the appearance of a powerful centralized state in the Old Kingdom, it seems to me that the robbery of the tomb of Hetepheres illustrates the kind of thing which can happen anywhere in the best policed locality. It would not be too difficult to give examples from any modern country of fantastic robberies that are carried off, as it were, under the noses of highly organized police forces. I do not think that the robbery of the tomb of the king's mother can have been a common phenomenon in the Fourth or the Fifth Dynasty, or scarcely even in the Sixth Dynasty. I would cite the tomb of Tutankhamon, which also was broken into almost immediately after the burial, as a close parallel. As in the case of the tomb of Hetepheres, when the robbery was discovered in the tomb of Tutankhamon some of the things that had been taken out were loosely thrown back in and the tomb was sealed again. Tutankhamon's tomb was finally preserved to us substantially intact because one of the Ramessid tombs—I think it was the tomb of Ramses VI—was dug directly above it, so that it was concealed beneath an immense pile of limestone chips. The entrance to Tutankhamon's tomb was forgotten, and within a relatively short time, between two and three centuries after Tutankhamon's death, all the rest of the cemetery in the Valley of the Kings was thoroughly plundered.

GIBB: I should like to shift the axis of this discussion a little, taking up certain points about towns which underlie our discussions in this and previous sessions. While on some questions that have come up I have been unwilling to intervene by introducing Islamic parallels, there are one or two cases, I think, where Islamic history and tradition are relevant. Although historically speaking Islamic cities are late, nevertheless the earliest Islamic cities were, in the majority, new foundations, except for Damascus and some Persian examples. Hence we are fortunate in being able to distinguish quite clearly what went into their foundation and how they were articulated, even though we cannot answer all the questions which arise in this connection. The early Islamic cities are of two kinds, which I shall distinguish as, first, "organic" and, second, "arbitrary." The latter term refers to the foundation of royal capitals without regard to economic or ecological relationships. The organic cities were originally settled in the main by Arab tribesmen who were themselves organized in kin groups. The settlements so made naturally attracted old social economic organizations within the region, and this set a problem of integration.

Seemingly to diverge for a moment, Islam arose within a society which was structured upon and intensely conscious of kinship ties. But Islam as a religion, and Muḥammad as its founder, by recognizing the individual outside his clan ties, by attributing personal responsibility to the individual as distinct from the clan, introduced a disturbing and potentially disastrous element into the pre-existing kinship structure. In the new Arab cities the Arab social tradition fought a relentless battle against these disintegrating or disturbing factors; consequently it was within the general structure of the kin group that the problem of integration was faced. Professor Von Grunebaum in his background paper refers to the *walāʾ* organization (p. 443), the means by which the conquered were first related to an Arab tribe by clientship, and, as I see it, this clientship organization was not merely a social device but was also in part economic. Here I must confess that I am a little beyond the evidence, having been made more conscious than ever during these discussions that Islamic history is terribly backward in comparison with ancient Near Eastern history. While there is a large body of data, they are not yet adequately mobilized; hence a great many of our constructions still remain somewhat arbitrary. In short, I am a little shy about being definite on the matter of the *walāʾ* organization, but it does seem fairly clear that its purpose was not solely to attach non-Arabs to Arab clan organizations. In addition, it served to attach specific economic occupations, which, from one point of view, were exploited by the clan or, according to another point of view, were integrated into the clan. One must remember that these economic occupations were practiced not by Arabs but by the Christian and Jewish inhabitants of the area. While those who remained Christians and Jews continued to be organized in their own religious organizations, those who became Muslims had, as a consequence of the predominance of the Arab clan idea, to become members of an Arab clan. Professor Louis Massignon,[20] in a brief study of the city of Basrah, for example, has shown that the weavers in the adjoining areas were adopted by the clan of Tamim as a whole. The integration of the urban industries into the Islamic community through the clans therefore falls into a kind of pattern. We know, of course, that the *walā'* system broke down not only with the increasing numbers of the clan members but also with the gradual conversion of the old Arab troops into citizens and the suppression of their old pension privileges, but it is as yet premature to attempt any kind of precise description of the mechanisms by which the city populations were ultimately leveled out into economically and socially diversified groups. We do know the end result, which appears to have been still within a framework of kinship structures. However, those kinship structures must have been remolded considerably during the two or three centuries of turbulent settling-down following the Arab conquest, because at the end we find an emergence of guildlike artisan organizations articulated quite clearly in the manner of the clan group. And these functional groups, in course of time, actually became organic or genuine kin groups through intermarriage. It is remarkable that even the later Muslim slave armies were articulated in the same manner, in artificial, if you like, kin groups from the period of their cadet training. I was reminded very forcibly of this articulation by the description which was given in the previous session by Professor Landsberger of the *edubba,* in which the head is the father and the elder cadets, if I may use that term, are elder brothers; this strikingly resembles, even in detail, the actual structure of a military cadet group in the later Islamic empires. So much for the organic city, structured more and more upon kinship groups.

As to the royal city, the city arbitrarily organized and laid out by the rulers, we are fortunate not only in having the actual archeological remains of such a city at Samarra but also in having fairly extensive descriptions as to how that city was constructed. We know exactly how it was planned by the caliph and his officers, with respect both to their own quarters and to the subventions which were made to military and administrative officers for the building of their own sections of the city. We know how the new canals were constructed to supply the necessary water, what ideas dictated the gen-

20 "Explication du plan de Basra," *Rudolph Tschudi zum 70th Geburstag üburreicht* (Wiesbaden, 1954) p. 160.

eral layout, and, furthermore, how the artisans and cultivators who were necessary for the economic maintenance of the city were simply swept into it from raids on the resources of other cities and areas. Certain groups of artisans were brought en masse from Syria, for example, so that an entirely different kind of town structure must have resulted. And then, of course, the counterpart of the rapid artificial construction of a royal city was that, in an incredibly short space of time, the whole agglomeration was deserted. The capital could be suddenly moved without the slightest notice, and the elaborate structure simply fell to pieces. What happened to the unfortunate artisan and agricultural populations is not recorded. The artisans presumably moved to the new capital or back into their old cities; the agricultural population presumably continued to cultivate the land so long as the canals remained operative. We have in the Islamic material, therefore, something like a technical description of the way in which these two types of cities were articulated.

GÜTERBOCK: Mr. Wilson may want to respond to some of these observations and theories.

WILSON: Mr. Chairman, because of the time I will take a cowardly way out. I have noted so many points requiring comment that if I take them all up no one will have any more time this morning. In the interest of opening the session for general discussion, I will limit myself to three comments.

First, I agree with Professor Edgerton that our evidence is extraordinarily spotty. I plead guilty to having taken little pieces here and there and built them into a concept rather like a structure above ground without any foundations underneath. But it is obvious that if we try to summarize so much in twenty or thirty minutes, any such construction is going to be false in ways which we cannot guess.

Then I want to comment to Professor Parker on an element of irony in this situation. He and I, both being humanists, have resorted to two different kinds of determinism; I think I had a kind of geographic determinism in mind and he a kind of economic determinism, and certainly neither of us believes in this approach as having any full and ultimate validity. We believe that there must be unseen things which are very difficult to state and can only be guessed at.

My third comment is that in all our discussions we are involved in difficult problems of semantics. The word "security" was handled by Professor Oppenheim and also by Professor Edgerton in ways which were different from the way I had used it. Professor Oppenheim spoke of the omens as reflecting a kind of security by conveying warnings, and Professor Edgerton referred to the emphasis on afterlife as being a kind of desperation. I would like to change his wording a little here: "desperation to try to secure the goods of this life." I think we are all in a kind of general agreement, but, having different approaches, we feel important semantic differences. This applies to my grossly exaggerated thesis "civilization without cities." Of course I do not believe it. When this symposium was first framed as a discussion of the processes of urbanization I had to say "we can't do it for Egypt the way you people can do it for Mesopotamia," and to emphasize this I said "there is no city in Egypt until Alexandria." Later I tried to build up a substitute analogy for the image of the city as a nerve center, using the idea of a shifting, dividing cell nucleus. It is clearly not a matter of the presence or absence of a phenomenon but perhaps only a matter of degree.

I apologize to Dr. Adams; if time permits at the very end of this session I will return to his questions. But I think we really should give others an opportunity to talk now.

BRAIDWOOD: What Professor Parker invites us to think about is a precondition rather than a condition for civilized life. And this was properly a concern of the second session. In order not to divert this discussion after Professor Wilson's fine introduction, I suggest that Professor Parker, Professor Reed, and I go into his point in private session.

However, let me just make two short points. First, I am impressed with the potentialities for thought in what Professor Parker suggests, even though I am sure he consciously overstated it in setting up a dichotomy between "Asia, cereals" and "Africa, animals." Second, although I of all people should walk gently on the broken-glass floor of radiocarbon dating, it is increasingly impressive that the dates are bulking up to indicate a late start for food-production in Egypt. For the earliest village complex that we know in Egypt, in Fayyum A, there are dates, two only, which cluster around 4200 B.C. An equivalent catalogue in the hilly-flanks zone of western Asia clusters around 5700 B.C. But this does not detract from the interest of what Professor Parker invites us to think about, which is that a great variety of alternatives are possible in a subsistence pattern.

ALBRIGHT: My respect for Professor Wilson as an Egyptologist is equaled only by my admiration for him as a true gentleman; hence

I can cheerfully insist that nearly all his evidence is of negative type. I should like to remind this conference that we knew nothing about law from law codes in Babylonia and Assyria until just fifty-seven years ago this month, when the code of Hammurabi was discovered. Moreover, I suggest that we not only have all kinds of decrees of great length from both the Old and the New Kingdom in Egypt, but we also have a specific reference to codes of laws in the New Kingdom. There is also the so-called "demotic" law code, not yet published, which was copied down into Roman times from much earlier sources.

With regard to divine kingship, the Egyptian god-king is simply a specialized case of a universal human phenomenon found in Babylonia, among the Hittites, among the Hellenistic Greeks and Romans, among the Chinese, the Japanese, the Incas, and so on. As to the statement crediting the formation of the first bureaucracy to Djoser of the Third Dynasty, I would like to ask Dr. Wilson about the great number of titles found in sealings of the First Dynasty, which certainly presuppose an elaborate officialdom of some kind. I would also like to emphasize what Professor Oppenheim said about the Assyrian and Greek evidence for tremendous cities, Thebes and Memphis, in the early first millennium B.C. The fact that all these cities or virtually all of them now are buried almost completely under the alluvium, except for a few temples and fewer palaces, does not deny their original existence. As Professor Edgerton said, how little we really know about what actually went on in Egypt is stupendous.

Similarly, in my opinion, the arguments against early empires are based solely on negative evidence, every bit of which can be explained; I think that there was indeed an empire of sorts in the Old Kingdom and again in the Middle Kingdom as well as in the New Kingdom. Nubia had to be occupied if the Egyptians were to guard their precious caravan routes to central Africa; in order to protect the sources of gold and ivory and other treasures, they had to establish settlements in Nubia, quite aside from a possible desire for domination. In the same way they had to protect the caravan routes and the seaports in Asia, and in my opinion execration texts furnish a surprisingly continuous and well-attested series of testimonies for Egyptian control of a loose empire of sorts which extended as far as northern Phoenicia and southern Syria.

THRUPP: While listening to this symposium, I have been speculating on what would become of the knowledge of western medieval society, my own field, if overnight our material were to shrink to the character and dimensions of that of the ancient Near East. But I think my feelings of dismay are partly due to the fact that most medieval archeologists are relative amateurs compared to their colleagues in your field, and what you might call our philologists are able to concentrate largely on individual writers. At any rate, if this catastrophe were to occur and we were to draw up a program of future study, it would certainly not be as sociological or anthropological as Dr. Wilson's brand of humanism. One thing that struck me was that the only individual who has wandered into these discussions so far is Abraham, and he was encouraged to wander out again very quickly.

A few questions come to mind that are directed toward a pulling-together and comparison of the different societies under consideration. I take it for granted that the real objective of comparison is to see at what points differences arise and how deep-seated certain differences really are. I take it for granted also that it is not very useful to compare isolated things like soil, but that instead we must examine the kind of use made of this within a certain social organization in order to arrive at a fruitful unit of comparison. For one thing, a description of wadi-terracing interested me as indicating a kind of symbiotic relation between the nomadic economy and at least a certain kind of agricultural economy. In my ignorance of the historical context, I am unaware whether this kind of adaptation occurred fairly widely and whether such symbiotic relations applied only to marginal areas or were spread through trade or other means into the heartlands of alluvial cultivation.

A question which interests me particularly in my own medieval research is the relation between tax collectors and other bureaucrats, on the one hand, and the local social structure, on the other. Is it possible to get any evidence as to the nature of the resistance to paying taxes? This is an economic subject, but resistance to paying taxes and resistance to bureaucrats seem to me perhaps equally to concern the human spirit, at least for twentieth-century man.

RHEINSTEIN: The question of law in Egypt has been brought up repeatedly, and it has been stated repeatedly that the fact that we have not yet found any codes of law such as have been discovered in Mesopotamia is not conclusive evidence that there were no laws in Egypt or that there was no law in Egypt.

What do we mean when we speak of law and when we speak of laws in the plural? In a comparative view we might say that law is the combination of a government plus fixed rules according to which this government will deal with its subjects. Wide variation in these respects clearly is possible. There are societies which have neither government nor rules. We know of societies with intermittent government, and it was most interesting to hear from Professor Jacobsen that this was exactly the type of society associated with the so-called primitive democracy of Mesopotamia. It was a society which functioned on the basis of kinship relations, traditions, customs, habits, and religious ideas, but governmental officers were established only in times of emergency such as war. When the emergency was over the government disappeared; obviously, with the government the law disappeared, if indeed that government had had any law to go by at all.

Apparently in Egypt we do not know of any period of no government or of intermittent government, such as we can establish from the Mesopotamian texts. It seems that at the first entry of Egypt into history there was full-blown, full-fledged government. But what do we know, if anything, about the curbing of this government by any rules according to which it was supposed to proceed? It is possible that it was a completely arbitrary government, but it is much more probable, for as orderly a country as Egypt seems to have been at the very beginning, that there were rules. Again, however, how were the rules enforced and what was their nature? If we look over various other types of societies we find that certain rules were enforced by self-help, that the individual had to go out and enforce a judgment as best he could, perhaps after adjudication by a government officer. This system prevailed in Rome in surprisingly late times. Do we know anything about such a situation in Egypt? Was there adjudication? If so, was there any enforcement of the judgments?

Another situation, for which we find illustrations in China, I think, and more particularly in England, as far down as the early nineteenth century, involves administration of justice in the sense that there was a strict prohibition of self-help and a governmental enforcement of the judgments for the great of the realm, the great men. For the masses there was also a strict prohibition of self-help, but there was hardly an adjudication according to fixed rules; instead, there was a paternalistic taking-care of the affairs of the masses by justices of the peace who merely followed rough, general precepts. From what we know about Egypt it seems to me not impossible that such a situation may have prevailed there. A court, perhaps the pharaoh himself, might have seen to it that disputes among the great of the realm were decided in an orderly way according to rules, but the masses might have been handled in a different, more paternalistic fashion.

Now a brief word on the Mesopotamian codes. They are mysterious, for a code of great laws is not a necessary ingredient of a legal order. There may be a well-running legal order without fixed laws, for instance a law precedence, and even a system of laws—but customary laws which are not written down. Thus the mere fact that written laws in the sense of these codes are absent in other civilizations does not say much about the character of the administration of justice. But what were these Mesopotamian law codes? In oral conversation after the previous session, the opinion was voiced that they may have been internal administrative directives for the royal domain, somewhat in the nature of the capitularies of the Frankish kings. But the Mesopotamian codes contain provisions which go far beyond what would seem necessary for the management of a domain in that they contain numerous rules on what we call the law of torts: if A hurts B in such and such a way then such and such reparation has to be made. It would be strange if rules of this sort were limited to the members of the royal household and the royal manors and did not apply to the people at large. And why were these laws written down? Does this indicate that there was a need of reform? That is possible. Or does it indicate, as might also be possible, that there was a period of weakening of the general legal consciousness, that customs, habits, and traditions which had been strongly felt were decaying and therefore it seemed necessary to write down what had been regarded as self-evident?

Finally, I would like to suggest that we might perhaps try to use the legal aspect as a kind of chronology of a civilization. It is much less reliable, of course, than dating based on radioactive carbon, but if we know to what extent in a society self-help, private feuds, and so on were not permissible, we know a great deal about the general state of that society. Do we find in Mesopotamia or in Egypt any evidence for the direct prohibition of self-help? Certainly one of the most impressive phenomena of Mesopotamian history is that at a very early time we find a record of a murder trial carried on by a governmental authority. It seems that generally in society murder is one of the events which are among the latest to be taken care of by government; it is left to revenge rather than to adjudication. What other evidence of that kind do we have in either Mesopotamia or Egypt?

KANTOR: So much has been said about lack of evidence that I would like to note that we can fill in a few details. Professor Wilson began by speaking of the recalcitrance of Egypt in its lack of material. Some of our problems are caused by the archeologists' unfortunate dislike of dealing with less spectacular types of evidence. However, pertinent archeological material does exist. I would like to mention some of it briefly.

First, we may consider all that is pertinent to the crystallization of the Egyptian civilization and state at the beginning of the First Dynasty. Our evidence for pots and pans and the like, the ordinary material of daily life, is fairly extensive. On the basis of that material we can see that in prehistoric Egypt there were two cultural areas: a relatively well-known one in Upper Egypt and a less-known but clearly distinct one in Lower Egypt. And it is, as has already been mentioned, the Upper Egyptian culture that expands and provides the basis for the material culture of the First Dynasty.

I might mention in passing that it is exceedingly difficult for me to visualize the Gerzean period as one of stagnation. It seems to me that we have evidence for a very well-established complex culture and at intervals can find, in hiding almost beneath the level of everyday objects, hints that there is a background in prehistoric Egypt for the First Dynasty. For instance, a sherd of an ordinary prehistoric pottery ware has on it in relief one of the two characteristic crowns of later Egypt. An ordinary type of predynastic object, a slate palette with no trace of foreign influence, bears reliefs showing a hunt carried on by men who are representatives of political or geographical units, for they hold certain standards which we know in historical Egypt; on the same palette a little shrine is rendered in a form which later appears as a hieroglyph and which obviously is a representation of a prehistoric shrine such as existed in Egypt but was too flimsy for traces to have survived. A prehistoric wall painting of Gerzean style shows a remarkable group consisting of a man smiting three smaller-scale bound figures kneeling in front of him. This is exactly the theme that is used throughout pharaonic Egypt to symbolize the might of the king. My point, then, is that we must not be misled by any incompleteness in our material to forget that there is, under a surface which is sometimes hard for us to penetrate, evidence for the growth in the Gerzean period of various features typical of historical Egyptian civilization and even of some social or political stratification. Such evidence does much to make the appearance of the Egyptian state in the First Dynasty less sudden and mysterious.

Second, I would like to raise a question concerning possible concentrations of population at various periods in ancient Egypt. I would like to ask Professor Wilson about two sites. We know from religious written sources that Hierakonpolis was an important prehistoric center, both political and religious. This site has been tested in various spots, but there has never been any real exploration of about a kilometer's length of desert fringe which has been greatly wind-eroded so that it is heaped high with potsherds. According to Brunton it is not a cemetery area. Apparently it was a prehistoric township. If this indication of the existence of a relatively large settled area at the site itself is combined with the later written evidence can any conclusions as to Egyptian towns or cities be drawn? The other site which I have in mind is Thebes. We do have in this area from Middle Kingdom times on great temple complexes whose location on the east bank of the Nile implies that they existed in the midst of settlements. Furthermore, in New Kingdom tombs are represented houses of several stories, which seem appropriate for crowded cities. Could we not perhaps rescue some proofs for the existence of cities in ancient Egypt from such evidence as that from Hierakonpolis and Thebes?

SINGER: Dr. Wilson, your hypothesis that security leads to an interest in the afterlife and immortality, while insecurity leads to immediacy, realistic narrative, colossal architecture, and love poetry should perhaps be theorem number three in Professor Speiser's new science of "psychoceramics." This is an interesting approach. In the case of India, however, the interest in afterlife and in nirvana is generally connected with a sense of insecurity and escape from the evils of this life. Perhaps we do not have a theorem here, perhaps we have two theorems. In any case I think you are offering a generalization of the kind that social scientists love to make, and I think I feel more comfortable now that you have made it.

Your development of the physiological metaphor of the loosely structured organization as a basis for comparing Egypt with Mesopotamia and perhaps other civilizations as well is very suggestive.

John Embree, anthropologist, introduced some years ago the concept of a loosely structured society, applying it to Thailand,[21] and recently two young sociologists have attempted to apply the same concept to Ceylon.[22] In its application to your problem, one obvious basis of tracing the structure has already been mentioned, namely the kinship structures and networks. And do they differ in Egypt and Mesopotamia? Another basis of tracing it, perhaps more directly relevant to the urbanization theme, is the so-called structure of the urban hierarchy. That is to say, we are interested not merely in the question of whether there were cities or not but also in the character of the cities, their distribution, their functional classification. Along the lines of Sir Hamilton Gibbs' suggestion, were there royal cities, organic cities, commercial cities in Egypt? Is there a difference in the way in which urban patterns were structured in relation to the surrounding village patterns in the two cases of Egypt and Mesopotamia that may be significant?

WILLEY: While listening with great interest to Professor Wilson's exposition of a civilization without cities, I have been considering what possible comparisons might be drawn with the one American area where I think there was indeed civilization without the formal container of the city. To be sure, I find myself somewhat on the defensive about the civilizational status of the Maya as a result of Professor Gelb's comments in a previous session. I can only say that, whatever the nature of Maya writing, if one looks at the five 200-foot high temples of Tikal or the refined cynicism on the face of the priest as he interviews some cowering neophytes from behind his mask, one sees reflected the aspirations and the attitudes of something I believe we could agree upon as civilization.

What are any possible similarities, then, in function or nature between Egypt and the Maya? I really see nothing deterministic; they seem so very far apart in space, time, and setting. In Egypt, as I understand it, the river was exploited by small scattered populations more or less in independent segments, perhaps each with some kind of ceremonial center. In the case of the Maya a possibly comparable factor might be the green sea of the jungle, apparently also exploited by isolated groups in a segmented fashion, with a low level of agri-

21 J. F. Embree, "Thailand, a loosely structured social system," *American Anthropologist* LII (1950) 181–93.

22 B. F. Ryan and M. A. Strauss, "The integration of Sinhalese society," *Research Studies of the State College of Washington* XXII (1954) 179–227.

cultural techniques, and in a very similar but independent fashion throughout. Whether or not there was any political or national unity in Maya civilization is still a question, but there was indeed a commonality, a nationality, of culture. It is reflected in uniform art, writing, and architecture over an area some 200 miles in diameter.

This Maya pattern was at least fifteen hundred years in formation, and after that it crystallized and flowered for about six hundred more. In this span of six hundred years I think there was a civilization which had some interesting parallels with Egypt in form and content. For example, there was the feeling of harmonious balance and certainly there is evidence for consideration of great ranges of time. There was also a sense of omen: "Walk carefully, the gods are watching you. You perform and lead a very circumspect and balanced life and you can get by." But in the background, too, there was always a threat of danger. This Maya Classic period of six hundred years was essentially a self-contained cell. During its earlier part, there is evidence of some trade with other parts of Middle America. Moreover, we find some clues in the little scattered hamlets that suggest a very sophisticated peasantry; the same kind of highly ornate pottery occurs in both the hamlets and the ceremonial centers, although in the hamlets one does not find evidence of writing. There was a change in the latter half of the period, with a complete cessation of trade with the outside, with what looks like an attempt to reinforce the prerogatives of the leadership, with the building of more ceremonial centers; in other words, there was a kind of hardening of the cell walls. While we do not know all the factors involved in the collapse of Maya civilization some five hundred years before the Spaniards arrived, it would seem that its vitality had been destroyed even before Mexican invaders penetrated this cell, to continue with Professor Wilson's phrase. I am inclined to think that the Maya may illustrate the kind of tragic fate that may befall social and civilizational systems that achieve such precise inner balance and static harmony in ecological, social, and cultural forms.

THORNTHWAITE: I felt at the outset that I should come here primarily to listen and not to speak, because of my almost complete ignorance of the evidence dealt with by the conference. But in this session alone both Professor Wilson and Professor Edgerton have referred to the need for consultation with physical scientists. Perhaps, very briefly, I can suggest a way in which hydrology and geography might contribute to some of the problems that have been raised. Professor Wilson explained that in Egypt irrigation was quite a simple matter, carried on easily by small groups of people. I would remind you that the waters of the Nile come from two great sources. One is the plateau of Tanganyika and Kenya, where a number of enormous reservoirs such as Lake Victoria and Lake Albert tend to regulate the flow. The rainfall in that area, too, since it is right athwart the equator, is quite uniform in that it tends to result in a relatively continuous flow of water. The other great source of the Nile is the Ethiopian plateau, where a very definite seasonal rhythm is produced; from there the waters drop down into an enormous swamp, the Sudd, which again acts to maintain uniformity of flow. In consequence, while the Nile in Egypt is hardly uniform it is predictable; it comes year after year, in such a manner that the small farmers can presumably make use of it in their small way.

The situation in Mesopotamia is quite different. There are two rivers; the water originates mainly in the very rough country of eastern Turkey; the rhythm of flow is more erratic; the rain comes mostly in winter and dries up in summer. If there were more time to develop this, I think it could be shown that irrigation cannot be expected to have developed naturally in the midparts of Mesopotamia in the same way that it might have in Egypt.

SPEISER: As Professor Oppenheim stated so aptly earlier, similarities are less significant for our problem than differences. In this case the differences are highly characteristic, and they seem to go to the heart of the matter. I shall list just a few of them, as time permits, without developing any of the themes very far. First, there is the basic difference in cosmogony; it is from this, from the concept of the universe in each instance, that so much else seems to flow. Law, for instance. There is no question that Egypt had law, whether we have codes or not. It could not have maintained an efficient government without law. The important thing is the attitude toward the law, the concept of the law, in each instance. In Mesopotamia, the king was a servant of the law. In Egypt, could he have been anything but the master of the law? Take the question of the attitude toward history. Professor Edgerton may or may not accept Frankfort's bold characterization of Egypt, in contrast to Mesopotamia, as a country that had no history, that did not believe in history; but there are some sober and incurable Egyptologists, like Gunn and Gardiner, who say the same thing in different words.

Another important difference is the attitude toward the ruler. Hammurabi goes into every little instance of the problems of his subjects; Sennacherib tells us—I admit that there is a coefficient of mendacity in what rulers say, past or present—that he had to clamber up mountains like a mountain goat. Could an Egyptian king do this or even say this about himself? During the celebration of the new year, the Babylonian ruler got up early in the morning to be slapped by the officiating priest in order to learn due modesty. Again, would this be possible with an Egyptian king? Professor Wilson in one of his many lucid papers tells of Thutmose III in the battle of Megiddo, where all the details are given until the king arrives on the scene, then silence. The majesty has appeared, everything is settled, it is the best of all possible worlds.

In short, it seems to me that there is a chasm between these two great civilizations. They faced each other from opposite sides of a curtain, even if not an iron curtain, or at least from opposite ends of a crescent.

BRONEER: In hearing the title of Professor Wilson's introduction and listening to his very lucid discourse, I was struck with an analogy for his "civilization without cities." In the Aegean countries, and in the mainland of Greece in particular, we know of a large number of graves belonging to the period from about 1100 to 600 B.C. In studying the archeology of graves of that period one gets the impression that the people died but never lived. In the city of Athens, for example, from those five hundred years we can point to no more than one small foundation, which is so haphazard and so poorly preserved that it took a well-trained archeologist even to discover it. We have considerable remains from all the three Bronze Ages, actually extending back into Neolithic times; obviously the area was occupied. But it seems to me that a society which focused its attention upon the welfare of the dead must somehow have been rather skimpy in its attention to the living. Although I have no specific knowledge about the situation in Egypt, I cannot help but be reminded by it of the misplacement or displacement of emphasis that I have mentioned in Greece.

GRENE: I would like first of all to express my appreciation to Professor Wilson for his luminous analysis of the civilization of Egypt. The two points that I have to make are applied to quite different aspects of this discussion.

The first is a brief comment on biological models. Professor Wilson spoke a good deal about Egypt as a biological entity, metaphorically or otherwise, and Professor Singer continued that theme. It seems to me that probably this is a good analogy; it serves to convey facts that are otherwise difficult to bring into focus. But when one thinks in more substantive detail, certain difficulties emerge; the model fails to suggest the extent of historical variation that is possible. Suppose, for instance, one were to compare Egypt with the Roman Empire in its life and death. At once, it seems to me, one is struck with a tremendous difference in organization. In that Professor Wilson has stressed the rigidity of the late system, in which the pharaoh became a captive of his army and his professional classes, the parallel is clear enough. But the Roman Empire was a system with an exactly opposite feature at its top, that is to say, a system which never entirely lost its sense of being an elective monarchy, and yet the same sort of rigidity set in. In other words, the rigidity of the structure underneath, if that is the factor which eventually led to destruction, does not have to extend to the person who ostensibly was at the head of the whole structure.

My second point concerns the theory or, better, the suggestion by Professor Parker that one should consider animal husbandry as an alternative to cereal-growing at the origin of the Egyptian civilization. About the evidence for this from the ancient Near East I naturally know nothing, but Professor Parker clearly regarded animal husbandry as easily accessible to all, at a variety of stages leading to civilization, whereas perhaps cereal-growing was not. This view does not seem to correspond with a different sort of fact; as far as is now held on the basis of experiments by animal geneticists who have been interested in domestication, only certain strains of animals are in fact domesticable. The theory of a big game reserve and a lot of hungry sheep and goats who come along and obediently harness themselves for purposes of domestication does not seem to be correct. For instance, thirty generations of wild rabbits that have been kept and bred in captivity are still totally undomesticable, in the sense that they do not willingly permit handling or man's appurtenances and arrangements for their lives. The prevailing view of these specialists is that, in regard to the major animals like cattle and the various members of the horse family, the same thing was true; only very special strains were domesticable at all, or others were only domesticable with difficulties far beyond the resources of early man. This is merely a comment on the assumption that underlay Professor Parker's suggestion as I understood it.

GELB: Some years ago, Passarge, a German geographer, published a monograph in which he defended the proposition that it was in the area of the Delta that Egyptian civilization arose originally.[23] While I do not recall his detailed arguments, this view seems to be consistent with the inference from Toynbee's challenge-and-response hypothesis that the Delta provided a greater stimulus to cultural growth than did Upper Egypt. In short, I question the conclusion stated earlier that the growth of civilization necessarily proceeds most quickly where environmental conditions are most favorable.

There is another point, however, that is of greater importance with respect to the Delta, and that is the security the Delta offered in the struggle between the desert and the sown, to borrow the immortal saying of Breasted. I sometimes describe this struggle metaphorically as the struggle between the goat and the tree; in a denuded or deforested area young saplings can reappear and grow into trees only if they are protected from grazing herds. Such protected areas, needed for survival, must have been sought by the sedentary villagers as security from hungry roaming nomads. Could not the wide Delta, with its marshes and many islands, have had a positive attraction as a refuge for early farmers far beyond that of the narrow Nile Valley in Upper Egypt?

WILSON: To summarize the discussion: Mr. Wilson made a brilliant synthesis which was wrong at every individual point. I have written down eight pages of tightly cramped comments, and it is clearly impossible to deal with them all. I apologize to each one who contributed comments or questions which time does not permit me to refer to.

I did promise Dr. Adams that I would return to some of his questions if possible. The first, the reality behind the assertions of full political control, is a faint and evanescent thing. I think it is possible for people in their public protestations to surrender themselves to a charismatic leader without following him blindly in their daily life. The dogma in Egypt insisted that there was a god and that every operation—perhaps better, every important operation—having to do with the state was under his divine direction. In actual practice, of course, this was nonsense. Surely there were counterforces who, while

---

[23] S. Passarge, "Die Urlandschaft Ägyptens und die Lokalisierung der Wiege der altägyptischen Kultur," *Nova acta Leopoldina* IX (1940) 75–152.

loyally protesting that they were entirely subject to his word, worked against him. We see this, for example, in that there are times when they do protest too much. The Middle Kingdom was not tightly centralized, but one of the most devoted statements of absolute adhesion to the god-king comes out of the Middle Kingdom. The instruction of Sehetepibre says: "If you want to know what to do in life, cling to the pharaoh and be loyal to your oath to him, because he comprises in his own person all the divine attributes which are listed"; but at the time this was a fiction. Similarly, going down into the Nineteenth Dynasty, I think one can see another overprotest in the Kuban stela of Ramses II. Already the army was becoming a kind of independent power, the civil bureaucracy had its domains of power apart from the king, the priesthood was using the oracle of the god to inhibit the king, but the courtiers grovel before Ramses II and say: "If you just speak the words, the water will come up under the mountain top." The reality had ceased to correspond to the claim, although the claim of divine power had been a cohesive force to which people had adhered for several thousand years and to which they happily continued to adhere in words even while operating against it. I think such a situation is not unknown in some societies today; there may be willing and verbal adhesion to a central authority with independent action unverbalized.

I want to go back to the problem of cities and take up some specific examples. We have very few to look at. A little thing near Lahun which was once called a workman's village but is now I believe called a priest's village, an entirely artificial construction, put up next to the pyramid for the priests who served the pyramid, has to be brushed aside as being atypical. Then there is the tremendous example of Tell al-ʿAmarnah, where a desert bay was to be converted into a garden city, the model city. A garden city, incomplete in its construction, having a colossal plan which was never achieved, is not what we are looking for. There is a great deal of evidence from such places as Memphis and Thebes, but that evidence is not for the city of the living. Let us take Thebes. The poor tourist visiting Luxor at the present time is galloped around a tremendous area. He is paraded through the Temple of Luxor and thrown into an arabiyah and taken a little over a mile to the colossal Temple of Karnak, then the next day he is pitchforked into a boat and carried across the river, where he gets into an ancient motor car and goes all the way up to the Valley of the Kings and comes back to Hatshepsut's temple and then is rushed through the Ramesseum and two private tombs and the Temple of Medinet Habu and pushed back through the Colossi —exhausted. The physical space is extraordinary. This is not a city. On the west side of the river, with the colossal temples that stretch out for a long distance, there were houses. As I recall, among the tomb-robbery papyri there is a list of the houses. I cannot remember the exact number, but it is around seventy; for the expanse of space this is not heavy occupation.

The capital city, to be sure, was on the Luxor-Karnak side. And there you have the two great temples that I have mentioned; they were connected by some kind of artery, with the Avenue of Sphinxes and so on; scholars debate as to whether these temples were connected by a canal or by a road, but, in so far as the area has been tested, there is no particular evidence that a city occupied this stretch of a mile and a quarter. As I remember it, Charles Nims, reviewing a book by Otto on the topography of Thebes, says that the evidence seems to suggest some urban development south of the Temple of Luxor. But in the great stretch between Luxor and Karnak there was no very extensive settlement. Thus, we cannot at present identify this organism of the capital city of Thebes south of the Temple of Luxor. It has not been tested by excavation; perhaps it could not be tested by excavation. The Egyptian government currently is cleaning out the space north of the Temple of Luxor and going through Coptic down into Roman materials; the pharaonic materials are still deeper, and the excavators will not penetrate to them. All of this suggests to me that Thebes was not particularly large in area. Thus it appears that we are misled when we think of Thebes as being of colossal extent because of its scattering of monuments. Similarly, we may also be misled when we think of Memphis as extending for a great distance along the desert cliff with the wonderful things on the top of Saqqarah. We just don't know, we don't have the evidence. Certainly there were nerve centers which perhaps we may properly call cities, but we cannot make the comparison we should like to make with the nerve centers, the cities, of Mesopotamia.

GÜTERBOCK: Thank you very much, Professor Wilson, first for your introduction and then for the really wonderful way in which you picked up some of the main strands of the discussion. It is rather sad that, in the interest of those who follow us in the next session, we have to leave so many motifs unused.

III

The Development of Culture in the
Great Empires

ASSYRIA AND PERSIA

SINGER *(chairman)*: Empires have already been mentioned at a number of points in the symposium. Yesterday morning Professor Jacobsen raised the question whether, with the empires of the ancient Near East, there is a degree of expansion of society which differs qualitatively from the preceding phases of expansion in that it becomes a threat to culture, its continuity and its unity. I think this indicates a certain ambivalence which we all feel toward that degree of expansion which presupposes an expansion of power, an expansion of power which both attracts and repels us. Accurately to record our feelings on this problematic phase of human expansion perhaps our title should have been "The Development of Culture in the Great and Terrible Empires." Empires are no longer popular; they become commonwealths or unions. Those of us who are not specialists in the ancient Near East particularly look forward to this our sixth session because we think that the discussion may throw some light on problems with which the tremendous expansion in the present-day world confronts us. Professor Güterbock.

GÜTERBOCK: Mr. Chairman, ladies and gentlemen: I would like to start with what I think is both an apology and a *captatio benevolentia* by saying that the task of introducing today's discussion was more or less thrust upon me. It appears in the program that I am to talk of the Assyrian and Persian empires, but I want to confess my very great ignorance in both of these fields. I am a little more at home with the Hittite empire, and perhaps also with what little we know of the Mitannian, and I hope you will forgive me if I bring them in at times through what may seem to be the back door. At any rate, I want to say that I hope to learn more than I can myself contribute from those speakers who, I hope, will later take up the discussion.

We are concerned here with civilization as an expanding society, and we have taken the ancient Near East as the focus for obvious reasons. The idea behind our program is, of course, the truism that Western civilization had its roots in the ancient Near East, and therefore it is only natural that we should conclude with the Greek and Roman world and the form that its civilization took. As you all know, it was characterized, at least in part and for the regions and periods that concern us here, by empire in one way or another, and Dr. Kraeling will deal with this in his presentation. It seems to me, therefore, that I must provide a bridge, as it were, between the earlier stages of Babylonia that we have discussed and the time when the Greek and Roman world came into contact with it, a period taken up by the great empires of Assyria and the Achaemenians.

Dr. Jacobsen gave us a very clear description of the development in Mesopotamia that began with cities in the south and extended to the north, including the appearance of what he called the "Kingir League." He used the word "empire" for the Agade period, while applying the term "territorial state" to the later Ur III and Old Babylonian periods. Even for the Ur III period the term "empire" has been used. Hence, we may very well ask what we mean by "empire." We have heard also, in Dr. Jacobsen's presentation, that the king asserted his power through an army, and we may therefore ask whether there is just a difference of quantity rather than of quality. Is an empire merely a larger kingdom with more power? This question I want to put before us, but I do not claim to have the answer.

Theories about the rise of empires as a consequence of nomadic invasions have been advanced by Röpke, Rüstow, and certainly others, all of them perhaps long ago anticipated by Ibn Khaldun. The argument is that generally such cases involve the superimposition of one ethnic group upon another as a result of conquest. For many of the older empires this explanation no doubt applies. In a sense, perhaps, it may apply to the Agade "empire," when Semitic-speaking Akkadians, although they had long been in the country, for the first time asserted themselves as rulers. It seems obvious that the Mitannians and the Hittites are among the best examples in support of the theory. Both empires were built up on the basis of a feudal structure by people who, as we know from their language, were newcomers; perhaps they were conquering immigrants, although we do not know the details of their coming. The fact that these states were based on an aristocracy of "chariot" warriors influenced their whole development. They were of a feudal nature not only in matters of landholding but also in their broad structural elements, inasmuch as they largely incorporated conquered territories into their realm as vassal states. Certainly the Kassite kingdom of Babylonia also shared many of the characteristics of a feudal state with large estates and with a dynasty of foreign origin. Professor Landsberger already has mentioned the relation of the Kassite rulers to the rest of civilization; school training, at least, was carried on independently and entirely by the native Babylonians. On the other hand, it is worth noting that the Kassites, although in some respects they can be described as conquerors and newcomers, did not achieve what may be called an empire.

It is more difficult to account for the rise of Assyria, a question which, as you know, has been discussed over and over again. An ethnic, or even more specifically a racist, point of view was introduced by Von Soden. This is certainly wrong in the particular way in which he introduced it, but one may very well ask whether some of the differences between the Assyrians and the Babylonians, particularly in their expression of political power and their building-up of their empires, had something to do with different ethnic subtrata. Here one thinks of the large admixture of Hurrians in the population of Assyria and perhaps also of the fact that Assyria itself was apparently part of the Mitannian empire at some time and hence might have drawn its inspiration from the earlier model. Still another factor of empire-building has been mentioned by Dr. Wilson with regard to Egypt, where the New Kingdom grew out of the Hyksos rule, or in other words as a reaction against foreign domination and as a logical outcome of the primary necessity of driving the foreigners out. The fact that the first great Assyrian conquerors of the Middle Assyrian period, such as Adad-nirari I, Shalmaneser I, and Tukulti-Ninurta I, almost immediately followed that dark age of Assyria for which we presume a Mitannian domination might point in the same direction. In the case of the Assyrians, however, I think the need was not so much to drive out an overlord as to defend the realm against pressing external enemies. These enemies were, first, the Arameans and, somewhat later, the equally menacing kingdom of Urartu to the north. Certainly another factor is the internal dynamism that any empire has; once it has reached a certain point, there will always be borders, there will always be unconquered enemies on the outside who must be dealt with. The applicability of this factor to the Assyrians is so commonplace that I need not discuss it.

All this has to do mainly with quantitative change, and my suggestions as to possible causes behind such change were meant as no more than questions. About the possibility of qualitative change, I must confess that I have not been able to arrive at a clear picture. Certainly there was marked centralization. With regard to cities, we may say that in the Assyrian empire it was primarily the capital which continued to be a city, in which cultural life was concentrated. We find in the Assyrian empire the phenomenon which Sir Hamilton Gibb mentioned with regard to the Islamic rulers, namely their founding of new capitals. In Assyria there were Dur-Sharrukin, Kar-Tukulti-Ninurta, Nimrud, and many others. Assur remained a spiritual and cultural center even when the royal residence was elsewhere, yet Nineveh, as far as I understand, was taking over that role in the latest period of the Assyrian empire. It became by far the largest city, and because of its sheer size may be the one that most deserves the term "city," even in the modern sense.

Centralization of culture in the main city may have been a generic characteristic; centralization of government seems to have been a long and gradual process. In the Assyrian empire the first stage involved raids upon neighboring tribes, princelets, or small kingdoms. Tribute was imposed in two forms: one to be paid on the spot and one to be paid yearly. The system of annual tribute obviously was not satisfactory; whenever the king turned his back, the local rulers tried to reassert their independence by ceasing to pay the tribute. Thus there were repeated raids, repeated wars, repeated conquests. The next step was the conversion of the raided territories into real provinces. And this went on gradually, expanding outward from the nearest territories until the whole of what we call the Assyrian empire was under control. The process was not without relapses, as you know, but in principle centralization was achieved by the time of Sargon.

Another point in connection with the central administration has to do with its efficiency. Since the development was not in a straight line and since there were intervening periods of weakness while the Assyrian empire was slowly growing, we hear of times when provincial governors wielded more authority than it was thought they ought to possess or more than was in the interest of the king. Tiglat-pileser III conteracted this tendency by splitting large provinces into smaller ones. We also know of the fixed rotation of provincial governors in their role as eponyms and thereby get an insight into the operation of the hierarchy.

Art as an expression of culture is still another phenomenon which we have to draw upon in connection with empires. It may be said, and I think it is a truism, that what makes Assyrian art distinct from the art of other regions is that it is imperial art, that it expresses the idea of the conqueror-king, that it involves what has been termed the "calculated frightfulness" which was not only practiced but also depicted in the palace reliefs to impress visitors. The Hittites very often are praised for their relative mildness, but it is known, for example, that they deported the populations of conquered regions just as the Assyrians did. There was a difference perhaps in emphasis but certainly not in principle. Yet in Hittite art there is nothing that can be compared with Assyrian art, not a single war scene, not a single representation of the king as conqueror. Again, the Achaemenian sculptures at Persepolis express the power and the grandeur of the king not by showing him in battle slaying his enemies but by showing his retinue and the peoples of his realm coming to his court with tribute. I cannot give reasons for this difference; I can only mention it as meriting discussion.

The systematic deportation of conquered populations, which I have mentioned, certainly made for unity in a sense, a forced unity, because it destroyed the individuality of the subjugated peoples and possibly melted them into a larger unit. Whether this policy had lasting success is another question. The practice of forcibly populating a new royal residence, mentioned by Professor Gibb in the previous session, certainly is known in Assyria, for instance in the case of Ashur-nasirpal's building-up of the capital at Nimrud.

Another kind of unification, through the inherent power of a certain ethnic group, is exemplified by the Hittite empire. Certainly its rise is an example of the superimposition of one ethnic group upon another. When the speakers of the Indo-European language which we call "Hittite" and which the Hittites themselves called "Nesian" entered Anatolia, they did not enter a vacuum. The natives—let us call them Hattians—had a well-developed culture which the Hittites, or the Indo-European element, fully assimilated. The cultural features that they took over in many cases were really the fundamentals not only of the material culture but more particularly of the religion. The one distinctive expression of the new ruling group was their language. This Hittite or Nesian language exerted its special influence to the very end of the empire in spite of the fact that the empire, with all its vassal states, included peoples with widely varying ethnic and cultural backgrounds. The Syrian vassals, for example, spoke Semitic languages, while in part of the former Mitannian empire the population was mostly Hurrian. In Anatolia itself there were the Luwian and Palaic languages, related to Hittite but different from it. Particularly in religion, there was from the beginning a tendency to unite the disparate elements in a national system, not by extinguishing them but rather by taking them over, by equating foreign gods with native ones, by creating a kind of a syncretism. It seems that toward the end of the Hittite New Kingdom the Luwian- and Hurrian-speaking elements became more and more powerful in the administration, among the scribes, and, so it appears, even in the royal family. There was also the increased—and toward the end, continually increasing—role of the hieroglyphic writing, which I have already mentioned in this connection (see p. 122). Yet, with all this, the Hittite language remained the dominant vehicle of expression for the central government and for what we call Hittite culture or Hittite civilization. Unfortunately this was cut short by the downfall of the empire as a result of the great migrations around 1200 B.C.

To come back to the empires with which we are mainly concerned, the principle of superimposition might again be invoked as an explanation for the growth of the Neo-Babylonian empire, since the Chaldean Arameans, who had been settling in the southern part of Babylonia for centuries, now for the first time asserted themselves as the dominant political group. However, in this instance I do not believe a good case can be made for this principle. A more important factor, I would say, is that the Neo-Babylonian empire grew out of opposition to the Assyrians; once Nineveh had been destroyed, the Assyrian empire almost automatically fell to Babylon as a heritage. In cultural expression, the Babylon of Nebuchadnezzar had all the characteristics of a time of restoration; it tried to imitate the great Hammurabi even to such small details as the type of old Babylonian script used in royal inscriptions. The concentration of most of the cultural life in the capital certainly was very pronounced in spite of the fact that the old schools continued in other places, such as Uruk.

And finally we come to the Achaemenian empire. The Indo-Iranians, the Arians, the Medes and Persians were certainly newcomers from whom the new empire might have arisen by superimposition. The process of centralization certainly was carried farther than it ever had been previously. Particularly with Darius the administration of the empire was very thoroughly enlarged and reorganized. Another feature that frequently has been mentioned as characteristic of the Achaemenian empire is its religious tolerance. Perhaps this is best exemplified by the attitude of Cyrus, who immediately tried to become a legitimate Babylonian king not only by worshiping Marduk but also by restoring Marduk as against the heretic moon cult of the last Babylonian king, Nabonidus. Moreover, as we know from the Old Testament, he gave orders for the restoration of the temple in Jerusalem. There were exceptions to this tolerance, but they seem to have occurred in cases in which religion was connected with political claims; the destruction of the temple in Babylon by Xerxes has been shown to be such a case. With greater centralization, with unification of the whole realm, with the contacts between the Achaemenian empire and Greece in the centuries following Darius—and I mean peaceful and intellectual exchanges as well as the Persian wars —and with the appearance of new religions, new mystery cults and others, we have reached the point from which Dr. Kraeling will carry on.

SINGER: Thank you. I will now call on several scholars to comment briefly.

GOETZE: To be called upon to say something about the presentation we have just heard reminds me of that student who was called before the "assembly of the masters" for examination. But I venture to present a few remarks.

Let me first say a word about my conception of the expanding of the Assyrian empire, about the dynamics behind this process, and then a word about the organization of Hittite towns.

I think it is quite correct to state that there was inside Assyria a pressure that called for expansion at the time when the Assyrian kingdom "exploded." And here I think we can profitably recall a point which Mr. Delougaz made earlier, namely that this expansion began at a time of weakness, as a reaction against an epoch of constriction. The structure of society which existed in Assyria at the time could not maintain itself with the resources that its limited realm offered. To remain static, to tolerate this restriction, would have meant a lowering of the standard of living, perhaps even extinction, or at least extinction as a political force. To change the situation the Assyrians had several alternatives. One was expansion toward the south, where Babylonia probably was similar in structure and roughly equal in power. Whatever the reason may have been, this alternative was not chosen. The Assyrians turned westward instead. Their decision may reflect a reaction against the Mitannian domination which had preceded this period or even against the earlier Amorite domination at the time of Shamshi-Adad. But I think there were other impelling reasons which have not been mentioned at all, namely economic motives, above all the quest for raw materials. Mesopotamia was a curious country, particularly lower Mesopotomia where there was really only one raw material in abundance which was basic for Mesopotamian civilization, and that was mud. There was no wood, there was no metal, there was not even stone; these materials had to be imported in exchange for other commodities. This process had been going on for a long time. There were established lines of communication, which certainly had never been forgotten. In addition to the waterways, there were caravan routes along the northern fringe of the great plain where it merges into the hill country. All these factors were no doubt influential in directing the Assyrian expansion toward the west, that is to say, toward Syria. And here another factor enters the picture, because Syria was the center where the trade routes from Mesopotamia, Egypt, and Asia Minor met and crossed. Here was the timber needed for temples, palaces, and houses; here was metal brought from Anatolia; here, too, stone was available. Stone, of course, was to be obtained closer at hand, but we know from the sources that the Gudeans, for instance, floated their stone down the Euphrates River from far to the west. Therefore Assyrian society as it was then constituted could hope to exist only if it dominated Syria. It was not competition with the Urartians which brought the Assyrians to Syria. It was rather that the Urartians themselves wanted to have an important part in this world trade by dominating Syria. It is of great significance that Assyria won out over Urartu. Thereafter the process of expansion continued almost automatically. Having Syria, the Assyrians held a kind of corridor to the west which was exposed on both flanks. The effort to protect the flanks led step by step to the establishment of a system of provinces along the Taurus, with some provinces even beyond forming a kind of glacis toward Asia Minor on the northern side of that magnificent mountain range. Similarly, the conquest of such places as Damascus and then Samaria and Jerusalem was necessary, leading finally and inevitably to conflict with Egypt.

With reference to town organization in Asia Minor, we may begin

with a factor which has already been mentioned, namely the deportation of populations. The Babylonian captivity of the Jews is an
example. The practice, of course, was quite common in the Hittite
empire. Deported people were called *nam.ra,* a Sumerian expression
(Akkadian *šallatu*). These *nam.ra* were, I believe, not allowed to
move from one place to another. For the most part they were artisans
and the like who lived in towns; when the towns were conquered the
nam.ra were taken by the conqueror to populate what might be
called industrial centers in other places.

The historian of the Near East is often asked how he comes to
know these things, since there is no real book, no systematic presentation in the text material that he receives. That is largely true; we
have to piece together from single occurrences an integrated picture
of the whole. But we are rather fortunate in dealing with the question at hand. Among Hittite sources at least one text is preserved
that tells, admittedly a little indirectly, how a town was organized.
There existed on the northern flank of the Hittite empire something
like a Roman limes, within which there were towns. This limes had
to be defended against the Kashkeans, who lived on the shore of the
Black Sea and who continually threatened the Hittite empire. The
military commander in this area received instructions from the king
on how to behave, and his duties are actually described in this text.
He had to see that the people were fed, that they were provided with
fuel and water, that there were sanitary installations, that justice was
done, passing cases which he himself was not able to solve along to
the higher courts, and so on. Certainly these duties were the same
as those of a civilian governor in places which were not under military control. Thus, from this text we obtain real insight into the
administration of a city. It was, for instance, prohibited that a Kash-
kean, one of those terrible people from the north, should enter the
city. The common term for towns and cities was *ālu* in Assyrian.
No difference is expressed between villages and cities. Characteristic,
I think, is the Hittite term, *happira,* which goes together with the
word for "to trade." The town was actually the market place to begin
with, but it was surrounded by a wall as protection against invasion
and had a rather tightly knit administration.

OPPENHEIM: From what Professor Goetze said, one might receive
the impression that the Assyrian empire grew from a conquest of
trade routes, that the Assyrians, so to speak, conquered what they

could not trade. I would like to amplify this view in the following way.

For both the Assyrian and Neo-Babylonian empires there seems to be some evidence for actual trade routes, which somehow were governed from the capital or at least fed raw materials and money into the capital. But as usual we have very scanty evidence, a little information here, a little there. A recently published text, for instance, indicates that Sargon (721–705 B.C.), when he first came to the Egyptian border, erected something which could be called a trading post, something which would enable the Assyrian caravans to exchange goods and establish trade with Egypt. This is recorded in a historical inscription and hence must have been of some political importance. It suggests that one of the objectives of the Assyrian wars was to secure trade routes. Another bit of evidence comes from Babylon, a Neo-Babylonian inscription[1] which is rather typical except that it mentions the entire personnel of the Babylonian court, including a man who is called *rab tamkaru*, "the chief of the merchants." His name is Hanunu or, in Phoenician, Hanno; there is no doubt about this equivalence. If a Phoenician was the minister of trade in the court of Nebuchadnezzer, there had to be trade relations. Yet we know nothing directly about these trade relations because we have no pertinent documents from either the Assyrians of that period or the Babylonians. In fact, there is no Babylonian reference to such texts; except for a small group of Babylonian private legal documents, everything we know comes from temples and administrative centers. The same is true for Assyria. Nevertheless, we do have indications that there was indeed trade between the Persian Gulf and the Mediterranean, between Iran and Egypt, and that the Assyrians were good traders. Of course, they had been even before they became conquerors, as we know from their so-called "Cappadocian" texts.

My other point has to do with the nature of the Assyrian dynamism. There are two strange things about Assyrian history, the sudden expansions of the empire and its sudden collapses. The Assyrians and their political power disappeared at times with astonishing speed, the empire crumbling like an empty shell, and after a generation or two they came back to full-fledged domination. There was an inner dynamism, an inner potentiality to recuperate, which is astonishing. Of course one can offer ethnic explanations, but there was another source of Assyrian strength. I am inclined to think that the entire

[1] *Forschungen und Fortschritte* III (1927) 1 ff.

Assyrian empire depended on a superstructure of enforced urbanization. The Assyrians collected people in cities all over the realm and exacted taxes, contributions, and military service from them. The power of the empire was in direct relation to its ability to collect taxes and levy troops from these cities, and at the moment communication stopped for some reason the empire collapsed. The Assyrian empire really lived and existed on its capacity to communicate, to receive information from the outside, to direct troops to the right point. It had, for example, a wonderful system of mail and road stations spanning the entire realm, and a very good system of intelligence based on spies all over the realm.

SINGER: The discussion so far has paid a good deal more attention to the Assyrians than to the Persians. I wonder whether Professor Cameron would care to restore the balance.

CAMERON: From the standpoint of culture, the Persian empire— this is not my phrase—reaped where it had not sown. There were some new features, and yet most of the Persian culture may be characterized more or less as an outgrowth of elements already present or at least incipient. It is interesting to note that the same observation, applied to a much earlier period, has frequently been used as a criticism of the concept of an "urban revolution." At any rate, there was already a very extensive base on which the Persians were able to build.

For example, consider Persian art. What difference is there, except in scale perhaps, between Persepolis and Khorsabad or between the Bisitun relief and the Bavian reliefs? In literature and science, again, there is very little that is new. Perhaps we might detect an innovation in the approach to the past; it seems to me that the Achaemenids felt very keenly their debt to the past and built upon past experiences more explicitly than did the Assyrians. One finds repeatedly the attitude: "Here is something new, something good for what was not good before, justice where there was injustice."

Since there is no doubt that the Persians became empire-builders, it is worth while to consider their motives. Professor Singer, I would like to take you to task for the comments in your background paper that there is a stage when "expansion becomes 'expansionism' " and that "the dream of empire is usually dreamed before the empire is gained" (see p. 256). These are only partially true, if at all, of the Near East before Alexander. At least, I am unable to find support for them in any of the material I know. I hope the fact that you are acting as chairman will not prevent your commenting on this point during the discussion.

SINGER: I shall be glad to abuse the privileges of the chair.

CAMERON: Conceivably one might adduce a "dream of empire" in Esarhaddon's conquest of Egypt, but I think there were more valid motives which might have led the Assyrians into Egypt. Similarly with the Persian conquest of Greece; it can be fully explained without that motive. I would see the Greek episode of the Persians as did Eduard Meyer and A. T. Olmstead, stressing the relative unimportance—and most of what there was with overtones of trade—of the Persian effort to control the unruly Greeks in a little and distant corner of the realm. As for the Egyption empire in Asia, I would follow Professor Wilson's analysis that after the Hyksos there came for the Egyptians a psychosis for security. This does seem to me to explain the Egyptian drive into Asia, primarily if perhaps not exclusively. With respect to the still earlier effort of Akkad to enter Anatolia, I would follow Professor Goetze's lead in seeing this as the flag following trade rather than the reverse. In other words, the expansion of the earlier empires possibly was based on fear more than on anything else. In addition, and quite personally and perhaps subjectively, I believe that most of the empire-building of the Persians, the Assyrians, and even the Egyptians was based in part on a continuing effort to keep the peace. But, as always, keeping the peace in one area meant expanding into other areas which threatened it. And peace in its turn permitted both trade and the expansion of culture.

LANDSBERGER: I am going to speak of the historical causes for the rise of Assyria as the first great empire. Those which were economic I leave to Professor Polanyi with only the modest remark that money was needed more than timber to sustain the armies and the palaces. I can relate only briefly—and this is not new—how the whole thing is said to have developed by the Assyrians themselves. The rulers who initiated the custom of annual expeditions were deeply concerned with hunting. In the records they say "I conquered this land" and then, in the same record, "I killed about fifty wild bulls." Thus expeditions began as the sport of the kings, to the very, very shallow eye of a philologist. Since Hattusili I was the first to cross the Euphrates, it was he who was imitated by the others. All of them were moved by adventurousness and belligerence of spirit, although this was never admitted. Instead they aped the great Sargon with his claim to the four quarters of the earth, professing to go as missionaries of god in Sargon's footsteps. So it was a petty little sport which was (again by my scribes, of course) expanded to the idea of the world conqueror. Whether the Assyrians were racially especially gifted is unclear to me. No doubt they were good soldiers, but it was very easy to be good soldiers with superior weapons and superior organization. No Assyrian king died in battle except the great Sargon. And we do not know whether the enemy or his own soldiers killed him; his son investigated, with the help of liver experts, but he never found out. I should say also that the real empire did not develop earlier than the time of Tiglat-pileser III. What was this empire? So to speak, a palace with a hundred arms. As you know from the Bible, the chief cupbearer played the role of the governor of a province, and so it went in other respects. It was an expanded palace, nothing else. And what was the palace? Nothing but a struggle, sometimes involving the killing of a father by his own son. In the whole succession there was no natural line in this great period.

Now only a word about how the Assyrian culture spread into the provinces. Only one attempt was made to have a whole empire worship a new god, the old and at the same time new Aramaic god Sin, combined by Nabonidus with Nannar and Ilteri in a great syncretistic effort that fused the Sumerian, Akkadian, Assyrian, and Aramaic roots of his people. But the Assyrians, although they took away the statues of the gods, never forced conquered peoples to revere the god Assur. They sought only to show their subjects that Assur was more powerful than any of the small gods they had. As to Assyrian cultural influence—a most abused term—even before the little princes were taken into captivity they were imitating the court style of the Assyrians. The Assyrians say a hundred times: "I made them Assyrians and they pay taxes to the gods and to the governors exactly as does the Assyrian." They even claim they imposed the *īnu*—I would have to look this word up in the dictionary, but it means something like culture or erudition—"*īnu* I impose on them and I make them Assyrians." But in this they did not succeed, as is best exemplified by the Bible.

JACOBSEN: I should like to take as my point of departure Professor Güterbock's question as to the difference between the city-empire of Agade and the later empire of the Assyrians. It brings us face to face with the problem of the character of empires in general. Off-handedly, it seems to me that force is the essence of empire. Force is based on an army, and the essential thing for a conqueror who wants to hold on to his empire is the loyalty and efficiency of his army. This the Agade rulers had; they developed a well-disciplined standing army that was stationed as garrisons in the major cities and at strong points along the roads.

Another requirement for empire is an efficient, loyal civil administration that reaches from the king down into the minutest provincial affairs in a connected chain. This the Agade kings did not develop. Its absence proved to be a continuing problem all through their successive reigns as again and again parts of the empire revolted and general disintegration threatened. When, later on, the territorial state of Sumer and Akkad was formed by the kings of the Third Dynasty of Ur, civil administration seems to have been one of the issues with which they successfully dealt. The difficulty that had confronted the Agade rulers was that on a local level the old city-states were very tightly organized structures. When they were incorporated in the newly formed empire, they kept their identities and local loyalties; hence the king could not rely on them. With the Third Dynasty of Ur the king successfully broke through this local autonomy; in addition to his army organizations throughout the realm, he had a civil administration based on city governors. The old *ensis* had now become governors appointed by and responsible to the king, and we have evidence that they could be shifted from place to place, so that they would not too easily take root in the local community and adopt the local loyalties.

Turning to the Assyrian empire, I think that one of the essentials I have mentioned was achieved by the Assyrians in a very rough manner: the establishment of a reliable system of local governors who were regulated in terms of office by the important system of rotation. As Professor Cameron so rightly said of the Achaemenians, the Assyrians reaped where they had not sown. This was particularly true in the sense that they reaped a very large area that was already organized. From the Assyrians on down, we see over and over again a persistent solid administrative system extending over an extraordinarily large realm. The ruling elite could change overnight, but the structure itself remained intact.

Because empire is based essentially on force, it is interesting to consider also the forces that opposed empire. In later times it seems that opposition to empire tended to centralize around religious symbols, that is, religion became the one thing in which a local group found its coherence and its opposition to the empire. I think that that can be seen in the role of the cult of Marduk in Babylon and in the curious attempt of the Assyrian kings after the destruction of Babylon to partially transplant the whole Marduk ritual to Assur. Of course, we are fortunate in having a non-Assyrian view of this in the Old Testament, but a discussion of the prophetic reaction given there to the Assyrian expansion I would leave to more qualified members of the symposium. This local opposition was so bitter and strong that it presumably would have been detrimental to the whole empire if its major themes had not been counteracted by the attitude of tolerance introduced by Cyrus. Without tolerance it would hardly have been possible to hold the large empires together. At the same time, it is clear that the evocation of tolerance implied a relaxation in the claims to absolute truth of autonomous local cultures. This movement toward relaxation of previously absolute commitments to a local group grows in volume as the history of empires progresses.

This leads me to the effects of the empire. An obvious consequence was that a kind of peace was imposed over a very large area, as already mentioned by Dr. Cameron. Peace, in turn, must have had many effects. One thinks of trade over a larger area, with the empire guarding the routes, and possibly relaxation of local duties imposed at local frontiers. Another effect may have been internationalization, to be sure on a very small scale, arising out of contacts between people from different parts of the realm and enhanced by the forced deportation of populations. I should not be surprised to find that activities like the Macedonian colonization had occurred earlier. Also one cannot help wondering whether, in addition to such wholesale uprootings of people, there were not individual movements. Private families, I should think, might have moved over the entire realm under the new conditions.

I think that the word "uprooting" implies another factor that tends to break down absolute commitment to a culture. Physical uprooting means also spiritual uprooting, and these large movements of populations must have relaxed the strong grip of a single, uniform, local culture on the individual.

A third and last element which I should like to stress as characteristic of empire is the rise of the metropolis. A classical historian commented that when the Macedonians came to Mesopotamia they were amazed at the fertility of the country and astounded to find that nevertheless there were only two cities, Babylon and Nineveh; all the other settlements were only villages. So here we see the tremendous expansion of the town or city into the metropolis, forcefully raising another question: What did all these people live on? The older cities we have studied here had an agricultural basis, but the metropolises force us to turn to things like trade, to administrative jobs, to a cultureless non-agricultural proletariat in Toynbee's sense of that concept.

ALBRIGHT: I think there is some justification for making cautious comparisons between republican Rome and Middle Assyria; in both we have the phenomenon of an originally small city-state which found itself exposed to enemies on all sides and had to lay tremendous stress on national defense. Even after republican Rome had freed itself from Etruscan domination it still was constantly threatened not only by the Etruscans but by the Oscans and Umbrians as well. Its location on the lower Tiber River and its control of the rich fields of Campania made it a constant target for these invaders. Thus we find an extremely solid development of the instruments of power in the state, the development of a *cursus honorum*, a citizen-army, and in addition to these features a remarkable stress was laid on legal sanctions of morality. Exactly the same thing occurred in the Middle Assyrian state. We have laws, found in the palace of Tiglat-pileser I, from about 1100 B.C. (but supposed by most scholars to belong somewhat earlier in the Middle Assyrian period) showing an almost Draconic attempt to enforce morality by extremely severe penalties, a process which offers a very close parallel to the situation in republican Rome. The causes, I suppose, are the same: both Romans and Assyrians simply had to maintain themselves against enemies from all sides. Yet in pursuance of their own defense they organized such strong military states that they both inevitably became aggressors.

Turning for a moment to the Chaldean empire, I should like briefly to supplement Professor Güterbock's remarks. I think we have to reckon with the fact that the Chaldeans were immigrants from the south who maintained associations with the nomads of the peninsula and were distinguished sharply from the Arameans, despite all obvious ties with the latter. The Chaldeans appear to have written their own inscriptions in South-Arabic, as we have recently learned, and their South-Arabic inscriptions contain exclusively Babylonian names. The campaigns of Nebuchadnezzar in North Arabia can most easily be understood when we remember that he was a Chaldean, a bearer of Chaldean traditions who maintained a sort of familial connection with the peninsula just as the Cossean kings retained their close connection with their own homeland in the Zagros Mountains. The Neo-Babylonian empire was thus a combination of older Babylonian traditions with a largely Aramean merchant population and a Chaldean military class or corps with its old desert associations, still closely maintained through the reigns of Nebuchadnezzar and Nabonidus.

SINGER: Professor Güterbock has indicated that he is willing for the discussion to go on before he comments. I will seek to enlarge the scope of the discussion by asking a number of people to continue the theme, not necessarily restricting it to the ancient Near East.

VON GRUNEBAUM: Since you must be aware that I have nothing to contribute to the analysis of Hittite, Persian, or other early empire-building, I take your call as a genial summons to elaborate several points dealing with the relation between urbanization and the unfolding organization of empires.

There are two paradoxes in the Islamic development. (As the cat always falls on its four feet, I cannot but come back to Islam.) The principal one is that the government in Islam is justified exclusively, one might say, through its function of making possible a perfect or complete religious life, while, at the same time, the Islamic institution (to use an expression that Sir Hamilton Gibb has inaugurated) as a religious institution is trying its best to become independent of the vicissitudes constantly besetting the state. In other words, it spurns the help of the state beyond a certain point and makes political power, as such, somewhat unjustifiable in terms of the Muslim law. The other paradox is that Islam quite clearly, it seems to me, is city-based, in the sense that the perfect religious life can be led only in a city environment and that part of Muḥammad's early success may have been due to the fact that he provided an ideological justification for certain attitudes that had become strong in Mecca. At the same time, however, the overwhelming majority of Muslims were and still are rural people. This paradox, or conflict, has been a permanent feature of Muslim life. It might be said that the canon law is the product of the urban aspect of Islam and is adjusted, or tries to be adjusted, to the requirements of city life. This is another way of saying that the influence of both the city and the canon law is apt to decline as one moves toward the rural, not to speak of the nomad, believers. The opposition which develops within Islam between the canon lawyer and the kind of piety which he articulates, on the one hand, and the kind of piety which is commonly identified as Sufi or mystic, on the other, expresses itself in the fact that it is not the lawyer-theologian's Islam that spreads into the rural districts. Instead it is the mystic orders that win the allegiance of the rural population for Islam, especially during the later period. Moreover, this is not to say that it was especially the Sufi orders that went out and converted non-Muslims to Islam; rather, it was through them that a more Islamic life percolated to those who had already been nominally converted.

When an empire or, shall we say, a Muslim state arises it is almost always city-based. It may well be that an encampment of a tribal group only gradually develops into something that we would recognize as a city, but, nevertheless, in the overwhelming majority of cases the Muslim governmental organization is city-based and reaches out through its various organs—military occupation, tax, farming, and so on—into the rural areas which it considers within its limits. If the state consolidates its power, the lawyer-theologians go out into what had been the domain of the Sufi orders alone and a certain adjustment in favor of the city-based *sheri'a* is attempted, if not always attained. What I have particularly in mind in formulating these generalizations is the North African history of perhaps the last six or seven hundred years. The progress of systematized Islam, of strictly traditional, legal Islam, is by and large contingent upon orderly city-based government; when such government breaks down, as for instance when the Mongols destroyed organized government in large parts of Persia, then these organs or aspects of Islam decline. The cultivation of Islam then shifts to the Sufi orders that occasionally remain as the only organized forces on the local scene. Perhaps this is comparable to the way in which, after the devastation of the Roman Empire, the representatives of the Roman church found themselves as the heads of the only organizations still intact and hence tended to take over not only the protection of the faith but also political power.

It would not be correct, it seems to me, to say that an Islamic state, or shall we say the expansion of Islamic civilization, is identical with and inseparable from the expansion of urbanization and urban culture. But historical experience does teach that the solidification and expansion of the legal and *sheria*-based aspect of Muslim life is inseparable from an expansion of the urbanized orbit.

HOSELITZ: I should like to express a certain bewilderment which perhaps is not surprising since my acquaintance with the Near East is essentially confined to four "paperbacks": Braidwood, *The Near East and the Foundations for Civilization;* Chiera, *They Wrote on Clay;* Wilson, *The Burden of Egypt;* and Frankfort, Wilson, Jacobsen, and Irwin, *The Intellectual Adventure of Ancient Man.* But there are two central elements here on which I would like to obtain some further clarification. One is the city, and the other is the empire.

I have written down in the course of the discussions five criteria by which one recognizes the city. The first criterion is size, mentioned by Professor Wilson with particular reference to Thebes. Again, Professor Jacobsen spoke of the metropolis, which I presume is a matter of size. Associated with physical layout, of course, is a second feature, the size of population. How large were these cities? What is the difference between a city and what Dr. Wilson referred to this morning as a focal town? The third aspect has to do with complexity, the occupational and social structure within the city. A number of references have been made to the greater complexity of social structure within cities than outside them. The fourth criterion is the legal status of a city; I think Professor Oppenheim has pointed out that the city-states of ancient Sumer were separate and independent in legal character. And, finally, Professor Wilson, in talking about Egypt not having a permanent heart but only a nervous system, alluded to the factor of continuity or durability.

I should like to know, first, whether we all mean the same thing when we talk about cities. Secondly, which are the most important characteristics of these cities? None of them, I think, are necessarily characteristic of a city in the modern sense, which implies at least certain industrial specifications. Perhaps some of our problems of cityless empires, city-states, empires with cities, and so on might be clarified if it became clearer what we really mean by "city."

Turning to the question of empires, I should like to make two comments. Professor Jacobsen has said that the characteristic feature of empire is power, military power. Others have spoken about the dynamics and motivations of empire. The one theory with which I am familiar relates to the dynamics and motivations for empire, and especially the ancient empires. Schumpeter, in *The Sociology of Imperialisms,* states that empires are essentially created by the existing warrior class or, as he puts it, wars created a class of warriors who then were instrumental in creating further wars. That is to say that during the Egyptian liberation from the Hyksos, or the Assyrian liberation from the Mitannians, a warrior class was created within the society, which then, in order to justify its continued existence, had to push for expansion, and, theoretically speaking, limitless expansion. If this is so, and I regard it only as a hypothesis which deserves critical comment here, expansion was due not necessarily to the conquest of economic goods but essentially to the dynamism of the class which only by extended conquest could justify itself.

My second comment concerns the relationship of empires once established as against empires coming into being. Under the technological conditions that existed in the ancient world I take it that sheer size was one of the old, well-known problems with which empires had to cope. This means that with any great increase in size—and I am talking now not about historical particulars but of what might be considered sociological or at least general questions—some of the most crucial and difficult points at which control by the center has to be exercised are the frontiers. In the first place, they have been most recently added to the empire, and, secondly, they are the most vulnerable to outside attack. Hence the administration of the empire's frontiers becomes an overwhelming problem. I can imagine only two possible ways of coping with this problem in the absence of modern communications facilities. One is in the nature of feudalism and implies that the governors of the frontier provinces are at the end of a long vassal relationship extending to the head of the state in the center. The second is the development of a bureaucracy instilled with an ideology which makes it faithful to the core of the empire. It is probably no accident that in many empires, after they had been established, attempts were made to develop all-embracing religious ideologies, such as Zoroastrianism by Darius in Persia, Buddhism by Ashoka in India, and so forth. In the absence of a religious ideology, the only other possibility I can see is what the Romans did, the instilling of an ideal of citizenship in a provincial governor as a *civis Romanus* or in the legions as *cives Romani*. As a matter of fact, with the breakdown of this ideal a religious ideology, Christianity, in a way was called into the breach.

In sum, I would like to ask whether, in the case of city, we know

184

really what we are all talking about and, in the case of empire, whether these various hypotheses help to order the available data.

LOEHR: I will try in the brief time available to sketch a rapid though pale image of China as an empire. It is chiefly a contrasting image, of course, and I start from Professor Güterbock's observation that in the ancient Near Eastern empires there was what Strzygowski called *Machtkunst*: the king impressively represented as slaying enemies or receiving tribute-bearers. In China there was no such art, no art intended to impress visitors. Even under the Shang Dynasty, when rule was in the hands of a chariot-warrior aristocracy, propagandistic imperial art was not known; nor did art expressing imperialistic pretensions appear in any later period.

In Otto Franke's *History of China* the manner of Chinese expansion is expressed in a very brief and enlightening formula. The Chinese conquered with the plow and held with the sword. Whenever members of the able Chinese mandarin bureaucracy appeared to take over as administrators or tax collectors in a new territory, a Chinese population was already resident in it, thus validating the claim that the territory was Chinese. Until very late, China fought no war of conquest. Such, indeed, were the Han Dynasty's first ventures northwest into central Asia, and later the T'ang in A.D. 648 established garrisons in the western and central parts of eastern Turkestan. But these were, on the whole, exploratory ventures on the part of the Chinese and did not actually mean conquest, nor was the penetration lasting.

The endurance of China as an empire seems to me to be related to the fact that it did not wage wars of conquest. This aspect of endurance is certainly valid in the case of China in spite of the absence of a state church or priesthood; it even had no central religious thought, except perhaps that which De Groot has formulated as universism.

KRAMER: From the discussion of empires we get the feeling that there was a Persian empire, a Hittite empire, an Assyrian empire. We also heard about an Agade empire, although that was mentioned rather softly, and about the Ur III empire we do not know. I would like to predict here, as I already have done in print, that we shall be able to demonstrate a still earlier, Sumerian, empire whose first emperor was Lugalannemundu. This view is based on an inscription which describes the size of his empire. While we have not been able to come to any conclusion as to what makes an empire, his was at least as big as the Agade empire and certainly bigger than the empire of Hammurabi. So please remember the name Lugalannemundu; I believe you will be hearing more of him during the next five or ten years.

While in principle I do not like to defend chairmen, I feel compelled to speak out for Professor Singer on the issue of "dreams of empire." It is true that economic forces, defense needs, trade relationships, and even love of war as a sport all make for empire. But there is good evidence that at least the Sumerians (of whom alone I am talking) dreamed of empire in Professor Singer's sense. The love of power and prestige and the ambition to be successful are very apparent in our evidence—available only in redactions five or six centuries later, of course, but there is no reason to assume it was invented or falsified during the interval. We have at least two epic poems in which a man says in essence: "I want to go to fight in order to subjugate the other man. He is going to build an empire; I want to subdue him." And the other man fights back because he does not want to be subdued or to lose his prestige. In another poem, which does not happen to deal with military conquest as such, the ruler says: "I am going to these places to place my name there." Could the dream of empire be clearer? Of course economic factors were involved, but the desire for full imperial power was indeed held by these people.

GIBB: I am going to jump with both feet into an area on which I have no special competence. A question was implied by Professor Cameron in relation to the Achaemenian empire: What is it in the Achaemenian empire that gives the impression that something new had appeared? As a hypothesis I suggest that there was complete freedom of trade for the first time in the Near East. In spite of the scarcity of documents, there seems to be evidence of state regulation of trade down into late Assyrian times. For example, the treaty of Esarhaddon with Tyre permitted the Tyrians to open trading stations in Assyrian possessions in Phoenicia and northern Palestine. Another example may be "the chief of the merchants" under Nebuchadnezzar, mentioned by Professor Oppenheim. Under the Achaemenids, on the contrary, so far as I know from my own reading, there was complete freedom of trade. And I suggest that the important new feature under the Achaemenids was the symbiosis of Persian government with principally Aramean trade, which gave a new sense of freedom in the whole of the Near East.

SPEISER: I would like to call attention to two paradoxes in connection with Assyria. Whatever the reason for the sporadic and partial deification of rulers in Akkad, in Ur, and elsewhere in southern Mesopotamia, such deification never became permanently established. Nevertheless, overtones of it are associated with kingship there. In Assyria, on the other hand, without a single exception the very strongest rulers, those with the very greatest concentration of power, never made any pretense to deification. Second, Assyria, even while she ruled western Asia, remained essentially parochial. And even though she made the strongest move up until that time toward a nationalistic state, she was more Babylonian than Assyrian in culture and outlook. I think that these paradoxes, while quite well known, are worth pondering about.

LANDSBERGER: Our discussion about Assyria would be quite incomplete if we failed to recognize an additional historical factor, the deep-rooted racial, ethnic, or cultural (call it what you will) difference between the Assyrians and the Babylonians. This was one of the main reasons of the sudden collapse of the Assyrian empire. To be very brief, we know that every Babylonian despised and hated the Assyrians. And the Assyrians feared the Babylonians and had to compromise with them for fear of losing everything. The first compromise was to make a superdeity named Enlil essentially a syncretism between the god Marduk of Babylon and the god Assur. This failed. The second compromise was to make Assur into a Babylonian god, Anshar. This also failed. Assyria, culturally speaking, could not conquer a cubit of Babylonia, whereas Babylonia's cultural supremacy, as Profesesor Speiser said, conquered almost the whole spirit of Assyria.

POLANYI: The early empires that we have been discussing are extremely difficult to study and to generalize about. They are very distant from us in time; we are forced to depend on fragmentary sources, and we are seldom able to obtain a really detached account of the operation of their major institutions. An interdisciplinary approach offers one means of overcoming these disadvantages.

As an example that is pertinent to our discussion of the Assyrians, we might consider the Kingdom of Dahomey in Africa. It flourished twenty-four centuries later than the Assyrian empire but was of an archaic type which justifies some comparisons. Its advantage for us is that we may view the motivations behind its expansion through the eyes of Western observers, namely, several English travelers.

Dahomey had a head who was regarded as an arbitrary ruler, and it engaged in extensive annual campaigns aimed at the capture of slaves. While it had a very effective standing army, we know from accounts of the army's origins that it was created by the king himself and had no vested interest in warfare. Schumpeter's analysis, that the army's basic interest was always to be successful but never to succeed in removing the threat of further crises which justified its existence, has little pertinence here. Nor does the promotion of trade seem to have been a factor in Dahomey's expansion; from the seizure of the coastal trading port of Waida in 1727 until the destruction of the dynasty in 1892 no king of Dahomey was sufficiently interested in trade even to visit the port. The king was, of course, questioned repeatedly by the European travelers as to his motivations in the yearly campaigns against the Yoruba to the east, and he laughed at suggestions that he conducted the campaigns in order to promote the sale of slaves. Some of the slaves were sacrificial victims at an annual ritual, while others were set to work on the plantations of the king and his major vassals. The latter even became citizens of Dahomey, and the king had no further power over them. The king, incidentally, is reported to have expressed his willingness to expand palm-oil production on the plantations by ending the sacrifices but to have indicated that he would not last a year on the throne if he dealt with his people's customs in that fashion.

My conclusion is that even if Assyria could be visited by a trained sociologist we would perhaps be just as puzzled about the character of its yearly campaigns as we are about those of Dahomey. But at least an interdisciplinary approach in this case may help to dispose of some overly simple notions about causes and motivations.

SINGER: While Professor Güterbock is collecting his thoughts to reply to the numerous questions, comments, and contributions that have been made on this last problem of empire, I shall take a minute to comment on Professor Cameron's challenge to the chair as to whether the dream of empire precedes the actual attainment of the empire. I am very grateful for the evidence that Professor Kramer has adduced. I myself am not a specialist on the ancient Near East, and I do not refer specifically to the history of the ancient Near East in my generalization; it is based on what I think is common sense, and I regard the statement as a truism.

I would like to cite ancient India in this context. In the earliest periods there was a kind of commonplace acceptance of expansionism as a normal activity which needed no special justification. In fact, it was not until the Buddhist period and the Jains that there was a doctrine of prudence which says that the sugar of persuasion should be used before the poison of force. Before that time there was even an institutionalized ritual of the horse sacrifice, the *aśva-medha,* in which a king who wanted to become ruler of the universe let one of his horses of a particular color roam over the countryside for a year. Any kingdom that the horse strayed into was thereby challenged, and the ruler of that kingdom had to submit or fight. In the end the conquering king brought back his horse and his retinue of rajas to the capital, where he sacrificed the horse, thereby becoming ruler of the universe. It was only with Ashoka, I think, that there was a remarkable reversal, with opposition to imperial expansion built around a religious doctrine. Ashoka's edict gives a wonderful expression of how he was going to replace military victory with victory based on righteousness, an empire of ideals and ideas rather than an empire based on force. I would like to read the last sentence of that edict because I do think that perhaps in this discussion we have not stressed enough the efforts to mitigate and oppose imperial expansion. "I have had this inscription of righteousness engraved that all my sons and grandsons may not seek to gain new victories, that in whatever victories they may gain they may prefer forgiveness and light punishment, that they may consider the only valid victory the victory of righteousness which is of value both in this world and the next, and that all their pleasure may be in righteousness."

GÜTERBOCK: I can be very brief because it seems to me that there is hardly anything I can add. I did not come before you with a set thesis but tried merely to invite comments and to raise questions. Now I can only express my gratitude to all those who contributed to the discussion by bringing up new viewpoints or elaborating on features that I omitted or only sketched. Dr. Hoselitz reminds us of the necessity of defining what we mean by city and by empire. I must confess that neither of these terms was too clear in my mind when I came here, and, after all the discussion, they are not much clearer to me than they were. I think we all would do well to devote some further thought to them. Finally, I should add that I am very much afraid that Professor Polanyi is right: we would be just as puzzled as we are now if we could talk to the ancients themselves. Thank you.

SINGER: I now turn the chair over to Professor Braidwood, who will take charge of the discussion dealing with the Greek and Roman periods.

THE GREEK AND ROMAN ORIENT

BRAIDWOOD (*chairman*): I do not intend to make a long introduction. I merely want to suggest that it may be symbolic of the Oriental Institute's consciousness of the relevance of its scholarly work for the modern world that its Director and the organizer of this symposium invites us to think about the impact of the cultural tradition of the West upon the older tradition of the ancient Orient. Mr. Kraeling.

KRAELING: Mr. Chairman, ladies and gentlemen: In the cultural history of the Near East, the thousand years that begin with Alexander's victory over Darius in the battle of Gaugemala in 331 B.C. and extend to the Islamic conquest represent a separable and in some respects a separate period. As things stood in the days of the last Achaemeneans, the Orient was still paying homage to the remains of an indigenous "great tradition" that survived in an ossified, if locally differentiated, form under a system of government concerned with its preservation for practical reasons but apparently unable to stimulate its further development. The advent of the Greeks marks the entrance into the Orient of a manifestly different and strongly individual cultural tradition that had already reached a classical formulation in the city-states of the Aegean area but that was proving capable of restatement in new and more comprehensive terms as it adapted itself to an imperial frame of reference. During the long period of its impingement upon the Orient, through a generation of soldiers of fortune, through a succession of Hellenistic dynasties, through Roman generals, merchants, and governors, and through Byzantine bureaucrats and *religiosi,* this extraneous tradition had a partly stimulating but always significant effect upon the cultural life of the Near East. Some of the aspects of this effect I shall try to develop in the brief time allotted to me.

Outwardly the Greek and Roman periods in the history of the Near East have many of the earmarks of colonialism, ancient and modern, and parallels from the later and the contemporary history of the Far, the Middle, and the Near East come readily to mind. But one aspect of the development gave it a particular character, serving both to ameliorate the effects of its colonialism and to intensify its cultural potential. This is the fact that it brought with it and worked through the growth and proliferation of cities. Not since the period of the national city-states in Sumerian times had cities (plural!) played so important a role in the cultural life of the Orient. The effect of the development that since those days had led to the pre-eminence of capital cities (Babylon, Assur, Nineveh) was by no means canceled out, for new metropolitan centers arose to take their place—Alexandria in Egypt, Antioch on the Orontes, and Seleucia on the Tigris. But alongside them hundreds of cities of moderate size came to exist as semi-autonomous entities throughout the length and breadth of the Hellenistic and Roman Orient. The remains of many of these lie deeply buried under their Turkish and modern successors and will probably never be exhumed. Those of others have been so pulled about in millenniums of political and military conflict that their form could not be established even if excavation were possible. But others have been resurrected by the spade of the archeologist, and the bones of still others are exposed for the venturesome traveler to see in remote areas thinly populated since the Islamic conquest.

That in the thousand years between Alexander and Muḥammad the cultural development of the Near East was so closely bound up with urbanization is the result not of chance and only partly of inherited establishments. Instead it is largely the result of program and of the nature of the new forces making themselves felt in the area.

Tradition has it that Alexander chose to plant Greek cities in the Orient as a means of Hellenizing the barbarians and credits him with the founding of no less than seventy-five cities. That the cultural purpose suggested was actually dominant in his case is questionable because many of Alexander's foundations were originally simple military establishments along the roads of communication with the far reaches of the empire he had carved out. Moreover, that every city that claimed Alexander as its founder had actual justification for this claim is naturally too good to be true. But it is inherently probable that in the lifetime of Alexander there were founded or re-founded in the Near East as settlements for colonists, for the retirement of veterans, for security and commercial purposes not less than twenty-five cities spread over the area between Alexandria on the Nile in the west to Alexandria on the Indus in the east. As a group they outline the vast pattern which subsequent foundations served to fill in, at least in the region west of the Tigris.

In the centuries after Alexander the urbanization of the Near East, so far as it is programmatic, divides itself into four periods. The first is that of the Diadochoi down through Antiochus IV and Ptolemy III, a period in which the palm belongs by all odds to the Seleucids, who were actually responsible for founding most of the seventy-five cities that are credited to Alexander. When the Egyptian control of the Aegean disintegrated upon the death of Ptolemy III and there was no further occasion for the planting of new Ptolemaic colonies outside Egypt, the role of Egypt in the urbanization of the Orient ended. Elsewhere in the second period, that is, in the centuries from Antiochus IV to the beginning of our era, urbanization continued, taking a different form and proceeding under the aegis of local dynasts such as the Pergamenes and the Commagenians in Asia, the Characenians and the Osrhoenians in Mesopotamia. Subsequently Roman generals and triumvirs and vassal kings like those of Homs, Emesa, and Ituria in mid-Syria and the Herodians of Palestine took a hand in the development. What is involved here is, of course, sometimes no more than the "modernization" of traditional cities, but examples of new foundations are not uncommon, for instance in Palestine. In the reign of Augustus, however, and particularly in the period from the Flavian to the Severan emperors, imperial policy again made a point of encouraging urbanism in the Near East, and the results were imposing. To this third period in the urbanization of the Orient there was a sequel in the centuries from Diocletian through Justinian, but its creations had a different character and function and, of course, a briefer life span.

The urbanization of the Near East in the thousand years that began with Alexander the Great was a multiform rather than a uniform development, but it had a clearly definable impulse behind it and worked itself out along recognizable lines. The impulse stemmed from the importance and the meaning that the institutions denoted by the words *polis* and *astu,* both of which we translate "city," had come to have for the Greeks in the centuries before Alexander. The former denotes that form of democratic government that the Greeks had developed, in which the free recognized members of regional and tribal groups expressed and administered their sovereignty under sanction of constitution and law and to which, in theory at least, the Greek man devoted virtually his entire life. The word *astu* had by Alexander's time developed the connotation of an urban establishment planned and purposefully developed to serve as the instrument for the life of the democratic community, with public buildings such as markets, council houses, gymnasia, stadia, theaters, and temples provided by the action of the community or of its members for the welfare of the group. When, in the period that begins with Alexander the Great, Greek veterans and colonists were settled in the Orient it was only natural that they should feel impelled to create for themselves there the institutions and installations of city life normative for their life in the old homeland. When the flow of Greek colonists ceased and Roman governors and emperors took over, basically the same purpose was still being served, namely the creation of communities with some responsibility for the administration of their own internal affairs and with some rights and privileges accorded by the central government in connection with the assumption of that responsibility. Only in the period that begins with Diocletian did the role and the foundation of cities begin to serve primarily the purposes of the central government.

What we know best about these Hellenistic and Roman cities of the Near East is their physical form. The cities built or rebuilt there in Greek and Roman times were planned cities, responding in whole or in part to the patterns that had been developed in the Greek world by architects since Hippodamos and that had been modified in the Roman West, supposedly in accordance with the layout of the Roman *castra*. There had of course been a certain amount of planning in the older cities of the Near East. We see it in the organization of ancient temple and palace precincts and in the provision made for the residence of administrative personnel at ancient Babylon; we see it again at Tell al-ʿAmarnah in the city of Akhnaton; we see it also in the Solomonic and succeeding levels at Megiddo. But basically the older Near Eastern city was organized, like the older acropolis city of the Aegean, with special provision only for the house of the god and the palace of the king and with no provision for the rank and file of the inhabitants except the girdle of city walls that protected the population of commoners that was necessary to the service and supply of the established order. By contrast, the Greek and Roman cities of the Near East were laid out in a regular gridiron of streets or along intersecting axial thoroughfares, with a public market place in an important central location where the commercial and the administrative life of the community had its focus. Included in the development of the plan were the meeting house of the "council," the stadia and later the hoppodromes and amphitheaters for sport and physical exercise, the theaters for competitions in the lyric and dramatic arts and for popular assemblies, and the shrines of special tutelary deities. Cities so organized and especially the public buildings and the installations for street drainage and for public water supply were new in the Near East, betokening a different way of life, a different conception of society, and ultimately a different conception of the world and man's place in it.

As to how these cities were administered and who participated in and benefited from their thriving life, we are less well informed. Located as they were within the confines first of Hellenistic empires, then sometimes of smaller free, federated, or vassal kingdoms, and finally of provinces of the Roman and Byzantine empires, they never had the autonomy of the Greek city-states. But, to the extent that they were at the outset not merely military posts on the frontiers or on the major arteries of communication, they commonly had a charter or a constitution and a *chora* or territory set apart from the *ager regius* and parceled out in whole or in part among the enrolled citizens. With the constitution went a degree of independence in the administration of internal affairs and in the payment of taxes and other *privilegia,* particularly when in Roman times some of the cities were given the rank of *municipia* and *coloniae.* At first, of course, the only ones to participate in and benefit from the life of the community were the Greek colonists, and indeed there never was a period in the history of the Hellenistic and Roman Orient when all inhabitants of a given city had some rights or privileges just by virtue of their residence there. It is interesting to note, however, how the number of local, particularly Semitic, names in dedicatory inscriptions and in private documents increases as time goes on. Through intermarriage of Greeks and Orientals, through the rise of a new mercantile class, and in many other ways the citizenry of the cities came to be recruited in even larger measure from the native population. Here an important change is manifesting itself in the life of the expanding Near Eastern society. The individual emerges on the scene as a responsible person, functioning now as a member of a semi-autonomous community and participating with other persons in determining a course of action for himself and with his associates. If we recall the sharp cleavage which the earlier stages in the cultural development of the Near East had gradually brought about in the social order, it will be obvious how radical a change the developments of the Hellenistic and Roman periods ushered in. The change, it cannot be repeated too often, was not uniform or equally shared by all, but it was at least available to many and enjoyed by not a few, and its effects can be traced in many aspects of life. Only in the light of this change can we understand what it meant for Orientals to immortalize themselves as individuals in the inscriptions that testify to their service in public office and their private contributions to the erection and maintenance of public buildings. This was a form of self-realization previously unthinkable except for members of the royal court and their highest administrative assistants and representatives. The pattern changed long before the end of the period in question here, when local public office became a burden imposed upon citizens by the state as a means of discharging duties no longer within the financial competence of either the cities or the central government. But by that time much of the light of Near Eastern culture had been dimmed and formed merely a reflection of the culture of the new capital of the eastern Roman Empire at Constantinople.

I do not wish to create the impression that the Greeks and Romans remade the Orient entirely or that the same influences remained at work everywhere throughout the entire thousand years. The myriads of agricultural villages and towns remained approximately as they had been for millenniums; the fortunes, the aspirations, and the horizons of their inhabitants were probably quite the same when the control of the villages rested in the hands of those who administered the older satrapies and the royal or temple estates as when they formed part of the *ager regius* or even of the *ager privatus* of the city territory. Some areas, moreover, especially the vast territory between the Zagros Mountains of western Iran and the Indus River, were cut off from the Seleucid Empire at an early date, so that the early impact of Hellenism upon them as represented by the Greco-Bactrian coins and its echo in the Ghandara sculptures of the Roman period did not long continue. In Egypt a local tradition strongly intrenched in the upper Nile Valley provided a screen that filtered out much of the Hellenizing influence. Elsewhere cities of hoary antiquity remained relatively unaffected by the new democratic institutions and the new building programs. Some of them, indeed, were "refounded," as the "styles" on their coins and the eras used in the building inscriptions indicate, but sometimes the changes did not stick; in other instances new and old settlements existed side by side, with the relative importance of the old and the new shifting as time went on.

But it is time to turn from the urbanization of the Near East in Greek and Roman times to its significance in the cultural sphere. Actually the effect of Hellenism on those parts of the Orient that were exposed to it over long intervals of time were not either universal, that is, thoroughgoing, or even universally positive. Many portions of the cultural spectrum remained relatively unaffected, it being the policy or the tendency of the new regional or imperial governments to preserve the traditions and the customs of the past. What had been Achaemenean policy in this particular was continued as the policy of the Diadochoi and their successors. There were also sharply negative reactions to Hellenistic influence and ideals, particularly in the sphere of religion and on the part of men of religious persuasion. We know how violent was the reaction of pious Jews in the Maccabean period against the Antiochene citizenship that had been bestowed upon certain of the more liberal inhabitants of Jerusalem and against the construction of a gymnasium there, where "advanced" young Jews disported themselves in the nude in the time of the high priest Jason (174–171 B.C.). We know how the pious Jews reacted to the construction enterprise of Herod the Great at Jerusalem and Samaria and to such works as the creation of the city of Tiberias by Herod Antipas. It is interesting to note that the Hellenized cities of Palestine, such as Tiberias, Sepphoris, Bethsaida-Julias, Gadara, Samaria, Caesarea, Livias, known to us from the records of Josephus, play no part in the Gospels as scenes in the life of Jesus. The inference is that the "boom towns'" with the "advanced" communities were not friendly to the prophetic teaching of Jesus. Indeed, some of them, for example Bethsaida, appear among those over which "woes" were spoken by him. This negative reaction to the new cities was only natural, for between the old-type cities and hamlets and the new-style cities there was a fundamental difference. The agricultural villags and the old cities, which provided little more than crowded shelter for the ordinary inhabitant, reflect the traditional Oriental and prophetic conception that "man is as grass and as the flower of grass." The Hellenized city and its culture reflect a train of thought that begins with the idea that this is the best of all worlds, that counts on the permanence of the world, and that regards it as both the desire and the duty of man to use his reason to achieve here and now a life devoted to and expressive of the highest good. It is obvious that this hither-worldly ideal and the prophetic ideal of the Orient should clash.

Judaism and Christianity continued for some centuries to reflect a hostility to many of the institutions of the new urbanism. We know that the rabbis had scruples about using the public baths of the new cities because of the nudity and because of the presence of statues of

Aphrodite. We have passages in the *Babylonian Talmud* that condemn the stadia, the theaters, the circus, and the "seat of the scornful," and we even have in *Midrash Rabbah* passages that describe what must have been comedy acts in the local theaters in which pagans poked fun at Jewish customs. Similarly we know that up to the days of Constantine the Christian apologists inveighed against the spectacles and the mimes. Eventually the antithesis softened, especially among the Christians, and at the end, when the circus factions of the Greens and the Blues became synonymous in the Near East with the Monophysites and the Orthodox, the adherents on either side could enjoy the satisfaction of supporting their religious belief by cheering their own charioteers and engaging in wholesale brawls with those of the opposition.

It is clear that the dominant trend in the cultural development in the Near East during the Greek and Roman periods was that of a continuous synthesizing of eastern and western traditions. To determine this major aspect of the development fully, we would have to take each facet or aspect of the total cultural inventory and examine it, if that were possible, in order to ascertain how much it owes to the indigenous and to the extraneous traditions and what fusions or new combinations appear in it. It is obvious that no one individual can claim mastery over all these facets, and I certainly would not do so. Perhaps Professor Welles would be willing to say something about law in the Hellenistic and Roman Near East—to what extent it was indigenous, to what extent it was traditionally Greek or specifically Rhodian, and to what extent it was invented to fit new circumstances. Perhaps Miss Perkins would give us some idea of the development of art and describe its component elements—Greek, Iranian, and Semitic—in the several regions and show what came of the art tradition as time went on. Perhaps Professor Brown would be willing to say something about the rise of the Parthians and the Iranian component in the cultural syncretism. Perhaps Professor Albright would comment on the developments in the field of religion as seen from the angle of the Dead Sea Scrolls. All this would help enlarge the picture. I would like to limit myself to one particular topic—literature, literacy, and learning in the Hellenistic and Roman Orient—which seems germane to the subject introduced by Professor Landsberger in the fourth session.

Seen in relation to the earlier cultural history of the Near East, the development of learning, literary production, and literacy in the thousand years that begin with Alexander the Great has its own special characteristics. Of fundamental importance for this development are, of course, such formal and material factors as the use everywhere of alphabetic writing and the availability everywhere of the convenient parchment and the somewhat cheaper papyrus as writing materials. More important are the influx and creation of new modes and forms of literary expression and, above all, the spread of the desire to record or express things in writing. The amazing growth and spread of this desire, which seems to reach its maximum in the centuries immediately following the beginning of our era, has no counterpart in the cultural life of the ancient Orient. It can scarcely be explained save as the result ultimately of an intellectual awakening in which the Greek conception of education and of the proper function of the individual as a responsible member of a community plays an important part.

In its broadest outlines the history of literary production and consumption in the Near East during the millennium that begins with Alexander can be divided into four parts. Beginning largely with the importation of a foreign cultural tradition as to both form and substance of the materials, the development next reflects the growing participation of those born in the Near East, then the growing strength of the Oriental component and viewpoint in a large part of the product, and finally a return to a restricted and severely localized manner of cultivation that recalls conditions as they were in the pre-Hellenistic period. In this as in so many other spheres of cultural development we begin with an energy-releasing impulse, move on to a vivid syncretism, and gradually return to something outwardly like the *status quo ante.*

The first stage in this development owes no little to the patronage of the Hellenistic monarchs who after Alexander's death divided up the Orient among themselves. Of prime importance is Ptolemy Philadelphus, whose creation at Alexandria of the great library and research center in the Museion is too well known to require further comment. It is a commonplace also that in the Hellenistic period, and except for the New Comedy and for speculative and moral philosophy, the center of Greek learning and literature moved from Athens to Alexandria, with secondary overseas hearths at Pergamum and Rhodes. The commonplace expresses properly the fact that what happened at Alexandria was that Greek scholars imported from Greek areas continued a Greek tradition. Of course the products were not the same. Poetry under the tutelage of Philetas of Cos launched out into new fields in the bucolic idylls of Theocritus and the hymns, elegies, and epigrams of Callimachus and ultimately, seeking an outlet to the wider public, turned more and more to the trivial, the genre piece and the erotic. Historiography adopted peripatetic strictures in the memoirs of Ptolemy Soter and Demetrius of Phaleron or indulged in the romantic extravaganzas of pseudo-Callisthenes. Philosophy turned from the speculative to the descriptive, the exact, and the physical sciences, as the names of Eratosthenes, Euclid, Hermophilus, and Erisistrades indicate, and philology and literary criticism began, particularly at the level of establishing acceptable texts of older authors. But save occasionally for the subject matter and the changed outward circumstances, everything was a logical development from what had gone before elsewhere.

Antioch on the Orontes, the more westerly of the capitals of the Seleucid Empire, became the center of a similar though much smaller and less influential group of writers. Seleucus I is said to have established there the library of Pisistratus that had been taken from Athens by Xerxes and to have set the pattern for his successors by inviting men of letters to his court. The names of the poet Aratos, who was there temporarily, Megasthenes the famous geographer, Patrocles and Demodamus, the poets Euphonor and Hegesianax, and the historian Mnesiptolemos are associated with the history of Seleucid Antioch down to Antiochus III.

The pattern that was thus created, of individual scholars and creative writers working in the Greek cultural centers of the Near East to the further development of Greek literature, philosophy, and science, continued to be a feature of Near Eastern cultural history until late in the period with which we are concerned. This the mere mention of such names as Meleager and Libanius of Antioch and Ptolemy the Geographer, Plotinus, and Hypatia of Alexandria will serve to show. And with production the attention paid by readers to classical and later literature kept pace. It is as natural, no matter how surprising it may be to us, that Oxyrhynchus should yield fragments not only of epics and Menander but also of Aeschylus and Pindar as that the Parthian king Orodes should have been viewing a scene from Euripides in Armenia when Crassus' head was brought to him and that Virgil was being read in the Wilderness of Zin in the Byzantine period.

But as time went on there came to exist alongside this aspect of the literary development, as an enhancing and enriching factor of the Near Eastern milieu, an aspect that shows the increasing participation of those who were born in the Near East, no matter whether of Greek or mixed or Oriental parentage, and the widening geographical distribution of literary production. It is true that many of the most promising and most talented thinkers and writers who were reared in the Orient left it to make their mark in the Western world, quite as the "bright young men" of the contemporary United States are drawn from the local scene to populate the offices of Madison Avenue, New York. But it is surprising how much talent remained, even though by and large what has been preserved is little more than lists of names and fragments of lost works.

Berossos in Babylonia and Manetho in Egypt were the distant forerunners of this second stage in the literary development, and their concern with their own local traditions was unusual and due to special circumstances. Generally speaking the second stage in the development belongs to the period of the decline and inner deterioration of the Hellenistic dynasties of Alexandria and Antioch. It is interesting in this connection to note that the excavations of Susa in remote Elymais have recently produced two metrical Greek epigrams of the first century B.C. and a hymn to Apollo from the first century of our era. More imposing is Tarn's compilation of the names of persons and places associated with literary production in lower Mesopotamia beginning with the Parthian period.[2] The list includes Archedemus, the pupil of the "Babylonian" Diogenes who returned from studies at Athens to found a school of Stoic philosophy in his own and his teacher's homeland, the astronomer Seleucus of Seleucia on the Erythrian Sea, Apollodorus of Artemita (near modern Baquba), who wrote a history of Parthia, the unknown writers who served as sources for Trogus and for Plutarch's life of Crassus, and the familiar geographer Isidor of Charax. Franz Cumont has made a similar compilation of what is known about writers and literary production in early Roman Syria.[3] The list includes Archias of Antioch, who wrote epics, the Platonist Antiochus of Ascalon, Nicolaos of Damascus, the historian and biographer of Herod, the Pythagorean Nicomachus of Gerasa, and Jamblichus, the author of a *Babyloniaca*. To these we may add a group of writers in Egypt and Palestine about whom we learn chiefly from the fragments preserved by Eu-

2 W. W. Tarn, *The Greeks in Bactria and India* (2d ed.; Cambridge, 1951) pp. 41–44.
3 *Cambridge Ancient History* XI (1936) 639–43.

sebius of Caesarea. They include the Demetrius and Eupolemos who wrote in Greek on the history of the Jews, the author of a five-volume work on the history of the Jewish revolt, used as a source for II Maccabees (presumably Jason of Cyrene), the Elder Philo and one Theodotus who wrote epics on Jerusalem and the Jews, the dramatist Ezekiel, who wrote on the Exile, and the historian pseudo-Hecataeus. Most of these writers were of Greek descent, though born in the Near East, and all concerned themselves with the application of Greek literary form to the materials of their choice. We are dealing, therefore, with a secondary development in the cultural and literary history of the Near East that stems from the circles established at Alexandria and Antioch by the patronage of the early Hellenistic monarchs and that shows the impact of the cultural tradition upon the more remote areas and a growing preoccupation with local materials and events.

In the third stage of the development we see, against an ever widening geographical background, the use of the written document by natives of the Near East for the expression and promotion of thoughts and beliefs that were essentially their own. Here traditional Greek literary form begins to lose its importance and here the substance of what is conveyed records the result of a process of cultural syncretism. Much of the literature produced belongs to the sphere of religion. This is only natural because it was in the sphere of religion that the destruction of the old political and national boundaries and the importation of Greek speculative philosophy were making their strongest impact and leading to ever more notable developments.

For the antecedents of this type of literary production we have to go back to such writers as the Artapanus who sought to combine Jewish and Egyptian religious tradition. More familiar, of course, are Philo Judaeus and his predecessor Aristobulos, who allegorized the Pentateuch. The whole development has been high-lighted recently by the discovery of the Dead Sea Scrolls, representing the literature of the Essene sect. Here we see another type of syncretism manifesting itself, and we have in the size of the library and in the physical remains of the scriptorium witnesses to the extent of the use of written documents for religious purposes. The fact that the languages are Hebrew and Aramaic does not affect the basic significance of the discovery as a testimony to the importance of the production and widespread use of the written religious literature. Seen in the light of the literary production of the Essenes, the creation of an early Christian religious literature appears in a new light and seems an altogether natural development.

But we must not tarry too long with these more or less syncretistic products of Palestine. In Egypt comparable phenomena are the corpus of Hermetic writings and at a later date, probably first in the Syrian area, the collection known as the "Chaldean Oracles." Between the two in time lies the whole development of the vast Gnostic literature. Most of this material was long thought to have been irretrievably lost owing to the opposition of the growing Christian church. We knew only the Simonian *Apophasis Megale* and the Ophite *Naasene Document,* both quoted extensively by Hippolytus. To them we could add catalogues of the book titles listed by the antiheretical church fathers, representing the literature of the Basilideans and of the Valentinians, and what could be learned about documents like the "Fundamental Epistle" of Mani from the quotations of Augustine. Now the picture has changed radically, and large bodies of such Gnostic writings are being brought to light. A vast quantity of Manichean writings has been revealed in Coptic and Sogdian and Vigurian texts during the lifetime of the present generation, and now we are beginning to know also from Egypt the large Valentinian literature.

All this material, to which the name "Gnostic" properly applies, pays homage to the Greek ideal of "knowledge" and reflects the loosening of traditional religious ties under the impact of an intrusive nivellizing cultural force, quite as it reflects also the Greek interest in speculative thought, the use of the Greek allegorical method of interpretation, and the Greek's insistence upon personal choice and conviction. Yet it operates with traditional Oriental materials, both mythological and magical, and is obviously syncretistic. These massive religious literatures—Gnostic, Essene, and Christian—represent a new phenomenon in the cultural and religious history of the Near East in that they brought the religious texts out of the temple archives and put them into the private houses where the conventicles met. The manuscript material was intended for and actually reached a vast reading public, as we know from the spread of the sects themselves and from the fact that the format used was that of the papyrus codex, which was in effect the counterpart of the modern "paperback."

The fourth and last phase in the production and use of written materials brings us closer to what we would be inclined to call "learning." It expresses itself in the appearance and workings of what can be called "schools" or "academies." Whether the basic conception underlying this development is Greek and reflects the schools of philosophy that sprang up first at Athens, whether it derives from the practices of the late Oriental *sopherim,* or whether it institutionalizes the figure of the wandering teacher and holy man of Hellenistic times that Lucian satirized in his *Peregrinus Proteus* is difficult to say; perhaps the roots are multiple and different in different areas.

Perhaps the earliest forerunners of such schools or academies are to be found in the circles that gathered around Johanan ben Zakkai, Gamaliel II at Jabneh, and Akiba at Lydda in Palestine. However this may be, there ultimately developed in Palestine at Tiberias a continuing circle of rabbinical scholars which under Judah ha-Nasi in the second century produced the great codification of Jewish religious practice that we know as the *Mishnah.* In the third century we witness the development of an analogous group of schools or academies in lower Mesopotamia under Rab and Samuel at Sura and Nehardea. Out of these and their successors came eventually in the fifth century of our era the massive *Babylonian Talmud.*

Meanwhile, closer to the Mediterranean, other schools more Western in orientation began to appear upon the scene. Familiar to all of us is the school of Alexandria that fostered and produced in the work of Ammonius Saccas and of Plotinus the last great formulation of Greek philosophy. Less familiar, perhaps, is that school of law that comes into view in the second century at Beirut and that Justinian characterized as the *nutrix legum.* Less familiar also is the school of rhetoric that developed at Gaza, that eventually produced Procopius, Choricius of Gaza, and Zacharias Scholasticus and that survived as one of the last outposts of classical learning in the Near East.

To these Jewish and classical academies of the Near East we need to add finally the Christian schools that grew up in the same region. The earliest is the Catechetical School of Alexandria, to which Pantaenus, Clement of Alexandria, and Origen belonged. An offshoot of the Catechetical School of Alexandria was founded by Origen at Caesarea in Palestine and was led by men like Pamphilius and Eusebius of Caesarea. Farther to the north, at Antioch on the Orontes, there soon appeared the Lucianic School, which had such profound influence upon the exegesis and the textual criticism of the Bible and upon theology through men like Paul of Samosata and Eusebius of Emesa. In its later history, after A.D. 360, it became more Alexandrine in its orientation and contributed to the development of orthodox theology through such men as Diodor of Tarsus, Theodore of Mopsuestia, and Chrysostom, who had been trained there. Farther inland, in what was then a part of Syria, a school with a more regional orientation began to emerge in the third century; associated with it in its earlier period was the name of Bardesanes, who wrestled with the problem of finding Syriac equivalents for the terminology of Greek speculative philosophy, and in its later period the name of Rabbula, who established the text of the Peshitta. Through Ephraem Syrus there came into being at Edessa in the fourth century the "School of the Persians" that eventually moved to Nisibis and through Narsai became, after the Council of Ephesus in A.D. 431, the theological center of the Nestorian form of Christianity that spread into distant China and maintained itself in inner Asia until late in the Middle Ages. In these schools of Edessa and Nisibis lies the fountainhead for the massive Syriac theological literature that forms the counterpart to what appears in the *Patrologia Graeca.*

As we move father and farther along in the period that saw these schools flourish, learning and the production and use of written literary materials become ever narrower in their content and ever more closely restricted in their application. Thus the great impetus that was originally given by the Greek cultural tradition to the intellectual life of the Orient through the importation of Greek scholars lost its liberating effect, its impact on large numbers of people in all walks of life, and its ability to create new syntheses of inherited traditions and acquired viewpoints. It survives eventually only as the force that serves to keep alive a new traditional theology in and through a new priestly class. Typologically things have returned at this point and in this sphere to the patterns of the earlier millenniums in the history of the ancient Orient.

And what about the cities of the Hellenistic and Roman Orient? The rise of Sasanian power in Iran and the restiveness of the tribes along the desert frontier of Arabia brought to an end the era of stability and wrought havoc as far west as Antioch on the Orontes. This and the critical involvement of the Roman Empire first on the Danubian and later on the Rhine frontier dealt severe blows to the economic life of the Near East. From the days of the Tetrarchy on the Empire used the cities as the media for the exercise of its control over the region, thus reducing them to the status of cogs in the machine of central government. Emperors like Anastasius and Justinian did what they could to repair the physical installations of cities laid in ruins by earthquakes or deteriorating with age. But the policy of requiring wealthier citizens to assume responsibility for what remained of the local self-government and to pay themselves the administrative expenses involved only led to the pauperization of what remained of the citizen group and caused its members to seek to escape into the farming communities or into the service of the central government or into the church. Thus there ultimately remained in the cities as a powerful local force only the church and its bishops. At the end of the story the bishops are the ones who repair the cities' walls, who rally its defenders, and who provide on church property the counterpart of the older city baths. With the Islamic conquest the power of the church also comes to an end, and a new pattern in the relation of urbanization and cultural development begins slowly to emerge. But this belongs to another phase in the long cultural history of the Near East.

BRAIDWOOD: Ladies and gentlemen: At this seventh and final session of the symposium I propose to organize the discussion by first calling upon the four members from whom Mr. Kraeling solicited remarks in his introduction and then throwing the subject open for comment by others. We will therefore now hear from Mr. Brown, Miss Perkins, Mr. Welles, and Mr. Albright in that order.

BROWN: Mr. Chairman: I would like to begin with some general observations which arise out of the very stimulating educational experience that we all have had while sitting here these last few days and out of Mr. Kraeling's presentation, which was in some sense the crown of that experience. We have been discussing the development of culture in the ancient Near East, and our terms of reference have been the social units—villages, cities, and empires—that we have conceived of as the generating agencies. W have attempted to define the kind and quality of the culture generated by these units, using those aspects that were most available to us and that we felt were most characteristic. I regret in this connection particularly the absence of Mr. von Simson, whose commitments elsewhere have robbed us of the voice of the history of art, for I believe we would all agree that in works of art the essence of a culture is distilled in greatest purity and refinement.

Looking back over what we have said and heard I wonder whether, if we were to approach the study of culture from the point of view of the study of its works of art, we might not find some of the perplexities that have confronted us readily resolved. I wonder, for instance, whether the difficulty that we encountered in trying to define the nature of a city or of an empire might not be resolved if we said simply that a city is what produces a high culture and an empire is what produces imperial art? I wonder further whether looking at things from the same point of view would not resolve still other problems that we have encountered, such as that of the reality to which a given culture trait corresponds. The value of a work of art is intrinsic; it is not conditioned. We do not need to inquire concerning the audience for which a work of art was intended. The artistic quality of an Egyptian tomb painting is the same, as is its value as a witness to the Egyptian culture of its period, whether or not it could be seen by anybody. Similarly, the literary quality of the Gilgamesh epic and its value as an index of Sumerian culture are the same whether or not anybody but its author read it in antiquity. A work of art cannot lie about the cultural value which it embodies. Its value is not only intrinsic, it is explicit. Hence it is quite useless to inquire what it was about the ancient empires of the Near East that made their cultures imperial.

More important, it would seem to me, is a phenomenon that manifests itself in the broader reaches of the Orient in the second of the divisions that Carl Kraeling made in his presentation of the Greek and Roman Orient, from the time of Antiochus IV to that of Pompey. Although from one point of view this period seems less intensely creative and less significant than that of the first flourishing of Hellenism in the newly conquered world and less vivid than that of Roman imperial domination, I think that seen from another point of view it was most significant indeed. The period witnessed the creation of a political frontier between the reduced Seleucid Empire and its successor the Roman Empire, on the one hand, and the inner Orient, on the other. The period was also in some particulars a turning point in cultural development. In this period and in the area between this new frontier and the older one that coincided roughly with the fringes of the Mediterranean we can study Hellenism—the impact of Western culture upon the Near East—in a purer form, so to speak, than on the other side of the line. The range and the nature of the cultural experience in this area were more comprehensively and continuously related to the West than they were farther inland. But we must not suppose that the area beyond the new frontier was barren of its own developments. Indeed, it would seem that precisely at this time new impulses were generated there that in effect made the period beginning with Antiochus IV a watershed between two types of cultural development. For when Oriental empires—Parthian and Sasanian—began to emerge again east of the new frontier they in some mysterious way generated a whole new series of cultural and specifically artistic forms. These are not the traditional forms of the ancient Oriental cultures, nor are they the traditional Greek forms, or any simple modification of the one or the other. These new forms were sufficiently potent to endure down through the centuries with which we are concerned here, down through the Islamic period, and practically down to modern times, so that the Parthian palaces of Hatra or Assur have more in common with the Taj Mahal than with either their Mesopotamian predecessors or their Greek counterparts.

I would suggest that the profound changes in sensibility and in the formal expression of artistic values on the far side of the eastern frontier beginning in Parthian times must have been due to the yeast of Hellenism, and I would therefore find here another example of the third type of interaction between East and West to which Carl Kraeling called attention—that of the creative synthesis of old and new.

PERKINS: Professor Kraeling has asked me to comment on the art of the Greek and Roman Orient, which covers a sizable area and a sizable period of time. So I shall speak on only one aspect of it, following the lead of my colleague Professor Brown, who has already begun the discussion. Professor Kraeling himself provided us yesterday with this one main point when he spoke of the mixture of influences that were visible in the Near East in the Hellenistic and Roman periods. In art particularly, as Professor Brown has said, these influences come together in a very sensitive and creative way, and there is a blending of four strains. In the first place, there are the old indigenous traditions which Professor Kraeling has loosely and in my judgment improperly spoken of as "Semitic art"; I believe with Professor Gelb that "Semitic" is a linguistic term and that it has no relevance in any other context. In the Near East before the Hellenistic and Roman periods there existed two major foci and traditions of art, namely that of Egypt and that of the great Achaemenean-Persian empire; the latter had borrowed from Greece, had borrowed from Assyria, had borrowed from Babylonia and had made a synthesis of its own. To my mind, neither of these "great traditions" had become rigid and ossified, although some of my colleagues think so. In any event, they existed. Then came the new impact of Hellenism, with Alexander's conquest. It was, of course, not the beginning of Hellenism in this area. That had occurred several centuries earlier in Persia particularly, but also in other areas. Later on there was some impact of Roman art in the period of Roman imperial expansion, but, as Professor Brown has said, there was not so much of it and it covered a much more restricted area. Hellenistic cities were founded in Bactria and as far away as India; Roman influence did not reach very far east of the Euphrates—Professor Brown's frontier. But the Roman influence cannot be completely discounted, and then, of course, came the new Near Eastern arts to which Professor Brown also has alluded, the Parthian and Sasanian arts, most noticeable to us in architecture but visible in other forms of expression also. Since Professor Brown has already mentioned architecture, I will consider sculpture and painting.

In the Near East we find at this time some very interesting products of artistic eclecticism, or syncretism if you will, which show western—mainly Hellenistic—and eastern influences. These products come particularly from the Parthian period, and we will not be far from right if we say that they show a Hellenistic influence and a Parthian influence. The two major groups of known sculptures of this time are, of course, those of Palmyra and those of Commagene, most noticeable at the site of Nimrud Dagh. In both cases, particularly at Palmyra, there are very interesting indications of influence from the east. One such indication is in the area of style; frontality appears for the first time in the Near East. I should perhaps digress to say that people have commonly spoken of frontality as something inherited from the art of the more ancient Near East. This is not correct if we use the term in the only way that makes sense, namely to refer to the fully frontal presentation of a figure. The Khorsabad bull, which we see behind us here in the Oriental Institute Museum, is not an example of frontality. We see its face from the front, but we do not see its body from the front. Entire human bodies seen from the front, without change of aspect, do not become a typical feature of Oriental art until the Parthian period. They do not come out of the Western tradition, and we can, I think, only assume—although we are here arguing from silence—that this frontality was developed in Parthia and spread from there to the west. It is very striking, of course, in the Palmyrene sculptures. The second indication of eastern influence is a somewhat simpler iconographic element, namely that the gentlemen are shown wearing trousers. This feature is, of course, not a western tradition, nor is it universally eastern. It seems to have begun in Achaemenean times, but it is particularly associated with Parthian art. I would call your attention to the very high level of technical and artistic achievement revealed by most of the sculptures from Palmyra, Hatra, and Commagene. The sculptors knew how to cut stone, knew how to model, and were at the same time combining different artistic traditions in a very interesting way.

Of Roman sculpture there is not very much, and I think we can happily leave it aside. Egypt is always on a slightly different level. The Egyptians have to be different, and so they are. The whole process of which I speak, the interaction of eastern and western elements, is almost unknown in Egypt. Egyptian architecture goes on being dynastic-type architecture and Egyptian relief goes on being dynastic-type relief, with very few exceptions. When we speak of syncretism we speak, therefore, mainly of Asia.

As regards wall painting, the documentation for the Hellenistic and Roman periods is superior to that for any of the preceding periods. The best example—and here local pride must raise its head—comes from what we at Yale refer to as "our own Dura." The largest and most important series of wall paintings has been recently published by Professor Kraeling; I refer, of course, to the paintings of the great third-century Synagogue at Dura. It is clearly obvious, and Professor Kraeling states it most eloquently, that all these different art traditions are combined in the paintings of this one small frontier city. We find here architectural background such as is seen in Pompeian wall paintings, though it is not done with the confidence that the Pompeian painter shows. Set against this background are figures dressed in Greek-type drapery, though, again, they are not done with the grace of a Greek painter. The figures themselves are done in the Parthian frontal manner, with faces whose tremendous eyes look straight ahead. The faces are done in a style which shows little or no painted modeling and which is more like that of the Fayyum portraits of Egypt than anything else we know. The tradition that we have here was destined to go on in some form or other—and we still do not know how—to develop the next great Hellenic art, the style of the Byzantine period. So this is a very crucial period in the history of ancient Near Eastern art, and I think we have a particularly nice note on which to end our discussion of it, for the syncretism in the art of the Greek and Roman Orient is not the end of anything. It is the beginning of a new tradition that was to become increasingly vital for the Western world through the developments of the Byzantine period.

WELLES: Mr. Chairman, fellow symposiasts: Mr. Kraeling has asked me to speak about law in the thousand years of Hellenism in the Orient. I do this rather reluctantly, since it is something of an impertinence for me to discuss the subject in the presence of a legal historian who has contributed to our meeting a document of such basic importance to the legal study of any period. The point that Professor Rheinstein makes in his paper on "Government and Law" (pp. 405–18) is one that I think we must adopt. Hence we must say that law is not a matter of codes alone. Law is, perhaps, a combination of three elements—authority, acceptance, and sanction. These three elements are what tie law in with the general subject of our discussion.

For a Hellenistic historian, such as I am, to sit here during these days and listen to the discussion of cultural history of the earlier Orient is a very enlightening experience. I think that all of us tend to limit our studies to the period of our primary concern, beginning where it begins and stopping where it ends. I am an Orientalist and an Egyptologist in my own way, but of course the period of my concern is one which the professed Egyptologists and Orientalists normally omit. For those of us who work in the thousand years between Alexander and the Arabs it is vital to know what went before, and this is particularly true for the study of law. As to what went on in the field of law in the Hellenistic Orient, I can perhaps offer a few generalizations.

The Hellenistic period in its broad sense has contributed an enormous number of legal documents to the sum total of our knowledge of ancient law, and the study of these documents has colored legal historical studies for the past seventy years or so, ever since the days of Ludwig Mitteis. The new sources are of various sorts. Of codes we have a few. Of diplomatic documents, that is, correspondence between political entities such as cities or between sovereigns and cities, we have a fair number. Of documents that show civil law in its practice we have an enormous number. It is, of course, impossible for me to do more than point to this material and speak of it in most general terms in relation to our topic.

The conquests of Alexander and the new kingdoms created by his successors did not necessarily change anything. I think that their purpose and intention was not to change but to control. In this sense the Macedonians and the Greeks who invaded the Orient are the successors and heirs of the Persians and the Hittites, perhaps of the Amorites, and possibly, for all we know, of the Sumerians. That is to say, their prime desire being to find in the Orient a good life under their own control, the Greeks permitted the system of law prevalent in Babylon as we know it from the tablets and the law prevalent in Egypt as we know it from the demotic documents to continue in force, just as they did the structure of governmental administration. For local administration in general was not changed either.

The new factor in the picture was that of the Greeks themselves, whose activity in the sphere of business, with which law is very largely concerned, had received a tremendous impetus not only from the opening of the Orient—this having already begun under the Persians—but also from the inflation that developed when the enormous stocks of silver accumulated by the Persian kings were freed for commercial use. The Greeks came in every capacity and from every part of the Greek world. This is shown very dramatically by such a document as our earliest papyrus, the marriage contract from Elephantine, where we have a man and a woman from different Greek places marrying, the marriage being witnessed by Greeks from still other Greek states. The fact that the Greeks who came to the Orient came from so many different localities had a profound effect upon the development of law in the Near East. To a Greek the law according to which he lived was the law of his city. It was not essentially a law enacted by legislation but rather a law given by a law-giver, either the founder of a city or someone who was especially designated for that purpose. It was not adopted piecemeal; it was adopted as a whole. In the newly founded or refounded Greek cities of the Near East a code of law was provided in some fashion still unknown to us, but certainly under the sanction of a king. It was the law of the city and its inhabitants. But what happened when Greeks from different cities came together for transacting business apart from their cities and not as members of a new city? In part they fell back on a *koine,* the legal *koine* that had arisen in the fifth century and was already flourishing in the fourth century B.C. as the agency of Greek trade throughout the whole Mediterranean world. Devices were thus supplied or invented to make contracts valid wherever they might be presented for enforcement. More was necessary, of course, and we know from the fargments of codes preserved to us that the Greek kings of the Orient enacted laws applicable to the whole of their kingdoms. The relation of these codes to the laws of the individual cities is a very obscure matter, quite as is the relation of these codes to the earlier laws of the area. In general, then, the whole program of Hellenistic law offers more problems than solutions, but it was an active field of development in the thousand years of cultural continuum that separated the ancient Oriental East and the Islamic Orient.

When the Romans came, they were presented with the same problems. Many of you know how active a discussion there has been among Roman legal historians as to the penetration of Roman law into the several sections of the Roman Empire and as to the influence of native laws upon Roman law during the period of the Empire. I would only point to one or two matters which seem to me somewhat new in this field. It is now, I think, generally recognized that in certain areas of family and social relationships Oriental elements can be specifically identified as having come into Hellenistic and Roman law from the east, one matter notably so. It was a characteristic feature of the Hellenistic period that women enjoyed a very large element of freedom in their legal relationships. This was not true of Greek law and it was not true of Roman law. It was true of ancient Egypt and of ancient Mesopotamia.

RHEINSTEIN: I would like to ask one question of Mr. Welles. He mentioned the position of women in Mesopotamia. I wonder whether he would add a few words about marriage and divorce and about any changes which may have occurred with the rise of Christianity?

WELLES: I think that the rise of Christianity made no difference as far as the legal developments were concerned. Actually I have not made an intensive study of the legal documents of the later periods. Surely during the first three centuries of the Christian era there was no change, and from what I know, for instance from the Byzantine papyri from 'Auja' al-Hafir, there was no essential change there either. That, however, is only an opinion.

BRAIDWOOD: We have one more comment on Mr. Kraeling's statement, from Mr. Albright.

ALBRIGHT: When Mr. Kraeling asked me to make some comment on the Dead Sea Scrolls, on their importance for the New Testament and related topics, I warned him that I was by way of becoming a heresiarch on a plane far below that of Valentinus and Marcion so far as professional New Testament scholars are concerned. He said he was well aware of that and would by no means be disturbed if I "stirred things up a bit."

As you all know, two groups of manuscript discoveries are currently revolutionizing the whole approach to the history of religion and the history of ideas in the Near East during the period between the third century B.C. and the third century of our era. These are the Hebrew and Aramaic Dead Sea Scrolls from Qumran and the Coptic Gnostic documents of Chenoboskion. The former date largely from the immediately pre-Christian centuries and include original religious writings, commentaries on biblical books, collections of testimonia, rules of order, psalms, prayers, and benedictions. The latter date from the third and fourth centuries of our era and contain over forty treatises of early and Valentinian Gnostics, apocryphal gospels, and Hermetic writings. We now have a fairly adequate idea of the Dead Sea Scrolls, though only about five per cent of the nonbiblical material has been published. Of the codices of Chenoboskion we have in published form today perhaps ten per cent, thanks to the publication of the Jung Codex in Europe and of one codex by Pahor Labib, Director of the Copitc Museum in Cairo. The fact is, however, that M. Jean Doresse, who with the late Togo Mina was the first to identify the Coptic documents and the first to call attention to them, has made extensive notes on and transcriptions from the texts and has materially added to our general knowledge of the codices by the first of a series of projected volumes.[4]

You have just heard about the cultural continuum of the Hellenistic and Roman periods in which the art, business life, and law of the vast region between Crimea and South Arabia and between Carthage and Bactria were held together. This same cultural continuum, which began with the period of Alexander, must be expected to have left important traces in the sphere of religious thought, more particularly in the creation of religious syncretisms. This has long been recognized, but some of us have felt for many years that the nature and extent of the phenomenon have been grossly misunderstood and underestimated. In the light of the new material I may say that, in my opinion, everything that was written on Gnostic syncretism before Chenoboskion must either be set aside as having

---

[4] *Les livres sécrets des Gnostiques d'Égypte.* I. *Introduction aux écrits gnostiques coptes découvertes à Khénoboskion* (Paris, 1958).

value only for the history of the discussion or must be completely restated. Let me illustrate with a few examples.

A good many years ago I became convinced that the Essene sect of Judaism was partially Mesopotamian in origin. My thought was that these Essenes were at least in part Jews from Parthian Mesopotamia who had either escaped or come of their own volition to Palestine. For one thing, I could not regard the bodily lustrations which the Essenes stressed as a typically Palestinian institution. The late Gustav Dalman, who directed the German Evangelical School for Palestinian Archaeology for many years and knew Palestine inside out, took reluctant groups of German pastors on long horseback rides through the country every year and recommended that they take no baths during these trips. I am not recommending this myself, but the fact is that one can get along quite well in the highlands of Palestine without baths, whereas in Mesopotamia and Egypt baths are absolutely necessary for elementary hygiene. It would be odd a priori to find that the Essene baths for purification originated in Palestine and, even worse, in the Jordan Valley. The Jordan is one of the dirtiest rivers in the world, with a very high mud content in the water. I do not deny that the Mandeans of Mesopotamia practice lustration in muddy canal water, as a result of historic circumstances.

The Qumran discoveries have provided corroboration of earlier inference in different ways. For one thing, the very first of the scrolls from Cave 1—the Isaiah Scroll—spells quite a number of Assyro-Babylonian names and words correctly, though the correct forms were unknown to the translators of the Greek Bible in the third and second centuries B.C. as well as to the Massoretic scholars who vocalized our Hebrew Bible a thousand years later. In other words, the Isaiah Scroll may have come from Babylonia, and textual considerations make it almost certain in my mind that it did, directly or indirectly.

But there are other arguments for the Mesopotamian origin of these Essene sectaries. The Essenes of Palestine clearly derived from the same source as the Pharisees, namely from the Hasidim of the early second century B.C. However, many of the specific views of the Essenes are not Jewish at all in origin but Zoroastrian. Typical of the Zoroastrian elements in Essene thought is the simple dualism between the two creative spirits, the spirit of good and evil, light and darkness, truth and falsehood. In the Qumran documents one sees the Druj appearing in the form of the spirit falsehood, the lying spirit. It has been maintained by several scholars—I think first by André Michaud—that a specific Zervante influence is involved here, in other words that the Essenes had been influenced by Zervanism, a form of Zoroastrianism that dates back in some form to the Achaemenean period. Another indication of strong Irano-Babylonian origin is the apparent absence of Greek loan words in the genuine Essene literature, though there are a good many Iranian loan words.

For the Roman period we can now document the religious syncretism that is part of the cultural development of the Hellenistic Orient anew, thanks to the recent Chenoboskion discoveries. Gilles Quispel of Amsterdam, in a brilliant little book,[5] recognized that the Church Fathers' accounts of Gnosticism are far more accurate than those of modern students of the subject and that we must actually consider the deacon Nicholas (of Antioch) and Simon Magus as pioneers in what we call Gnosticism. In other words, there was no such thing as the pre-Christian Gnosticism about which Bultmann and Reitzenstein have written so eloquently. But Christian Gnosticism did have roots and basic elements connecting it with the religious life of earlier periods. Jean Doresse[6] has collected details about the early Gnostic intermediary principle between good and evil, Greek *mesites*. This is not the pre-Christian Redeemer for which Bultmann and others have searched in vain, and it does not appear in the stage of syncretism represented by the Qumran scrolls. Rather, it is a product of the syncretistic process at a later stage of development, again representing the impact of Zoroastrian ideas on the later Orient. In the Manicheism of the third century of our era we have another, still later and the most consistent, expression of the same Iranian syncretism.

AL-ASIL: I wish to express my appreciation of the way in which the period between the coming of Alexander and the rise of Islam has been treated as a unit by Mr. Kraeling. This is indeed the right thing to do. Alexander's conquest marked the end of the indigenous culture of Mesopotamia but not the end of the process of creation which continued to go on bringing together new ideas, secular and religious, from different sources, Western and Oriental. I think it must all have been somewhat confusing, particularly to the artists of these later centuries.

[5] *Die Gnosis als Weltreligion* (1951).
[6] *Op. cit.*

We have two beautiful pieces of sculpture in the Iraq Museum that illustrate this. One, which we found at Hatra, represents the Arabian goddess Allat. One day when a classical historian from England was visiting the Museum I was trying, perhaps more than I should have, to show him how much this statue of Allat resembles statues of Athena. After I had pointed out that she has Athena's helmet and shield and spear and the Medusa on her breastplate, he said: "This is Athena, all right, but how do you know this is Allat?" My answer was that we had found the statue in a temple dedicated to Allat and that she is mounted upon the back of a lion, just as Assyrian and Babylonian deities are sometimes portrayed. The second piece is a statue of Mercury that we found at Nineveh. There was a small Greek colony at Nineveh after the conquest of Alexander. Compared to the statues of Mercury in the museums of Europe and the National Gallery at Washington, our Mercury is a very poor chap. It seems as though the artist tried to show the Greek messenger of the gods in a strange land looking for the strange Assyrian gods. In any event, he gives the impression of somebody who was not quite sure of what he was doing or how he would be received. The period of cultural syncretism must have had many moments of uncertainty for the peoples of the Near East.

LARSEN: I want to say a few words about the Greek polis, more particularly about the function of the market place (the agora) in the economic life of the Greek city-state. At this point my ideas tend to run contrary to those developed by my honored friend Dr. Polanyi in his paper (see pp. 329–50). Since much of what I would like to say concerns the period before Alexander the Great, suggesting that, except for some control of the food supply, there was freedom of trade at Athens as there had been in the Persian empire and the empire that preceded it, I would be glad to have my argument appended to this discussion as a footnote.[7]

[7] Since Dr. Polanyi emphasizes Athens, I shall confine myself largely to that city or, rather, city-state. Athens, like all Greek states, desired freedom for itself and domination over others. The other ideal connected with the city-state, that of *autarkeia* or economic self-sufficiency, was an ideal of theorists only, though even they realized that some trade with the outer world was necessary. Many Greek cities, Athens included, had to import much of their food. In addition, there was a considerable trade within the state both in goods produced at home and in imported goods. Was this trade as a whole free or regulated by government? Here it may be well to start from the statement of Professor Gibb concerning freedom of trade within the Persian empire. If this empire, more or less the heir of the old Oriental empires, allowed trade to go its own way, a fortiori we should expect the Greek cities to have done the same, and this is what we actually find except for some control of the grain supply. The customs duties were low, for revenue only,

POLANYI: I am prepared to agree beforehand to much of Professor Larsen's criticism, which I have expected because I am not myself satisfied with the way in which I describe the function of the Greek

---

and were the same on imports and exports. Such measures as protective tariffs do not seem to have been known to the Greeks before their use in Hellenistic times by the Ptolemies (see particularly W. W. Tarn and G. T. Griffith, *Hellenistic Civilisation* [3d ed.; London, 1952] pp. 190 ff.). An approach to protection of a sort is found in a prohibition by the city of Thasos against sale of foreign wines by Thasian ships along the coast of Thrace, but such regulations seem to have been very rare (see inscriptions published and discussed by Georges Daux in *Bulletin de correspondance hellénique* L [1926] 214–26).

The most important contribution of the government to trade was the minting of money, and it is clear that at Athens there were coins minted specifically for wholesale trade and others for retail trade and marketing. The foreign trade was mostly centered in Piraeus, the harbor town of Athens, which, by the way, should not be considered as distinct from Athens. It was, as it were, a semidetached part of Athens but, nevertheless, as much a part of it as the agora. At Piraeus was the *deigma*, the building in which importers could exhibit their goods. It was for the wholesale trade that the omnipresent silver tetradrachms were coined. To some extent coins themselves were objects to export. As Xenophon remarks (*Vect.* 3. 2), the merchants trading at Athens had the advantage that, if they did not wish to take on a return cargo, the Athenian silver money was itself a profitable object of export. (Note that, though the merchants obviously traded in Piraeus, Xenophon does not mention the port by name but speaks of Athens. When he later uses the name [*Vect.* 3. 13], it is to distinguish the Piraeus from the *asty*, the city of Athens proper.) The retail trade, on the other hand, was conducted in the agora and shops around the city. Objects produced by artisans apparently were sold in the shops in which they were made. Otherwise the trade was conducted largely in the agora. For this trade Athens coined tiny silver coins, some of them as small as an eighth of an obol. This has been called an "absurd little coin" (Charles Seltman, *Greek Coins* [2d ed.; London, 1955] p. 179), and so it may seem, but coins of such small denominations were needed for retail trade and marketing. An obol was not a penny or a farthing, as often translated, but more like a nickel or a dime or, in purchasing value, even a quarter. When bronze came into use, coins of even smaller denominations were minted. If we judge by such evidence as Aristophanes' *Acharnians*, the market was open, except in time of war, also to non-Athenians. Boeotians and Megarians came to the agora of Athens with their wares. Some fees were paid, and Xenophon (*Vect.* 3. 13) could urge the development of facilities for retail trade both in Athens proper and in Piraeus in order to increase the income of the state, but, except for grain, there is no indication of price regulation. Nor does there seem to be any particular connection between the development of democracy and the development of the market place. Aristotle, who excluded artisans, traders, and farmers from citizenship in his ideal city (*Pol.* 1328b39) and specified that there should be an agora unsullied by any commercial transactions (1331a30), nevertheless provided for another agora for trade with convenient access to goods coming by land and sea (1331b1). Nor is there any reason for believing that Pericles personally went marketing every day. This story seems based on a misinterpretation of Plutarch's *Life of Pericles*, chap. 16, where it is stated that Pericles annually sold all the crops from his lands at once and then later satisfied the current needs of his household by purchases in the agora, and all this he managed with the aid of one household slave. Naturally, the one who actually took care of the details, including the marketing, was the slave.

And now just one remark in connection with Professor Kraeling's interesting statements concerning the state. It is not likely that the Greek cities of the Near East in Hellenistic times had preserved much of any democratic tradition. Back of the democratic façade seen in many documents, the men of wealth ruled the cities. After the

[Footnote 7 concluded on page 218]

agora in my paper. My description is compressed to the point of imprecision, and its tone is somewhat categorical on questions which are known to be controversial. I intend to do something about this on another occasion, because I do not think that my presentation is adequate. But, as to my essential thesis, on which I have long hesitated before making up my mind, I would find it difficult to adopt a contrary position.

SMITH: I am not going to talk about the agora, which was a place for the promulgation of the laws, but I want to say a word about legal institutions, which I think have to some extent been neglected in our discussion. Mr. Landsberger has suggested that, although the code of Hammurabi existed, the magistrates or whatever judicial officials there were in the ancient Oriental empires probably continued to use their traditional procedures and to disregard the code. Then Mr. Rheinstein pointed out yesterday that the Mesopotamian codes deal largely with torts rather than with crimes and that homicide seems regularly to be one of the last things taken up by the state. In that connection he raised the question as to when self-help as a means of dealing with wrongs became disallowed. It seems to me that out of these statements and out of those of Mr. Welles this morning a pattern emerges that has analogies in Greece. In Homer we find the beginning of a fusion of self-help and state control. Self-help is still being practiced, but there is a tendency to at least voluntary arbitration, although I find no compulsory arbitration as yet.

Another interesting point that has been raised several times is that of the connection of law and religion. The theory has long been held that the codification of law generally grew out of religious sanction, but an analysis of the earliest Greek codes which we know shows no indication, to me at least, that this is true, even though the early codes very frequently are attributed to a divine source. Of course there were rules to take care of infractions of religious regulations. But otherwise religion comes in to no great extent except in cases of homicide, which seems regularly to be one of the last things taken

[Footnote 7 continued from page 217.]

rapid development of democracy in the 5th century, there was a process of change through which *demokratia* became a laudatory name for any republican government, which, in most cases, actually was oligarchic (A. H. M. Jones, *The Greek City from Alexander to Justinian* [Oxford, 1940] chap. x, esp. p. 170. For further discussion of change in the meaning of *demokratia* see Larsen, "Representation and democracy in Hellenistic federalism," *Classical Philology* XL [1945] 88–91; for evidence for the early stages of the change see Larsen, "The judgment of antiquity on democracy," *Classical Philology* XLIX [1954] 6–10.)

up by the state. Even for homicide the procedure is limited almost entirely to the family of the victim, and the act continues to be considered a tort. Religion comes into the picture when the state has created rules for dealing with homicide, and pollution doctrines become a distinct part of the feeling about homicide. But self-help is still a strong factor in that only a relative of the victim is allowed to prosecute before an Athenian homicide court. Thus there remains a good deal in the way of self-help and family solidarity. I am trying to point out merely that the codes which we have from Greece are secular in origin, that they grew out of purely practical situations and show little trace of religion. I would like to hear this point pursued by the Orientalists.

GELB: As I listened to Professor Kraeling's presentation I had the uneasy feeling that he was omitting something. He gave us an excellent picture of the cities in the Hellenistic and Roman Near East, of their literacy and literature, but nowhere did he say anything about the interplay of two great forces which were involved in the shaping of the society, the Greek language and the native languages of Syria. The differences between the languages of the newly-arrived Greeks and the native population provide a basic measure and touchstone of a difference on the social level. I recalled from my reading of classical authors that when the Greek writers speak of the natives of the Near East they refer to them either as Syrians (sometimes Assyrians) or as Arabs. Neither of these terms, however, is ethnical in connotation. Both mean what in earlier days the Greeks had called "barbarians." The attitude which the terms express is that of a group which looks on the natives as though they were of a lower cultural status than itself. I verified my reminiscence concerning classical authors by consulting George Haddad's *Aspects of Social Life in Antioch in the Hellenistic-Roman Period* (Chicago, 1949), where I was surprised to find a tremendous amount of interesting and important material bearing on this factor. Haddad speaks repeatedly of the haughty attitude of the Greeks in their relation to the local inhabitants. At the end of the process of integration we find statements by Libanius and John Malalas to the effect that they considered themselves Greeks, but by language only and not by descent. Such statements reflect exactly the point that I am trying to make, namely that language more than anything else provides evidence for the understanding of the process of cultural assimilation and interchange in the ancient Near East. I do not understand why Carl Kraeling did not take up this matter, because more evidence is available in the sphere of language development in the period under discussion than in any other sphere and because he has written a most enlightening article on the language situation at Antioch. I also have comments to make on remarks by Professor Von Grunebaum (see p. 86) and Professor Speiser (see p. 91). Nowhere have I meant to insist that either *ethnos* or language is the one paramount factor in the shaping of society, but I do want to stress consideration of the language factor as the basis of our studies. All of us who have spoken here today are basically philologians and still we neglect the basic elements that we work with, namely the language and the people who use it.

SINGER: Only a presentation as rich and stimulating as that of Professor Kraeling could have succeeded in keeping us awake, alert, and excited at the end of the last session. What was particularly stimulating to me was that in describing the mixture of many different traditions in the Near East in the Hellenistic and Roman periods Professor Kraeling was himself exemplifying so well a mixture of academic traditions. This feature has characterized this symposium, where geographers have been cautioning humanists not to push geographic determinism too far and where humanists have been cautioning social scientists not to rely too much on intuition and subjective impressions. I think that those of us who have worked a little bit in the field of urbanization and cultural change as seen from the point of view of anthropology have a great deal to learn from what the humanists have contributed. My only regret is that Robert Redfield, who was himself a pioneer in this field, beginning with his classic Yucatan study and continuing with his *The Primitive World and Its Transformations* (Chicago, 1941), is not here. I think he would have been greatly stimulated and pleased by the symposium and by Professor Kraeling's description of the cultural processes in the urban containers of the Hellenistic and Roman Near East. I myself carry away the conclusion that what happens to culture as cities expand cannot be studied simply in terms of the social scientist's dimensions of the size and character of the container, of the population, of trade, and so on but must be studied also in terms of the cultural life inside the container. Thus the anthropologist has to rely on the humanist for help.

BRAIDWOOD: I wish now to give Professor Kraeling an opportunity to summarize the discussion his remarks introduced and will turn the chair over to him, so that he can introduce the last speaker.

KRAELING: I am very grateful to Professors Brown, Perkins, Welles, and Albright and all those who with them participated in the discussion for their enlightening comments. The cultural life of the thousand years between Alexander the Great and Muḥammad has so many facets that it is difficult if not impossible for any one person to describe them all, especially in what could be at best only a few "well-chosen words" intended to introduce the topic. I think this provides at least a partial answer to Professor Gelb's question as to why I did not treat also the language problem. In matters of language as in matters of law, of economics, of art, and of religion we need the help that such scholars as Professors Gelb, Singer, Welles, Rheinstein, Smith, Brown, Perkins, and Albright can give and have given.

Several points raised in the discussion may call for a word of comment on my part. I confess, for instance, that the legal documents of the period, particularly from among the papyri, are to me something of a closed book. What Professor Welles said about the great gaps in our knowledge of the relation between traditional Oriental law and Greek city law provides some slight comfort for the inexpert. Of the fact that particular groups and societies bowed to the force of inherited ordinance other than their own I can cite one interesting example. It is the dictum of Rabbi Samuel, one of the Jewish sages of Mesopotamian Judaism in the third century of our era, who, while upholding the force of traditional Hebrew law for the members of the Jewish communities in Mesopotamia, enunciated the principle that *dina di malkutha dina,* "the law of the kingdom is the law." By admitting that the law of the newly established Sasanian Empire was valid and binding upon the Jews of lower Mesopotamia, he paved the way for amicable relations between the Jews and the Sasanians in a difficult period and for generations to come.

I accept, of course, what Miss Perkins said about the incorrectness of the term "Semitic art." It is not in the written text of my remarks and represents a *lapsus linguae.* In connection with her own lucid description of sculpture and painting from Commagene, Hatra, Dura, and Palmyra I would make only two comments. The first is that in addition to the Greek and Parthian elements identifiable in these works of art there is a lavish use of decorative ornament, a tendency to embellish by the addition of detail, which seems to me a third element in the syncretism, the derivation of which is not clear to me at all. My second comment is that geographically the art typified by the monuments of Dura, Palmyra, and the east is limited to the zone north of the Hauran and that it has no echo in southern Syria and Transjordan, for instance in the sculptures of Khirbat al-Tannur or the contemporary tomb paintings of Transjordan and Palestine. What this means to me, when taken together with the fact that Egypt always "had to be different," is that the syncretism in the sphere of art differed regionally. Thus it is doubly important to inquire how it was that certain stylistic features, such as frontality and denial of corporeality, became dominant in Byzantine art.

What interested me most in the discussion was Professor Brown's comment on the things happening on the two opposite sides of the Roman Euphrates frontier. This underlines the necessity of our seeing the cultural development of any period in its widest possible framework, even wider than that set for this symposium. It has been suggested by Rostovtzeff that the advent of Roman power in the Near East first interfered with the further development of Hellenism in the Orient but that eventually the Romans had to become the defenders and protagonists of Greek culture there. Professor Brown's comments suggest that we apply the same formula to the opposite side of the Roman Euphrates frontier and say that the growth of Parthian power east of the Euphrates in the period beginning with Mithridates I served at first to sever the connections with Greek culture but eventually led to a new cultural development in which the earlier Greek influence was preserved as an element of a new synthesis. Thus the coming of the Greeks under Alexander the Great is still more important as a turning point in the cultural history of the Near East, for it was the Greek element combining with the native traditions that led to the new syntheses on either side of the Euphrates frontier in Roman and Parthian times. West of this frontier we can follow the process more or less continuously and identify at least the major local elements. East of the Euphrates we are not so well fixed. In what form native Iranian art, for instance, survived in the period between the Achaemeneans and the Parthians is something of a problem.

In this connection the work of the Iraq Directorate General of Antiquities under Dr. Naji al-Asil at Hatra may take on even greater importance than it already has. The Hatra sculptures as we know them today fall into two categories. One category includes religious monuments like the Allat and the Mercury of which he has spoken and in which Greek and native traditions are clearly combined. The other category consists of representations of Parthian kings or princes which are technically and aesthetically superior to the religious sculptures and reflect a minimum of Greek influence. This second category is shown even by its subject matter to express the national tradition in its essential character. Perhaps further work at Hatra will produce in addition to these portrait statues historical scenes and compositions in the same style. Then we shall be better able to bridge the gap between Persepolis and Naqsh-i-Rustam.

IV
Concluding Address

KRAELING: We have given to Professor Mumford two difficult assignments: to introduce the subject of our symposium to a wider audience and to bring our discussions to some kind of conclusion. Coming at both the beginning and the end, he has necessarily had to try to follow the lines of thought of all of us as we have ranged over millenniums of time in the pursuit of our theme. The breadth of his own horizon is such that this was for him no new experience. If what we have said has at times not produced a coherent picture, he has every right to confront us with our own shortcomings, and whatever he adds we shall ourselves gratefully accept.

MUMFORD: Dr. Kraeling, ladies and gentlemen: You must not expect a summary of this conference in what follows. My real tribute to this conference, with its wide-ranging papers and acute discussions, is to acknowledge that it could not possibly be summarized, even by one better equipped to appraise its special contributions than I am. These papers and discussions leave everything open and fluid, ready to be carried into new channels, not to be condensed into a little *Reader's Digest* pellet and disgorged at the end.

I would like to go back to one of the themes that originally prompted this meeting, the part played by the city in development and expansion of cultures. In this field, as in every other, I speak not as a specialist but as a generalist whose special competence is to put the scattered and often arbitrarily separated parts together in meaningful relationships. There are certain rules of the game, of course, that a generalist must keep when he tries to put the pieces together. He must not manufacture any of the pieces himself in order to fill out the pattern. He must be willing to scrap the pieces as soon as one of the specialists discovers that they are inadequate or that they belong to another stratum and are unusable at the particular level under discussion. If there are not enough parts, I cannot give anything like a plausible picture. On the other hand, if my design will not hold all the parts presented to me, then that pattern is a faulty one and will have to be thrown out.

"What is the city?" Dr. Hoselitz asked yesterday. "When does it begin and under what conditions does it take shape?" I purpose to address myself to these questions. I share fully Dr. Jacobsen's timidity about going into the problem of chronology, if only because the beginnings of the city predate the written record; and the stratigraphic record, even if it were more abundant, would still not tell us what we most need to know. To come close to the origins of the city we must, I think, extrapolate backward from the fullest known urban remains to their original components, however remote in time and space from the actual city.

One is tempted too easily to say that the city has come into existence at the moment one finds, either below or above the surface, a visible ruin big enough to resemble a town as defined by the census today. That seems to me an oversimplified solution of the problem; in fact it begs the whole question as to the nature of the city by supplying only a physical, quantitative answer. I submit, as a working hypothesis, that all the essential parts of the city were in existence before the city itself took form and that their mobilization and concentration within an encircling wall helped bring about a radical change in neolithic culture.

Our problem, on these terms, is to find out what forces played a part in this transformation; for the form that it took was widely copied or reinvented in every part of the world and held together right down to the seventeenth century. One of the symbols of the end, I would say, was the building of Versailles. At that moment the original core of the city, the fortified citadel, escaped from the surrounding community and became a suburb of the city it had once dominated; the royal power, instead of being fortified by a masonry wall, was protected for a few generations by a hundred thousand armed men. But that was the beginning of the end. Within a few short centuries the city itself, instead of being an almost impregnable agent of military power, became a military liability, so that we now face a new situation culturally and politically—we must learn to live in an open world.

When I look for the origins of the city, I find myself happily close to the eminent scholar on my left (Albright), for I welcome his suggestion that we must go back to a far earlier stage of human culture than your actual diggings indicate—at least as far back as the earliest paleolithic findings of permanent graves. In the uneasy life of primitive man, the dead were the first to have a permanent dwelling place.

And perhaps the first form of the city is the cemetery, the city of the dead, a place to which people returned to keep a sense of family identity and continuity. As a matter of fact, one might write a whole interpretation of the city in this vein. I do not think that Egypt and China were so abnormal in their respect for the dead or that Abraham's concern to get a cave for family burial was not shared by much earlier peoples. In time, when the city at last develops, it serves as a kind of tomb, filled with dead institutions as well as dead bodies, so that, even when it is destroyed as often as Troy, the survivors return to the same spot out of piety to the dead.

If the cemetery was perhaps the first permanent meeting place, the cave, as a center of art and ritual, was another paleolithic contribution. Though these caves were not inhabited, Lascaux and Altamira seem to have been ceremonial centers of some kind, as much so as Nippur or Abydos. Here we encounter for the first time an art whose imaginative quality is not touched again till we reach the temples and palaces of a much later period. And if this art was, as some hold, only an incidental by-product of magic, did it not even at the earliest date exert a special magic of its own which drew men at intervals back to the sacred spot? This brings to mind other venerable shrines that embodied sacred powers: sacred stones, sacred groves, sacred single trees, sacred wells, fixed landmarks and meeting places for those who shared the same religious beliefs. In time these became the core of the city.

One must not, of course, overlook more practical needs that brought people together seasonally even in a collecting or hunting economy. Camp sites near a particularly good yield of water, perhaps medicinal water, or by waters heavily stocked with fish and shellfish seem to have served as bases for mesolithic settlements even before nontuberous plants were domesticated. Eventually we find the hunter's camp in the very heart of the city, next to a sacred shrine, a paleolithic enclave walled off from the neolithic villages at its base. But note that two of these three original aspects of temporary settlement have to do with sacred things: the sacred dead and the sacred ritual caves or shrines. Except where cremation was practiced, these were permanent components of the city.

The point I am making is that the city begins as a meeting place to which people periodically return; it is an object of pilgrimage, and this ceremonial function makes it a natural magnet, which at a later stage greatly facilitates the more practical functions of political organization and control of commercial transactions and industrial specialization. Unlike the village, the city from the beginning draws on a population larger than that which permanently gets a living from the near-by farming area. People come to the city for some special participation in the good life; it is Passover, and they go up to Jerusalem, just as today, for more secular reasons, they stream from every part of the United States to New York to see a popular musical comedy. The purpose is different, but the urban function remains the same. Thus the most typical phrase, the one dropped most often perhaps in the city, in all cities at all times, is "I'm a stranger here myself." That is true, even if the "strangers," like the rustics in Aristophanes, come from a near-by village. This merely emphasizes the fact that from its dimmest beginnings, the city is a meeting place. Meeting, intercourse, intermixture are the very breath of its life and the source of its special dynamism. But even when meeting is on a permanent basis, a year-round affair, it does not by itself bring the city into existence or encompass all its functions. So let us look further.

You are all, of course, sufficiently vigilant to the danger of taking strata too seriously. Respect for strata remains a necessity for archeology as a way of defining time limits and successions. But only material culture ever remains stratified. The nonmaterial culture is fibrous in nature; though the long threads may often be broken, they go through every stratum and, even when they are out of sight, they are continuously present. Thus we must remember, when we deal with the village's contribution to the city, that the mobile, restless, imaginative paleolithic hunter is coming back into the city. He does not disappear at any time; and probably the city would never have taken exactly the form it did but for his special gifts and special interests.

But now let us look at the village. There comes a moment, perhaps in mesolithic times, but certainly in neolithic culture, when the domestication of plants produces a more secure and abundant food supply, since the hard grains can be kept over from season to season; and with this a continuous life in one place becomes possible, with more opportunity for child nurture, greater scope for woman's role, a more rich and varied diet that probably abetted fertility, and with all this a great gain in order and regularity and general stability, if also a greater tolerance of repetition and monotony. As for the last, witness the change from the swift snapping of paleolithic tools to the slow process of grinding neolithic tools. The first characteristically needs skill and luck; the second needs dogged patience.

Here lies the beginning of domestication and permanent settlement. Without getting involved in the controversy over Bachofen's *Das Mutterrecht* we cannot doubt that woman exercised a great influence over neolithic culture, from seed selection and hoe cultivation to coiled pottery; but, above all, she domesticated man and thus contributed a new factor toward the formation of the city—hearth and home. This village element remains an essential part of every city, whether the house nestles under the wall of the citadel or like Rahab's house is part of the outside wall or whether it lies as much as five miles away from the center like the ancient Mayan villages. Without this village element, the ancient city could not be fed; and without its surplus children, it could not remain populated. Subsistence economies, collecting or hunting, do not produce that surplus.

From this village culture the city also gets an essential moral ingredient whose character Robert Redfield did so much to illuminate for us. In the more complex forms of the city, the village becomes disguised as a temple quarter, a parish, a neighborhood unit, sometimes, as in Greek and Moslem examples, a place to which a closely knitted group of families is transplanted, each quarter retaining its identity. What Fustel de Coulanges a century ago discovered about the foundations of the ancient city have now been carried back to a much earlier manifestation in Ur, with a family hearth, a household god, and even a mortuary chapel right at hand. The dead were never closer to the living.

The persistence of the village pattern both within and outside the city explains how people were able to survive the perversions and destructions that have accompanied the growth of great urban centers throughout history. For the neighbor is the new contribution of the village. He is not yet a citizen but one who dwells near by and gives help and succor when they are needed, because he in turn cannot survive without such help in times of stress. Remember what Hesiod says about neighbors?

> Call him who loves you to your feast.
> ... By no means least
> Invite a man whose house is near,
> For if upon a place comes hurt,
> The neighbors hurry out ungirt,
> But kinsmen dawdle o'er their gear.

The village breaks down to some extent the pure kin grouping and makes the neighbor more important; and in times of stress, in plague or war, the city may return to the undifferentiated state of the village, where rank, wealth, class, and caste cease to be important.

With the village comes a new technology, for the symbolically masculine weapons of the hunter, the spear and the bow and arrow, are supplemented by more feminine forms. In interpreting this contribution, I shall first approach the city itself from the standpoint of technology, though there is much one might add on the reciprocal effect of the city upon technology. I would like to call to your attention the technology of utensils, of utilities, of containers. We have no clue to the development of early cultures—or even of our own complex technology—if we concern ourselves only with tools and the beginnings of the machine. We must remember that the neolithic period is pre-eminently a period of containers, a great age of pottery, of vases, pots, jars, vats, cisterns, bins, barns, granaries, houses, and, not least, inclosed villages and cities.

Wherever a surplus must be preserved and stored, containers are important. Without the container, people could not store beer, wine, oil or carry water any distance. No wonder it is in containers that the neolithic inventors outdid themselves, and so well that we are still using their methods and preserving many of their forms, even though plastics have been invented! With storage there is continuity as well as a surplus to draw on in lean seasons. The setting-aside of unconsumed seeds for the next year's sowing was the first step toward capital accumulation; and the city derives this from the village. The hunter cannot save; he has to consume his game almost on the spot, for he has only human containers for transport and storage. He has no means of independent capital accumulation. But out of the neolithic village come, directly or by further elaboration of the same habits and function, the granary, the storehouse, the arsenal, the library, the archives, the reservoir. Remember that the irrigation ditch and the canal and the aqueduct are also containers, which enable a community to store and transmit a surplus. Without these inventions the ancient city would not have taken the form that it did, for it was a container of containers.

But I am going too fast. We are still in the village, and, as you know, village life has gone on for thousands of years almost untouched by the rise and fall of cities and empires. Max Sorré, the French geographer, has pointed out that four-fifths of the world's

229

population still live in villages. That will not be true much longer; but it should be chastening for us to realize that we still live in a world supported, physically and morally, by the old neolithic culture, though it is dominated by a late iron-age culture and threatened with premature extinction by an early uranium-age technology, whose lack of life-conserving taboos would disgrace the most primitive folk yet discovered. There must have been a fairly long period when nothing that could be called a city had yet come into existence but during which all the components of the city were already in being, crudely shaped, imperfectly related, waiting for the critical moment that would bring the fully dimensioned city into existence. Perhaps only by its area and the number of its inhabitants could this proto-city be distinguished from a village, though even at an early stage its growth may have been due to its being a special cult center.

But where is the paleolithic hunter? What has happened to him? He has been pushed out of the cultivated areas somewhat. If small game can be found there, it is snared or hunted by villagers probably; big game, though, is pushed back a little as the area of cultivation increases; it remains in the swamps and the highlands. But some of the hunting groups do not go along with the secure, orderly, methodical life of neolithic agriculture; perhaps they feel about it the way Huckleberry Finn felt about the "tarnation tidiness" of the "Widder." Did agriculture push the hunter back permanently, or did the growing scarcity of game make him feel that his own predatory life was becoming too insecure as long as he depended upon killing other predators? Was he perhaps lured by the comforts and sociabilities of the village? Before the city springs into being the hunter's camp turns into a permanent stronghold, held by someone a little too vaguely described as the "local chieftain."

Do I stretch the evidence if I suggest that this chieftain was a hunter who had partly abandoned his roving life for a settled one and a predatory life for what was at best a commensal relationship with the village community, at worst a parasitic-predatory domination? It seems to me that the hunter must have had a function in the early neolithic economy. With his mastery of lethal weapons, he protected the village against the lion, the tiger, the wolf, the rhinoceros, the hippopotamus. He knew how to handle these dangerous beasts, whereas the villager had perhaps lost the skill and probably lacked the weapons or, still more, the adventurous animus needed. Gilgamesh, that permanent chieftain, was a heroic hunter, was he not?

And is it an accident that the early culture heroes are hunters? Can we close our eyes either to the fact that kings, their lineal successors throughout history, practice hunting as *the* royal sport and are just as proud of their skill in slaying lions as of their prowess in capturing or slaying men? If the great royal metropolises of modern times have open spaces in their very heart, it is because these spaces were originally royal hunting parks or imitations of such parks and because the hunter insisted on preserving large tracts of open land for game, no matter how much the peasant might want it for cultivation.

And yet there is another side to the hunter's control of dangerous animals: one has to pay for protection. Our Victorian ancestors might not have understood this as well as we do. With one gang chieftain or another controlling an industry or a transportation union in our time, we know that we have to pay for "protection" lest the protector himself show even uglier teeth than the animals he is guarding us against. We began to learn this sad lesson under Prohibition, and we have been paying ever higher prices as the system has spread. Similarly, although the hunter had a function in the village economy, he had to be bought off; and, since he was in a minority, probably the function of his castle or fortress was as a holding point—not a protective retreat *for* the villagers but a means of defense *against* them. Do not your diggings suggest that the wall around the citadel preceded the wall around the city?

This is of course a mythological reconstruction; but, since you have no documents to show me, I have to insert a few suppositious events to make the visible data look plausible. Admittedly, it is easier to spot the hunter in the hills of Palestine or in Greece. Where did he hang out in Mesopotamia and Egypt, Mr. Wilson, Mr. Kramer, Mr. Speiser, and all the rest of you? I cannot find him on the map until the city appears; and by that time he has taken on other attributes, and the chieftain has assumed control not only of his own special territory but of the large-scale operations necessary to sustain a more complex life.

The proto-city might exist wherever there was either marginal farming or herding; it would not surprise me to find it on the uplands, away from any good source of transportation or communication. Jericho does not surprise me nor upset me, though what has now come to light in Jericho may still be buried, perhaps irretrievably, in Mesopotamia or the Nile Delta. Such an aggregation of houses might have kept on growing without producing the new

231

forms and institutional activities of the city. For the decisive change that creates the city is not just an increase in numbers but a transformation of its institutions and the creation of a new pattern of life. Thus the city is an emergent in the definite sense that Lloyd Morgan and William Morton Wheeler used that concept. In an emergence, the introduction of a new factor produces an over-all change, not a mere addition, but a change such as we see in the passage of relatively unorganized matter into a crystalline form, or of the small stable molecule into the large complex unstable protein molecule, or of reptiles into birds. On the new plane, all the old components are carried along, but they now have qualities and potentialities that they did not possess in their original state.

In the act of urban emergence other elements—the ritual cave, the holy shrine, the sacred mountain, the hunter's camp or stronghold, the primitive village "agora," the nest of peasants' houses—come together to form a new pattern in which each part is both more highly differentiated and greatly magnified in form or intensified in activity. In a sense, the city marks a real break in the neolithic economy but not a revolution. I do not like Childe's term "urban revolution." Revolution means turning things upside down and leaving the past order behind. But nothing was left behind in the city; on the contrary, more and more things were gathered there and preserved there. It was within the close quarters of the city that the human representatives of paleolithic culture and neolithic culture came together, reacting upon one another and influencing one another.

The dynamic, imaginative, audacious, violent, custom-breaking element we have to attribute mainly to the intruder from the outside, the hunter, and to his successor, the roving herdsman. There is certainly more imagination, a more exquisite aesthetic sense, in a paleolithic cave than there is in any early neolithic pottery or sculpture. A little sadly we must confess that the good, sober, industrious, utilitarian, life-oriented neolithic villagers were probably a little deficient in imagination. But, on the other hand, these docile villagers, with their stable custom-bound routine, had something that the hunter, by the very nature of his occupation, lacked: a tolerance of mechanical order or of repetitive humdrum activities. The marriage of audacity and docility, of competent individual command and collective regimentation, gave the city powers that neither the village nor the proto-city possessed.

Though the proto-city could grow anywhere, the full-grown city could come into existence only on one of the great natural channels of transportation and communication. The old lady who remarked that God was very kind because He always put rivers next to cities said something very profound. That is why the earliest indubitable examples of the city appear in the valleys of the Nile, the Tigris-Euphrates, the Indus, and the Hoang-ho, for the city demands a mobilization of resources and facilities that the immediate agricultural area cannot supply.

What made this mobilization and concentration possible must be our next concern, for it produced not only the city but a change in technology, in religious and political institutions that has colored every subsequent phase of civilization. The plow, the potter's wheel, irrigation, astronomy, abstract mathematics, writing and the permanent record, the permanent division of labor into single lifetime occupations, forced labor, slavery, bureaucratic and military organization, and, if I am correct, war itself as an institution all come into existence at about the same time, give or take a few centuries. In that total change in the pattern, the new urban centers were both agent and product.

What I am going to suggest as a key explanation I would hardly dare bring forward were I not merely carrying a little farther the work of one of your old compeers, whose absence we must all deeply regret. I am speaking of the late Henri Frankfort. Both he and Robert Redfield, from different sides, came very close to this explanation; but my main debt is to the author of *Kingship and the Gods*. Frankfort located the lock and provided the key; my function now is merely to turn the key and open the door. I suggest that the key agent in the foundation of the early city is the king and that one of the attributes of Ptah, that he founded cities, is in fact an all but universal attribute of kings.

Here I am very grateful to Mr. Wilson for using the figure of the cell, with the nucleus of the cell surrounded by the cytoplasm and its "wall." That is a good figure for the new urban unit, almost an exact description. I hesitate sometimes to use it, lest it be taken too literally, but even physicists have had to recognize the existence of a nucleus that seems to hold the charges of the atom in an orderly dynamic system. And because we know that the nucleus of a living cell carries the inheritance of the cell or the organism, the analogy is all the more apt in my definition of the city. The nucleus of the city is the citadel, the walled precinct of the palace and the temple. Frankfort's interpretation seems to me to point to a profound change that took place when secular power and sacred power were brought together permanently within a limited area. At that point the physical force exerted by a mere chieftain was enormously enhanced by close association with the thaumaturgic powers of a priesthood, so that what command and coercion could not do alone and what magic and ritual could not sufficiently effect by persuasion alone the two together could perform with an overwhelming power never before approached in any society. Since this change came before the written record, it cannot be satisfactorily dated. It may have needed only a few generations, it may have slowly accumulated over centuries before its elements reached the critical weight needed for a reaction. By 3000 B.C. the urban results are plainly visible. Here I find myself naturally using the current vocabulary of nuclear physics for perhaps an extra reason, namely that the forces that brought the city into existence were the products of a fusion reaction and, like that reaction, released an enormous amount of energy for collective work.

You know how suddenly, speaking in centuries, the little step pyramid became the overpowering Great Pyramid. But did not such expansion and magnification take place all along the line and would it not explain how a mere chieftain could become not only a king but likewise, in Egypt, a god? You know the magnitude of the physical works that are still visible or detectable—the great temples, the complex irrigation systems, the vast platforms above the flood, built out of the mud by hand, the mighty walls. No council of elders acting on precedent could have deployed vast bodies of men in such efforts; no mere desire for profitable trade could have created such an extravagant setting for life. Only a king identified as a god or treated as the human representative of a god, a god inflated to astronomical dimensions, could have brought about this transformation. The new powers often assumed paranoid proportions, with paranoid accompaniments of hostility, suspicion, aggression, delusions of grandeur, which may help explain how war repeatedly brought these great achievements to ruin. But it is more important here to recognize that the city endowed the collectivity with cosmic powers and almost superhuman potentialities. No similar magnification and intensification was achieved again until our own times.

This unification of heaven and earth, symbolized so widely, if not universally, by the man-made sacred mountain, completed ideologically the unification of paleolithic and neolithic modes of life. People were drawn to the city voluntarily, no doubt, to participate in these awe-producing powers that were not visible or viable elsewhere, though such participation might demand acts of submission, abnegation, and sacrifice not required in the meaner environment of the village. All the resources of art and technics were mustered in the city to reinforce the claims of kingship and priesthood with the overpowering symbolic representations of authority. Under these conditions the king gathered to himself and ultimately bestowed upon a favored minority a large part of the surplus of the new economy of abundance; and it is not for nothing that you so often find the royal granary within the citadel, for this monopoly of food gave the king the powers of life and death over the whole community. By the same token, the priesthood and the scribes monopolized the production and the transmission of higher learning; this monopoly was more or less maintained in all cultures until the invention of printing. But in return for heavy tribute and heavy toil, the king undertook large-scale public works, of drainage, irrigation, and river control, which were beyond the scope of any smaller community. Democratic communities notoriously shrink from taxing themselves, even for their own benefit, while the royal power, if extravagant and perverse, often had something to show at the end that exalted the humble and caused them to identify their fate with their master's.

In all this my debt to Frankfort is obvious, though even before I had been put on the trail, without guessing how far it would go, by Herodotus, who gives a much later version of how Deioces was turned from a village councilor into a king. That was a sort of shorthand version, not taking account of the earlier religious change, of the change-over from Jacobsen's Mesopotamian council of village elders to a unifying central agent capable of making quick decisions, meeting unexpected emergencies, breaking with ancient customs, capable of giving commands and exacting obedience not merely within its immediate ambit but at a distance, through his distant civil and military agents. From the earliest stronghold on, the walled city was a *Zwingburg* and played an essential part as an instrument of compulsion and control. Whether the wall was originally a religious or a military feature or, more likely, a combination of both, it lessened the need for coercion. In a cityless culture like that of the Spartans, who for long disdained to build walls, the ruling class was forced to remain alertly under arms at all times, lest it be overthrown by the Helots. But where the religious aspect played a relatively larger part, or was accepted with more docile faith, so that the ruler and his followers had less reason for anxiety and distrust, the physical means of ensuring control by a minority, including the wall itself, may have been less conspicuous and the form of the city a more open one, with the bulk of the population remaining in villages, whose number perhaps increased. This seems to hold for early Mayan culture and would indicate not merely an absence of war but perhaps an absence of class conflicts and resentments within the community. And perhaps the same holds for Egypt; if so, it would perhaps help to ease Mr. Wilson's difficulties in finding archeological evidence of the city to support the documentary references to the city's existence in Egypt. But note that one of Deioces' conditions for assuming rulership was that a city should be built for him and that an inviolable royal precinct should be established.

If there are parallels between the original magnification of power through a fusion of secular functions and sacred purposes and similar changes in our own time, with science substituting for theology, there are also important differences. Ours is an age of explosions; and, as a result of undirected technological advances, the city has burst open and scattered its organs and organizations incoherently over the landscape; even the surviving core of the city seems threatened with disintegration. We are witnessing a sort of devotion of urban power into a state of randomness and unpredictability. But the forces that originally produced the city moved in just the opposite direction; they produced not an explosion but an implosion by which a multitude of diverse and often conflicting and colliding particles were held together within a strong urban container. That very containment was perhaps one of the conditions under which the urban cultural potential was built up.

We must not lose sight of this difference when we try to understand the nature of the earliest cities. Whatever else they were, they were above all containers of religious and royal power; and it was that central nucleus of power, itself contained in the palace and the temple, that called people from a distance and united them in tasks that men had never attempted before. Thus the city became the great reservoir of manpower, available for digging, building, trading, fighting, engaging in the specialized trades and professions, the arts and sciences, no longer needed for agricultural labor. The market is a by-product of this concentration and this surplus; but it is the drawing power of the city that brings the trader, not the trader who creates the city. The trader, in time, appears wherever crowds gather, at festivals, funerals, shrines, games, but he does not by his own activities cause population growth nor does he produce the distant goods that circulate in trade. On this matter, Henri Pirenne's description of the extension of the medieval stronghold to include the merchant's suburb has caused many scholars to misinterpret the whole process; and Max Weber, who also looked at the city through medieval spectacles, colored by early capitalism, unfortunately reinforced him.

The attractive power of the ancient city comes not from its market but from its gods. Perhaps the shortest way to define a city, to distinguish it from any mere massing of buildings in a limited area, as at Kahun, is to describe it as the home of a god. But it is even more than that, as emphasized by Mr. Eliade; it is a replica of the universe or that part of the universe in which cosmic order has prevailed over chaos. This connection with heaven gives the city a sort of extra-territoriality, with special privileges and immunities. People put up with the discomforts and congestions of urban life in order to be at the ordered center of things. The city, then, is a model, so to say, of the real world, the significant world, the world representing a wider cosmic order.

Perhaps instead of making so many flat statements, which I have not the time to elaborate in a convincing manner, I should put what I am getting at in the form of questions; for on all these matters I cannot move farther without asking your assistance and gaining your assent. So let me ask: Was the change from the village or the proto-city possible without the institution of kingship, however feasible it was to dispense with that authority at a much later stage, as in Athens? Do you ever find cities of any size without discovering the castle or palace, along with the temple, in a sacred, usually fortified, precinct? Do you find any early cities in which there is not a dominant minority in control of the instruments of power and culture and a much larger group contained by the city but participating only vicariously in its higher activities?

If all these relationships were in fact present from the beginning of cities, as I suppose, and remained constant beneath various disguises and alleviations, they would perhaps point to the fact that the very form and contents of the city produced a result that has too often been overlooked: it minimized the need for application of external force and coercion to its own population, because its divine services and its sacred buildings did more than any pressure of police to polarize its activities and command obedience to its rulers.

Now I want to come back to the question we started with. What is the city? And first we must distinguish between the functions of the city and the purposes and goals that it embodied or made possible. I would say that the main function of the ancient city was the containment and control of a large population—perhaps ten to twenty thousand people—for the immediate benefit of a ruling class and for the ultimate benefit of a whole community whose capital resources and creative potential had been raised to a higher level by this ruling minority. In time the goods monopolized by the citadel, from immortality to water closets, from the written record to systematic science, would filter down to the rest of the community.

But once the urban container was created, it happily subserved many other functions. The special virtue of the container is that the old unchanging form easily adapts itself to new contents. And first, because the rivers were the main transportation routes of the early cities, cities not merely drew for raw materials, food, and manpower from their surrounding region but drained the whole valley and brought together, within a small area, such an intermixture of people, customs, languages and dialects, and craft skill and technicologies as could never have taken place between small isolated villages. The function of the small container is to multiply the opportunity for human contact and intercourse. People who would be lost to each other even a day's journey apart would meet frequently within a walled town and be aware of one another's existence even when they did not meet. The opportunities for cultural cross-fertilization were of many kinds; and even the widening of biological choices in mating may have given the city a special advantage. Without such interactions and transactions, practical and ideological, human cultures tend toward fossilization or toward perverse elaboration on a low level.

So much for the essential urban functions. But the purposes of urban culture transcend these functions to give the city a different role, namely that of adding new forms, values, and significances to the human heritage. In other words, the city is the means of transforming power and productivity into culture and translating culture itself into detachable symbolic forms that can be stored and transmitted. Without the organs and institutions concentrated in the city, it is doubtful whether a complex culture could be transmitted and, still less, continue to develop.

Yet the original form of the city—a self-inclosed container "holding its own"—is in some sense at odds with its function of widening the area of organization and control and bringing into a common center the people and the products of other regions and cultures. Or it might be said that the city is both a container and a magnet and that it plays at once static and dynamic roles, perpetuating its complex past but transforming itself too. This ambivalence seems particularly notable in the central nucleus, and it is has some bearing, I submit, upon the whole problem of the expansion of cultures and the expansion of political power in the form of empires. The very form of the city, with its tight encapsulated nucleus, its limited area, its walled periphery, makes it an excellent organ for one-sided control but a poor one for large-scale co-operation on a give-and-take basis. When royal power, by its very successes, began to expand, it came into conflict with similar concentrations of physical and magical force in other cities; and instead of producing a fusion reaction, with an increase in power, the collision would destroy the nucleus of the rival city and repeatedly wipe out all the co-operative institutions it had fostered. This is not, you will recognize, a mere metaphor; the first object of military attack was to destroy the rival city's god. Characteristically, the Aztec symbol for a captured city is a destroyed temple. Thus, at the moment of its expansion, the city tends to be the chief enemy of every rival city. All over the world, the archeologist has been uncovering the same sad picture: one destroyed city on the debris of another destroyed city. If the cemetery is the first sign of a permanent urban settlement, the necropolis is the last. When culture made one step forward, power too often took two steps backward.

The city, with all its advantages and achievements, was the product of a closed system; and the problem of civilization, still unsolved, is that of creating an open system without losing the important qualities that the first urban containers brought into existence. The size and form of the city must always bear some relation to the complexity and density of the culture it embodies. The ancient city, up to perhaps the beginning of the iron age, was capable of holding and transmitting the major elements of its culture, outside the orbit of agriculture. But it could not expand indefinitely without losing its inner coherence and without encroaching on the territory claimed as the sphere of another city. Given the nature of the container, neither federation nor empire solved this problem. The original isolation and confinement of the city, and the tensions, antagonisms, anxieties generated with it, always or almost always led to a destructive solution. If Egypt seems largely an exception, at least until the Hyksos invasion, this may possibly be because the Nile Valley itself was the main container, and desert, mountain, and ocean served as its walls. But even when the wall became the frontier of a great state, the institutional apparatus created by the city stamped the ampler unit. Perhaps that is why the periods of greatest cultural intermixture seem to be those of destruction and confusion.

But if the combination of sacred and secular power, in the institution of kingship, was responsible for the original form of the city, how is it that the city itself was not radically transformed by the weakening of these powers? The answer is, I think, that, even when one or another element dropped out of the original divine pattern or new factors like overseas commerce and specialized industry became important, the pattern as a whole nevertheless held. Perhaps Athens would seem an exception; but it was not. Athens was a pseudodemocracy, not a real democracy. Even when new institutions came into the city, like the gymnasium, the internal divisions remained. There was a rich man's gymnasium and a poor man's gymnasium; you followed Plato or you followed Antisthenes.

Such freedom and democracy as Hellenic culture knew were probably due to the fact that the village component remained stronger in the city and, with a sturdier development of what Mr. Albright calls "empiricological" thinking, the Greeks, as Herodotus remarked, were less given to nonsense than were their Near Eastern predecessors. More than once, through the offices of the Olympic games, the shrines at Delphi and Delos, and even the medical sanatoria of Cos and Cniddus, the Greeks seemed to be on the verge of breaking through the limitations of the old form of the city and its disruptive empire-building alternative. But the new federated pattern, more mobile, flexible, open, never got a hold on their best minds or even entered them for a receptive examination. Both Plato and Aristotle conceived of the ideal city as a closed container, in which all the higher elements of culture are monopolized by a dominant minority.

If this interpretation of the critical change that made the city possible should help account for the almost universal form of the historic city, from Babylon to Peking, it perhaps also throws a little light on something that the historian and the archeologist, seeking for evidences of human progress in the arts and sciences, too easily overlook, namely that the cult of kingship, with its overmagnification of power and absolute control, with its assumption of absolute sovereignty, also released aggressive and destructive tendencies that the sheer feebleness of earlier communities gave no scope to. These anxieties and delusions account for the invention of war as a typically civilized institution, indeed, as Plato remarked, the main business of states. I have not the time here to go into some of the fresh lines of thought that this opens up; it is enough to point out that by the time the record becomes visible, the original magical purposes of war—except among the Aztecs and the Maya—have been obscured by presumably sensible excuses for aggression in conflicts over territory or water rights. But in any event, the city, by its very form and original contents, institutionalized destruction and extermination as a condition for maintaining and perpetuating its (magical) sovereign powers.

As an instrument of culture, the city has proved indispensable; and if our age of explosions should blow all the ancient cities into thin amorphous suburban film, it will, I think, be necessary to reinvent the city if all the higher manifestations of human culture are not to perish. But as an instrument for monopolizing power and extending that monopoly, through a system of tribute, to other communities, the city bears the unfortunate stamp of its origins and has constantly torn down with one hand what the other hand built up. For this reason I regret that Toynbee wrote twelve whole volumes on the rise and expansion and destruction of civilizations without even mentioning the city, except in two incidental passages. If the perversions of urban power have not in the past proved fatal, that is probably because the mass of mankind continued to live outside cities. This factor of safety is disappearing before our eyes; and if mankind is to survive it must invent a new kind of urban container, on an open pattern, based on the realities of human association and development, not on paranoid claims to godlike domination.

I have merely tried to suggest that one of the chief keys to the development of civilization from about 4500 B.C. to about A.D. 1500—at the end rashly risking a few dates—lies in the radical change of pattern that took place through the implosion of many diverse and conflicting forces in a new kind of container, the nucleated city, and that the new institution of kingship by divine right and appointment may lie at the very center of that change even as it still lies at the heart of all the cant about the unlimited sovereignty of purely earthly governments today. Whether my hypothesis is worth examining or not, I hope I have given you the courage to go back and look more closely at the origins of the city—more closely than even Childe, with his somewhat Victorian antireligious bias, permitted himself to look. Whether these speculations hold water is unimportant. But if you look further, we, or at least our successors, may some day meet at another conference and come to grips with some of these difficult but deeply fascinating problems.

KRAELING: Thank you, Professor Mumford, for your intriguing, stimulating, and question-provoking remarks. They have lifted these discussions to a new plateau, from which I hesitate to recommend any downward pull toward the concrete and limited world with which specialists deal. We have half an hour before it is necessary to adjourn, and I propose that we give several of the gentlemen who provided the central themes of our discussions an opportunity first to say a few words. One is Professor Braidwood, the second is Professor Jacobsen, and the third is Professor Wilson.

BRAIDWOOD: I would like to say to you, Mr. Mumford, that I have never felt as comfortable with a picture painted by a generalist of the material on which I am considered a specialist as I have with yours. Your notion of the hunter still close to the village, for example, is an important idea. In archeology we are still somewhat bound by late nineteenth-century classifications, bar diagrams, neo-Grecisms such as "mesolithic" and "neolithic" for period terminology, and so on. These tend to establish an image of quick and all-pervading change from one level to another. I think the evidence increasingly instructs us otherwise: that different levels of complexity—hunting camp, village, city—intergraded with one another in their development; that the hunter in effect was always there; that in the early villages the proportion of food which was actually produced by agriculture, or the proportion of other bands in the cultural spectrum that responded to this subsistence pattern, was not at all bounded by a clear horizon. While I obviously do not have the time to develop it, this picture has consequences for our understanding of geographical environment—consequences that make me a bit uncomfortable with identifying a particular type or level too closely with a given ecological cubbyhole.

The other thing that came to my mind, and it is too bad that Professor Willey is not here this morning to discuss it with us, concerns your notion of cities adjacent to rivers. This, as Dr. Adams' background paper suggests, gets us into some difficulties in the New World, and, as Professor Gelb suggests, we may have to find some different words. I think Professor Kluckhohn might be willing to think briefly about this feature.

KLUCKHOHN: I was going to say, quite apart from the river business, that on the basis of the present evidence as I understand it, the suggested establishment of kingship as a necessary precondition for the growth of the city does not seem to apply very clearly to the civilizations of the New World.

JACOBSEN: I should like to say first that it is always tantalizing to close a discussion of the kind that we have had, and especially tantalizing after a statement so rich in fruitful ideas and viewpoints that command immediate agreement and demand immediate following-up for further insights that can be produced by them. Professor Mumford's comments were so stimulating in their totality that it is a pity to single out any one aspect, however important it may be in itself; I apologize for concerning myself only with the question of the role of the king in the origin of the city and for limiting myself to ancient Mesopotamia.

We are at the moment in a very difficult position because the evidence is such that we cannot get our hands on the things that are of greatest importance. The question takes us to periods before we have written evidence; it takes us to periods which we may perhaps skirt by using later myths and epics, but these data are very difficult to evaluate. What seems to be left is archeology; if we could find a clearly defined palace we would have something to go by. At the moment, however, we are frustrated because of the fragmentary nature of archeological investigation. No city has been dug in its entirety; there are extensive exposures in only a few spots. We cannot answer this question, therefore, as it should be done. One point that may have some bearing is that when the king emerges in the epics he seems to be connected always with a background larger than the city; he is always the leader in war of a region or of a larger group. Whereas, the *city* ruler, when he comes into full view, is much later. I only say that this is what the evidence suggests, not that there are not other possibilities.

WILSON: I would like to ask Professor Mumford a question and then to make two comments. In the analogy of cell and nucleation is it possible for a cell to have two nuclei? Suppose that there is in a culture one location which is pre-eminently sacred and one location which is pre-eminently political, Babylon and Nippur for example. Would they both be cities, one being the residence of the king and the other a source of power as a sacred city?

MUMFORD: That is a very difficult question to answer. I could answer very easily; the parallel is obvious with medieval cities, which also have the contrast between the cathedral and the castle. I suppose that any one ingredient of the city, any one component, can become the major formative influence and replace some of the other components. That is how we have commercial cities, market cities, industrial cities; but they are not the complete city. The complete city necessarily would include all the components.

WILSON: Occasionally some good citizen says that he and his wife are making a brief visit to Egypt and asks me to recommend a very brief description of the ancient Orient, its history, its monuments, etc. On one occasion I said I could take the time out to write it myself, and I took out a slip of paper and wrote "perhaps." I think this applies to much of the presentation of ancient Egypt. If we think of how different it might have been fifty years ago, or even thirty years ago, we can see how tentative we must of necessity still be. Thus we are not going to arrive at a good, firm, fine answer now; we are merely going to understand more clearly what are the most significant questions and deal with them in the next five to fifteen years, working toward only a new series of questions.

I think I assumed for myself the role of the devil's advocate in saying that Egypt had civilization without cities. The role of the devil's advocate is recognized as a holy role but not as one of full personal commitment. As the devil's advocate, I have been partly persuaded by this meeting but not fully convinced.

KRAELING: I am sure there are others who would like to comment on some of the many interesting facets of Professor Mumford's presentation.

KLUCKHOHN: This is only partly relevant to Professor Mumford's argument, but in these meetings, which to me have been profoundly instructive as well as enjoyable, there has been one curious omission. The theme has come up again and again as to how we may understand cultural distinctiveness as well as similarity. There has been, from my point of view, an extraordinary silence on one possibility. I suspect this is a case where a particular baby has been scrubbed so hard in the last generation or so that it has been poured away with the bath water. The absurdities and extravagances of certain nineteenth-century conceptions of race and the intellectually and morally abhorrent versions of such doctrines in this century should not blind us to the fact that populations differ in their genes. Not generally on an all-or-none basis, but certainly, in terms of the marker genes on which we now have a considerable amount of information, they differ appreciably in the incidence of certain genes. Assuming that capacities of various sorts and, shall we say, "temperamental proclivities" are not precisely identical in all populations, should we not at least allow for the possibility that along with environmental, geographical, and cultural influences that make for distinctiveness there may be a biological element? Frankly, I think it is extraordinary that in these meetings this particular issue has never been mentioned.

SPEISER: I wish that Mr. Mumford's fishhook had been thrown out earlier. In that case we might have followed up some important lines of discussion that it is now too late to do much about. I would like to make just one suggestion about a possible criterion for the definition of a city. What counts is not the physical shell but the society inside it. It is a question of a state of mind. Cities in the biblical society, no matter how large they may have been, did not house an urban society. Biblical society was basically a tribal society, as can be shown by both its law and its terminology. On the other hand, in Mesopotamia from the very beginning the terminology was that of an urban society. The basic unit, the *awīlu,* legally is a citizen of a state and not merely a member of a family.

ALBRIGHT: I will seize this opportunity not to say anything new but merely to remark that I have never attended a conference from which I learned as much as I have from this symposium.

KRAELING: Thank you very much. I hope I may be excused for calling an end on this flattering note. Professor Mumford has put us deeply in his debt with a provocative presentation which give us much food for future thought. Perhaps next time we meet we should slay the sacrificial lamb first and then, as high priests, exercise the prerogative of sitting around at the banquet and devouring him.

Professor Mumford said one thing which particularly stuck in my mind. He stressed the importance of the meeting place, the place to come back to, as an element in the growth of established settlements and of culture. I am sure I speak for all of its staff when I say to all of you that the Oriental Institute is most grateful for the time you have taken to come here and be with us and for the contributions you have made to the discussions. We hope that, to a worth-while degree, this hall, this Oriental Institute, has fulfilled the functions of a meeting place in Professor Mumford's sense. If so, it deserves to be returned to. Let us hope that other meetings, as useful as this one, may be held here in the future.

THE BACKGROUND PAPERS

I

The Expansion of Society and Its Cultural Implications

By MILTON SINGER

Archeology, History, and Social Anthropology

The symposium papers deal with three distinct spatio-temporal contexts of societal expansion:

(1) The context of prehistory, in which, after about 450,000 years of food-gathering and about 50,000 years of food-collecting, mankind achieved on the hilly flanks of the Fertile Crescent in southwestern Asia by about 8000 B.C. an incipient cultivation of wild wheats, barleys, and legumes, domestication of the dog and of food animals, manufacture of flint sickle blades and good stone tools, and the building of settled village-farming communities. This is the "prelude to civilization" described by Braidwood and is also the context frequently mentioned in Adams' and Eliade's papers.

(2) The context of the historic civilizations, the early ones of the Old and the New World as well as the later ones of Byzantium, Islam, and the West, which grew out of them. Most of the papers in the symposium take this as their primary context; Braidwood's and Kluckhohn's are clearly outside of it.

(3) The context of the ethnological and sociological present, of the villages, towns, and cities directly observed by students of tribal, peasant, and urban societies within the last hundred years. Only Kluckhohn takes this as a primary context, although there are incidental references to it in some of the other papers, particularly in Rheinstein's.

These contexts involve different time perspectives, different kinds of methods and evidence for their exploration, different levels of cultural development. Kluckhohn, for example, prefers to restrict his inquiry into the effects of societal expansion on the moral order to the third context because of the difficulties of reconstructing the prehistoric moral order from archeological evidence. He finds it equally difficult to reconstruct the moral order of preliterate societies prior to a few centuries ago because of the absence of written records and the "interfering" effects of colonialism, religious proselytization, and worldwide communication.

Kluckhohn's restriction of the field of inquiry to the last few centuries represents the critical methodological viewpoint of contemporary social anthropologists. Nineteenth-century anthropologists were much less critical in this respect. Sir Henry Maine (1861, 1876) compared the customs of Indian village communities he had personally observed with early Roman law. Lewis Henry Morgan (1877) compared the Iroquois kinship and political structures with early Greek and Roman precedents. In fact, the nineteenth-century anthropologists used "primitive," "ancient," and "archaic" almost interchangeably and moved back and forth among the three contexts with the greatest of ease. What predisposed them to do so was the belief in a theory of linear social and cultural evolution and in "laws of progress" which ordained that monogamy, private property, monotheism, and constitutional government were the culminating achievements of a cosmic process beginning in primitive hordes with a community of property, wives, and decision. The twentieth century's critical reaction to this naïve faith (as it now seems to us) largely accounts for the critical circumspection with which contemporary social anthropologists approach the kind of comparison and integration of archeological, historical, and ethnological data proposed in the present symposium.

Redfield has observed that the separation of social anthropology from history and archeology, as represented for example in the work of Durkheim, Malinowski, and Radcliffe-Brown, was in fact a phase in a dialectical development which is just ending and which is beginning to be superseded by a new phase in which social anthropology once more seeks closer articulation with historical and archeological studies (Redfield, 1955). Redfield's own work bears out and contributes to this sequence of development.

Not all the conceptions of the earlier period have been superseded in the later. In modified form, some of the earlier conceptions have continued to be useful. Redfield himself acknowledged the influence of the evolutionary theories of Maine and Morgan as well as of the theories of Durkheim and Tönnies. All these writers attached fundamental significance to the differences between small-scale communities based on kinship ties, on the one hand, and large-scale societies which transcended such ties, on the other. Each of them introduced a special set of terms to mark this basic distinction: "status" *vs.* "contract" (Maine), "Societas" *vs.* "Civitas" (Morgan), "Gemeinschaft" *vs.* "Gesellschaft" (Tönnies), and "mechanical solidarity" *vs.* "organic solidarity" (Durkheim). Made more precise and systematic, this distinction was the heart of the folk-urban typology which Redfield (1941) applied so effectively to the particular facts of Yucatan. Kroeber's general summary on the significance of kinship in primitive and early societies as contrasted with its role in complex civilizations is consonant not only with Redfield's findings but with those of the nineteenth-century evolutionists as well:

> In the grand sweep of cultural growth, . . . successful technological and political developments, which characterize the more complex civilizations, are secondary and late products reared upon social forms or devices centering immemorially around kinship. Some measure of these kinship forms persists into higher civilization because kinship is biologically inescapable and perhaps equally inescapable psychologically. But the kinship structures of complex civilizations are often reduced, almost always divested of excrescences and luxuriances of pattern; they have become humble, simple, subserving real ends. The experimentation, inventiveness, and instability so evident in the social forms of primitive societies are transferred to the technological and political fields in higher civilization [Kroeber, 1942].

Not many anthropologists today would accept Herbert Spencer's theories of social and cultural evolution. Yet his theories and organic analogies served as the provocative stimuli to much later development, as is made particularly clear in Durkheim's *Division of Labor in Society* (1933), where Spencer figures so dependably as an antagonist. Durkheim does not accept unchanged Spencer's formulation of the relation of the size of a society to its structure, but the changes he introduces are easier to understand with these formulations in mind. Here is Spencer:

> . . . along with increase of size in societies goes increase of structure. . . . It is also a characteristic of social bodies, as of living bodies, that while they increase in size they increase in structure. . . . The social aggregate, homogeneous when minute, habitually gains in heterogeneity along with each increment of growth; and to reach great size must acquire great complexity [*Principles of Sociology,* 1876; see also Schnore, 1958].

This is the root idea, minus the evolutionary assumption, from which Durkheim (1933) develops his distinctive theory of "segmentary" and "organic" social structures. In the segmented small societies, Durkheim posits little differentiation beyond that defined by age and sex, by the basic social units founded on kinship, by the lack of control over the environment, and by a "mechanical" solidarity springing from the likeness of each segment to every other segment. In large complex "organic" societies, there are, on the contrary, increased specialization and division of labor and interdependence among the parts; basic social units are no longer restricted to kinship units but include territorial and professional organizations; and social solidarity is "organic," springing from functional differentiation as well as from a core of similarity.

The increase in the social division of labor, according to Durkheim's theory, depends not just on the increase in size or in physical density of the population but on its "moral density," that is, an increase in social interaction:

The division of labor develops . . . as there are more individuals sufficiently in contact to be able to act and react upon one another. If we agree to call this relation and the active commerce resulting from it dynamic or moral density, we can say that the progress of the division of labor is in direct ratio to the moral or dynamic density of society.

"Moral density" in turn results either from an increased concentration of population, as in cities, or from improvements in the means of transportation and communication.

Chiefly through the influence of Radcliffe-Brown, Durkheim's analysis of "segmentary" societies has been intensively applied to the social structure of primitive societies. Through Redfield, the interrelations of isolation, homogeneity, and "moral density" have been studied in the changing structures of primitive, peasant, and urban societies.

In Redfield's *Folk Culture of Yucatan* (1941), the context of societal expansion is that of the ethnological present. Through a simultaneous comparison of four communities in Yucatan, which exhibit increasing size and complexity (a tribal village, a peasant village, a town, and a metropolitan city), it is established that their positions on the map, in relation to the city as a major center of influence, correspond to a regular association of certain of their cultural characteristics. Redfield's most general formulation of the nature of this association is that as the isolation and cultural homogeneity of a community decrease, cultural disorganization, secularization, and individualization within the community increase. This generalization is asserted only in relation to this area of Yucatan. Whether it may also be asserted as a universal generalization applicable to other societies and cultures is discussed as a question for further research, and some evidence is presented from Tax's Guatemalan studies to raise doubts about the universality of the association. All that is implied as to universality is "the assumption that other communities, similarly situated in other parts of the world, might be similarly ranged according to the same guiding conceptions and so make possible a comparative study of the problems sketched in this report" (p. 345).

In keeping with the contemporary and functional emphasis of the Yucatan study, the relations among the different cultural characteristics are seen as interdependent, natural, and, in a sense, timeless. Although several historical implications of the study are noted, Redfield prefers to understate these; "the contribution made to the history of Yucatan is small" (pp. 342–44) because the chief purpose of the study is not historical but a systematic comparision of the "folk" and "urban" types of society:

. . . The simple comparison of contemporary communities is not a method to be recommended to those wishing to do historical research in Yucatan, in view of the availability of documents and in view of the opportunity to determine the recent history of any community studied by consulting old informants as to earlier conditions. It is, however, a satisfactory way somewhat to clarify certain problems as to the nature of isolated-homogeneous society as compared with mobile-heterogeneous society [pp. 343–44].

In Redfield's *The Primitive World and Its Transformations* (1953), what were previously separated are now brought together—archeology, history, and social anthropology. The folk-urban typology applied to a contemporary cross section of four contemporary communities in Yucatan is now applied longitudinally to the history of the human career as well as to the particular histories of Mayan and Roman civilizations. The value of this longitudinal analysis goes beyond the many illuminating contributions which social anthropology makes to historical and archeological problems; it is equally valuable for the contributions that archeological and historical analyses make to social anthropolgy. What was hidden in the cross-sectional analysis shows up clearly in the longitudinal analysis. The Mayan civilization now reveals a primary phase of transformation in folk societies from tribal to peasant levels within a single local cultural tradition which is missing from the secondary transformations induced by contact with Western civilization. This led Redfield to make a sharper differentiation between peasant and primitive folk societies and to add an important analysis of indigenous civilizations in which new styles of life and new types of specialists, idea systems, and cultural centers appear.

The omission of the Mayan indigenous civilization from the cross-sectional study of Yucatan, it might be argued, resulted not from the limitations of the functional analysis of social anthropology but from the fact that the Spanish Conquest "decapitated" the indigenous Maya elite and the cultural centers. A contemporary cross-sectional analysis of a civilization whose great traditions have survived into the present, as in India, would reveal, according to this argument, elements of the indigenous civilization. We may grant this possibility without relinquishing the general conclusion of our discussion that where a culture or civilization has experienced significant change, a cross-sectional analysis made at some limited phase of its career will need to be supplemented by a longitudinal historical analysis, or at least by an analysis of several cross sections taken at different periods in its career. In practice, then, close co-operation among social anthropologists, historians, and archeologists will be required.

Cultural Causality and the Formation of Cultural Traditions

The relation of culture to societal expansion is a peculiarly difficult one to analyze because of its mixed objective-subjective character. Expansion can be expressed quantitatively in terms of increases in population size, density, territory, and the like. Its effects on the essentially mental and subjective phenomena of language, law, literature, art, religion, and other spheres of culture are, however, difficult to formulate in precise and objective terms. As in the analogous case of the individual body-mind problem, although interaction occurs, the exact nature of the interaction is not clearly understood. This difficulty is appreciated by all contributors to this symposium, and none of them attempts to reduce the problem to a simple causal theory or form of determinism. Each of them is, indeed, rather careful to avoid such theories in his formulation. Eliade's statement that "it is not the natural phenomenon of vegetation which is responsible for the appearance of mythico-religious systems of agrarian structure but rather the religious experience occasioned by the discovery of a mystical solidarity between man and plant life" (see p. 359) is typical of the level of methodological sophistication to which I refer.

Nevertheless, the papers taken together do contain, at least implicitly, a tenable view of cultural causality, which I should like to make explicit and to develop a short way beyond the authors' intentions. There are indeed several different kinds of cultural causality discussed in the papers, each particular kind assuming a special significance for each context of societal expansion. In the context of prehistory, Braidwood sees the imperious demands of the local environment imposing an *ecological causality* on the society and culture of the precivilized small community. This ecological causality does not remain constant, however; certain variations on the "ecological theme" occur: an increase in extractive efficiency, which makes possible a "living into" the environment; an increase in technological complexity, which makes possible adaptation to a greater variety of environments; and an increase in sociocultural complexity, which mitigates the necessity for an ecological balance. The net effect of these variations is a change in the nature of the ecological causality, for *natural history* becomes under their influence *cultural history* about 3,000 or 4,000 years before the "coming of civilization."

Much the same conclusion is arrived at by Adams in his comparative analysis of the ecological basis of four early civilizations of Peru, Middle America, Egypt, and Mesopotamia. Although he finds a common ecological basis for these civilizations in the surpluses made available by sedentary, diversified, and intensive agriculture, he is equally impressed by the ecological and institutional differences among them and by the fact that many of these differences and much of the sociocultural development seem to proceed on their own terms. The natural environment recedes to a backdrop as ecological causality is increasingly controlled by improved technical development.

Something more than the natural ecological balance is transcended with the coming of civilization. As Kluckhohn, following Redfield, observes, the balance of the technical order and the moral order now also undergoes a change. The moral order ceases to dominate the expanding technical order and itself becomes an object of deliberate policy and self-conscious reform. Ideas become forces in history.

One of these ideas, already foreshadowed in the earliest civilizations and a commonplace of modern civilizations, is the idea of ethnic and cultural imperialism. Gelb documents it for ancient Mesopotamia, and Von Grunebaum for Islam. Eliade suggests that it may even have a prehistoric precedent in the ancient belief that a new or unknown territory needs to be "cosmized," that is, sanctified in accordance with the cosmogonic myths in order to assure the "openness" to the world of the gods and to make possible orientation in space. Perhaps this idea is the basis for planting a national flag on newly discovered or conquered territory.

In any case, the imperial idea reverses the direction of the causal relation between societal expansion and culture. Expansion now becomes "expansionism," a doctrine or idea which may precede the actual fact of expansion. The dream of empire is usually dreamed before the empire is gained. Ethnic and cultural imperialism, however, contain intrinsic limitations which prevent them from functioning creatively in historical development. These limitations have been well described by Redfield:

A consciousness in a people that it is their mission to extend their rule, their customs, their kind of law and justice, over peoples different from themselves is such an idea as now supplements and guides the automatic extensions of the technical order. It controls and it justifies an expansion engineered by power—commercial, military, political. Surely, as in the extension of Hellenic culture into Asia through Alexander, or in the expansion of Western civilization with the aid of such ideas as the white man's burden or the manifest destiny of the United States, it has great consequences for the moral order, and it may, as in the conception of Roman law, have an ethical component within itself. But these ideas are not primarily ideas of religious and ethical creativeness; they are ideas after the technical fact. And all of them contain an assumption as to the superiority of right or privilege of the expanding people over others. And one ventures to say that all of them fail in the long run [Redfield, 1953, pp. 78–79].

Redfield also notes that expanding political institutions tend to create new moral orders, or at least to initiate a process which creates them. The dynamics of such a process stimulate ideas of ever more inclusive moral orders, and these ideas in turn become influential in history:

The unit of political life tends to become identified with a people who share a common moral life, including the sense that they share one. So the tribe, the city-state, the nation are such approximate identifications of equivalent units of society, peoples that are both a technical and a moral unit. Yet as one looks at any one of these politico-moral societal types as it appears to predominate at some place or time, one sees that the technical order, in the form of exchange of goods and in the conflict of war, has already gone beyond the politico-moral unit, which is already inadequate to keep people from enjoying the fruits of the exchange or even the security of peace; and one begins to look forward to the extension of the moral order to larger societal units, which will in turn call for political inventions. . . . The idea that a world community is necessary is an idea created by developments in the technical order. This idea in turn influences the actual moral order to develop in its direction, and helps to bring about political inventions, United Nations, or possible charters of a universal federal government that would both express and create the enlarging moral order [*ibid.* pp. 74–75].

To ecological, technical, and ideological causality, social anthropology adds a notion of *functional causality*. This is the causality that obtains among the interdependent parts of a functioning society or culture. Kluckhohn's statement that "the association of type of economy with a specific kind of social organization and of these and other aspects of culture with one sort of moral order as opposed to another is by no means altogether a random one" implies functional causality and is the basis for his anticipation that "there will ordinarily be some determinable relationships between the size of social groups and characteristics of their value systems" (p. 392 below). The abstract character of a moral code in a non face-to-face urban society, for example, he explains in terms of the necessity of maintaining a minimum of social order and predictability under conditions "where many persons never encounter certain other persons at all and where numerous contacts that do occur are casual and transitory" (see p. 394). The interrelations of isolation, density, and homogeneity postulated by Durkheim and Redfield are further examples of functional causality. The context in all these cases is that of the ethnological present, but the functional analysis of causal relations may also be applied to prehistorical and historical contexts, as it is to an extent by Braidwood, Adams, and Von Simson.

Standardization of Cultural Diversity

A functionally causal analysis in social anthropology usually begins with an ongoing social and cultural system; it does not seek to trace the processes by which the system was established or how it may have grown out of a previous system. So long as the context is that of the ethnological present and of short-run changes within it, the method is adequate. When the context is broadened to embrace the expansion of society from the beginnings of agriculture through the historic development of different civilizations, functional analysis needs to be extended. It is just at this point that historical and archeological analyses make an important contribution to our understanding of cultural processes concomitant with societal expansion. The process revealed by these analyses is the formation of cultural traditions through the standardization of cultural diversity. The results of this process are not always uniform, but its operation is sufficiently general to apply to all contexts of expansion.

The operation of this process is explicitly noted in Rheinstein's paper on the growth and development of law when he writes that "the need for law arises with the need of correlating in one society different modes of human existence, and that need grows with growing complexity" (see p. 417). The increasing heterogeneity of modes of existence which accompanies expansion, rather than the sheer growth of numbers and space, has influenced the rise and growth of law. The development of legal norms and of enforcement procedures may thus be seen as a series of efforts to standardize the increasing diversity of an expanding society.

With only slightly less explicitness, the other symposium papers indicate the operation of a similar process in other spheres of culture—economic organization (Polanyi), political administration (Gelb, Adams), language (Gelb), literature (Grene), art (Von Simson), religion (Eliade, Von Grunebaum), morals (Grene, Kluckhohn). In each case a particular kind of diversity is standardized through the development of particular kinds of standards, norms, and institutions for managing that diversity (e.g., money, a bureaucracy, a lingua franca, an art form or art style, a religious ideology, an abstract moral code). The process is both concomitant with the expansion of society and a means of furthering such expansion. It underlies the formation of those cultural traditions which together make up a developed civilization. In rudimentary form it is probably also the basis of the earliest cultural development, as Braidwood's discussion of a "standard tool" that can be made at will for a specific purpose suggests (see p. 300). Presumably a similar process of cultural standardization was involved in the domestication of plants and animals, for this required the selection and cultivation of particular varieties from generation to generation. Edgar Anderson's contemporary observations on this process in the Guatemalan highlands and in Assam call attention to the rigid selection exercised by primitive farmers:

In Mexico I worked almost exclusively with farmers of European or partly European ancestry. Even those who had strikingly Indian features were mostly Spanish-speaking and did not consider themselves Indians. In Guatemala I worked with such people but also with Indians who had retained their old languages and their own cultures. I found, to my surprise, that their cornfields had been more rigidly selected for type than those of their Latin-speaking neighbors. Their fields were quite as true to type as had been prize-winning American cornfields in the great corn-show era when the American farmer was paying exquisite attention to such fancy show points as uniformity. This fact was amazing, considering the great variability of Guatemalan maize as a whole, and the fact that corn crosses so easily. A little pollen blown from one field to another will introduce mongrel germ plasm. Only the most finicky selection of seed ears and the pulling out of plants which are off type could keep a variety pure under such conditions. Yet for Mexico and Guatemala and our own Southwest the evidence is clear: wherever the old Indian cultures have survived most completely the corn is least variable within the variety.

Much later I grew a collection of corn made among an even more primitive people, the Naga of Assam, whom some ethnologists describe as still living in the Stone Age in so far as their daily life is concerned. Each tribe had several different varieties which were sharply different from one another, yet within the variety there were almost no differences from plant to plant. Furthermore, some of the most distinctive of these varieties were grown not only by different families but by different tribes, in different areas. Only a fanatical adherence to an ideal type could have kept these varieties so pure when they were being traded from family to family and from tribe to tribe. It is apparently not true, as has so frequently been stated, that the most primitive people have the most variable varieties. Quite the opposite. It is rather those natives most frequently seen by travelers, the ones who live along modern highways and near big cities, the ones whose ancient cultures have most completely broken down, who have given rise to the impression that primitive people are careless plant breeders [Anderson, 1952, pp. 218–19].

The process of standardization operates, in all probability, in primitive and in prehistoric societies as well as in the civilized. In the case of civilization, however, there is more of it. The increasing cultural variety that follows expansion requires a countervailing increase in standardization. Among its other functions, this requirement expresses man's need to live in a meaningful world, in a "cosmos," a need which Eliade says is to be found in all religions. But standardization does not follow automatically because there is a need for it. The need must be perceived, and ways to meet it must be found or created. Civilization is the story of these perceptions and of the cognitive responses to them. The standards so developed differ from those developed under precivilized or primitive conditions in being more autonomous and specialized, more self-consciously elaborated by a professional intellectual class.

In their earliest form, cultural standards follow the broad lines laid down by the local "paleo-environment." At this stage the "cultural types" are replicas of local "natural types." In its later forms, the standardization becomes progressively more autonomous. Autonomy of development means not necessarily a development of each cultural sphere but only a decreasing dependence of a particular culture on a particular local environment.

Increasing specialization of the different cultural spheres and increasing systematization of the standards peculiar to each go with explicit verbalization and cultivation by full-time specialists. The standardizing process is thus lifted from a subliminal level of "typical unawareness," where the canons of choice are largely unconscious, to a self-conscious and reflective level of formulated criteria, rules, values, codes, arts, and sciences. For example, Emeneau (1942, 1955) has noted how in ancient India a science of grammar, a highly elaborated gesture-language for the dance, and yoga have all resulted from the bringing up to a conscious level of unconsciously patterned systems of behavior.

The general tendency to self-conscious standardization in Indian civilization finds parallels in other civilizations. It may operate unequally on different cultural spheres in different civilizations—on law and government in one, on astronomy and mathematics in another, on language and literature in still another. Whatever the cultural spheres, the continuous operation of a process of autonomous, systematic, and self-conscious standardization under the guidance of a group of specialists transforms a given body of local cultural traditions into what Redfield has called a "great tradition."

The foregoing sketch of the formation of cultural traditions through a process of standardizing the increasing cultural diversity concomitant upon expansion tries to synthesize the concepts and methods of the archeologist and the historian with the social anthropologist's concepts of functional causality, culture patterns, and cultural values (especially Sapir, 1927; Benedict, 1934; Kluckhohn, 1941). I shall now consider how such a cultural process may be related to the particular form of societal expansion that comes with urbanization.

Urbanization and Cultural Change

The attainment of civilization, as Braidwood and Adams and other contributors to the symposium agree, is expressed in the growth of towns and cities, in an "urban revolution." Yet it would be hard, as Adams notes, to imagine a sharper contrast "than that between Sumerians clustering in cities and Classic Mayans living in dispersed, essentially rural, hamlets while only a small elite permanently inhabited the elaborate religious centers" (p. 273 below). All that these two kinds of "cities" may have in common is an average density higher than that of their respective hinterlands. The great variability in the distribution of population and settlement units in the different civilized areas challenges any effort to generalize about the relation of urbanization to types of culture change. Two distinct and complementary methods are available: the functionally causal analysis of the sociologist and social anthropologist and the historical-contextual analysis of the culture historian and archeologist.

Durkheim (1933), Redfield (1941), Simmel (1951), and Wirth (1951) employ the first method by seeking to establish functionally causal relations between the physical and "moral" density of settlement units and the social and cultural characteristics generally associated with them.

The second method recognizes that urban centers of similar density may differ in important social and cultural characteristics if they are located in different historical and environmental contexts and if they play different cultural roles in the network of settlement units in which they happen to be embedded. This method views a city as a locus of interaction of diverse cultural traditions and tries to trace the conditions and consequences of such interaction in the formation and transformation of new cultural traditions through standardization and other processes. Since Kluckhohn has given an excellent and lucid summary of the major results of the first method, I should like in this concluding section to confine my remarks to the second method and to indicate how several of the symposium papers contribute to it.

Applying the second method, Redfield (1953; Redfield and Singer, 1954) has suggested two basically different roles which cities may play in relation to cultural change: (1) to carry forward into a systematic and reflective dimension an old culture and (2) to create original modes of thought which have authority beyond or in conflict with old cultures and civilizations. The first or "orthogenetic" role is predominant in the administrative-cultural cities (e.g., Uaxactun, Kyoto, Liége, Banaras) where the native literati convert local folk cultures into a civilized dimension of a "great tradition." The second or "heterogenetic" role tends to predominate in cities of native commerce (e.g., Bruges, Marseilles), in metropolitan cities (London, New York, Osaka, Bombay), and in cities of modern administration (e.g., Washington, D.C., New Delhi, Canberra). In these cities, in which live large populations of diverse cultural origins removed from the indigenous seats of their cultures, a new class of intellectuals, the intelligentsia, arises to cultivate new states of mind indifferent to or inconsistent with the states of mind associated with the local cultures of the indigenous civilization.

Cultural change takes place in both the orthogenetic and the heterogenetic cities, the difference consisting in the character of the predominant changes:

Insofar as the city has an orthogenetic role, it is not to maintain culture as it was; the orthogenetic city is not static; it is the place where religious, philosophical and literary specialists reflect, synthesize and create out of the traditional material new arrangements and developments that are felt by the people to be outgrowths of the old. What is changed is a further statement of what was there before. Insofar as the city has a heterogenetic role, it is a place of differing traditions, a center of heresy, heterodoxy and dissent, of interruption and destruction of ancient tradition, of rootlessness and anomy. Cities are both these things, and the same events may appear to particular people or groups to be representative of heterogenesis. The predominating trend may be in one of the two directions, and so allow us to characterize the city, or that phase of the history of the city, as the one or the other. The lists just given suggest that the differences in the degree to which in the city orthogenesis or heterogenesis prevails are in cases strongly marked.

The presence of the market is not of itself a fact of heterogenetic change. Regulated by tradition, maintained by such customs and routines as develop over long periods of time, the market may flourish without heterogenetic change. In the medieval Muslim town we see an orthogenetic city; the market and the keeper of the market submitted economic activities to explicit cultural and religious definition of the norms. In Western Guatemala the people who come to market hardly communicate except with regard to buying and selling and the market has little heterogenetic role. On the other hand the market in many instances provides occasion when men of diverse traditions may come to communicate and to differ; and also in the market occurs that exchange on the basis of universal standards of utility which is neutral to particular moral orders and in some sense hostile to all of them. The cities of Group 2, therefore, are cities unfavourable to orthogenetic change but not necessarily productive of heterogenetic change [Redfield and Singer, 1954, pp. 169–70].

This difference in the cultural role of cities is particularly well illustrated in the symposium papers by Von Simson, Polanyi, Gelb, and Grene. Von Simson regards the city as "the most important prerequisite for a significant development of the arts." The art of peasants, nomads, hunters, and seafaring people, he believes, is only a "marginal art" and adornment. But it is a special type of city he has in mind—one which offers tradition, social stability, cultural cohesion, a widespread demand for and appreciation of art products. In the metropolitan city lacking a community of tradition and changing too rapidly to allow the development of cultural homogeneity, he does not find great art or any distinctive art styles.

Polanyi's analysis of the relation of the city market (the agora) to the city-state (the polis) in fifth-century Athens similarly identifies some of the characteristics of an orthogenetic city by showing how the close political, religious, and cultural integration of the "market" with the "state" prevented either from expanding and produced a deep-seated fear of ethnic and religious dilution.

In marked contrast, some of the city-states of ancient Mesopotamia described by Gelb dominated their neighbors and grew into small kingdoms and then into empires, embracing a diversity of peoples and cultures. However, even this rapid development of the heterogenetic role depended, in part at least, on the continuation and extension of orthogenetic functions. Some of these links with the older cultural traditions are emphasized in Gelb's analysis: the maintenance of allegiance by all the city-states to a religious center, Nippur, which was not directly involved in their political rivalries; the striving to extend the language of the dominant people over an entire kingdom and the instability of bilingual compromises; the persistence of Sumerian and Akkadian as cultural languages after their disappearance as spoken languages; and the disappearance of the Sumerians and the Akkadians with the disappearance of their languages as living languages. The sequence of development of political allegiance which Gelb finds in Mesopotamia—first to small city-states and small kingdoms, then to a religious center, and finally to a *demos* based on a dominant *ethnos*—not only marks the phases of an expansion beyond the original ethnic, linguistic, and religious social units of the city-states but marks as well the creation of new ethno-linguistic units. Under the influence of imperial expansion, orthogenetic cities become heterogenetic in cultural function, and they in turn serve as starting points for the development of new cultural traditions and a new cycle of orthogenesis.

Viewed in the perspective of imperial expansion or the growth of metropolitan centers, an orthogenetic city like fifth-century Athens appears as a case of arrested development. When viewed, however, in the perspective of the more archaic traditions which it transformed into the great Athenian traditions in philosophy, drama, art, and literature, it appears to play a more creative cultural role. Grene's account of the influence of Homer on the fifth-century tragedians describes in detail several steps in this transformation. There is continuity in both subject and technique with the archaic period. "The three tragic poets must have had an inner acquaintance with the myths and a capacity to reconcile them and their personal ideas and impressions rather like the relation existing between the epic min-

strel and his story." And this may also be the manner, Grene suggests, of Shakespeare or a modern playwright: "No doubt the idea
for the play came to him out of a scene in a street, a sentence in a
story, or a public happening. But for his audience this must be
enlarged and accommodated, archaized and still left contemporary,
in the dress of a myth of altogether unhistorical times." The myth is
"also the touchstone of the validity of the idea gained conceivably
from another source" (see p. 378). Aeschylus, Euripides, and Sophocles reinterpret the myths, each in his distinctive way, and create a
new medium of tragedy. Stimulated by the interest in war and
slavery among the urban, largely illiterate audience at the popular
festivals for which the plays were written, the dramatists restate the
Homeric tragic philosophy "for a whole people." Within the Homeric framework they raise questions of justice and injustice unknown to Homer's heroes, lifting, in Aeschylus at least, the solution
of the blood feud to the abstract notion of justice within the community. These questions bring to the surface, Grene believes, the
philosophy of justice criticized by Plato, a philosophy buried so deep
in Homer's epics that everything else seems more important. The
dramatists are thus literati who carry forward into new dimensions
of a reflective urban culture elements of an "archaic" and "poetic"
world view.

In twentieth-century Madras I recently had an opportunity to
observe some of the cultural processes—though the quality of the
product may differ—which Grene describes in fifth-century Athens
(Singer, 1958). Dramatists, reciters, performers, and producers in
other media adapt and enlarge the themes and techniques of epic
and myth for mass urban audiences interested in the relation of this
"archaic" material to contemporary social problems and democratic
ideology. Madras is not an exact parallel to Athens, of course; it is a
modern metropolitan center, and the great Sanskrit traditions of
drama and philosophy to be found in the city are already very old.
Nor is there in these traditions a world view similar to Homer's
tragic philosophy. In the Hindu outlook, as in the Greek, there is
a widespread belief in the inexorableness of fate and in the futility
of trying to circumvent it in this life, but in Hinduism the individual
can do something about it. He can escape from his "existential" condition by following a regime of ascetic austerities, a good life of
ritual observance, or a path of devotion—the three traditional paths
to release and merger with the Absolute. Within such a practical

and optimistic outlook there seems little need for the stance of direct confrontation of fate and of ultimate defiance struck by the Homeric hero.

In contemporary Madras, and in the other metropolitan centers of India, Greek tragedy, Shakespeare, and the modern tragedians are well known and appreciated by the educated class. The importation of these Western cultural forms has not yet led to any sharp break with the traditional Indian outlook. Instead, elements of these Western forms and of the mass media are combined with the traditional media to produce a distinctively modern Indian culture. In this culture, the great traditions of Sanskritic Hinduism and local and regional cultural traditions continue to exercise an important influence, not in their traditional forms but reinterpreted to serve the newer demands of social reform, ecumenical religion, and advancing scientific knowledge.

This brief comparison of the fifth-century polis Athens and the twentieth-century metropolis Madras suggests that the relations of urbanization to culture change may depend not only on factors of size, density, and cultural heterogeneity but also on the social and cultural structure of the traditions undergoing urbanization and upon the nature of the world view expressed in these traditions. I have neither the time nor the competence to compare ancient Greece and modern India in these respects, but it seems to me quite likely that the striking continuity of the old and the new in Madras depends on the resiliency in the structure and content of Indian cultural traditions. This resiliency has permitted continuous absorption into and modification of the dominant orthodox traditions by a great variety of heterodox, tribal, local and regional traditions. Its operation seems to depend on and in turn to create such features of structure and world view as flexibility in applying scriptural canons to particular cases, tolerance for the diversity of creeds, a long-run cosmic view of change, and a highly pragmatic attitude toward religion, science, art, and political ideologies. I do not mean to assert that every civilization which persists in the face of societal expansion and change will have just these characteristics; I am saying that these are some of the decisive characteristics which enabled Indian civilization to endure and expand. The persistence and expansion of other civilizations may or may not depend on just these characteristics. In Von Grunebaum's analysis of the persistence of Islamic civilization, for instance, there are also noted the capacity to integrate heterodox beliefs into the orthodox position and a flexibility in applying canon law, but other features, such as the transformation of the religious law from an operational to a moral code, unilateral conversion, conception of the religious community as a timeless far-flung community freed from territorial ties and unified only at an abstract level by a minimum requirement of belief and practice, are not very prominent in Hinduism, although they seem to have played an important part in the persistence and expansion of Islam. How far these characteristics of Islamic culture were related to urbaniza-tion Von Grunebaum does not happen to say in his present paper. From his other writings on this subject, however, I have the impres-sion that he would link these characteristics with the fact that Islam was essentially a religion of urban origin.

In any case, we may conclude that urbanization is associated with varied patterns of cultural development in different civilizations, and that the question of why the net balance of development should sometimes be culturally anabolic and sometimes catabolic remains a problem for further research.

WORKS CITED

Anderson, Edgar. 1952. Plants, man and life. Boston.

Benedict, Ruth. 1934. Patterns of culture. Boston and New York.

Durkheim, Émile. 1933. The division of labor in society, being a translation of his *De la division du travail social* (Paris, 1893), with an estimate of his work, by George Simpson. New York.

Emeneau, Murray B. 1942. Review of La Meri, *The gesture language of the Hindu dance* (New York, 1941). American Oriental Society. Journal LXII 148–50.

———. 1955. India and linguistics. American Oriental Society. Journal LXXV 145–53.

Kluckhohn, Clyde. 1941. Patterning as exemplified in Navaho culture. *In* Language, culture, and personality: Essays in memory of Edward Sapir. Menasha, Wisconsin.

Kroeber, Alfred L. 1942. The societies of primitive man. Reprinted in Kroeber, The nature of culture (1952). Chicago.

Maine, Sir Henry. 1861. Ancient law. London.

———. 1876. Village-communities in the East and West. New York.

Morgan, Lewis Henry. 1877. Ancient society. New York.

Redfield, Robert. 1941. The folk culture of Yucatan. Chicago.

———. 1953. The primitive world and its transformations. Ithaca, New York.

———. 1955. Societies and cultures as natural systems. Royal Anthropological Institute of Great Britain and Ireland. Journal LXXXV 19–32.

Redfield, Robert, and Singer, Milton. 1954. The cultural role of cities. Economic development and cultural change III 53–73.

Sapir, Edward. 1927. The unconscious patterning of behavior in society. *In* The unconscious: A symposium. New York.

Schnore, Leo F. 1958. Social morphology and human ecology. American journal of sociology LXIII 620–34.

Simmel, Georg. 1951. The metropolis and mental life. Paul K. Hatt and Albert J. Reiss, Jr. (eds.), Reader in urban sociology, pp. 563–74. Glencoe, Ilinois.

Singer, Milton. 1958. The great tradition in a metropolitan center: Madras. Journal of American folklore LXXI 347–88.

Wirth, Louis. 1951. Urbanism as a way of life. Paul K. Hatt and Albert J. Reiss, Jr. (eds.), Reader in urban sociology, pp. 32–49. Glencoe, Illinois.

II

Early Civilizations, Subsistence, and Environment

By ROBERT M. ADAMS

This symposium has accepted as its central problem the cumulative, if hardly constant, tendency of human society to grow in size and complexity. Its major substantive foci, of course, are the roots of our own Western tradition in the early civilizations of Egypt and western Asia. At the same time, it is clear that processes and institutions appearing first in the ancient Orient subsequently have recurred, with varying degrees of similarity, in widely separated regions and at different times. A better understanding of some of these recurrent features may help to clarify not only the picture of developing Egyptian and Sumero-Babylonian societies but also the cumulative development of society at large.

My task is to describe briefly some of the major ecological relationships which sustained the growth of civilizations in a number of "nuclear" areas. In addition to Mesopotamia and Egypt, the choice of pre-Spanish Mesoamerica and Peru seems most appropriate. It is supported not only by the volume and historical-archeological depth of relevant data that are available from the latter two areas but also by the likelihood that extreme geographic separation reduced their dependence on Old World precursors to a minimum. In spite of this separation there is a striking similarity, in scope and form, of nuclear American sociopolitical attainments to those of the Fertile Crescent area at a much earlier time.

J. H. Steward has argued convincingly that even the demonstrated fact of diffusion between two cultural traditions is insufficient to "explain" their likenesses. "One may fairly ask," he maintains, "whether each time a society accepts diffused culture, it is not an independent recurrence of cause and effect" (Steward, 1955, p. 182). From this point of view, it is possible to regard all four areas as historically distinct examples regardless of the ultimate "origins" of particular traits. This is especially true for our purposes, since cultural-environmental relationships within an area are pre-eminently a matter of independent adjustment to local conditions and resources.

Moreover, the substantive evidence in these cases for the presence of diffusion from some outside source as a determinative factor is either lacking or at best equivocal. Each of the four areas stood out over its surroundings as a highly creative rather than a passively receptive center. While the complete absence of trans-Pacific stimuli for New World high cultural development cannot be assured, the conclusion of most Americanists today is that the latter "stands clearly apart and essentially independent from the comparable culture core of the Old World" (Willey, 1955, p. 571). There is certainly no suggestion of any New World–Old World contact as important as the relatively brief but catalytic influence of Mesopotamia on Egypt at about 3000 B.C., yet in the latter case Frankfort took pains to point out the selective, qualified, and generally transient character of the borrowing (Frankfort, 1951, p. 110). With respect to interrelations between Peru and Mesoamerica, it is sufficient to state that not a single object or record of influence or contact between these areas has been accepted as authentic from the long time span between the Formative (or Early Village) period and the coming of the Spaniards, although the over-all tempo of development in each is remarkably similar (Strong, 1951, pp. 278–79). In short, it is both reasonable on a priori theoretical grounds and justified by present evidence to use Mesopotamia, Egypt, Mesoamerica, and Peru as essentially independent examples for a discussion of their internal ecological relationships.

Within the limits of this discussion it is neither possible nor necessary to explore fully the similarities in cultural development among these four areas. All clearly became civilizations, in the sense in which that term is defined here as a functionally interrelated set of social institutions: class stratification, marked by highly different degrees of ownership or control of the main productive resources; political and religious hierarchies complementing each other in the administration of territorially organized states; a complex division of labor, with full-time craftsmen, servants, soldiers, and officials alongside the great mass of primary peasant producers. Each was a complex, deeply rooted cultural tradition displaying most or all of V. G. Childe's more inclusive civilizational criteria as well: monumental public works, the imposition of tribute or taxation, "urban" settlements, naturalistic art, the beginnings of exact and predictive sciences, a system of writing suitable at least for rudimentary records and accounts (Childe, 1950). The attainment of civilization, from a diachronic point of view, was expressed in each of the four areas by a series of parallel trends or processes: urbanization, militarization, stratification, bureaucratization, and the like (Adams, 1956a). Of course, these processes were truncated in the New World by the Spanish Conquest—as a plausible approximation, after a level of development had been reached which was functionally equivalent to Old Kingdom Egypt or southern Mesopotamia under the Dynasty of Agade. However, this does not affect our comparisons here, which will be limited to earlier periods in the Near East for which New World equivalents are available.

It thus seems possible to group the four civilizations as representatives of a single type or class of social system. (Other members of the class would include the unknown Indus Valley polity of Harappa and Mohenjo Daro, Shang China, and perhaps certain West African city-states.) To be sure, this stress on structural and functional similarities needs supplementing by the traditional humanistic emphasis on the unique and relatively timeless qualities of each civilization for a properly balanced view. One example of the latter emphasis is the invocation of particular environmental features of different civilizations to account in part for their differing views of the natural world as reconstructed from works of ancient literature or art, for the distinctive structuring of their formal cosmologies, and perhaps even for dominant psychological attitudes (cf., e.g., Frankfort *et al.*, 1946, pp. 31 ff., 125 ff.). A typological approach necessarily neglects, although certainly cannot deny, the unique total patterning of every culture irrespective of what proportion of its constituent elements may have close parallels elsewhere. Probably this patterning is expressed most systematically, concisely, and impersonally in stylistic or configurational terms. But in any case these widely ramifying, largely ideational, aspects of the interrelations between man and the natural world are beyond the scope of this paper. Here we are concerned only with the generalized social order common to a group of autochthonous civilizations and with its relations to the environment.

Climate, Physiography, Resources, and Population

Beyond the limitation of each of the nuclear areas to subtropical latitudes, the combined gross catalogue of environmental features is characterized mainly by its diversity. If Egyptian and Sumero-Babylonian civilization are restricted to great arid or semi-arid river valleys, no such uniform description holds for the zones occupied by either Mesoamerican or Peruvian civilization. Both of the latter range from sea level to high mountain slopes, with tropical, temperate, or even cold-temperate climates corresponding to their altitudes. If coastal Peru and much of highland Mesomerica are sufficiently dry to be closely comparable with the Old World centers, this is progressively less true in the Peruvian sierra with increasing altitude and distance from the Pacific coast and not true at all in the Gulf Coastal lowlands of Middle America.

Both of the New World areas lack great inclusive river systems comparable to Egypt and the Nile or Mesopotamia and the Tigris-Euphrates. Instead, short, steeply descending watercourses that drain relatively small watersheds are common, and many of the largest of these are reduced in their pre-Hispanic importance by geographic factors. The main valley of the Rio Balsas and the intermontane basins of the Bajío on the Rio Lerma in Mexico, for example, were lightly occupied before the Spanish introduction of draft animals and the iron-tipped plow made it possible for agriculturalists to deal with heavy soils and sod (Poole, 1951, p. 36). The Amazon headwaters in the eastern sierra and Montaña of Peru may be found to provide a more significant exception when they have been explored more adequately (Bennet, 1946, pp. 67–68), but at least the lowland rain forest of the Amazon basin proper acted as a major ecological barrier to the expansion of Peruvian civilization. Since the potentialities of the Old World rivers for disastrous floods, for large-scale irrigation, and as arteries of commerce are often thought to have promoted political unification and the growth of trade in the ancient Orient (Childe, 1941, pp. 106 ff.), it is worth noting that the same cultural phenomena appeared independently in regions where these potentialities were absent or at last far less important.

With respect to natural resources, it is sufficient to recall the absence of even stone in the alluvial soil of southern Mesopotamia, as well as the extremely poor quality for building of the soft and quick-growing woods that alone were available locally. In contrast, parts at least of the New World nuclear regions were well favored, although with great altitudinal variation local self-sufficiency was often replaced by patterns of regional specialization and exchange.

As with climate and terrain, then, we cannot identify a fixed constellation of raw materials which acted as a necessary precondition (much less as a "cause"!) for the emergence of civilization in every area.

While relatively continuous settlement in linear patterns coinciding with the positions of the watercourses was possible in southern Mesopotamia and Egypt, enclaves of dense occupation separated by stretches of relatively inhospitable terrain were more characteristic of Mesoamerica and Peru. The best known and largest of the Mesoamerican enclaves is the interior drainage basin called the Valley of Mexico, which has provided the bulk of population and subsistence resources successively for the great religious center of Teotihuacan, the Toltec realm with Tula as its capital, the widespread conquests and incipient empire formation of the Aztecs, and present-day Mexico City. Yet in spite of the unparalleled importance of this region its area does not exceed 8,000 sq. km. In Peru the areas of intensive settlement and cultivation were all still smaller. Perhaps the largest of the mountain basins able to support a concentrated population is that of Huancayo, in the central highlands, with an area of only 1,200 sq. km. The arable area of the Chicama Valley, the largest in the North Coastal lowlands, is approximately the same.

In all of nuclear America, only along the Gulf Coast and on the low-lying Yucatan Peninsula were the conditions suitable for relatively uniform and continuous settlement. There, too, the rivers most nearly resemble the Nile or the Euphrates in regularity of flow and ease of control. But the lateritic soils and heavy rain-forest vegetation impose a very long recovery period after brief use for slash-and-burn agriculture, which materially reduces population density (Sanders, 1953; Palerm, 1955) and perhaps helped to postpone for a considerable time the onset of urbanization processes which had been initiated in adjacent Mesoamerican highlands. A sharper contrast would be hard to imagine than that between Sumerians clustering in cities and Classic Mayans living in dispersed, essentially rural, hamlets while only a small elite permanently inhabited the elaborate religious centers (Willey, 1956, pp. 109 ff.). Yet both were civilized. In short, the distribution of population and settlements within the nuclear areas appears to have been as variable as the general environmental conditions within which they occurred, although average density in each case was surely much higher than in surrounding areas.

273

Variations in Agricultural Subsistence Patterns

While the essential basis for subsistence in every civilization is obviously to be found in sedentary agriculture, this rubric covers impressive technical, botanical, and zoölogical differences when it is applied to the high cultures of both the New and the Old World. Largely following C. O. Sauer (1950), we may summarize these differences briefly.

New World agriculture, in the first place, essentially did not involve stockbreeding or the utilization of such animal products as dung fertilizer or milk. Domesticated Andean camelids such as the llama were used mainly for transport and were largely confined to the higher slopes; hence they cannot be regarded as important exceptions. Also missing in nuclear America, therefore, is the unique and powerful ambivalence of relations between herdsman and farmer, involving both symbiosis and hostility, which has shaped the social life, tinctured the history, and enriched the literature of the civilizations of the Fertile Crescent.

Second, nuclear American agriculture involves an entirely different range of cultivated plants, which nonetheless seem to have provided as balanced and adequate a diet as the cereal-date-vegetable-livestock complexes of the ancient Orient.

Third, basically different methods of cultivation were employed in the New World. In the absence of draft animals, the major implements were the digging stick and the hoe instead of the plow. Instead of a definite brief harvest season, crop-gathering was prolonged by the use of the major food crops also as green vegetables during earlier stages of their growth and by the widespread practice of interspersing different crops within a single field.

Finally, corresponding to the greater variations in climate because of altitude, New World agriculture was far more variable. There is little difference in at least the potential yields of the Assyrian uplands and the Mesopotamian alluvial plain other than that due to the inability of the date palm to flourish beyond the northern limit of the alluvium and to the greater (but not exclusive) reliance on barley rather than wheat south of that limit. By contrast, coastal Peruvian agriculture essentially revolved around a maize-beans-squash-cotton-fruits complex, while in the sierra subsistence depended on an entirely different complex composed of root crops like potatoes, oca, and quinoa. Similarly, maize, beans, and squash were the staple foods in both highland and lowland Mesoamerica, but they had been differentiated very early into altitudinally specialized varieties. Moreover, the cultivation of cotton, cacao, and many fruits was restricted to the lowlands.

Similarities in Subsistence Patterns

In spite of these profound differences, common features are not lacking. Perhaps something can be learned of the general place of subsistence in the growth of civilizations by outlining three common elements which seem to be of greatest importance.

One such significant common feature is that "farmers were persuaded or compelled to wring from the soil a surplus above their own domestic requirements and [that] this surplus was made available to support new economic classes not directly engaged in producing their own food" (Childe, 1942, p. 69). It must be understood that the notion of a surplus is related to fixed biological needs and the level of productive efficiency only in very general terms and that both the kinds and the quantities of available surpluses were determined to a considerable degree by the broad social contexts—"noneconomic" as well as "economic"—within which they occurred (cf. Pearson, 1957; Harris, 1959). Yet the institutional forms for the concentration and redistribution of surpluses show a high degree of uniformity among the early civilizations and serve to distinguish the latter sharply from societies in which no full-time activity other than primary food production finds sanction. Although it is impossible to quantify, it is only reasonable to assume that the proliferation of nonagricultural specialists common to all the early civilizations was correlated with a general increase in agricultural efficiency. It is, of course, quite another matter to assume that improved efficiency was independent of and prior to the whole ramifying network of concurrent social changes. Even purely technological advances, which in most instances these increased surpluses probably do not reflect, are usually linked with the social and cultural milieu, as Kroeber's (1917) study of independent and relatively simultaneous inventions was first to show.

A second common feature of some importance may be the complexity of the subsistence base on which each of the civilizations seems to have rested. We are dealing in no case with a single-crop economy or with one in which the bulk of the population normally could supply the entire range of agricultural produce for themselves.

Perhaps the diversity of resources is partly to be understood as the protection against natural calamity necessary for long-term cultural growth. But also in part it must have been responsible for the development of trade, exchange, and resdistributive institutions which in turn enhanced the growth of some form of centralized authority.

Mesopotamia is perhaps the best-documented example. The complementarity of dates and grain finds symbolic expression in the alabaster "Uruk vase" (Heinrich, 1936, pp. 15–16, Pl. 3), of late Protoliterate date, where alternate palm and cereal shoots in the bottom register figuratively support the abundant ceremonial life illustrated above. Fishing was another essential subsistence pursuit; of the 1,200 or so members of the Baba temple community in Girsu in the mid-third millennium B.C., more than 100 were fishermen (Deimel, 1931, p. 98). The precise role of fishing in earlier times is difficult to ascertain, but quantities of fish offerings found in a late Ubaid temple at Eridu (Lloyd and Safar, 1947, p. 104) may indicate that it had already attained considerable importance by that remote period. Slightly less numerous than the Baba temple fishermen were its shepherds and herdsmen, but their numbers in that specific case do not adequately reflect the crucial position of sheep, donkeys, and oxen in the mixed economy of ancient Mesopotamia for plowing, transport, wool, and fertilizer as well as meat. Surely the prominence of the shepherd-and-byre motif in Protoliterate glyptic art reflects a high antiquity for husbandry as an essential part of the configuration of subsistence activities. In all of these cases it is interesting to note that the temple and state institutions played a vital part in the collection and redistribution of the agricultural produce.

To the far more limited degree to which there are pertinent data on diversification and specialization of subsistence in Old Kingdom Egypt, the picture is at least not inconsistent with what has been described for Mesopotamia. The idealized representations in the tombs of life on the estates of court officials record a great variety of craft activities and subsistence pursuits; since an organization of the work under foremen is sometimes illustrated, there must have been at least a partial specialization of function in the real world as well. While the great bulk of the peasant's caloric intake may always have been derived from grain, the cultivation of vegetables and fruits and fowling, fishing, and animal husbandry also play a substantial part in the tomb scenes of Old Kingdom officials (cf., e.g., Steindorff, 1913; Duell *et al.*, 1938). The importance of herding, in particular, may have been obscured by its limited modern role under very different conditions of land use. For obvious reasons the main center of husbandry was in the Nile Delta, and the close concern of the state for husbandry is clearly to be seen in the emphasis on livestock in lists of claimed tribute and loot, in periodic censuses of the herds, and in the appointment of numerous officials charged with responsibility of one kind or another for domestic animals (Kees, 1933, pp. 18 ff.).

In the New World the differentiation of subsistence pursuits seems to have been mainly on a regional basis, perhaps as a consequence of the greater environmental diversity that has previously been alluded to. But the necessity for a wide interchange of agricultural products remained the same, and the organization of this interchange similarly must have helped to expand and consolidate the position of centralized social authority. In North Coastal Peru, for example, llamas from the sierra were already being ceremonially buried in a community shrine or public building in Late Formative times (*ca.* 800 B.C.; Willey, 1953, p. 56). In another case, the only llama bones from a contemporary site of the same period were found in association with the burial of an individual whose relatively elaborate *Beigaben* suggest a priestly status (Willey and Corbett, 1954, p. 19). By the succeeding Florescent era, the relative abundance of llama bones, wool, and droppings indicates that trading contacts with the highland centers of domestication for these animals had been regularized and enlarged (Strong and Evans, 1952, p. 213). Presumably cotton, maritime products, peppers, fruits, and coca were among the commodities moving in the reverse direction, as they were at the time of the Conquest. To some degree, regional specialization with regard to subsistence extended into craft production as well, as is implied by the importation of a colony of Chimu craftsmen to work for the Inca government in Cuzco (Rowe, 1948, p. 46). It is interesting to note that a high degree of specialization still characterizes the Quechua community (Mishkin, 1946, p. 434).

Similar patterns of differentiation in specialized production can be identified in Mesoamerica. Cotton from the lower-lying valleys of Puebla and Morelos was already being interchanged with the Valley of Mexico in Early Formative times (*ca.* 1200 B.C.; Vaillant, 1930, p. 31; Armillas, 1951, p. 21), and the securest archeological dating horizons of later periods are provided by distinctive pottery wares that were traded widely from their different centers of manufacture. For the Conquest period these traces of evidence can be greatly amplified with eyewitness accounts of, for example, the great and diversified market at Tlatelolco with its separate vendors for many varieties of fruit, meat, maize, vegetables, and fish (Maudslay, 1908–16, II 70–73) and with a reputed daily attendance of 60,000 persons (MacNutt, 1908, I 257–59). From a different point of view, the heterogeneity of native resources is also underlined by the *matricula de tributos* (Barlow, 1949). Although it accounts for tribute levied by the Aztecs rather than for trade, the general concentration of assignments for particular kinds of produce (other than the ubiquitous mantles) to a very few provinces surely reflects earlier patterns for the interchange of normal regional surpluses. And by Aztec times, if not earlier, the integration of interregional trading with the needs and policies of the expanding state is well known (Acosta, 1945, pp. 10–11).

A third significant feature common to the agricultural pursuits of the early civilizations was the development of some degree of intensive land use. Whether or not this was accompanied by a general increase in agricultural efficiency (output/labor input), certainly it must have increased at least the total agricultural output. However, the point of current interest is not so much the effect of intensive methods of cultivation on the volume of available surplus as their effect directly on social organization. The argument, following Ralph Linton's (1939) lucid portrayal of the introduction of wet rice cultivation in Madagascar, is that under conditions of intensive cultivation plots of land acquire different values based, for example, on cumulative improvements and the availability of water. Since water, or good bottom land, or some other similar resource was almost always relatively scarce, well-favored and improved plots came to be regarded as capital investments. While unimproved land was allotted equitably among all members of the village or extended kin group, under conditions of intensive cultivation the cohesiveness of the older social units broke down and tended to be replaced by a small number of individual families as the hereditary landholding units. The emergence of an authoritarian "king," of rudimentary social classes including nobles, commoners, and war-captive slaves, and increasing expenditures on warfare are some of the further consequences which Linton traces to the basic shift in cultivation practices. Under at least some circumstances, in other words, the social processes we have identified with the beginnings of civilization are closely interconnected with the beginning of intensive agriculture.

No necessary distinction into "cause" and "effect" is implied, be it understood, between subsistence change and institutional change. The investment of labor in land improvement and the adoption of intensive cultivation techniques were as much influenced by contemporary social forms as they influenced the latter.

Intensive agriculture, in the case of the earlier civilizations, usually is taken to be roughly synonymous with irrigation. Indeed, without some kind of irrigation agriculture is and probably always was impossible in southern Mesopotamia, Egypt, and coastal Peru. But we shall attempt to show that in most cases irrigation was part of a broader range of intensive techniques and that some of the assumed implications of irrigation as a single, gross category are misleading when applied to the four nuclear areas where the civilizations with which this paper is concerned had their beginnings. Here, then, irrigation is subsumed under the general rubric of intensive cultivation rather than equated with it.

It is important to distinguish between the functional significance of different kinds of irrigation if we are to understand better the relations between ecology and cultural growth. Small-scale irrigation, including flood-water techniques and the construction of short lengths of canal serving small landholdings, does not seem essentially different in its social effects from those observed by Linton in Madagascar. It may make available for agricultural purposes only a fraction of the potentially irrigable land surface, since it will seldom extend very far from the streams and since short canals will not be sufficient everywhere to bring the water to fields at a high enough level. Alluvial situations, in which rivers tend to raise their beds above the level of the surrounding land, are particularly favorable for small-scale irrigation. For the same reason, they invite destruction of existing canals by silting and flooding, although this is not critical where canals do not represent a heavy investment in labor and can be quickly replaced. The construction and maintenance of this kind of irrigation, we submit, requires no elaborate social organization and does not depend on labor resources larger than those at the disposal of the individual community, kin group, or even family—or, at most, those easily available locally through patterns of reciprocity. To the extent that this kind of irrigation is important, its chief influence on social development would seem to arise from its encouragement of stratification based on differentiation of landholdings. Perhaps also it encouraged the growth of militarism associated with increasing competition for developed canal networks and the most fertile and easily irrigated lands.

Large-scale irrigation, on the other hand, imposes technical and social demands of a different order. Masses of labor must be mobilized from many scattered communities, and their activities need close co-ordination. The problem of maintenance and supervision is a continuous one and again demands a superordinate authority. Some kind of equitable distribution of the available irrigation water must be imposed on many competing communities, and disputes must be adjudicated. Since downstream users are inherently at the mercy of those higher up, large-scale irrigation networks are only durable where the entire area they serve is a politically integrated unit. As has often been observed, large-scale canal networks can only be associated with formal state superstructures in which the ultimate authority rests with an administrative elite.

The problem for us is an absolutely basic one, however sparse, refractory, and ambiguous most of the present evidence may be. To the extent that large-scale irrigation is found to have begun very early, its social requirements may be adduced as a convincing explanation for the origin of primitive states in the ancient civilizations. Processes of class stratification associated with intensive agriculture then might be a secondary and derivative phenomenon on this reconstruction; because of its monopoly over hydraulic facilities, the state bureaucracy is identified as the strongest social force. Largely following Karl Wittfogel (cf. now Wittfogel, 1957), Julian Steward took this position in a recent symposium (Steward *et al.*, 1955, p. 63) with respect to Mesopotamia and Peru although not to Mesoamerica. Our view is firmly to the contrary. It is beyond the scope of a paper dealing with cultural ecology to argue that the primitive state is mainly linked instead with the emergence of a stratified society (cf. Adams, 1956*b*), but at least it will be suggested here that the introduction of great irrigation networks was more a "consequence" than a "cause" of the appearance of dynastic state organizations—however much the requirements of large-scale irrigation subsequently may have influenced the development of bureaucratic elites charged with administering them. The admittedly still inadequate evidence for this proposition now needs to be briefly summarized.

Our present understanding of the antiquity of irrigation in Mesopotamia is derived mainly from surface reconnaissance in Akkad and the Diyala basin (Jacobsen and Adams, 1958) and is obscured by the heavy and continuous alluviation with which the northern part of the alluvial plain has been particularly affected over the millenniums intervening since Sumerian times. At least in this region, however, there appears to have been little change in settlement pattern between the beginning of widespread agricultural occupation in the Ubaid period (*ca.* 4000 B.C.) and the end of the third millennium B.C. or even later. There is historical documentation for the construction of occasional large canals and irrigation works as early as the Protoimperial period, but on the whole the settlements followed closely the shifting, braided channels of the major rivers.

In other words, for a long time irrigation seems to have been conducted principally on an *ad hoc* and small-scale basis, which would have involved periodic cleaning and perhaps straightening of clogged natural channels, adjusting the location of fields and settlements in the closest possible conformity with the existing hydraulic regime, and for the most part constructing and maintaining only relatively small-scale field and feeder canals that were wholly artificial. Where the king explicitly claims credit for initiating dredging operations on either a canal or a natural watercourse (as in modern Iraq, the same word is used for both!), it is noteworthy that the aspect of canals as providers of irrigation water is entirely unmentioned (Adams, 1956*b*, p. 117). Moreover, whatever the rhetoric of the king's claimed responsibilities, the necessary labor forces for the maintenance work were apparently organized and directed by the individual temples (Falkenstein, 1954, p. 797). No Early Dynastic or Protoimperial record has survived of the mode of allocaton of irrigation water, but at least in Ur III times this was separately handled in each temple constituency by a special official in charge of sluice gates (Schneider, 1920, pp. 45 ff.). In short, there is nothing to suggest that the rise of dynastic authority in southern Mesopotamia was linked to the administrative requirements of a major canal system.

There are very few data yet available on the character or extent of Egyptian irrigation during the period for which it might be compared with New World equivalents, that is, up to the beginning of the Middle Kingdom. Prior to the opening of the Fayyum depression to irrigation in the Twelfth Dynasty, there is nothing less ambiguous to demonstrate state responsibility for irrigation than the statement of a Sixth-Dynasty royal architect that he had dug two canals for the king (Dunham, 1938, pp. 2–3). Unfortunately, the inscription fails to make clear whether the canals were intended for irrigation or only for the movement of royal supplies like building stone, as was the case with five contemporary canals dug to bypass the First Cataract of the Nile (Breasted, 1906, pp. 146 ff.). Still another possible explanation of the significance of the passage is that it refers to land reclamation by swamp drainage, much as a very late (and therefore doubtful) tradition credits Menes with having drained the territory around Memphis (Kees, 1933, p. 31). Yet swamp drainage began long before any pharaoh appeared on the scene—if the obvious meaning is attached to the claim of a Third-Dynasty official that he "founded" twelve estates in nomes of Lower Egypt (*ibid*. p. 77)—and continued afterward without the necessity of royal initiative. In considering alternatives other than irrigation we are also confronted with a protodynastic scorpion macehead ostensibly showing the king breaking ground for a waterway of some kind (Quibell, 1900, Pl. XXVI *C*). Again, an immunity charter of Pepi I protects the priesthood of the two pyramids of Snefru against any obligation for labor service on what may be a canal (Borchardt, 1905, pp. 6, 9); here it is neither clear that the putative canal was for irrigation nor that the pharaoh was responsible for its construction. Interestingly enough, the same charter continues with an injunction against enumerating canals, lakes, wells, hides, and trees belonging to the priesthood for tax purposes and thus suggests that all of those categories were under purely local jurisdiction.

In short, considering the number of known records of royal building activity in the Old Kingdom, it seems only fair to regard their silence on the construction of irrigation works as strange if the demands of large-scale irrigation had indeed been responsible for the initial emergence of a pharaoh at the head of a unified state. On the assumption of a centrally administered irrigation system, the failure of officials with long and varied careers of public service to refer to administrative posts connected with canal maintenance or water distribution is equally puzzling. To the degree that an *argumentum ex silentio* ever carries conviction, the Egyptian case parallels that of Mesopotamia.[1]

Although there is serious danger of overgeneralizing from it, the data on Peruvian irrigation are reasonably consistent with what has been adduced from Mesopotamia and Egypt. Drawing principally

[1] I am indebted to Dr. Klaus Baer for supplying and checking many of the Egyptian references.

from Gordon Willey's (1953) pioneer study of settlement patterns in a typical small valley transecting the arid North Coastal strip, we cannot presently trace large-scale irrigation earlier than the Florescent era (beginning probably at about the time of Christ). The distribution of Late Formative sites suggests, however, that small-scale experimentation with canal-building had begun in a few advantageous locales several centuries prior to this time, and some success with at least flood-water irrigation on the river flats is implied by the slow expansion inward from the valley mouth which began a millennium earlier. The Early Florescent (Gallinazo) canals, it is interesting to note, were built as integral parts of an elaborate and impressive complex of monumental construction which included fortifications and ceremonial pyramids as well; on present evidence, both of the latter types of monumental construction antedated the large canals. By mid-Florescent times at least, valley-wide systems of irrigation were in use on the North Coast (although our particular example comprises only 98 sq. km. of arable land!), and some individual canals are large by any standards: the canal of La Cumbre in the Chicama Valley, for example, is 113 km. long. A subsequent development, probably dating only from the Militaristic era (beginning after A.D. 700), was the still more extensive reshaping of natural drainage patterns through the introduction of intervalley irrigation systems in which urban zones occupied by a governing elite were set off from areas for agricultural exploitation (Schaedel, 1951, p. 240).

Irrigation apparently developed more slowly in highland Peru than on the North Coast, although the sharpness of the contrast may be a reflection in part of the lesser amount of archeological attention that the sierra has received. Terraces for soil conservation have been reported first for the Tiahuanaco horizon, at the outset of the Militaristic era (Bennet, 1946, p. 21). In the characteristically steep and narrow Andean valleys rapid runoff was perhaps a more serious problem than paucity of rainfall, but in general the later terraces seem to have been associated with irrigation channels as well. The elaborate, well-cut, and extensive terrace-irrigation systems for which Peru is famous all were products of the labor-service obligation imposed by the Inca state as a tax in the final century or so of its successful expansion before the coming of the Spaniards. Even the Early Inca terraces, probably postdating the onset of the Tiahuanaco horizon by four or more centuries, have been described as "small and irregular, and probably the work of individual family groups" (Rowe, 1946, pp.

210–11). As in North Coastal Peru, Egypt, and southern Mesopotamia, we seem to have evidence here of a very gradual evolution of irrigation practices beginning with local and small-scale terracing which emphatically did not require political organization embracing a large group of communities. Large-scale, integrated programs of canalization and terracing apparently were attempted only after the perfection of the Inca state as a political apparatus controlling the allocation of mass-labor resources. They are consequences, perhaps, of the attainment of a certain level of social development; we repeat that they cannot be invoked to explain the processes by which that level was attained.

For Mesoamerica the situation is more complex and not a little contradictory. The traditional view is that "there is little evidence that irrigation was of basic importance anywhere in Mexico, in pre-Spanish times, and that it is erroneous to speak of maize culture as having flourished most in arid or subarid regions of that country" (Kroeber, 1939, p. 218). Recently this conclusion has been controverted effectively by a number of investigators, although the full significance of their empirical findings is still open to dispute. On the whole though, the situation seems to be quite similar to that described for the other nuclear areas; in fact, it was primarily the recent findings in Mesoamerica which stimulated the reconsideration of irrigation that this paper represents.

The question of the role of irrigation in the formation of Mesoamerican civilization takes us back at least to the beginning of the Classic era (*ca.* A.D. 100?), if not earlier, and revolves particularly around the population and ceremonial center of Teotihuacan in the Valley of Mexico. The Pyramid of the Sun there, one of the largest pre-Hispanic structures in Mesoamerica, apparently antedates that era. It has been estimated that before its abandonment in Late Classic times (*ca.* A.D. 700) the site occupied 750 hectares or more of religious and civic buildings, residential "palaces," workshops, and clusters of ordinary rooms and patios housing "at least" 50,000 inhabitants (Sanders, 1956, pp. 124–25). True, the observed limits of surface debris may reflect only the aggregate area of the center over a period of several centuries and not its maximum size at any one period. Moreover, the proportion of residential units within the built-up area of the site is still not at all clear. But even if the estimate is scaled down considerably, it certainly reflects an urban civilization in being. To what extent, if at all, did it depend on irrigation agriculture? No direct evidence for canal irrigation has yet been reported. Instead, we have the observations that irrigation is necessary today for cultivation of even a single yearly crop in the subregion of which Teotihuacan is a part, that according to paleoclimatic studies based on pollen analysis and fluctuating lake levels it was even more necessary during the time of emergence of Teotihuacan as a great center, and hence that the use of irrigation must be assumed (Millon, 1954). The difficulty is that a center of the enormous size of Teotihuacan must have developed on a sustaining area far larger than its immediate subregion and that a major contribution from its immediate surroundings cannot be assumed to have been indispensable for the growth of the site. Monte Alban, Xochicalco, and other examples can be found which approach Teotihuacan in size but which lie at some distance from their main agricultural hinterland. A second argument is still less conclusive. It consists of the suggestion that irrigation is implied by representation of cacao and fruit trees along the banks of streams or canals in a mural from a Teotihuacan "palace" (Armillas, 1949, p. 91). Even if the identification of cacao is accepted as correct, the location of the scene is unknown and the crucial question of whether the waterways are natural or artificial is unanswered. There remains only a distributional argument, based on the wide extent of Mesoamerican irrigation practices at the time of the Conquest. Like all distributional arguments, it is loaded with presuppositions and provides no real clue to the antiquity of the trait in question. And so for Formative and Classic times the existence of canal irrigation still remains to be demonstrated.

For the final, or Historic, era (beginning *ca.* A.D. 900 with the founding of Tula), on the other hand, the evidence for large-scale irrigation agriculture and other hydraulic works is incontrovertible. Perhaps such works are already implied by the legendary account of the formation of Tula in the Codex Ramirez which describes the damming-up of a river in order to form an artificial lake stocked with fish and waterfowl (Radin, 1920, p. 73). In any case, the Spanish conquerors were full of admiration for the scale and intricacy of the system of dikes and aqueducts that by 1519 was both supplying Tenochtitlan with potable water and controlling fluctuations in the salt- and fresh-water levels of the lakes surrounding the city (MacNutt, 1908, I 262 ff.). The sequence of construction of these works can be traced in some detail in historical sources, and the conclusion seems justified that they should be viewed "not so much as the result of many small-scale initiatives by small groups, but as the result of large-scale enterprise, well-planned, in which an enormous number of people took part, engaged in important and prolonged public works under centralized and authoritative leadership" (Palerm, 1955, p. 39). Elsewhere in the Valley of Mexico, an irrigation complex in the Old Acolhua domain has been described that was roughly contemporary with the Aztec construction and also seems to have been initiated by a dynastic authority and carried out as a planned large-scale enterprise (Palerm and Wolf, 1954–55; Wolf and Palerm, 1955). Finally, an impressive list of places, with a wide distribution throughout Mesoamerica outside the Maya area, can be assembled for which irrigation is definitely identified or can reasonably be inferred in Spanish contact sources (Armillas, 1949; Palerm, 1954). In short, the position that irrigation was not important anywhere or at any period in pre-Spanish Mexico no longer seems tenable.

It needs to be stressed again, however, that distribution is a highly unreliable index to antiquity and that even the examples from the Valley of Mexico appertain only to the final century before the Conquest. Moreover, with the exception of the above-mentioned Aztec system all the known Mesoamerican irrigation networks are quite small in comparison with those of the Old World and Peru. On present evidence, then, Wolf and Palerm rightly tend to regard planned large-scale canal irrigation not as a primary cause of Mesoamerican civilization but merely as its culminating activity in the economic sphere. They recognize, to be sure, that political controls in turn probably were centralized and intensified by the introduction of major irrigation works (Wolf and Palerm, 1955, p. 275).

But if large-scale canalization is late in Mesoamerica, there are indications that other forms of irrigation and intensive cultivation—as in Peru and Mesopotamia also—can be traced to a more remote antiquity. Canal irrigation probably never became as important a technique in the Valley of Mexico as chinampa agriculture, that is, the cultivation of artificial islands made out of plant debris and mud scooped from the lake beds (West and Armillas, 1950). Modern chinampas are largely devoted to truck gardening, but, since the tasks of construction and maintenance do not require extensive organization and capital, they may have been used aboriginally as highly productive subsistence plots for kin groups or even families. The only example of an apparent chinampa so far subjected to archeological scrutiny contained occupational refuse dating to about the beginning of the Classic period and suggests that the technique is sufficiently old to have been a factor in the subsistence of Teotihuacan. The means were at hand early enough, in other words, for differential returns from specialized farming to have provided the material basis for the growth of a stratified society.

Since chinampas were unknown elsewhere in Mesoamerica (or depended on conditions not repeated elsewhere), their high and perennial productivity may not have been a direct factor in the development of civilization throughout the whole area. At the same time, the Valley of Mexico was in many other respects the key area of development for the greater part of Mesoamerica, for a very long time the center of its most advanced political forms, its widest and most closely intercommunicating trade network, its densest population (Armillas, 1951, pp. 20–21; Sanders, 1953, pp. 74–78). To a degree, then, it may have set the course of development which elsewhere was merely followed with more or less local innovation. To that degree, chinampa agriculture may far exceed in importance its highly circumscribed geographical limits. Unfortunately, having largely set aside simple diffusion studies, anthropologists are only beginning to develop more functional approaches to the analysis of interregional relations, through which the supposed primacy of the Valley of Mexico might be understood and evaluated.

Another, and broader, aspect of intensive cultivation in Mesoamerica is perhaps to be seen in the maintenance of dooryard garden plots in close symbiosis with individual houses, which augment the production of foodstuffs through the use of leavings as fertilizer and encourage stability of residence (Palerm, 1955, p. 29). Although not subject to archeological confirmation at present, this practice was apparently well established at the time of the Conquest and is possibly very old (Palerm, personal communication). Again, crudely made terraces for erosion-control purposes have been observed at many places in highland Mesoamerica and in at least one instance in the lowland rain forest of the Yucatan Peninsula. Certainly in many cases of considerable pre-Spanish antiquity, they suggest agricultural regimes of greater intensity than the milpa system as it is practiced today. Although at present impossible to document for pre-Conquest times, a more intensive application of labor in the form of hand-weeding would have prolonged cultivation and increased output, particularly in the tropical lowlands. This might make less inexplicable or even "explain" the extraordinary cultural achievements of the Classic Maya in the lowlands (Steggerda, 1941; Hester, 1952–54).

By assisting in the establishment of residential stability and in the production of surpluses, all the above-mentioned practices would have provided at least a receptive hinterland within which the new and more complex social forms could expand and consolidate. The origin of innovations such as the primitive state might then be sought in a few small strategic regions such as the Valley of Mexico where the inducements to accumulate surpluses and institutionalize class differences were probably greatest. In a wider sense, it may be granted, the florescence of the state could only take place where conditions in the hinterland were also propitious, so that the pinpointing of precise points of origin is probably misleading.

Briefly to recapitulate, we have attempted to show that developments in modes of subsistence within Mesoamerica were substantially similar to those in Mesopotamia, Egypt, and Peru in that large-scale canal irrigation was a culminating, rather than an early and persistent, form of intensive cultivation. It is conceded that differences in the rate of development existed, probably in large part because of the fewer inducements and opportunities to depend on irrigation that Mesoamerica offered. But these, we suggest, are quantitative and not qualitative differences. In North Coastal Peru the culmination came in the mid-Florescent era—or even later, in the Militaristic era, if the introduction of intervalley irrigation systems is accepted as a significant later innovation. In Mesoamerica it came in late Historic or Militaristic times, as it also seems to have done in *highland* Peru. According to our Mesopotamian data, admittedly inadequate in detail and based on a possibly retarded Akkad instead of Sumer, the onset of large-scale artificial canalization did not occur until after the time of Hammurabi. Even in Sumer itself there is no justification for supposing that this process began any earlier than the late Early Dynastic or the Protoimperial period—a sound equivalent for the New World Historic or Militaristic era. In *no* area, then, at least on present evidence, was large-scale irrigation early enough to "explain" the emergence of the great theocratic centers of the Classic era or the dynastic states which closely followed them. The concern of Wolf and Palerm (1955, p. 275), and latterly of Steward (Steward *et al.*, 1955, pp. 62–63), over the distinction between "Theocratic Irrigation States" (Protoliterate Mesopotamia and Florescent

Peru) and "Ceremonial Trade States" (Classic Mesoamerica) thus seems groundless.

Reciprocal Effects of Human Culture on Environment

This discussion so far has assumed that the natural physiography and resources of the four nuclear areas were relatively stable. The different cultural traditions have been regarded implicitly as evolving successive patterns of ecological adjustment and land use entirely according to some internal dynamic of their own. The effect of environment, in these terms, is merely that of providing a fixed framework of potentialities and limiting conditions which somehow is then exploited selectively by the creative cultural growth within it. Such a view is obviously an oversimplification of the processes of interaction between man and the natural world, even if decisive climatic shifts no longer are regarded as likely to have occurred during the span of time that led to the emergence of any civilization.

Unfortunately the reciprocal effects of changing patterns of human activity on the land and flora cannot be traced continuously for any area. Perhaps the clearest and best-documented example is provided by recent work in central Mexico, where it has been shown that intensive hill-slope cultivation during the last centuries of Aztec dominance had gone far to destroy the capacity of the soil to sustain agriculture even before the arrival of the Spaniards (Cook, 1949*a* and 1949*b*). But the more remote history of occupance in even this relatively well-studied region is still insufficiently known for its environmental effects to be understood. The abandonment of the central Peten region by the lowland Classic Maya furnishes an even more dramatic case, with ecological processes such as sheet erosion, the silting-up of fresh-water sources, and the gradual replacement of forest vegetation by uncultivable savanna in the course of slash-and-burn agriculture all having been suggested as contributing factors. But in spite of a generation of speculation and interest these factors still exist only as hypotheses, and in a recent general work on the Maya it is interesting to note that they are largely rejected in favor of an explanation of the collapse of at least the elaborate ceremonial life in purely historical terms (Thompson, 1954, pp. 85 ff.).

In the alluvial valleys of the Old World civilizations, processes of erosion are less likely to have affected directly the course of cultural development. It is not impossible, however, that deforestation at the headwaters of the Tigris and Euphrates increased both the silt loads carried by those rivers and their flooding potential. In turn, this would have affected the continuity of occupation in the alluvium and the problems associated with constructing and maintaining irrigation systems. But, although deforestation undoubtedly went on, there are no empirical data at present on its rate nor on its consequences for the alluvial plain as a whole. Even the traditional assumption that the area of the plain has been continuously enlarged by the deposition of silt along the margin of the Persian Gulf has now been challenged by evidence that extensions of the land have been roughly counterbalanced by subsidence (Lees and Falcon, 1952).

On the other hand, a group of different and important reciprocal effects is likely to have been initiated directly by the introduction of various techniques of intensive cultivation. Depletion of soil nutrients by inadequate crop rotation or fallowing cycle is one example. Salinization of poorly drained land as a result of continuous irrigation is another. Still a third may be the disturbance of natural patterns of drainage by the slow rise of canal beds and banks as a result of silting. To some degree all of these processes must have gone on, but their importance can only be gauged against the background of a far better understanding of ancient agriculture than we have at present for any area. To begin with, empirical studies are necessary of changes in the intensity of land use and of the exact nature of the full agricultural cycle over a long period in the past. At the time of this writing, a study along these lines has been undertaken for a small section of the Mesopotamian plain but not for any other nuclear area.

For the present, therefore, the distortions of a picture in which cultures are conceived as having evolved within a static environmental framework must remain uncorrected. If several possible types of correction have been mentioned, their effects cannot even be demonstrated satisfactorily with the evidence available from most areas, and in any case they are virtually impossible to quantify. One can only conclude that attempts to invoke changing ecological factors as "causes" of cultural development—however convenient they may appear as heuristic hypotheses—are still no more than a priori speculations.

In a broader sense, the lack of data on population density and land use underlines the purely speculative character of all those heuristic hypotheses which regard cultural change as an adaptive response to

290

direct environmental forces. One account of the rise of militarism, for example, sees it as a consequence of the displacement of a population surplus (Childe, 1942, pp. 66–67, 99, and *passim*), although there is absolutely no evidence of a concurrent reduction in the sustaining capacity of the environment or of a trend toward overpopulation in any of the nuclear areas. Another recent synthesis, going still farther, attributes not only the rise of large-scale warfare but also the cyclical character of the early empires in large part to population pressure (Steward, 1955, p. 204). How population "pressure" can be defined usefully except by reference to real patterns and intensities of land utilization and settlement pressing against clearly defined ecological limits—for which, we must emphasize again, the evidence is still almost entirely lacking—is not apparent.

There is always an attraction for explanations of historical and cultural phenomena that stem from "outside" the immediate field of study. They have the advantage of providing fixed points from which analysis may proceed in a straightforward chain of cause-and-effect processes. But on closer inspection many such fixed points will be found to dissolve into shifting relationships which are not as separate and distinct from cultural influences as they may appear. Premature dependence upon explanations in terms of the external environment only diverts the historian or anthropologist from unraveling the complex stresses within human institutions. In all but the simplest societies, it is forces within the social order rather than direct environmental factors which have provided the major stimulus and guide to further growth.

Conclusion

In retrospect, the significant common features of land use among the early civilizations of the Old and the New World are so general that they are almost trite. If we have attempted to define the terms more closely than is usual, there is certainly nothing unusual about finding that all the great civilizational traditions rested on surpluses made available through sedentary, diversified, intensive agriculture. In addition, of course, it is implicit in this discussion that the common social institutions and processes of development identified in each of the four civilizations were bound up together with this general constellation of subsistence practices in a functionally interacting network which characterizes early civilization as a sort of cultural type.

Against this simple and limited finding of regularity, the diversity of other environmental subsistence features and the huge proliferation of cultural forms stand in sharp contrast. History is not a mathematical exercise in the application of "laws," and the meaning of human experience is not to be found by suppressing its rich variety in the search for common, implicitly deterministic, denominators. From this point of view, perhaps the lack of closer specificity in the ecological relationships that are common to the early civilizations is the single most important point to be made. Much of sociocultural development seems to proceed very largely on its own terms, including even some important aspects of ecological adjustment. Societal growth is a continuously creative process, conditioned far more by past history than by directly felt environmental forces. On the whole, then, one may reasonably conclude that for an understanding of the meaning of the early civilizations—both in their own terms and for the modern world—the natural environment serves as no more than a backdrop.

WORKS CITED

Acosta Saignes, Miguel. 1945. Los Pochteca Acta antropologico I, No. 1. Mexico, D.F.

Adams, R. M. 1956a. Some hypotheses on the development of early civilizations. American Antiquity XXI 227–32.

———. 1956b. Level and trend in early Sumerian civilization. Unpublished Ph.D. dissertation. University of Chicago.

Armillas, P. 1949. Notas sobre sistemas de cultivo en Mesoamerica. Mexico. Instituto Nacional de Antropología e Historia. Anales III 85–115.

———. 1951. Tecnologia, formaciones socioeconomicas y religion en Mesoamerica. Tax (ed.), 1951, pp. 19–30.

Barlow, R. H. 1949. The extent of the empire of the Culhua, Mexica. Ibero-Americana XXVIII. Berkeley.

Bennet, W. C. 1949. The Andean highlands: An introduction. Steward (ed.), 1946–50, II 1–60.

Borchardt, Ludwig. 1905. Ein Königserlass aus Dahschur. Zeitschrift für ägyptische Sprache und Altertumskunde XLII 1–11.

Breasted, J. H. 1906. Ancient records of Egypt I. Chicago.

Childe, V. Gordon. 1941. Man makes himself. London.

———. 1942. What happened in history. Harmondsworth.

———. 1950. The urban revolution. Town planning review XXI 3–17.

Cook, S. F. 1949a. The historical demography and ecology of the Teotlalpan. Ibero-Americana XXXIII. Berkeley.

———. 1949b. Soil erosion and population in central Mexico. Ibero-Americana XXXIV.

Deimel, Anton. 1931. Sumerische Tempelwirtschaft zur Zeit Urukaginas und seiner Vorgänger. Analecta orientalia II. Rome.

Duell, Prentice, *et al.* 1938. The masataba of Mereruka I–II. Oriental Institute publications XXXI and XXXIX. Chicago.

Dunham, Dows. 1938. The biographical inscriptions of Nekhebu in Boston and Cairo. Journal of Egyptian archaeology XXIV 1–8.

Falkenstein, Adam. 1954. La cité-temple sumérienne. Journal of world history I 784–814.

Frankfort, Henri. 1951. The birth of civilization in the Near East. London.

Frankfort, Henri, *et al.* 1946. The intellectural adventure of ancient man. Chicago.

Harris, M. 1959. The economy has no surplus? American anthropologist LXI 185–99.

Heinrich, Ernst. 1936. Kleinfunde aus den archaischen Tempelschichten in Uruk. Ausgrabungen der Deutschen Forschungsgemeinschaft in Uruk-Warka I. Leipzig.

Hester, J. A. 1952–54. Agriculture, economy, and population densities of the Maya. *In* Carnegie Institution of Washington Yearbook Nos. 51–53.

Jacobsen, Thorkild, and Adams, R. M. 1958. Salt and silt in ancient Mesopotamian agriculture. Science CXXVIII 1251–58.

Kees, Hermann. 1933. Ägypten. Kulturgeschichte des alten Orients. 3. Abt., 1. Teil, 3. Bd., 1. Abschnitt (Handbuch der Altertumswissenschaft I). Munich.

Kroeber, Alfred L. 1917. The superorganic. American anthopologist XIX 163–213.

———. 1939. Cultural and natural areas of native North America. University of California. Publications in American archaeology and ethnology XXXVIII. Berkeley.

Lees, G. M., and Falcon, N. L., 1952. The geographical history of the Mesopotamian plains. Geographical journal CXVIII 24–39.

Linton, Ralph. 1929. The Tanala of Madagascar. Abram Kardiner, The individual and his society, pp. 251–90. New York.

Lloyd, Seton, and Safar, Fuad. 1947. Excavations at Eridu. Sumer III 85–111.

MacNutt, F. A. (tr. and ed.) 1908. Letters of Cortes. 2 vols. New York and London.

Maudslay, A. P. (tr. and ed.) 1908–16. The true history of the conquest of New Spain. By Bernal Díaz del Castillo . . . 5 vols. London.

Millon, R. 1954. Irrigation at Teotihuacan. American antiquity XX 177–80.

Mishkin, Bernard. 1946. The contemporary Quechua. Steward (ed.), 1946–50, II 411–70.

Palerm, Angel. 1954. La distribucion del regadio en el area central de Mesoamerica. Ciencias sociales V 2–15, 64–74.

———. 1955. The argicultural basis of urban civilization in Mesoamerica. Steward *et al.*, 1955, pp. 28–42.

Palerm, A., and Wolf, E. 1954–55. El desarrollo del area clave del Imperio Texcocano. Revista mexicana de estudios antropologicos XIV 337–50.

Pearson, Harry W. 1957. The economy has no surplus: Critique of a theory of development. Karl Polanyi, Conrad M. Arensberg, Harry W. Pearson (eds.), Trade and market in the early empires, pp. 320–41. Glencoe, Illinois.

Poole, D. M. 1951. The Spanish conquest of Mexico: Some geographical aspects. Geographical journal CXVII 27–42.

Quibell, J. E. 1900. Hierakonpolis I. London.

Radin, Paul. 1920. The sources and authenticity of the history of the ancient Mexicans. University of California. Publications in American archaeology and ethnology XVII 1–150. Berkeley.

Rowe, J. H. 1946. Inca culture at the time of the Spanish Conquest. Steward (ed.), 1946–50, II 183–330.

———. 1948. The kingdom of Chimor. Acta americana VI 26–59.

Sanders, W. T. 1953. The anthropogeography of central Vera Cruz. I. Bernal and E. Davalos (eds.), Huastecos, Totonacos y sus vecinos (Revista mexicana de estudios historicos XIII, Nos. 2–3) pp. 27–69. Mexico, D.F.

———. 1956. The central Mexican symbiotic region: A study in prehistoric settlement patterns. Willey (ed.), 1956, pp. 115–27.

Sauer, Carl O. 1959. Cultivated plants of South and Central America. Steward (ed.), 1946–50, VI 487–543.

Schaedel, R. P. 1951. Major ceremonial and population centers in northern Peru. Tax (ed.), 1951, pp. 232–43.

Schneider, Anna. 1920. Die Anfänge der Kulturwirtschaft: Die sumerische Tempelstadt. Essen.

Steggerda, Morris. 1941. Maya Indians of Yucatan. Carnegie Institution of Washington. Publication No. 531. Washington, D.C.

Steindorff, Georg. 1913. Das Grab des Ti. Leipzig.

Steward, J. H. (ed.). 1946–50. Handbook of South American Indians. Bureau of American Ethnology. Bulletin No. 143. 6 vols. Washington, D.C.

———. 1955. Theory of culture change. Urbana, Illinois.

Steward, J. H., et al. 1955. Irrigation civilizations: A comparative study. Pan American Union. Social Science Monographs I. Washington, D.C.

Strong, W. D. 1951. Cultural resemblances in nuclear America: Parallelism or diffusion? Tax (ed.), 1951, pp. 271–79.

Strong, W. D., and Evans, C. 1952. Cultural stratigraphy in the Virú Valley, northern Peru. Columbia studies in archaeology and ethnology IV. New York.

Tax, Sol. (ed.) 1951. The civilizations of ancient America. Twenty-ninth International Congress of Americanists, New York, 1949. Selected Papers I. Chicago.

Thompson, John Eric. 1954. The rise and fall of Maya civilization. Norman, Oklahoma.

Vaillant, G. C. 1930. Excavations at Zacatenco. American Museum of Natural History. Anthropology papers XXXII, pt. 2.

West, R., and Armillas, P. 1950. Las chinampas de Mexico. Cuadernos americanos L.

Willey, Gordon R. 1953. Prehistoric settlement patterns in the Virú Valley, Perú. Bureau of American Ethnology. Bulletin No. 155.

———. 1955. The prehistoric civilizations of nuclear America. American anthropologist LVII 571–93.

———. 1956. Problems concerning prehistoric settlement patterns in the Maya lowlands. Willey (ed.), 1956, pp. 107–14.

———. (ed.) 1956. Prehistoric settlement patterns in the New World. Viking Fund publications in anthropology No. 23. New York.

Willey, G. R., and Corbett, J. M. 1954. Early Ancón and early Supe culture. Columbia studies in archaeology and ethnology III. New York.

Wittfogel, K. A. 1957. Oriental despotism: A comparative study of total power. New Haven.

Wolf, E., and Palerm, A. 1955. Irrigation in the old Acolhua domain, Mexico. Southwestern journal of anthropology XI 265–81.

III
Prelude to Civilization

By ROBERT J. BRAIDWOOD

What To Expect of Prehistory

The focus of interest of the present symposium lies with events which began to take place as prehistory came to an end. With the appearance of *civilization* or "the urban revolution"—by whatever criteria this may manifest itself in the primary documents of archeology (see above, pp. 269–92; Childe, 1950*a*)—the range of conventional "history" has begun. Usually the criteria include writing, although the instance of the Inca civilization suggests it need not always be included. While the philological imponderability of most early writing leaves much to be desired, if the goal is full-bodied cultural interpretation, the boundary line between prehistory and conventional ancient history is generally set at the point where writing makes its appearance.

The function of this paper is taken to be a consideration of how the stage was set for the appearance of civilization (including most if not all of the criteria inferred above). Understanding of the prehistoric past depends entirely upon elucidation of the very incomplete archeological record of half a million years of preliterate human development. Much of this development took place in remote and relatively unexplored—for prehistoric purposes—parts of the world. Clark (1957) and Wheeler (1954) have recently considered the factors of the accidents of discovery, the variables affecting the preservation of antiquities, the difficulties of establishing a chronology, and the human element of the competence of the excavator himself, all of which must be taken into account in the assessment of the relative incompleteness of the archeological record.

For Henri Frankfort (1938), archeology's goal was "the reclamation *and interpretation* of the material remains of man's past" (the italics are mine). The interpretation of a very incomplete collection of material remains, representing most of the habitable world and a very great depth of time, presents exasperating difficulties. It is dangerous to assume that a "primitive" archeological assemblage or catalogue of material remains may be given direct explication by reference to the culture pattern which includes some apparently similar assemblage possessed by one of our remaining primitive contemporaries, for example the South African Bushmen or the Australian aborigines. And it cannot be assumed that reference to some unilinear evolutionary scheme makes the most reliable basis for interpretation. It has been maintained (Braidwood, 1959) that the conventional neo-Grecisms "paleolithic," "mesolithic," and "neolithic" show the dead hand of Gabriel de Mortillet's first two "laws," the "loi du progrès de l'humanité" and the "loi du développement similaire." Given what we have learned and are learning about the natural and cultural environments of the last half-million years, it is quite clear that human progress has not been evenly progressive and universally similar.

Throughout their prehistory, men had to adjust to the fluctuations of climates and natural environments which were sometimes worse than those of today and sometimes better. The title of Reginald Daly's (1934) classic account of the Pleistocene period, *The Changing World of the Ice Age,* very aptly describes what was going on. But part of the gratifying increase in the attention being given to the details of at least late-glacial/early-postglacial climatic and environmental history is a growing realization that all our present climatic and vegetational zones did not simply shift southward, in consecutive order, as glaciers built up in the northern latitudes and shift neatly back into their present positions as the glaciers disappeared. A more variable and irregular picture is beginning to appear. The field of human "paleo-environment" (Braidwood, 1957a) is only now being developed as a serious cross-disciplinary effort; its success will depend on the establishment of easy intercommunication and field co-operation between archeologists and natural scientists.

To biologists (e.g. Rogers, Hubbell, and Byers, 1952) man is an organism, an animal, a vertebrate, and a mammal, subject to strict ecological ties with the organic world about him. In a recent article Edward Deevey (1956) thoughtfully considered man's low efficiency as an organism, with vivid examples. But man became man by acquisition of culture. I believe that even if the major theme of all human prehistory were conceded to be primarily an ecological one (which I will not concede), three important variations on that ecological theme would appear, which could be paralleled in the history of no other organism. These variations would be additive and much less divisive than their separate listing makes them appear at first sight. A long overview of the details of man's prehistoric past—however incompletely known these details may be—would suggest the following as the three variations on an ecological theme:

(1) Evolving subsistence patterns showed an increasing extractive efficiency through time and an increasing ability to "live into" a given environment.

(2) But with the passage of time (especially during the last 50,000 years—since the appearance of anatomically modern man) increasing technological complexity made possible adjustments to variable environments and began to free men from painful dependence on one given type of environment; with increased technological complexity, regional ways of doing things came more to the fore.

(3) Increasing sociocultural complexity gradually tended to mitigate the necessity for an immediate ecological balance for an increasing number of—but not all —people of any given group.

This view is no doubt both a cumbersome and a trite way of saying that man's prehistory is the history of the species' acquisition of culture and of the increasing dimensions of culture. In this sense, Kroeber's (1917) description of culture as "the superorganic" is apt. There were obviously two themes during the perhistoric prelude to civilization. The first concerns the natural history of the species, its biological evolution, and the success with which it adapted itself ecologically. The second theme concerns the cultural history of the species and sets man apart from all other organisms. It would be satisfying to assert that the second and peculiarly human theme superseded the first, but dust bowls, exhausted lands, polluted streams, and the ever necessary war on insects and on disease and famine constantly remind us that this is not so.

Thus, to a prehistorian—whose raw data very seldom show him traces of the individual—human history appears as a struggle for the establishment of adequate checks and balances between the two themes of natural and cultural history as well as the attempts of men to cope with or take advantage of forces inherent in each of these themes. The archeologist's training makes the reclamation and interpretation of the documents of cultural history congenial to him, and there are some hopeful signs that the field of human paleo-environmental study will increasingly gain respectability among the natural scientists. Only by means of a joint effort will the whole story be unfolded.

The First Nine-tenths of Human History

For present purposes, the first approximately 450,000 of the half-million years of prehistoric time need not hold us long. Many animals *utilize* tools, but it now appears that the australopithecines—of lower Pleistocene times and at least in Africa if not in southeastern Asia—were already beginning to *fashion* tools. In several charming essays, Kenneth Oakley (1956, 1957) has developed the idea that "Tools Makyth Man," and it is generally conceded by human paleontologists that the fashioning of tools for use by the earlier fossil men forced the biological pace of human evolution.

For middle Pleistocene times, the *standardization* of at least chipped stone tool types is assured. This means that men had developed notions of an ideal standard form of tool for some particular job (or jobs) and could reproduce it at will—often in much more intractable materials than flint. It also means no doubt that tools were made in anticipation of some need in the immediate future. I have suggested elsewhere (Braidwood, 1957*b*), although of course I cannot demonstrate it, that the notion of standard tool types or "perfect tool for good job" already suggests symbol-making, with all its broad cultural consequences. An impressive thing is the apparent uniformity, over vast areas of the middle latitudes of the Old World, of essentially the same tool-preparation traditions.

Nevertheless, subsistence appears to have been at a most basic level of gathering and scavenging alone. From conversation with Clark Howell, who in 1957 in Tanganyika made the most extensive exposure yet available of a "living site" with Acheulean tools, I gather that the word "hunting" would be somewhat too dignified for what the evidence suggests of subsistence. Only with the onset of upper Pleistocene times do we have traces of such suggestions of human activity beyond subsistence alone as intentional burials and the "bear cults" (purposeful arrangements of the skulls of bears). And it would be only toward the end of this long range of time that we could guess that extractive efficiency and the "living into" an environment was beginning to increase.

My own preference for a name for this long range of beginnings is "the food-gathering era," the first era in the over-all "food-gathering stage." The era did not come to an end at exactly the same moment in all parts of the then habitable world. Contrary to De Mortillet's second "law," we also know that not all the tool-preparation traditions of the era were exactly similar, although the broad distribution of the core-biface and the flake traditions in southwestern Eurafrasia is impressive.

Anatomically Modern Man and Cultural Diversity

About forty or fifty thousand years ago, there begin to appear in the available prehistoric record the traces of two significant events. One of these is the appearance of anatomically modern man, the other a new tool-preparation tradition. It is not impossible, on present indications, that both these events had their beginnings in southwestern Asia (Braidwood, 1958). There is not, however, anything yet —in the admittedly very restricted evidence—to suggest that the two events were interconnected, save for their coincident occurrence.

Current understanding of the details of this time range—the latter half of the upper Pleistocene and all of what is conventionally called "upper paleolithic"—is best for western Europe and especially France. The word "hunting" may now certainly be used advisedly; the suggestions of organized drives or stampedes (such as the mass of horse bones at Solutré) indicate impressive increases in extractive efficiency. It is usual, and no doubt somewhere near the mark, to interpret the magnificent Franco-Cantabrian cave art as "increase magic," although that old phrase certainly oversimplifies the broad functional dimensions which the art must have had in Franco-Cantabrian culture of that time. The type names and the sequence established in France are so well known and broadly borrowed and the heritage of De Mortillet's "loi du développement similaire" is still so strong that the true nature of this era is often missed.

As a name for this era I prefer simply "the food-collecting era." It, also, did not begin at the same moment everywhere, nor did it end abruptly at the same moment everywhere. In fact, certain derivatives of the era still persist in a few out-of-the-way parts of the world. The blade-tool tradition, one of the two events which announces the appearance of the new era in western Eurasia, apparently did not spread over the whole habitable world. Anatomically modern man, the other hallmark of the era, did presently spread over the globe. During the development and spread of the era, the New World and the higher latitudes were occupied.

Cultural diversification seems to be the thing which distinguishes the era of food-collecting from the much longer era of food-gathering. Even within the great area of western Eurasia, where the blade-tool tradition was itself at home, the catalogues of the regional industries produced on blades show considerable regional variability. This was clearly in Dorothy Garrod's (1953) mind when she wrote:

> The speeding-up of change and development which begins to show in this period is reflected in some areas, not only in the greater number of industries having enough individual character to be classified as distinct cultures, but in their restriction in space, since [cultural] evolution now starts to outstrip diffusion.

What seems to be involved here is the coming into play of our second—as well as an intensification of our first—variation on an ecological theme, namely that increasing technological complexity made adjustments to new environments possible. A vividly instructive example, were there space to document it, could be made by reference to the remains from latest Pleistocene times on the plains of central Europe and Russia. Here, at least thirty thousand years, ago, lived groups of accomplished mammoth-hunters. They had certainly discovered how to "live into" a bitter environment, with sewn skin clothing and subsurface huts (e.g. Klima, 1954). Architecture is conventionally assumed to have begun at the time of the appearance of the settled village-farming community. Actually, the origins of constructed shelters in encampments of some degree of permanence go back well into the food-collecting era (Childe, 1950*b*).

I have little to say regarding the biological aspects of the appearance of anatomically modern man beyond S. L. Washburn's (1957) idea that the important differentiation of biological races has happened since fifty thousand years ago. In this view, a "race" is a population of genetically similar composition, more or less geographically restricted, but intergraded about the edges of its area with its neighbors. Culture allowed the geographical "restriction" (or, better, "localization") and seems still to have been setting the pace for biological evolution.

There is increasing evidence (cf. Braidwood, 1958) that, *for the more northerly latitudes* of both the Old and the New World, the date of the late-glacial/early-postglacial time boundary can be placed at about ten thousand years ago. What followed—in the northerly latitudes—was a cultural readjustment to the sequence of early postglacial environments, *on a food-collecting level*. In fact, this level often shows traces of very intensified extractive efficiency. Such traces are usually classified under the rubrics "mesolithic" for northwestern Europe and "archaic" for North America. I am not myself of the opinion that an entirely new era had begun. There appear to have been climatic and environmental changes within the preceding thirty or forty thousand years which must have been just as traumatic as those which happened ten thousand years ago (in the regions where we are sure they happened!). But there might be value in considering a terminal "sub-era of intensified food-collecting" (cf. Braidwood, 1958, Fig. 6 *C'*).

I believe it is important to bear in mind that this sub-era—quite contrary to De Mortillet's second "law"—may not have taken place everywhere. The implication of radioactive-carbon chronology is increasingly that it did not take place everywhere and, in fact, that in certain favored regions of the world a new era of potentially greater importance for what was to follow replaced it (Braidwood, 1958). This new era is that of "incipient cultivation," the first era of the new "food-producing stage," which is considered briefly below. It is probably worth remarking here, however, that there may have been some as yet very poorly understood linkage between the sub-era of intensified food-collection and the era of incipient cultivation. Both appear to have commenced at about the same time, roughly ten thousand years ago. Both imply an increasing "living into" a given environment and a technology-bound increase in extractive efficiency in utilizing it. The understanding of this range very particularly demands the close co-operation of archeologists and natural scientists.

Grahame Clark (e.g. 1952, 1954) has given much attention to the sub-era of intensified food-collecting in northwestern Europe, and Joseph R. Caldwell (1958) is one of the Americanists who has attempted its delineation in the New World. It is to this sub-era that the traces of really specialized and concentrated collection of smaller animals and plants pertain (the more "important" ones usually of a rather restricted number of species). The great shell mounds of both the Old and the New World begin at this level, as does adequate tackle for the taking of fish and waterfowl. It is probable that the first constructed dugout canoes are no older than this level, as are skis and the use of the dog as a hunting companion and possibly even the first general use of the bow and arrow. Ground stone tools and crude vessels for the crushing and preparation of seeds or acorns are also evidenced. In drier portions of North America, Willey and Phillips (1958, p. 111) note ". . . widespread seed-gathering . . . which . . . tended to anchor populations in favored localities, and, by conditioning them to greater dependence on vegetal foods, prepared the way for the adoption of agriculture at a later time." The traces of settlements in the earlier phases of this sub-era suggest small seasonal encampments, whose inhabitants had at best only a relatively efficient level of extraction (cf. Star Carr; e.g. in Braidwood and Reed, 1957, p. 23). It could be maintained, however, that the classic "salmon-reapers" of the northwest coast of British Columbia represented the ultimate in intensified food-collection.

There is one factor which needs to be taken into account in considering the scheme at this point. The instance of the Northwest Coast peoples suggests that intensified food-collection persisted in some places well into the ethnological present, and it is usually granted that some of the more spectacular of the Northwest Coast traits may have been based on borrowing. No culture in the world ever lived in a complete vacuum. It is likely that we shall find earlier cases of peoples, still at a level of intensified food-collecting, who borrowed traits from neighboring contemporaries with more developed extractive efficiencies. For example, I suspect such may have been the case with Carleton Coon's "mesolithic" and earlier "neolithic" cave dwellers at Belt and Hotu on the Caspian coast (Braidwood, 1958, Figs. 5–6).

The Food-producing Stage

It is my thesis that in certain regions of the world which were blessed with potentially domesticable animals and/or plants, the subsistence aspect of human culture took a new and alternate direction about ten thousand years ago. The result was the development of the food-producing stage. It is not conceivable to me that civilization could have appeared without a fairly well-developed level of food-production. However "intensified" food-collection might have become, it does not seem possible that civilization and true urbanization could have eventually attended it.

There are exquisite difficulties in delineating the first era of the food-producing stage, that of incipient cultivation. In the first place, as suggested above, there must have been some subtle linkage between the sub-era of food-collection and that of incipient cultivation. It is only reasonable to suppose that incipient cultivators also did a great deal of food-collecting. Such was certainly still the case in the next era, that of "the settled village-farming community," for which our documentation is much clearer. In fact, such is still the case, however industrialized our fisheries become—to take one example.

It must also have been the case during the era of incipient cultivation that the morphologies of both the plants and the animals being taken under domestication were little different from those of their wild contemporaries. Moreover, the artifacts—which were eventually developed to cope with the whole new subsistence pattern—were in their most elemental forms at best. A fair amount of "making-do" with older items of the tool kit must have obtained. Hence it is understandable that both the archeologists and the natural historians may have some difficulty in recognizing what they deal with during this era.

One clear implication of the notion of an era of incipient cultivation is that it would only be manifested within the natural habitat of the potentially domesticable animals and/or plants. Karl Narr (1956) has also considered this implication independently. Here again it should be obvious that increase in our knowledge depends as much on the interest of natural scientists as on that of archeologists.

With the study of human paleo-environments only in its infancy, it is not at all clear how many pertinent natural habitats there may have been nor even whether all the possibilities actually were the scenes of independent experiments in domestication. Carl Sauer has championed the case for an early development and spread of the domesticated vegetatively reproductive plants in southeastern Asia (1952) and has also considered many of the factors which must have conditioned the appearance of cultivation in the New World (1950). G. P. Murdock (1957) makes a case for an early center of cultivation in the great bend of the Niger River in West Africa. Both the Southeast Asian and the West African cases seem to me quite reasonable, but there is neither archeological nor paleo-environmental documentation for their reality. The same is true of China, for which it would certainly not be completely unreasonable to expect a range of incipient cultivation, and it is not yet clear whether a separate case will eventually be made for peninsular India—as distinct from both southwestern and southeastern Asia.

For the New World, much attention has been given to the history of maize (e.g. Mangelsdorf, 1958), and the pollen of one of its possible antecedents has been found in an early geological context in Mexico, but maize does not appear in the typologically earliest "village" sites so far available. Both Irving Rouse and Gordon Willey (cf. Willey 1958, p. 372) are sensitive to Sauer's (1952) suggestion for the early development of a premaize root-crop "horticulture" in low-land South America. R. S. MacNeish's (1959) earliest "incipient ag-ricultural" horizon in Tamaulipas appears to have been a combina-tion of squash and bean cultivation along with food-collection. The "preceramic agricultural period" mound sites of coastal Peru (e.g. Hauca Prieta; Bird, 1948), which probably pertain to the beginning of the next era in any case, were inhabited by people who depended on such cultivated plants as squash, aji peppers, and canavalia beans as well as on collected wild plants and fish. It is my present under-standing that from the point of view of maize as the most potentially effective New World food crop, the location (or locations?) of the natural habitat of the eventually domesticated form (or forms?) is not yet known.

The New World situation is further complicated by the fact that on various occasions in the area of what is now the United States, at least, there were prehistoric attempts at the cultivation of such seeds as pigweed, giant ragweed, sunflower, and so on. M. L. Fowler (1957) has reconsidered this evidence and concludes that these local cultiva-tions refer to the level of the "archaic" or our sub-era of intensified food-collection. Apparently the yield from these plants was not suffi-ciently impressive from the point of view of extractive efficiency to lead to a truly new subsistence pattern. It is of course possible that the same sort of thing happened at various times and places in the Old World and may correspond in part to a recently postulated (Braidwood and Reed, 1957) level of "vegeculture," the conception of which probably overemphasizes the matter of vegetatively repro-ductive plants and semitropical situations.

It is southwestern Asia that provides what little substance the era of incipient cultivation—as a true prelude to food-production—now has beyond pure theory. Within the biotic zone of the hilly flanks of the Fertile Crescent, a beginning has been made in a sophisticated study of the paleo-environment and suggests that the hilly-flanks zone was in fact a natural habitat of great potential. While the exact boundaries of the zone and the details of its climate and environ-ment some ten thousand years ago are far from fixed, the zone does appear to have been the home of the wild wheats, barleys, and cer-tain legumes and of the important food animals of the basic Western cultural tradition. Within this zone also appear the archeological traces known in Palestine as the "Natufian" and other traces found in Iraqi Kurdistan at Karim Shahir, M'lefaat, and Zawi Chemi Shanidar (Braidwood, 1958). These are the materials which I take to manifest the era of incipient cultivation. They show modest indications of architecture and settlement, the first flint sickle blades, perhaps the domesticated dog, and a variety of ground stone tools reasonably implying digging, grinding, and food-preparation. At the same time, implements implying food-collection also appear in the assemblages. The implications for incipient cultvation gain some force from the fact that the sites occur in the zone of the natural habitat and also by extrapolation backward from the earliest known phases of the next era—that of the settled village-farming community.

Clearly, a great deal more of both archeological and paleo-environmental study is needed before the era of incipient cultivation gains fully acceptable substance. But the place, the implications, and even the time seem to be about right. While there is as yet no radiocarbon determination for the Natufian (*senso stricto*), the termination of the Zarzian levels at Shanidar cave and determinations for the open site of Zawi Chemi Shanidar itself (Solecki and Rubin, 1958) both fall at about 8750 B.C. This is, in fact, somewhat before the conventional date for the late-glacial/early-postglacial time boundary (and for the beginning of the "mesolithic"—our sub-era of intensified food-collection—in northwestern Europe).

Unsatisfactory as its documentation remains for the moment, the conception of an era of incipient cultivation is taken to be useful as a model for further research in prehistory. It emphasizes a clean break from De Mortillet's "loi du développement similaire" and also the proposition that a new set of culture patterns (implying with it a new type of subsistence pattern) may have been developing at the same time as was the sub-era of intensified food-collection in other regions. It emphasizes the necessity for the reclamation of evidence in the realms of both archeology and paleo-environment if real understanding of the prehistoric past is to be achieved.

The next era, that of the established village-farming community, is somewhat more generally familiar (often under the rubric "neolithic"), although its beginnings are being pushed backward in time in both hemispheres. Since the era had intensifications in favored regions as time went on, we have sometimes referred to its earlier phases as "primary" (Braidwood and Braidwood, 1953).

The beginnings of this level of extractive efficiency are difficult to characterize simply and in a world-wide sense. If any definition of the "neolithic" were to be acceptable (though to me none would be, for the word has had too many meanings ever to regain precision), it would be in Childe's (1953) sense of " 'a self-sufficing food-producing economy.' " But the presence of great bulks of snail shells and traces of pistachio and acorn hulls as well as the bones of wild animals would make me uncomfortable about the possibility of self-sufficiency on the basis of *produced* food alone at the site of Jarmo. Even my choice of a name for the era, that of "the village-farming community," no doubt shows my predisposition toward the materials of southwestern Asia. There, architecturally well-expressed villages of fair permanency (as their depths of deposit show) seem to have been present from the beginning of the era. But it is not yet completely clear whether the roughly equivalent level in Mesoamerica followed the same type of settlement pattern (see e.g. Willey, 1956, p. 108), although the early mound sites of coastal Peru apparently do so. The presence of pottery as a "standard" trait for identifying the appearance of the "neolithic" has now clearly gone by the board in both the Old and the New World. There are even traces of preceramic village communities in Thessalian Greece and in Baluchistan, which suggest that expansion away from the zone of the natural habitat had already begun before the era witnessed the appearance of pottery.

The fact is that, while the names of many of the sites of this era in both the Old and the New World are generally familiar, in no case —within the areas of potential nuclearity for the appearance of the recognized ancient civilizations—are we really well informed in either culture-historical or natural-historical terms. It would be almost pure guesswork and extrapolation to attempt to answer the question: What was the subsistence pattern of the people of a Halafian village in the upper Tigris-Euphrates basin? There are actually few enough sites, although the names of the known sites may be familiar. I grow increasingly uncomfortable because we archeologists who deal with later prehistory have also been in the clutch of De Mortillet's dead hand (see e.g. Braidwood and Braidwood, 1953, Table I). We make our chronological tables as bar diagrams, never dreaming that some of the Hassunah phase, some of the Halaf phase, and perhaps even some of the Ubaid phase may have been in fact contemporaneous.

I do not take it to be my business here to detail the known sequences of the era. This has been done fairly recently for southwestern Asia (Braidwood and Braidwood, 1953; Braidwood, 1957*b*) and for the New World (Willey and Phillips, 1958). Max Loehr's (1954) short account of China is probably the best available. The new implications of radiocarbon determination for southwestern Asia have been briefly considered recently (Braidwood, 1958), but there do remain a few points of interest for our present purposes.

It is my understanding of the situation in southwestern Asia, at least, that the transition from the era of incipient cultivation to the era of the primary village-farming community took place within the zone of the natural habitat of the potentially domesticable plants and animals. Soon after this, presumably, the "permissive mutations" and/or "introgressive hybridizations" (Braidwood, 1958, esp. Fig. 6) allowed expansion of peoples (with their plants and animals) outside the zone of the natural habitat. Probably one important aspect of this expansion was the "fingering down the mud flats" of the Tigris and Euphrates toward alluvial Mesopotamia. Very presently, and no doubt most importantly in southern Mesopotamia although not exclusively so, the era began to take on intensified dimensions. We begin to find, for example, the remains of town-sized establishments with temples of some degree of monumentality.

It is here that I become uncomfortable with my attempt to delineate further eras or sub-eras (as Fig. 6 of Braidwood, 1958, tries to do) on the primary basis of subsistence patterns and extractive efficiencies. I believe my difficulty lies with the fact that by about this time, our third variation on an ecological theme, namely that increasing sociocultural complexity gradually tended to mitigate the necessity of an immediate ecological balance for an increasing number of people, began to become effective.

This does not mean that the natural-historian, working with the culture-historian, no longer has a role in the elucidation of events at the very threshold of civilization's appearance. The recent work of Adams and Jacobsen in southern Iraq merely serves to emphasize how important it is that we understand the natural (as well as the social) ecology of ancient Mesopotamia. Jean Perrot (1958) has convinced me of the importance of his conception of a "submarginal" culture pattern of rather mobile farmer-traders, as seen in the Beersheba-Ghassul type sites in Israel and Jordan—a culture pattern which seems to have achieved a neat balance with life well below the 200-mm. rain line. But the point remains that increasingly, as we move nearer the time of established civilizations, a scheme of classification based primarily on subsistence tends to blur rather than aid understanding.

As for the archeology of Mesopotamia in the threshold range, we still know far too little of it. In terms of Delougaz's very reasonable reclassification, we have a fair grasp of portions of the Ubaid assemblage on a few sites but know precious little of the Warka phase and certainly not yet enough of the Protoliterate phase from a full-bodied culture-historical (and natural-historical!) point of view. We do, very fortunately, begin to benefit by such extrapolations backward from "historical" times as those of Jacobsen (1946) and Wilson (1946, 1951). Childe (1952) gives a relatively good account of the archeology of both Mesopotamia and Egypt, but it must not be read alone or without Jacobsen and Wilson and certainly Frankfort (1951). Adams (see above, pp. 269–92) makes his own very important contribution to our understandings, especially in playing down *irrigation* as a determinate factor in the early formation of civilization.

Summary

Any prehistoric reconstruction must, given the nature of the available data, remain a thing of threads and patches. It will also be quite idiosyncratic and depend on the experiences and opportunities for observation which the particular prehistorian has had as well as on the degree to which he allows himself imaginative flights with respect to his data. Should Gordon Willey attempt to trespass into the Old World, as I have into the New (and I certainly hope he will attempt it!), he would be bound to come out differently. I myself am quite unashamed of a tendency to make imaginative models as a framework against which to set problem-oriented field research. I trust I am just as ready to abandon them when the data show them to be in error; I have already had to cease, with apologies, my scolding of Miss Kenyon for her preference for a "long" chronology (Braidwood, 1958, n. 47). I also have a tendency to think in terms both of multilinear evolution and of diffusion, as Richard Pittioni (1958) has noticed! If I understand Pittioni correctly, he does not believe diffusion took place effectively until a considerable cultural potential was built up, but not all anthropologists demand that the word "diffusion" refer to such an accomplished level (cf. Joseph Birdsell's [1957] important study of the rapid aboriginal peopling of Australia). For some curious reason, one of Carl Sauer's (1958) misconceptions of our general position is that American anthropologists do not find diffusion "reputable" (cf. e.g. Braidwood, 1957*b*, p. 139).

To the degree in which the reader agrees or disagrees with my tendencies, he may find this brief reconstruction acceptable or unacceptable. It seems to me that the long view of prehistory taken here suggests an obviously more direct man-nature relationship at the beginning. As time went on and technology gave man more control of nature, the relationship began to acquire more "human" proportions. As time went still farther and most importantly, although not necessarily exclusively, with the appearance of food-production, the increasingly complex sociocultural aspects of life further altered the man-nature relationship. Given the biological nature of man, the relationship must obviously continue to exist, and its balance, however subtle, must be maintained if the species is to survive. Perhaps a great part of human history could be said to be concerned with the developing subtleness of balance between man and nature as the dimensions of culture increase.

WORKS CITED

Bird, Junius B. 1948. Preceramic cultures in Chicama and Virú. Society for American Archaeology. Memoirs IV 21–28.

Birdsell, Joseph B. 1957. Some population problems involving Pleistocene man. Cold Spring Harbor symposia on quantitative biology XXII 47–69.

Braidwood, Robert J. 1957a. Means towards an understanding of human behavior before the present. Walter W. Taylor (ed.), The identification of non-artifactual archaeological materials (National Research Council Publication No. 565) pp. 14–16. Washington, D.C.

———. 1957b. Prehistoric men. Chicago Natural History Museum. Popular series. Anthropology, No. 37. 3d ed. Chicago.

———. 1958. Near Eastern prehistory: The swing from food-gathering cultures to village-farming communities is still imperfectly understood. Science CXXVII 1419–30.

———. 1959. Archeology and the evolutionary theory. The Washington Anthropological Society, Evolution and anthropology: A centennial appraisal pp. 76–89. Washington, D.C.

Braidwood, Robert J., and Braidwood, Linda. 1953. The earliest village communities of southwestern Asia. Journal of world history I 278–310.

Braidwood, Robert J., and Reed, Charles A. 1957. The achievement and early consequences of food-production: A consideration of the archeological and natural-historical evidence. Cold Spring Harbor symosia on quantitative biology XXII 19–31.

Caldwell, Joseph R. 1958. Trend and tradition in the prehistory of the eastern United States. Illinois State Museum Scientific papers X *and* American Anthropological Association Memoir LXXXVIII.

Childe, V. Gordon. 1950a. The urban revolution. Town planning review XXI 3–17.

———. 1950b. Cave men's buildings. Antiquity XXIV 4–11.

———. 1952. New light on the most ancient East. 4th ed. London.

Childe, V. Gordon. 1953. Old World prehistory: Neolithic. A. L. Kroeber (ed.), Anthropology today, pp. 193–210. Chicago.

Clark, J. Grahame D. 1952. Prehistoric Europe: The economic basis. London.

———. 1954. Excavations at Starr Carr. Cambridge, England.

———. 1957. Archaeology and society. Cambridge, Massachusetts.

Daly, Reginald. 1934. The changing world of the Ice Age. New Haven.

Deevey, Edward S., Jr. 1956. The human crop. Scientific American CXCIV 105–12.

Fowler, Melvin L. 1957. The origin of plant cultivation in the central Mississippi Valley: A hypothesis. Paper read at the 1957 meetings of the American Anthropological Association, Chicago.

Frankfort, Henri. 1938. Course lectures in Near Eastern archeology, Chicago.

———. 1951. The birth of civilization in the Near East. Bloomington, Indiana.

Frankfort, Henri, *et al.* 1946. The intellectual adventure of ancient man. Chicago.

Garrod, Dorothy A. E. 1953. The relations between South-West Asia and Europe in the later Palaeolithic Age. Journal of world history I 13–38.

Jacobsen, Thorkild. 1946. Mesopotamia. Frankfort *et al.*, 1946, pp. 125–219.

Klima, Bohuslav. 1954. Paleolithic huts at Dolni Věstonice, Czechoslovakia. Antiquity XXVIII 4–14.

Kroeber, Alfred L. The superorganic. American anthropologist XIX 163–213.

Loehr, Max. 1954 (and following editions). Archaeology: China, Southeast Asia, and Japan. *In* Encyclopaedia Britannica. Chicago.

MacNeish, Richard S. 1958. Preliminary archaeological investigations in the Sierra de Tamaulipas, Mexico. American Philosophical Society. Transactions XLVIII, pt. 6.

Mangelsdorf, Paul C. 1958. Ancestor of corn. Science CXXVIII 1313–20.

Murdock, George Peter. 1957. Culture areas of Africa. Paper read at the 1957 meetings of the American Anthropological Association, Chicago.

Narr, Karl. 1956. Early food-producing populations. William L. Thomas, Jr. (ed.), Man's role in changing the face of the earth, pp. 134–51. Chicago.

Oakley, Kenneth P. 1956. The earliest tool-makers *and* The earliest fire-makers. Antiquity XXX 4–8 *and* 102–7.

———. 1957. Tools makyth man. Antiquity XXXI 199–209.

Perrot, Jean. 1958. L'aube de l'histoire à Beersheba. Bible et terre sainte IX 8–19.

Pittioni, Richard. 1958. Zur Urgeschichte des Bauerntums. Österreichische Akademie der Wissenschaften, *Wien,* philos.-hist. Klasse. Anzeiger, Jahrgang 1957, No. 14:323–41.

Rogers, J. S., Hubbell, T. H., and Byers, C. F. 1952. Man and the biological World. New York.

Sauer, Carl O. 1950. Cultivated plants of South and Central America. J. H. Steward (ed.), Handbook of South American Indians (Bureau of American Ethnology. Bulletin No. 143) VI 487–543. Washington D.C.

———. 1952. Agricultural origins and dispersals. New York.

———. 1958. Letter *in* Antiquity XXXII 187–89.

Solecki, Ralph S., and Rubin, Meyer. 1958. Dating of Zawi Chemi, an early village site at Shanidar, northern Iraq. Science CXXVII 1446.

Washburn, Sherwood L. 1957. Some speculations on the significance of tools in human evolution. Paper read at the 1957 meetings of the American Anthropological Association, Chicago.

Wheeler, *Sir* Mortimer. 1954. Archaeology from the earth. Oxford.

Willey, Gordon R. 1956. Problems concerning prehistoric settlement patterns in the Maya lowlands. G. R. Willey (ed.), Prehistoric settlement patterns in the New World (Viking Fund publications in anthropology No. 23) pp. 107–14. New York.

Willey, Gordon R., and Phillips, Philip. 1958. Method and theory in American archaeology. Chicago.

———. 1958. Estimated correlations and dating of South and Central American cultural sequences. American antiquity XXIII 353–78.

Wilson, John A. 1946. Egypt. Frankfort *et al.*, 1946, pp. 31–121.

———. 1951. The burden of Egypt. Chicago.

IV

The Function of Language in the
Cultural Process of Expansion
of Mesopotamian Society

By IGNACE J. GELB

The Scope of the Study

The scope of the present study is to investigate the linguistic situation of ancient Mesopotamia through about three thousand years of its long history, with special reference to the mutual relationship between its two most important languages, Sumerian and Akkadian; to discuss the relationship of the languages with the peoples (*ethnos*) who used them; to trace, if possible, the growth of the peoples (*ethnos*) into nations (*demos*).

The area here studied is Mesopotamia. It is planned to include in an enlarged study the results of an investigation of parallel developments in other parts of the ancient Near East as well as in the worlds of Greece and Rome.

Definitions

Before discussing the main topic we should take care of such preliminary matters as definitions. It is my firm persuasion that omission of definitions is the main cause of the unbelievable confusion which exists in almost all the articles dealing with the present subject. The terms to be defined are "people" or "folk" (Greek *ethnos*), "nation" or "state" (Greek *demos*), "race," and "civilization."

In a previous study[1] the terms "nation" and "people" were defined as follows:

> The definition of "nation" is relatively easy: "nation" is a political term denoting a body of persons linked together by a state or by the common will to a state. Definition of the ethnic term "people" is more difficult, as the traits characterizing a people are more numerous and more complex. The main traits of a people are

[1] Gelb, *Hurrians and Subarians* ("Studies in Ancient Oriental Civilization," No. 22 [Chicago, 1944]) p. v.

community of tradition, customs, religion, culture, language, and geographic position. Not all of these traits are of equal strength, and indeed some of them may even be absent. Quite influential are the ties of common tradition in respect to descent. Compactness of geographical position is an important factor, even though parts of the same ethnic unit may at times inhabit widely scattered areas. Religion as an ethnic tie varies in strength. Language as the vehicle of tradition is one of the strongest foundations of a people. As an outward expression language becomes the symbol with which a people is most easily identified. For a people to give up its language in favor of another normally means the renunciation of its own ethnic identity and subsequent assimilation into the ethnic group from which the new language has been taken.

These brief remarks seem to me as valid today as they were in 1944, and, except for some qualifications discussed below, I believe that *lingua fecit gentem*. And *quid fecit nationem?* In other words, what are the factors leading to the origin of *the* nation? The answer is not easy. Older sociologists, such as Sir Henry Sumner Maine and Lewis H. Morgan, sharply separated two principles by which individuals are united for governmental purposes, one principle based on the tribal or social tie and the other based on the territorial or political tie. According to them, the tribal tie, founded on persons and personal relations, is old and universal, and from it developed in the course of time the territorial tie, founded on territory and property. These conclusions are contested by Robert H. Lowie, who assumes that the two types of ties, however antithetical, were not mutually exclusive and could have existed side by side within the same society. To Lowie, the main problem is to establish the process by which an originally weak but perceptible territorial sentiment, at first subordinate to the tribal tie, was intensified to the point of assuming the dominant role.[2]

The term "race" is relatively easy to define. "Race" represents a grouping of human beings linked together by certain common physical (anatomical) characteristics, such as color of skin, hair, and eyes, texture of hair, stature, form of head, etc. The study of races is the task of the physical anthropologists. It is up to them to decide which non-anatomical characteristics, all conditioned by laws of heredity, are pertinent. For example, to what extent is the Negroes' aptitude to excel in sports conditioned by such inherited physical characteristics as favorable stature and corporal structure? But most such alleged *geistige und seelische Merkmale* of the races as *Gerechtigkeitsgefühl, schauspielerische Begabung, lebhafte Phantasie*, so em-

[2] Robert H. Lowie, *The Origin of the State* (New York, 1927) pp. 51 ff.

phasized at one time by the Nazi anthropologists, belong in the realm of metaphysics.

Our knowledge of the physical anthropology of the ancient Near East is based on findings of skeletal materials, representations of human beings in art (reliefs and paintings), and references in literature. Scant as all the three classes of sources are, they do show quite clearly that the ancient Near Eastern peoples belonged to such different subdivisions of the white (Caucasoid) race as the Oriental Mediterranean, Armenoid (*vorderasiatisch*), and Nordic.

It is in the identification of these racial groupings with ethnic groupings that the greatest confusion reigns. The old-fashioned idea that races are divided into peoples and peoples into tribes is still followed by all those scholars who speak about the "Semitic race" and "Semitic characteristics," mixing the two levels of analysis, physical anthropological (races) and sociological (peoples and tribes), and showing little understanding of the plain facts that the Semites are simply peoples who speak Semitic languages and as individuals may belong not only to any of the three races (or subraces) which were prevalent in the ancient Near East but to any other race.

Among the few scholars in the field of ancient Oriental studies who separate distinctly the terms "race" and "people" (distinguished by language) are Eduard Meyer[3] and Giuseppe Furlani.[4] But an article by Hilary G. Richardson,[5] often quoted as a good characterization of the problem, is vitiated in a number of places by his confusion of matters of race with those of language. The confusion is compounded in all those languages in which the term "race" has many loose connotations, as for example in English, where the term is used to include almost any grouping of humans, whether they are linked by common ancestry, or habits, or interests, or mental characteristics. This difficulty comes best to the fore in the writings of that great master of English prose, Winston Churchill. Owing to the ambiguity of the term, it is often difficult to ascertain in the writings of all those scholars who interpret the conflict between the early Sumerians and

3 Eduard Meyer, *Geschichte des Altertums* I 1 (5th ed.; Stuttgart and Berlin, 1925) pp. 73 ff.

4 Giuseppe Furlani, "Lingua e razza nell'Asia Anteriore antica," *Silloge linguistica dedicata alla memoria de Graziadio Isaia Ascoli* (Torino, 1929) pp. 12–22.

5 Hilary G. Richardson, "The Semites," *American Journal of Semitic Languages and Literatures* XLI (1924/25) 1–10, esp. pp. 7 and 9, where he writes about the alleged racial differences between Hebrews and Phoenicians and between Hebrews and those who spoke languages which differed only dialectically from theirs.

the Akkadians (Semites) as due to differences in "race," whether the term stands for race in the anthropological sense or is simply loose talk. The truth is that there never was such a conflict between, let us say, the representatives of the Oriental Mediterranean and Armenoid races (or subraces), or between the Sumerians and the Akkadians as representatives of one or the other of the two races, or between any two peoples as representatives of any two races. The plain fact is that nowhere in antiquity, neither in the Oriental nor in the classical world, did racial groupings become a factor of political conflict. Such a royal title as "leader of the Sumerian race" was impossible not only because there was no such thing as a Sumerian race but also because the leaders were not aware of being at the head of any racial grouping which might have been in contrast to or in conflict with another racial grouping. Talking about the conflict between Sumerian and Akkadian races is talking "dolychocephalic politics"; like the "dolychocephalic grammar," made famous by Max Müller, it should be buried in limbo.

"Culture" or "civilization" represents a state or structure of a society distinguished by certain material and mental (spiritual) characteristics. Although the terms are sociological, like *ethnos*, they refer to groupings of an entirely different class, since the boundaries marking certain cultural entities do not necessarily coincide with those marking certain ethnic entities. The unity of a civilization may be marked by such material characteristics as the use of metals (copper, bronze, iron), of tools, of pottery and the potter's wheel and such mental (spiritual) characteristics as religious beliefs, customs, the use of a cultural (international) language and writing. Cultural changes can and do happen without regard to ethnic changes. It is very probable that the ancient Hebrews, once they settled in Palestine, were closer in their way of life to the neighboring Phoenicians or even to the faraway Assyrians and Babylonians than they were, for instance, to the Bedouins of central Arabia. In terms of culture-analysis, the differences between "the desert" and "the sown" seem to overshadow ethno-linguistic ties.

I omit from the discussion certain human characteristics which were once connected with the concept of race. Typical of that trend were the opinions of the famous Swedish botanist Carolus Linnaeus[6]

---

[6] See e.g. Linnaeus' characterization of the four main "races": "Der Amerikaner ist rötlich, cholerisch, aufgerichtet, der Europäer weiss, sanguinisch, fleissig, der Asiate gelb,

and, in the field of Semitics, of the great French writer and Orientalist Ernest Renan.[7] With the significance of racial background generally discredited, the modern trend is to link such characteristics with ethnic groupings, as best exemplified in the field of Semitics by the writings of T. Nöldeke,[8] G. Levi della Vida,[9] and S. Moscati.[10] Their individualistic-subjective approach to the problem and the lack of criteria by which such characteristics can be objectively connected with races, peoples, or cultures make me feel hesitant about the constructiveness of the results.

The Earliest Mesopotamian Period

The most ancient Mesopotamia comprises the southern part of the area of modern Iraq, situated roughly between Baghdad and the Persian Gulf. Within these limits we can distinguish a southern and a northern part. The southern part is called "Sumer" after the Sumerians, who spoke a language of unknown linguistic affiliation, while the northern part is called "Akkad" after the Akkadians, who spoke a Semitic language. The time covered is from the beginnings of Mesopotamian history, about 3100 B.C., down to the end of the reign of Lugalzagesi, king of Uruk, about 2340 B.C.

The written sources covering this period are limited in both kind and quantity, and the farther back we go in history the fewer sources we have at our disposal. The sources are inscriptions of historical character; building and votive inscriptions of rulers, officials, and private individuals; economic and legal texts; and letters, both private and official. From a much later period we have the Sumerian

---

melancholisch, zähe, der Afrikaner schwarz, phlegmatisch, schlapp. Der Amerikaner ist hartnäckig, zufrieden, frei, der Europäer beweglich, scharfsinnig, erfinderisch, der Asiate grausam, prachtliebend, geizig, der Afrikaner schlau, träge, indolent. Der Amerikaner ist bedeckt mit Tätowierung und regiert durch Gewohnheiten, der Europäer ist bedeckt mit anliegenden Kleidern und regiert durch Gesetze, der Asiate ist gehüllt in weite Gewänder und regiert durch Meinungen, und der Afrikaner ist mit Fett gesalbt und regiert durch Willkür."

7 See e.g. Renan's description of the "Semitic race" in his *Histoire générale et système comparé des langues sémitiques* (4th ed.; Paris, 1863) pp. 1 ff., as characterized by monotheistic trends, intolerance, lack of curiosity and mythology, lack of plastic arts, military inferiority, etc.

8 Theodor Nöldeke, "Zur Charakteristik der Semiten" in his *Orientalische Skizzen* (Berlin, 1892) pp. 1–20 and *Die semitischen Sprachen* (Leipzig, 1899) pp. 7 f.

9 Giorgio Levi della Vida, "Per una caratteristica dei Semiti" in his *Storia e religione nell'Oriente semitico* (Roma, 1924) pp. 10–42.

10 Sabatino Moscati, *Chi furono i Semiti?* (Roma, 1957) pp. 10–13.

King List, an important document listing the rulers of Sumer and Akkad from the earliest period down to about 2000 B.C.

The earliest historical picture of Mesopotamia shows a net of small city-states, scattered through the south (Ur, Uruk, Eridu, Larsa, Lagash, Girshu, Umma, Shuruppak, Adab, Nippur) as well as the north (Kish, Sippar, Akshak). At one time or another one of the city-states grew sufficiently in power to be able to establish its hegemony over the rest of the country. Among such city-states, Ur and Uruk in the south and Kish in the north played the most prominent roles. The extent of the control exercised by the dominant city-states at various times cannot be established within geographical limits owing to the scarcity of sources. It is rather probable that it was not until the time of Lugalzagesi, king of Uruk, at the end of the period under discussion, that the first unification of the country was achieved.[11]

The political allegiance of the population of Sumer and Akkad was thus first to a particular city-state and then to the city-state which succeeded in establishing some sort of hegemony over larger parts of the country. In addition, we can observe in this early period some form of religious allegiance to the Sumerian god Enlil of Nippur by the city-states grouped under what may be called the "Nippur amphictyony."[12] Nippur itself never had a king, never formed a city-state, and was not directly involved in the political strife between the various city-states.

The written sources of the period are all preserved in the cuneiform writing developed by the Sumerians in the south and borrowed from them by the Akkadians in the north.

The language of all the written sources in the south is exclusively Sumerian.[13] While the attestation in the north is not adequate to allow dogmatic conclusions, it may appear that in the early periods the written language of the north was also Sumerian, which was largely supplanted by Akkadian in later periods. Note that the very early inscriptions from Jamdat Nasr (near Kish) are written in

[11] Cf. the inscription of Lugalzagesi in François Thureau-Dangin, *Die sumerischen und akkadischen Königinschriften* (Leipzig, 1907) pp. 152–56, No. 2.

[12] It corresponds to what was called the "Kengir (Sumer) League" by Jacobsen in *Zeitschrift für Assyriologie* LII (1957) 106.

[13] In accordance with William W. Hallo, *Early Mesopotamian Royal Titles* (New Haven, 1957) p. 28, I believe that the Akkadian curse formula, occurring in Arno Poebel, *Historical and Grammatical Texts* (University of Pennsylvania, University Museum, "Publication of the Babylonian Section" V [Philadelphia, 1914]) No. 34, col. x, was added to the Sumerian inscription copied in the Sargonic period. Cf. also Jacobsen in *Zeitschrift für Assyriologie* LII 137, n. 104.

Sumerian, while the economic inscriptions on stone and some votive inscriptions dated to the end of the period under discussion are written largely in Akkadian.[14]

While the rulers of the city-states situated in the south bore Sumerian names,[15] the rulers of the northern city-states bore names the majority of which are Akkadian and the minority Sumerian.

The population of the south was almost exclusively Sumerian in the early part of the period under discussion, as best evidenced by the personal names in the economic texts from Ur and Shuruppak. In the latter part of the period, while in the south the Sumerians were still definitely in the majority, a steadily growing number of persons bearing Akkadian names can be observed in the economic texts from Ur, Adab, Lagash, and Nippur. As far as can be judged from the economic inscriptions on stone and from votive inscriptions (see n. 14), the north was almost completely Akkadian.

Mutual cultural-linguistic influences between south and north are exemplified by a very large number of Sumerian loan words in Akkadian and a sizable, though much smaller, number of Akkadian loan words in Sumerian.

The geographic names offer no basis for conclusions in respect to the relative distribution of the Sumerians and the Akkadians because almost none of them can be explained on the basis of the Sumerian or the Akkadian language, leading to the conclusion that the earliest Mesopotamian settlements were those of a population of unclear linguistic affiliation which anteceded both the Sumerians and the Akkadians in Mesopotamia.

The Sargonic Period

While certain northern cities, such as Sippar, Akshak, and, above all, Kish, occasionally played a dominant role in the earliest period, it was only under Sargon, the first ruler of the northern city-state of Akkad, that the north, and with it the Semitic Akkadians, established a firm and long-lasting rule over the whole of the country, both north and south. After his conquest of Elam, Assyria, and Syria, far beyond

14 Cf. pp. 2–4 of the forthcoming 2d edition of Gelb, *Old Akkadian Writing and Grammar* ("Materials for the Assyrian Dictionary," No. 2).

15 The only exception is the name of *La-ba-aḫ-šum*, king of the 1st dynasty of Uruk; this new reading was suggested by Gelb, *Glossary of Old Akkadian* ("Materials for the Assyrian Dictionary," No. 3 [Chicago, 1957]) p. 92, in place of a nonunderstandable *La-ba-aḫ(?)*-ɪʀ of Jacobsen, *The Sumerian King List* ("Assyriological Studies," No. 11 [Chicago, 1939]) p. 90.

the confines of Sumer and Akkad, Sargon could justifiably pride himself on having established an empire extending "from the shores of the Upper Sea (the Mediterranean) to the shores of the Lower Sea (the Persian Gulf)."[16] The reigns of Sargon and his successors, which comprise the Akkad dynasty, lasted from about 2340 to 2159 B.C.

The language of the royal inscriptions of the Sargonic kings was either Akkadian or Sumerian. As many royal inscriptions appear in both languages, it seems very probable that the official inscriptions of the empire were issued in bilingual form.

The language of the non-royal and non-official inscriptions, such as economic texts and letters, was exclusively Akkadian in the north, that is, in Akkad. In the south, that is, in Sumer, the Sumerian language dominated, although even there Akkadian letters and economic texts are found frequently. The growing bilingual character of the south is indicated by the fact that in the unpublished correspondence of Mezi, the governor of Adab, two letters are written in Akkadian and two in Sumerian. Outside Sumer and Akkad, that is, in the conquered areas of Elam, Assyria, and Mari, the only written language appears to have been Akkadian.

One of the most striking features of the Sargonic period is the standardization of the Akkadian language and writing used throughout the empire. This standardization, observed not only in the official documents but also in private letters and economic texts, is evidence of the controlling power of the central chancellery and of the high level of administrative organization in the Sargonic period. Nothing like it was ever known in the preceding period of Sumerian domination.

Just as the names of all Sargonic rulers were Akkadian, so also were those of the general population of the Akkad area. In certain areas of the south, such as Nippur, Sumerian names are found almost exclusively, while in others, such as Lagash, there is a substantial percentage of Akkadian names.

The attitude of the Sargonic rulers toward Sumerians manifested itself in two ways. On the one hand, Sargon recognized the paramount position of the god Enlil in Nippur, as shown by his title *ensigal Enlil*, "the great governor of Enlil,"[17] by his having "puri-

16 Poebel, *loc. cit.* cols. iv, viii, xii.

17 Poebel, *loc. cit.* col. ii and elsewhere.

fied" the temple of Enlil in Nippur,[18] and by the fact that he deposited his statues and inscriptions in that temple.[19] On the other hand, Sargon followed the policy of destroying the walls of the fortified cities in Sumer[20] and of appointing Akkadians to gubernatorial positions not only in Akkad but also in Sumer.[21] The anti-Sumerian policy of the Sargonic kings is clearly expressed in a late Sumerian composition entitled "Curse of Akkad," according to which the political disaster which befell Akkad at the end of the Akkad dynasty was the direct result of the sacking of Nippur and the desecration of Ekur, Enlil's great sanctuary, by Naram-Sin, the fourth ruler of the dynasty.[22]

The picture sketched above of an assumed conflict between the Sumerians and the Akkadians as representing two different ethnic groups is not in accordance with the reconstruction of Jacobsen,[23] who denies the existence of either racial (wherein I follow him; see p. 318) or ethnic conflict between the Sumerians and the Akkadians and assumes instead that the conflict was of a political nature, between one city-state and another irrespective of their racial or ethnic background.

The Ur III Period

Weakened by the invasion of the barbarian Gutians from the mountains, the Akkad dynasty, and with it the Sargonic empire, came to an end in the twenty-second century B.C. and was replaced first by the ephemeral fourth and fifth dynasties of Uruk and then by the Third Dynasty of Ur, all three originating in the south. In terms of geographical extent and administrative organization of the far-flung provinces, the Ur III empire closely resembled the structure of the Sargonic empire. The time covered is from about 2158 to 2008 B.C.

---

[18] Leon Legrain, *Royal Inscriptions and Fragments from Nippur and Babylon* (University of Pennsylvania, University Museum, "Publications of the Babylonian Section" XV [1926]) No. 41, col. x.

[19] *Passim.*

[20] *Passim.*

[21] Poebel, *loc. cit.* col. iv, and Legrain, *loc. cit.* col. ix. Cf. also Jacobsen in *Zeitschrift für Assyriologie* **LII** 137.

[22] Cf. Samuel N. Kramer, *From the Tablets of Sumer* (Indian Hills, Colorado, 1956) pp. 267–71.

[23] "The assumed conflict between Sumerians and Semites in early Mesopotamian history," *Journal of the American Oriental Society* **LIX** (1939) 485–95.

This is a period of renaissance of the Sumerian language, as attested by hundreds of thousands of documents, mostly economic, written in Sumerian. The number of texts written in Akkadian is limited to a few dozen. While the Sumerian renaissance affected the written language, the country as a whole continued in the direction of total Akkadization and elimination of Sumerian elements. This can be clearly established by the growing number of Akkadian personal and geographic names in the south and of Akkadian loan words in Sumerian and by the fact that the last three rulers of the Third Dynasty of Ur bore Akkadian names, while the names of the first two rulers were Sumerian. The title borne by the rulers was "king of Sumer and Akkad."

The Old Babylonian Period

Toward the end of the Ur III period, the political picture of Mesopotamia underwent a radical change when a new ethnic factor, namely the Amorites, began to play a prominent role in the history of western Asia. These Semitic nomads, spreading from the desert areas south of the Euphrates, brought an end to the Third Dynasty of Ur and succeeded in establishing themselves as a dominant political force in the ancient lands of Sumer and Akkad. The emerging political structure was that of a small number of independent kingdoms, among which Isin, Larsa, and Babylon played the most important roles. Gradually, the dynasty of Babylon, especially under its most prominent ruler, Hammurabi, succeeded in uniting the whole country. The city of Babylon became the capital of the united country, and Babylonia was named after it. The time under consideration for the whole Old Babylonian period is from about 2025 to 1725 B.C.

The importance of the Amorite ethnic elements in the affairs of Babylonia can be recognized from the following factors. A large number of persons bearing Amorite names and/or calling themselves "Amorite" occur in the sources. Most of the kings of Larsa and Babylon bore Amorite names; the others were Akkadian. King Hammurabi, besides several other titles connected with Babylonia, bore the title "king of all the land of Amurru." Two ethnic groups, Akkadians and Amorites, are recognized in the well-known Old Babylonian *Seisachtheia*.[24]

We do not know the extent to which the Amorite language was or

24 F. R. Kraus, *Ein Edikt des Königs Ammi-ṣaduqa von Babylon* ("Studia et documenta" V [Leiden, 1958]) pp. 27 ff.

may have been used among the Amorites after they established themselves in Mesopotamia. Its influence on Akkadian was negligible, and it was never used as a written language.

The dominant language of Babylonia was Akkadian. While Sumerian continued to be used side by side with Akkadian in royal inscriptions, legal and economic texts, and religious literature, all the known correspondence, whether public or official, was in Akkadian. This fact is the best evidence that Akkadian became the commonly spoken language of the country and that Sumerian was relegated to traditional usages in historiography, law, and religion.

Toward the end of the Old Babylonian period, with the gradual assimilation of the Sumerians and the Amorites into the Babylonian *ethnos,* the political boundaries of Babylonia coincided rather well with the ethnic boundaries.

The Kassite Period

After a period of gradual infiltration, the Kassites, whose original home was in the mountains east of the Tigris and whose language was of unknown linguistic affiliation, replaced the Hammurabi dynasty and ruled Babylonia up to about 1171 B.C. Their kings and their warriors bore Kassite names; no written records in the Kassite language have ever been discovered, and its influence on Akkadian in the sphere of loan words was very limited.

During the Kassite period the Akkadian language became the established lingua franca of the whole Near East. While in the Old Babylonian period Akkadian was used outside Mesopotamia in Elam, Syria, and Asia Minor, in the Kassite period its use in international relations was extended to Egypt and Palestine.

The New Babylonian Period

In the years 1170 to 538 B.C., when Babylonia was again under the rule of local dynasties, a new ethnic factor, namely the Semitic Arameans, was making an imprint on the political scene. Coming from desert areas, like the Amorites of the preceding periods, the Aramean tribes infiltrated the whole of Mesopotamia. In contrast to the Amorites, the Arameans lived peacefully in the country side by side with the Akkadians, leaving largely unaffected the political set-up of Mesopotamia. In contrast to the Amorite language, the Aramaic language succeeded gradually in establishing itself as the spoken and written language of Mesopotamia and in relegating Akkadian to the status of a written cultural language, limited in its use to religious, legal, and scientific literature. The spread of Aramaic in Mesopotamia, as well as in Syria and Palestine and to a smaller degree in Egypt, Asia Minor, and Persia, is one of the great mysteries in the history of ethno-linguistic developments, for it was achieved not by direct conquest but by a process of peaceful infiltration by nomads culturally inferior to the sedentary peoples who gradually accepted the new language. The spread of the Aramaic language is connected by Forrer[25] with its use of a simple writing, which the Arameans borrowed from the Phoenicians when they became established as a sedentary population in Syria and Mesopotamia.

With the replacement of Akkadian by Aramaic as the living language of Babylonia and the subsequent conquest of Babylonia, first by the Persians and then by the Greeks, the Akkadians ceased to exist as an *ethnos*.

The Assyrian Empire

The ethno-linguistic developments in Babylonia, in southern Mesopotamia, were paralleled by similar developments in Assyria, situated in northern Mesopotamia around the important cities of Assur and Nineveh. The time covered is from the Old Assyrian period (corresponding more or less to the Old Babylonian period in Babylonia) to the fall of the Assyrian empire in 612 B.C.

The linguistic situation of Assyria presents a simpler picture than that of Babylonia, for Assyria was not affected by foreign invasions to the extent that Babylonia was. From the very beginning the language of Assyria was Akkadian in a form known as the "Assyrian dialect," to be contrasted with the "Babylonian dialect" used in Babylonia.

While the Assyrian dialect persisted as the spoken language of Assyria throughout the whole span of Assyrian history, beginning in the Middle Assyrian period it became gradually limited in its written usage by the inroads of the Babylonian dialect. We find that in the New Assyrian period the Assyrian dialect was limited to certain types of records, such as contracts and letters, while the Babylonian dialect was used in historical inscriptions and religious literature.

All written attestation, both Assyrian and Babylonian, disappears in Assyria after the fall of the empire, and we may assume that the country became Aramaized.

With the exception of a short time during the reign of Hammu-

25 Emil Forrer, *Reallexikon für Assyriologie* I (Berlin and Leipzig, 1932) 139.

rabi, king of Babylon, Assyria was politically independent of Babylonia. The Middle Assyrian period is marked by a steady growth of Assyrian military power, which culminated in the New Assyrian period, when Assyria first established undisputed hegemony over the whole of Mesopotamia and then extended its political power over practically the whole Near East, including Syria, Palestine, Egypt, and vast areas of Anatolia and Iran. The political hegemony of Assyria was achieved by a high level of military and administrative organization previously unparalleled in the history of the Near East.

With the political linking of Assyria and Babylonia a new type of *demos* emerged under the leadership of the Assyrians, based on the symbiosis of the two closely related ethnic groups.

General Observations

The following general observations should be regarded not as final conclusions but as points which may merit discussion in the light of parallels from elsewhere. They are presented in concise form because of the limitations of space.

1. In the established sequence in the linguistic development of ancient Mesopotamia—from the dominance of the Sumerian language, through the bilingual Sumerian-Akkadian stage, to the dominance of the Akkadian language—we find that the intermediate bilingual stage was of an ephemeral character and that there was a striving to achieve a monolingual society based on the language of the dominant *ethnos*.

2. Sumerian as a written, cultural language continued in use after its disappearance as a spoken language. The same is true of Akkadian after its replacement by Aramaic.

3. The Gutian, Amorite, and Kassite languages, introduced into Mesopotamia by peoples culturally inferior to the Akkadians, had ephemeral life, were never used in writing, and exercised negligible influence on the Akkadian language.

4. The Aramaic language, introduced into Mesopotamia by a people originally culturally inferior to the Akkadians, succeeded in replacing Akkadian as the dominant language.

5. The Babylonian dialect of the culturally dominant Babylonians succeeded in replacing the Assyrian dialect in Assyrian official usage, even though Assyria was politically stronger than Babylonia at all times after the Old Babylonian period.

6. The language of the culturally dominant Babylonians, having

become the lingua franca of western Asia, contributed an important aspect to the unity of western Asiatic civilization in ancient times.

7. The Sumerians disappeared as an *ethnos* with the disappearance of Sumerian as a living language; the same is true of the Akkadians when the Akkadian language was replaced by Aramaic.

8. The growth of political bodies in Mesopotamia was from small city-states to kingdoms to empires. At the same time we can observe the growth of administrative organization and centralization of power, first under Sargon of Akkad, and most strongly developed in Assyria.

9. The development of political allegiance in Mesopotamia was first to small city-states and small kingdoms, then to a religious center ("Nippur amphictyony"), and then to a *demos* based on a dominant *ethnos* (Sargon of Akkad). The concept of *demos* was most strongly developed in Assyria.

10. Lower-class ethno-linguistic relationships were recognized from the earliest historical beginnings, as shown by the existence of the term "Sumer" (KI.EN.GI or KALAM) for the country inhabited by the Sumerians, irrespective of its political subdivisions.

11. Higher-class ethno-linguistic relationships played little if any role in Mesopotamia. There are no terms in Sumerian or Akkadian for any over-all ethnic groupings or linguistic families, such as Semites or Semitic languages. There is no evidence for the existence of any special attachments between peoples speaking different though related languages.

V

On the Comparative Treatment of Economic Institutions in Antiquity with Illustrations from Athens, Mycenae, and Alalakh

By KARL POLANYI

Tools of Analysis

A broad indication of the different ways in which we find the economic process institutionalized in society may, eventually, throw some light on the role of the economy in the territorial spread of the cultures that may or may not accompany the process of social growth. No frontal attack on the problem of size appears as yet promising.

Two features of the economy have been selected for inquiry: the relations between the economic and the political system in society and the manner in which the uses of money are instituted, primarily in palace economies. In either case some random reflections on territorial expansion seem possible, yet the main emphasis must lie not on these reflections but rather on the conceptual tools employed in the comparative treatment of economies as we meet them in history.

The economy, then, in our reading, is an institutionalized process,[1] a sequence of functional movements that are embedded in social relations. The function of the movements is to supply a group of individuals with a flow of material goods; the social relations in which the process is embedded invest it with a measure of unity and stability. The movements are either locational or appropriational or both. That is, the things move either in relation to other things, which movements include production and transportation, or in relation to the persons who need them or dispose of them.

Process and institutions together form the economy. Some students stress the material resources and equipment—the ecology and technology—which make up the process; others, like myself, prefer to point to the institutions through which the economy is organized.

[1] See *Trade and Market in the Early Empires*, edited by Karl Polanyi, Conrad M. Arensberg, and Harry W. Pearson (Glencoe, Illinois, 1957).

Again, in inquiring into the institutions one can choose between values and motives on the one hand and physical operations on the other, either of which can be regarded as linking the social relations with the process. Perhaps because I happen to be more familiar with the institutional and operational aspect of man's livelihood, I prefer to deal with the economy primarily as a matter of organization and to define organization in terms of the operations characteristic of the working of the institutions.

I am conscious of the inherent limitations of such a treatment particularly from the point of view of general sociology. For the process is embedded not in "economic" institutions alone—a matter of degree, anyway—but in political and religious ones as well; physical operations do not exhaust the range of relevant human behavior, either. But it helps roughly to disentangle the economy from other subsystems in society, such as the political and the religious, and thereby make reasonably sure that we know what we mean when we so confidently talk about "the economy."

In the first approximation, economies form a going concern mainly by virtue of a few patterns of integration, namely reciprocity, redistribution, and exchange. A historically important fourth pattern might be seen in householding, that is, the manner in which a peasant economy or a manorial estate is run, though formally this is actually redistribution on a smaller scale. By itself, or together with the others, each of the three patterns is capable of integrating the economy, ensuring its stability and unity. Whether or not integration raises technological problems, mainly of physical communication, or rather organizational problems such as the merging of smaller groups into bigger ones, size may be the essence of the matter; typically such merging occurs whenever peasant economies link up to form a larger society.

In early societies integration happens as a rule through the redistribution of goods from a center or through reciprocation between the corresponding members of symmetrical groups. The goods may be appropriated for distribution by peasant or chief, by temple or palace, by lord or village headman through physical storage or through the mere collecting of rights of disposal of the goods. Both the deliveries to and the awards from the center are largely assessed as a function of a person's status, and the actual allocation is made through administrative decision. Reciprocity, as between kin or neighborhood groups, may link individual partners or comprise a whole sequence of symmetrical situations "in turn." Numerous combinations of reciprocity and redistribution occur. A third way of integrating the economy is by exchange or barter. To have an integrative effect, this pattern needs the instrumentality of price-making markets, as in nineteenth-century society where a supply-demand price mechanism produced integrative prices. The mere presence of market elements or even of nonprice-making markets in a peasants' and craftsmen's society does not produce an exchange-patterned economy.

No "stages theory" is here implied; a pattern may appear, disappear, and recur again at a later phase of the society's growth. Admittedly, exchange resulting in an integrative effect only appeared with the self-regulating system of competitive markets inaugurated in the nineteenth century. Where prices are "set," "fixed," or otherwise administered, they are produced not by the market but by administrative action. Redistribution was regularly practiced in primitive tribes at the hunting and collecting stage; eventually it became a function of archaic administration, while in modern times it is a feature of industrial planned economies. Reciprocity was widespread among kinship-organized societies and still survives as the *raison d'être* of Christmas trade of Western cultures. Only integration through price-making markets, as we have said, was unknown until recent times.

These patterns do not—and this should be stressed—supply us with a classification of economic systems as a whole; rather the coexistence of patterns, notably of reciprocity and redistribution, is common. Also markets which do not integrate the economy may fit into either pattern. And any of the patterns may predominate, may reflect the movements through which land, labor, and the production and distribution of food are merged into the economy. But other patterns may obtain alongside the dominant one in the various sectors of the economy and at varying levels of its organization.

In the second approximation, patterns of integration are necessarily accompanied by the institutions through which the economy is organized. No complete theory of economic institutions is here intended. Some institutions are inherent in the pattern itself, such as a symmetrical structure for reciprocity or a degree of centralization for redistribution or price-making markets for integration through exchange. And already at this level institutional variants offer, for instance, temple or palace as a redistributive center. In addition, the patterns are as a rule accompanied by characteristic institutions, such as the drawing of lots for the division of booty or for the assignment of land or the allocation of burdens "in turn" under a reciprocity pattern. Storage arrangements, rations, and equivalents go with re-distributive patterns. Less important institutional traits, of which there are many variants, tend structurally to adjust to these "characteristic" ones.

It must be apparent that just as the economy forms only a part of society, so the economy itself consists of differently patterned parts, each of which may have its characteristic institutions combined with a variety of traits.

Hence there is need for circumspection before one attempts the task of mapping the changing place of concrete economies in actual societies. One should distinguish between the society as a whole, in which the economic, political, and religious spheres meet, the economic sphere itself, which sometimes combines several patterns of integration, the institutions characteristic of those patterns, and, finally, variants of other institutional traits. The inquiry may thus come closer to the attainment of more ambitious aims, such as systematically relating the territorial spread of cultures to the economy. At any rate, it should point to some of the potentialities—and limitations—of the economic historian at the present stage of our knowledge.

The two problem groups that follow will serve to illustrate what we call the institutional analysis of economies. To simplify matters, we have selected examples from the economic history of ancient Greece, with references to Alalakh. The first group connects subsystem to subsystem, economy to polity; the second treats of palace economies from the angle of money uses.

Classical Athens offers an example of interaction between economy and polity. By the beginning of the fifth century the agora, in the sense of a market place, had become part of the economic organization of the Athenian polis, as magistracies and other offices and bodies were parts of her political constitution. Both the Athenian city-state's strength of resistence in an emergency and its incapacity to expand territorially sprang from this conjunction of agora and polis government. The agora was not, as our market system is, an open supply-demand price mechanism disciplined through competition and interdependence with other markets. It was (in modern terms) an artificial construct of limited access and dependent for supply, rates of currency, and price control upon the sanctions provided by the polity. The power of the democratic jurisdiction formed a frame of authority, which alone enabled the agora to function but at the same time marred the chances of its expansion by limiting its scope to the confines of the polis. And, conversely, the agora was the mainstay of the democracy, which was the driving force of territorial expansion, yet the self-same agora time and again frustrated such endeavors through its jealous nativism. These mutually restrictive features of economic structure and polis constitution accounted for many of the vicissitudes of the Hellenistic polis. Neither the polis as such nor its agora had aptitude for growth. Hellenism was essentially polis-culture of empire size gradually spreading over the Near East by virtue of the "barbarian" government of the countryside, the *chora* (see below).

The palace economies of Mycenae and Alalakh are relatively new additions to our knowledge. For a comparative study of antiquity, the mesh of our patterns offers no more than a rough orientation. In order to study institutional structures we require a finer texture. At least one further determinant should be added to the economy, namely the dimension of quantitativity. Statements that ignore the quantitative connotation of the movements that make up the economic process are seriously inadequate. Thus the development of the monetary sphere, in the widest sense, should offer a heuristic avenue to the analysis of economic institutions in early societies. A "monetary" approach of this kind will be attempted here in the comparison of Mycenae and Alalakh. On such a sharpening of our conceptual tools hinges, as will appear, the separation of submonetary devices from money proper, in Mycenae (see pp. 340–46), as well as the differentiation of western Asian palace economies in terms of money uses, as shown by Alalakh (see pp. 346–50).

Economy and Polity: Agora, Polis, Chora

The Athenian agora may well have been the earliest market in the West which might be called a "city market." Yet such use of the term is slightly anachronistic. For the agora was historically not primarily a market place, but a site for meetings, and the Greek polis was not a city in the modern sense, but a state.

First, the agora. From about the end of the sixth century Attica apparently possessed in the town of Athens some kind of market place where food was retailed. Previously only Sardis, the capital of

Lydia, seems to have been credited with such an open space, which was crossed by the gold-bearing Pactolus. Gold dust presumably was employed there for the purchase of prepared foods, while coins of electron were used for trade. In Athens, where gold was absent, small denominations of silver coins served the purpose of retailing. Without some such monetary device, distribution of food throughout the market would not have been practicable. Hot meals offered in the inn, cuts of tepid meat and snacks to consume in the alley, foodstuffs to take home for the kitchen were the province of the *kapelos* (of authentically Lydian origin), to whose lowly figure was owed much of the famous ease of Athenian life. In the wake of the downfall of the tyrannis and its palace economy the agora eventually filled up with a variety of figures, male and female, selling mostly their own produce, self-raised or self-made. They rarely acted as middlemen, with the important exception of the grain trade, in which wheat imports were sold by supervised retailers.

Second, the polis. Athens the town had no resemblance to our medieval towns with their privileged citizenry lording it over the *banlieue*. True, the acropolis was an impregnable rock that overawed the flatland for a full day's ride. But the town of Athens had nevertheless no territory of its own, no legal or constitutional status, no juridical personality, no autonomy. Its agora could be put out of bounds to the unfriendly neighbor, but neither voters nor office-holders derived rights from their domicile in Athens. The privilege of keeping a stall in the agora was probably most of the time reserved for citizens, that is, citizens of Attica or Athens, not persons residing in Athens. Hence our hesitation to speak of the agora as a city market.

In what manner, then, did the agora assist the Athenian city-state in its political rise, while at the same time hampering its territorial expansion? And, conversely, how far was the polis constitution favorable to the growth of the market habit, while forming an obstacle to its expansion into a market system reaching beyond the state boundaries?

The agora, even from its beginnings, was an asset to the state. Solon's reforms would hardly have prevented debt bondage from becoming a normal part of the labor structure but for the timely emergence of the market habit. The edge of debt sharpened by the recent spread of currency was blunted by the market. There the farmer could turn some of his produce into money, and the citizen-artisan could find food to keep body and soul together by picking up a job away from home. The chance of selling part of his crop in the market would save the indigent peasant from having to work off his debt; the possibility of getting food at the cookshop would rescue him from bondage to a neighbor to whom he otherwise would have to turn for bread in late winter. The market relieved the pressure of unemployment once foreign beaches began to be closed to overseas colonists; it helped to carry the floating population which provided the nerve of the navy in wartime. Thus the domestic peace for which Attica was famed and which made her eventually feared abroad owed much to the agora.

But the reverse was true as well. The market, which bolstered domestic solidarity and stimulated the forces of a maritime democracy, was also a source of parochialism. Market-fostered popular feeling, which defeated on the battle field the organizing capacity of the redistributive empire of Persia and acquired a thalassocracy for Attica, was haunted by a xenophobia which denied even the semblance of equity to allies and associates and thereby undermined the military strength of that very empire which patriotism had helped create. Yet nativism was inborn to the agora. To keep a stall in the agora was just as much a citizen's prerogative as was his claim to jury fees. The market place offered modest but easy earnings to the poorer part of a necessarily small citizenry, a feature that was to prove a fateful handicap to a polis way of life in its attempt to conquer the Oriental monarchies.

Let us now view the problem from the opposite angle and regard the growth of the agora as a function of the polity. Again, the two subsystems were out of step.

The agora formed part of the popular platform and was favored by the democratic faction. Cimon, the aristocratic leader, preferred to pamper the conservative voter by offering the genteel poor modest hospitality at his table. Pericles, as the chief of the democratic party, supported the novel market habit; an Alcmaeonid himself, he gave it a fashionable coloring by personally shopping for his large and distinguished household. Democratic policies included daily fees paid from the treasury to citizens for jury and other public services, so that no one would be prevented by poverty from availing himself of his rights and performing his duties as a citizen. This policy fitted well with the practice of having food retailed cheaply in the market. The navy's popularity with the democratic faction reinforced the demand for an opportunity of spending oarsmen's pay on ready-made provisions. Plutarch's account of Pericles' and Cimon's contention spotlights the agoraphil line of policy followed by the friends and partisans of democracy. By the first decade of the Peloponnesian War this trend was so popular that even Aristophanes—assuredly no demo-crat—had to moderate his sallies against the market. After the war, polis management of this meeting place of commerce became perva-sive. The currency was closely supervised; contact with the Piraeus was under check and control; prices were watched; retailers' profit was limited; the time and place of dealing were set out publicly; grain continued altogether under administrative control; the activity of the money-changer, the trapezite slave squatting behind his bench, was closely policed. Credit transactions in regard to foreign trade had to conform to rule and regulation. The resident alien was still barred from the acquisition of land and consequently from lending on urban property. Implicit in all this was the principle underlying the existence of the agora: he who appeared in the market must obey the law without hesitancy or reservation. There was no room here for our modern concept of the "laws of the market" as contrasted to the "laws on the statute book." Nor was there any sign of the medieval distinction between the "law of merchants" (*ius mercatorum*) and the "laws of the market place" (*ius fori*). Not the merchant's privi-leges but the authorities' ordinances were binding. The sanction of the market place was engraved on the heart of the citizen, a word that spelt loyalty to the common gods, not to the invisible god of the Per-sians nor even to the gods of the Hellenes, whose seat was on high Olympus, but to the local deity whose statue stood in the temple and whose aura maintained the identity of the polis. The boundaries of the market were as immovable as the gods.

It is worthy of notice that these results did not come about through the economic effects of the agora on the standard of life. Only in-directly—through its social effects—did the positive contributions of the agora and, perhaps even more, its negative ones affect the fate of the polis. Material welfare was but slightly influenced by its working. Neither the intense patriotism nor the monopolistic exclusiveness generated in the populace can be said to have greatly added to, or de-tracted from, the resources or supplies of the country. The market-induced attitudes were felt directly in the life of the community as forces of *anomie* as well as of social cohesion, the balance of which may well have determined the course of national history without any significant change in the national product having been registered.

As a wealth-creating organ the agora was not a determining factor of growth. Producers' goods were not on sale; metals, marble, timber, pitch, flax were not among the commodities available; wholesaling was barred; deals in land were made indoors and were announced by the public herald. Farmers and craftsmen as such were the sellers; the general public with their small daily needs were the buyers. Most manufactures bypassed the market. Many were designed for use in public works, while others went through private contractors to the armament industries or directly to the manorial hall or the exporter, as did the big jars for oil. Bankers were not engaged in financing market purchases, and no documents were issued to testify to such deals. Business was in cash. The rich man had his money carried by his servant; the poor who had no cash turned even for small sums to Theophrastus' petty usurer, who made the rounds collecting his mites of interest. Payment for market purchases was not to be postponed. Even neighboring markets were unconnected. There was no arbitrage. When Cleomenes of Naukratis began to practice it in the interest of the Egyptian state, an outcry was raised in Athens.

The far-reaching consequences of the agora were, therefore, in the social and political field. Together with the introduction of coinage, it worked for equality of status and a self-reliant type of personality. The husbandman did not have to tremble for fear his landed creditor would auction him off to foreign parts as a defaulter. Similarly to Berber markets in Northwest Africa and the multitudes of small markets in the central and western Sudan,[2] the market place was primarily a social and political institution providing facilities for the people's livelihood.

The market mechanism as such did not create the well-known "economic" obstacles to welfare which are summed up under protectionism. Domestic producers apparently did not insist on tariffs; no farmer's pressure for higher prices is on record; foreign competition only seldom aroused hard feelings, thus forcing the government's hands in its dealings with allies, and no awkward effects of a competitive price mechanism interfered with national policies. If the demands of businessmen proved a hurdle to a successful empire policy, it was less on account of monopolists' interests than those of a majority of the small men. For opposition rallied at the mere threat of

2 See Rosemary Arnold, "A port of trade: Whydah on the Guinea coast," and Francisco Benet, "Explosive markets: The Berber highlands," *Trade and Markets in the Early Empires*, pp. 154–75 and 188–213 respectively.

an increase in the population, particularly if the threat stemmed from a policy of enfranchisement. Parochialism would paralyze any welcoming gesture to immigrants and freeze any influx of new citizens, even from the ranks of the allies. Not market forces, but deep-seated fears of ethnic and religious dilution seem to have been at work. Herodotus, Thucydides, Plato, Aristotle, the pseudo-Aristotelian *Oeconomica One*—none of them elaborate on the economic advantages or disadvantages of the agora. Even the Xenophontian praise of Athenian affluence refers to the Piraeus rather than to the agora. Plutarch, almost five hundred years later, still dramatized the role of the agora in Athenian politics without so much as mentioning the part it played in the economy. The Funeral Oration, an emphatically Athenian pronouncement, takes the agora for granted, as do the Viennese their coffeehouses. Pericles obviously included the agora among the scenes of liberal thought and social amenity and of that blossoming of a free and easy way of life that earned Attica the name of the "Education of Greece." Antedating the Funeral Oration, Herodotus in his history of the Persian Wars (i. 153) prophetically elevated the uncommercial understanding of the agora into a criterion of the enlightened mind. And even Cyrus the Great, his hero among "barbarians," fell down on the test.

The division that eventually established itself between the Greek and the Persian parts of the Empire was to Rostovtzeff's penetrating mind among the sources of the disturbance in the Successor states of Alexander the Great. And he added this enlightening comment:

> The main difficulty with which the Successors were faced did not lie in their Oriental territories. There they had inherited a solid and reliable system of administration, taxation, and economic organization from Alexander, who in his turn had taken it over, at least in part, from the Persian kings. *Their real difficulty lay with their Greek subjects in the East.* [Italics mine.][3]

The *poleis* of Asia Minor were dissatisfied with their rigorous treatment at the hands of Lysimachus and Ptolemy and even with the much more liberal regimes of Antigonus and Demetrius. Eternally struggling to regain their freedoms "the leading Greek cities shifted their support from one pretender to another, so that stability in this respect was never attained." In vain did the Successors create or recreate federations or leagues of cities as "a device directed against the isolation, political, social, and economic, of the single cities." The

[3] M. Rostovtzeff, *Social & Economic History of the Hellenistic World* (Oxford, 1941) I 152 f.

same is true of the synoecisms, "the attempts of many of the Successors to merge several small cities in a larger, richer, and more reliable State. . . . Synoecism was carried out on a very large scale by
Lysimachus in the case of Ephesus, Colophon, and Lebedus." The
synoecisms, we assume, were carried out particularly in order to ease
the economic and financial plight of "small cities with small territories and a restricted population" overloaded with debt and bur-
dening their own people with liturgies and compulsory loans—permanent sources of civil wars, lawsuits, and wars with neighbors.

The incurable particularism of these minute subdivisions "en-
deavouring to live in economic self-sufficiency" was to Rostovtzeff
the canker of the polis system:

> The rulers believed that one of the main reasons why the cities were poor and
> in distress was that there were too many of them. . . . They therefore tried to con-
> vince the cities of the merits of their remedy and to induce them of their own will
> and decision to carry out a union with their neighbours. In this they mostly failed,
> and thereupon *had recourse to compulsion, under the cloak of benevolent guid-
> ance.* [Italics mine.]

Only through compulsion, then, could the polis be induced to give
up its individuality. . . . Nevertheless Rostovtzeff put the blame for
what he regarded as the unpardonable political and economic non-
co-operativeness of the Greek coastal strip in Asia Minor squarely on
the polis.

This judgment sprang in our view from a one-sided approach to
the economic nature of the polis. The agora, which today is falsely
regarded as the germ of an institution capable of linking up with
similar entities to form a market system of limitless scope, was in its
origin nothing of the sort. It was a creation of the polis which territorially walled it in. It was not born out of random transactions of
unattached individuals whose collective attitudes eventually merged
in the market as an institution in its own rights. Such a germination
of markets, as anthropologists and sociologists have taught us, is unhistorical. Rather, markets were the result of deliberate policies of a
kind of authority that even in bush and jungle enters into the shaping of all structured human behavior. To expect the polis to relin-
quish its individuality implies among other things the abandoning
of the agora, which was its organ of breathing and nutrition. On the
other hand, to expect the agora to expand in a way that some fifteen
centuries later the local market was capable of would imply that an
institution can transcend its given structural limitations.

Rostovtzeff himself may have felt this contradiction, for he introduced his argument with a well-nigh invalidating admission. "The Successors," he wrote, "tried in various ways to get rid of . . . the particularly unsound and mischievous" elements in the polis tradition, *"though they never attempted to change the type of economic system established in the Greek city-states."* (Italics mine.)[4] Yet short of that nothing could avail.

This concludes our discussion of economy and polity in classical Greece. In justice to two eminent minds who, separated by two millenniums, dealt in their own ways with the subject of polis and *chora*, it is meet to remark on the depths of this still unresolved controversy.

Rostovtzeff, in his appreciation of the pseudo-Aristotelian *Oeconomica One* summed up:

> . . . at this time two types of economic and political organization balanced each other in the ancient world; that of the Oriental monarchies, represented by Persia, and that of the Greek city-states. Each had behind it a long and glorious evolution, longer in the East, shorter in the West. . . . *Each endeavoured to extend its form of economic life to the rest of the ancient world.* [Italics mine.][5]

Rostovtzeff, it would appear, was at this point very near to penetrating the historical issue of polis and *chora*.

Aristotle's encomium of the small polis has been under a shadow in modern times. He appeared to lavish praise on the irretrievable past at the very dawn of the great empires. But the polis, far from fading out, as modern critics appear to postulate, persisted for several centuries in the expanding Hellenistic universe, unchanged and, indeed, unchangeable as Aristotle had upheld with so much conviction, while the ancient empires readjusted their own methods at the hands of the new Hellenic rulers who continued to pour forth from the training centers of the polis.

If Aristotle failed to give the *chora* its due, he at least did not underrate the staying power of the classical polis, provided it did not grow in size.

Palace Economies from the Angle of Money Uses

Submonetary Devices in Mycenae

Michael Ventris, the decipherer of Linear B, has asserted the absence of money in the palace economy of Mycenaean Greece.[6] The

---

[4] See *ibid.* p. 154.   [5] *Ibid.* p. 75.

[6] See Michael Ventris and John Chadwick, *Documents in Mycenaean Greek* (Cambridge, 1956) p. 198.

term "Mycenaean Greece" derives from the earliest excavation of Mycenae and comprises that site and Pylos, in the Peloponnese, together with Knossos, in Crete.

Mycenae, as we shall briefly call all of Mycenaean Greece, flourished in the thirteenth century. Its palace economy was of an extreme type. For it may well be the only case on record in which a literate community eschewed the employment of money for accountancy. Mycenae is, then, of singular interest to the student of early monetary institutions. In the absence of "anything approaching currency,"[7] the actual means of accountancy employed in the Mycenaean palace economy may offer a clue to a very early phase in the development of money.

The economic historian of antiquity cannot make use of the concepts of money, price, etc. inherited from nineteenth-century market economies without a considerable refinement of these terms. "Money," it is suggested, should be defined as "fungible things in definite uses, namely payment, standard, and exchange," while "price" should be replaced by the broader term "equivalency," which transcends markets.

Operational definitions of money take their start from a particular use to which fungibles may be put. Under Roman Law, *res fungibiles* are things *quae numero, pondere ac mensura consistunt*. In terms maybe more acceptable to the economist, they are durable objects that are quantifiable, whether by counting or by measuring. The payment, standard, and exchange uses of such objects are defined in a manner which avoids any implicit concept of money creeping into the formulations. This requires *sociologically* defined situations in which the fungible objects are put to any one of those three uses in an *operationally* defined fashion. "Payment" is defined as a handing-over of fungibles with the effect of ending an obligation (always on the assumption that more than one kind of obligation can be ended by the handing-over of one kind of fungible). In their "standard" use fungibles serve as numerical referents; two different kinds of fungibles, like apples and pears, that are "tagged" to the standard can then be added up. In their "exchange" use fungibles are handled as middle terms (B) in indirect exchange, where C is acquired for A through the medium of B. "Being under an obligation," "adding up apples and pears," and "exchanging indirectly" are thus sociologically defined situations, while the manipulations of "hand-

7 *Ibid.*

341

ing over," "referring to" or "tagging," and "exchanging twice over" are operationally defined. To state that money was absent in Mycenae strictly means that none of the staples were handled in a situation and manner that would amount to their use as payment, standard, or exchange. Not even metaphorically, as in regard to the attractive brides of the epics, are cattle named as a standard of appreciation in the Mycenaean tablets. Apart from a list of small weights of gold, the precious metals are hardly mentioned, though small uniform objects of gold similar to Egyptian units of treasure were found in the Mycenaean Acropolis. Silver—the term *chrysos* we are told is of Semitic derivation—hardly occurs in the tablets at all. Bronze is repeatedly mentioned as a raw material for weapons weighed out to the smiths from the palace but otherwise occurs only once and then not in a valuational context; prestige goods such as tripods serving as elite tool-money in the epics are absent in our accounts, as are also ornamental shells or beads. As to staples more commonly employed as money, such as barley in Sumer and Babylon or cacao in pre-Conquest Mexico, Ventris' unqualified negative settles the point. On the face of it, all this is surprising indeed. Yet its full implications can be gauged only if the scope of the accountancy is considered.

The authentic core of the Mycenaean economy was the palace household with its storage rooms and its administration which listed personnel, land-ownings, and small cattle, assessed deliveries in wheat or barley, oil, olives, figs, and a number of other staples (largely unidentified), and handed out rations. The rest is conjectural: Homer's nine towns that belonged to the king of Pylos have been found, surrounded by a considerable number of villages with their common land and peasant holdings. There were slaves, a class of dependent laborers, also soldiers and oarsmen, who were sometimes recipients of rations, which, however, mostly went to women and children. Manufactures were carried on by craftsmen and artisans, many belonging to the palace and others only supplied with raw materials from there. The products may have been partly employed in trading for the palace. Yet the outstanding fact about the inventory and the accounts is and remains the complete absence of money. One kind of goods can never be equated with, or substituted for, an amount of goods of a different kind. Accounts were strictly separate for each kind.

But how, then, was the palace's administration maintained over an economy of the extent of a good-sized city-state? The answer lies in devices which up to a point could be substituted for money and thus make possible a staple finance which allowed an elementary form of taxation without the intervention of money.

Staple finance is the dealing with staples on a large scale, involving inventories and accountancy, for the purpose of budgeting, balancing, controlling, and checking. As a rule—and this must be clearly understood—staple finance requires the use of money. This comes about with the help of equivalencies that are set up between the staples and by the use of one or another of them as a standard which thereby acts as money. Staple finance is, then, always in kind, whether its accountancy makes use of money or not, but the absence of equivalencies necessarily reduces the handling of staples to a moneyless "finance." Only within one kind of staple is budgeting, balancing, control, and checking then possible. The vital operation of collecting goods at a center through the device of taxation is performed almost blindly. The accounts fail to show the total burden that is put on the contributing unit, whether individual or village. It is not possible to say how much its burden would be increased or diminished by changes made in any one kind. Neither is there a measure at hand by which to raise the taxes proportionately to an increase in population or to maintain equity in the burdens imposed on bigger and smaller communities.

A fairly obvious remedy, still on a submonetary level, obtains as long as the taxation in kind happens within an ecologically homogeneous region. A composite unit consisting always of the same main staples in definite unchangeable physical proportions can be there formed for purposes of taxation. Tax is then assessed according to the size of each village in multiples of this unit. The physical proportions which obtain between the goods in no way mean that the staples can be substituted one for another in those proportions and that the taxpayer is permitted to deliver one kind of staple instead of another. Nothing of the sort is involved. But the totaling of each kind of revenue is made much easier by the composite unit, as is the adjustment of the tax to changes in population. Moreover—and this should not be forgotten—some serious disadvantages of monetization are avoided. The chief requirement of a balance in kind is certainly that at any given moment rations and other obligations that are due are actually available in kind. But any equivalency that has been accepted as a standard may act as an inducement for the substitution of one staple for another, whether in delivery or in handing out, and thereby frustrate that basic requirement. Any assurance of "effective liquidity" would be gone. A composite tax unit avoids this danger.

Linear B, the script in which Mycenaean accountancy was done, shows proof of just such a device. In two cases we have explicit statements of the physical proportions in which the composite tax contained the staples. One is shown in the Pylos *Ma*-tablets:

> . . . A number of townships are put down for a contribution of six different commodities, mostly so far unidentified. The scale of the total contribution varies for each town, but the mutual proportions of the six commodities remain constant at $7:7:2:3:1\frac{1}{2}:150$.[8]

The other occurs in the Knossos *Mc*-tablets, which

> . . . contain lists of four commodities, one of which Evans identified as the horns of *agrimi* goats for making composite bows. Their amounts conform, with rather wider variations than on the Pylos *Ma*-tablets, to a ratio of $5:3:2:4$.[9]

Yet, we repeat, nowhere is there an equivalency nor anything approaching a standard and, a fortiori, money.

A submonetary device acts in a purely operational fashion. Complex arithmetical results, which in the economic sphere are usually gained through calculations in monetary terms, appear to have been attained in early society by means of operational devices without intervention either of money or of reckoning. In the light of these considerations we shall try to penetrate further into the earliest history of money.

From times immemorial wheat has been distributed in the Indian village community[10] to the various claimants—tillers, craftsmen belonging to their respective castes, village officials, and, last but not least, the landlord and the prince—by the simple means of handing out grain from the heap in a certain sequence which combines portions of absolute amounts with a number of unit measures that go to each in turn. The traditional sequence is extremely intricate. Yet the method is of utmost simplicity. There is no need to know how many units the heap contains, nor to how many units each claimant has a right, nor how much he actually gets, for once the heap is gone such questions are rather pointless in view of the certainty that each received his due, neither more nor less. No money and no reckoning enter into the operation.

---

[8] *Ibid.* p. 118. [9] *Ibid.* p. 119.

[10] See Walter C. Neale, "Reciprocity and redistribution in the Indian village," in *Trade and Market in the Early Empires*, pp. 224–27.

Another submonetary device, this one regarding trade and very different from that of the grain heap, is indicated in passages from Ezekiel, chapter 27, and some 250 years later in Aristotle's *Politics*. The Old Testament prophet describes the many-sided foreign trade carried on by Tyre, Queen of the Seas, while Aristotle offers an analysis of the role played by monetary objects in long-distance trade. Ezekiel speaks of the traders as "reckoning" one another's goods in their own, while Aristotle says that money sets the limit and the pace to trading. They both appear to have had the same operational image before them. He who sells a cargo of grain from his ship's bottom, sheep from the corral, or oil from the store beneath the temple makes his ware come forth from the stock—unit by unit—and makes his trading partner move his goods at the same pace in the opposite direction—unit for unit—until one or the other stock is exhausted. Again the method could not be simpler. There is no need for any knowledge of how many units of goods either of them possesses, nor —if the rate happens not to be 1:1—of how many units of the other's goods each of them is supposed to receive, nor even of how many each actually receives, as long as the rate at which the operation progresses is the agreed one, since both necessarily have received the right amount at whatever moment the transaction is discontinued. And, as in the former case, neither money nor calculation is required.

These two instances of submonetary devices stem from very different situations. The one may have been common in pharaonic Egypt, with its storage economy, the other in the Fertile Crescent, which could not survive without extended long-distance trade. The one belongs in the realm of redistribution, the other in that of exchange.

Surely it is more than a coincidence that Linear B deviated from the original Linear A precisely at a point which mirrors in a striking fashion this type of difference. Linear A was a fairly primitive script of the Minoan-speaking natives of Crete (whose language is still unknown to us). The invading Greeks continued and developed it in Linear B, for the purpose of writing their own language and with a greater wealth of syllabic signs and ideograms. These changes were accompanied by just one other innovation, which can hardly be unconnected with the shifting from the native Minoan economy to that of the Greek newcomers, namely, a different notation of fractions. While Linear A used numerical notation akin to that of the Egyptians, Linear B changed to the wholly different system of fractional measures used exclusively in the Fertile Crescent. The numerical notation employed figures, such as 1/2, 1/4, 1/3, 1/6, 2/3, while the fractional measures carried names comparable with modern hundredweights, pounds, and ounces or bushels, gallons, quarts, and pints. The simultaneous change-over to the Greek language and to fractional measures happened about the middle of the second millennium B.C. at a time when redistribution of grain from pharaonic stores was dominant in Egypt, while between mainland Greece and western Asia trade was on the rise.[11] It seems obvious that the Greek seafarers were more interested in trade with the East than were the Minoan-speaking natives whose script they borrowed and whose economy resembled that of Egypt.

For an analytical study of early money the disentangling of fractional measures in Linear B by Emmett L. Bennett, Jr.,[12] should therefore prove a most promising beginning. It may, as he suggests, throw light on the early history of the Mycenaean Greeks. It certainly seems to prove that among the multiple origins of money we must also list manipulations of an elementary character which do not assume any arithmetical operations whatsoever, not even counting. The composite tax unit that is present in traces in the Mycenaean tablets seems to be such a submonetary device.

The Prestige Sphere in Staple Finance

The first to call for a comparison of Mycenae with the palace economies of West Asia was Michael Ventris himself. Again and again he named those of Sumer, Ur, Babylon, Assur, the Hittites, and Ugarit as parallel instances, not omitting Alalakh from the list. Our own survey of Alalakh, restricted to secondary sources, is in line with that suggestion. To our surprise we found that the differences between Mycenae and Alalakh in regard to money uses were at least as worthy of note as the general similarities between these two palace economies. Ventris naturally centered on the redistributive character common to palace economies, since the role of money had not yet moved into the over-all picture. Otherwise he could not but have remarked on the singularity of Mycenae, which knew not money (a fact which he was first to state), in contrast to the West Asian civilizations which employed money in more than one way.

Still another surprise was in store. Alalakh, which at first glance seemed monetized as much as its Mesopotamian partners, on a closer

[11] See W. F. Albright, "Some Oriental glosses on the Homeric problem," *American Journal of Archaeology* LIV (1950) 162.

[12] "Fractional quantities in Minoan bookkeeping," *American Journal of Archaeology* LIV 204–22.

view turned out to resemble moneyless Mycenae with its Greek culture and Minoan script, a thousand miles away, rather than its own eastern neighbors, whose cuneiform writing and Akkadian official language were first cousins to those of Alalakh.

Several questions arise. Was the original assumption of Alalakh's monetized accountancy well grounded? And, if not, how should the evidence which seemed to point in that direction be interpreted? Secondly, how, then, did its palace economy function? If Mycenae's hidden strength lay in submonetary devices, what lesson could be drawn from Alalakh?

Alalakh was a small but long-lived North Syrian kingdom, whose external relations from both the political and the economic angle were far from simple. Its economy and even more its finance reflected up to a point the complexity of these conditions.

Sir Leonard Woolley, the excavator of Alalakh, tells us how the city lay in that crowded stretch of the Fertile Crescent where in the second half of the second millennium B.C. the Hittite and Egyptian great powers met. The Hittites had once raided Babylon and eventually defeated Egypt in the battle of Kadesh, on the Orontes. A fourth power, Mitanni, with its mainly Hurrian population, was mostly wedged between the land of the Hittites and Babylonia. Alalakh was in the eighteenth century B.C. closely dependent upon the city of Aleppo. (In the fifteenth century Alalakh appeared as a semi-independent state.) The key to the over-all situation, in which Alalakh benefited from the balance between the great powers, was its geographical location. It formed the hinterland to the port of al-Mina, at the mouth of the Orontes, which together with its southern neighbor on the coast, the port of Ugarit, represented a vital access to the Mediterranean for the inland empires, whether Hittite, Babylonian, or Mitannian. Ugarit was, moreover, Egypt's maritime point of access to the caravan routes of the Fertile Crescent. This configuration resulted in a coastal area of relative peacefulness in the middle of the second millennium. The inland empires traditionally avoided conquest of the coast for fear that the "riches of the sea" would cease to flow through militarily occupied ports;[13] they preferred most of the time to exert but mild pressure in the direction of the sea, agreeing to keep the coast unoccupied and the caravan roads to it open or maybe even tacitly arranging for zones of influence. Such an arrangement might, for instance, have left southerly Ugarit

---

[13] Cf. Anne M. Chapman, "Trade enclaves in Aztec and Maya civilizations," *Trade and Market in the Early Empires,* pp. 114–46.

in the Egyptian zone and northerly al-Mina in the Hittite zone, while allowing the eastern powers, Mitanni and Babylon, transit to either. Hence there may have been a network of international treaties by which a militarily weak and semidependent Alalakh secured its position in the midst of rival empires.

In regard to staple finance and trade the situation of Alalakh was, then, in all probability more complex than that of the Mycenaean cities of Pylos, Knossos, or Mycenae itself. Records show a flow of silver during the eighteenth century, large amounts of annual regional revenue collected in silver and passed on to higher administrative authorities; royal visits, betrothals, and other ceremonial occasions requiring a display of valuables; a drain on precious metals exerted by the temples; sums paid out as awards within the related ruling families; expenses of the local prince, particularly for raw materials to the "goldsmiths" (mostly dealing with silver); numerous other requirements of diplomacy and etiquette; purchases of land tracts comprising many villages in the course of adjustments involving exchanges of territory between contiguous administrations; caravan trade in transit, apparently requiring the military protection of nomadic chiefs. All these factors involved a movement of precious metals, whether acquired from foreign mine-owning rulers or indirectly through tributes and taxes. Such was the eighteenth-century picture to which our data refer.

We are here concerned, of course, not so much with the economic as with the financial aspect of Alalakh. According to D. J. Wiseman[14] the silver shekel was in the eighteenth century "a true currency" and "the principal medium of exchange." It seems very doubtful to us, however, that the level of accountancy in Alalakh was actually much higher than that of Mycenae, where money was altogether absent. Only in the prestige sphere, apparently, was silver widely employed for payment and certainly established as a standard of account. Outside that sphere accountancy was "in kind," each species of commodity being totaled separately (as in Mycenae). But the evidence seems to point to an intermediate state of affairs in which a prestige sphere, accounted in silver, formed the core of the staple finance while the subsistence sphere was accounted "in kind" without the intervention of money.

The sixty to seventy texts mentioning silver shekels would then

[14] *The Alalakh Tablets* ("Occasional Publications of the British Institute of Archaeology at Ankara," No. 2 [London, 1953]) pp. 13–14.

appear to be satisfactorily explained by the concept of prestige goods. Silver, being treasure, was employed for uses that befit prestige goods, and expenditures made for such purposes were accounted in silver shekels. In other words, since the prestige sphere—sacral, royal, diplomatic, or relating to top-ranking civil and military bureaucracy—was the traditional field for the use of treasure, accountancy in silver shekels was the given form of bookkeeping in this sphere. The frequent mention of silver accounts merely proves the presence of important hoards of silver in the possession of king, temple, or treasury and of a rigorous accountancy in regard to it.

Admittedly, much is still unexplained. The use of silver shekels as money of account in the prestige sphere would seem to imply the existence of some silver equivalencies in that sphere. Yet, with a very few unimportant exceptions (see below), no equivalencies in silver are indicated, nor can such be implied. The main group of transfers of silver represents physical amounts of silver given either by weight or as objects for which the silver served as raw material and which are listed by weight in terms of shekels. There follow yearly totals of tribute amounting to over one thousand and over two thousand talents respectively, that is, several millions of shekels each. (These two items are from fifteenth-century tablets.) The third group comprises shares in the great king's booty, in royal inheritances, in awards between royal relatives; a fourth large group comprises plain gifts to gods, sovereigns, and other important persons, with no counterpart in evidence. The fifth group consists of the prices of villages and territories bought from neighboring sovereigns. In striking contrast to all these massive transfers of silver without any equivalencies, there are small conventional items such as tips to servants, perhaps according to their master's rank, a day's provisions to a messenger or the fodder for his mount, and similar trivial expenses. The origin of these not too impressive equivalencies is obscure. However, they seem to derive largely from the equivalency of 1 shekel of silver to 1 *PA* of grain, to which we shall return presently. Finally, there is a group of silver items which appear to belong not to the treasury but to the household of the palace itself. An amount of 10 shekels goes as a "loan" to craftsmen and artisans engaging them for lifelong service in the palace; employment in the palace seems to have conferred status, in a modest way. Distinctly larger loans of 20, 30, and 60 shekels apparently go to persons of higher status, distinguished by mention of their patronymic, "family," or sons' names. In still other cases either apprenticeship or supervision of training appears to be involved; in these "middle-class" loans there is a curious practice of lending a round sum plus 1, such as 21 or 31 shekels.

All this referred to silver accounts. But by far the largest number of items concerned staple finance in kind, such as deliveries to the palace and rations handed out from there. Nevertheless no equivalencies either for the various staples or for silver can be traced, with the following exceptions: 1 shekel of silver = 1 pot of best beer = 2 *parisi* of emmer[15] and 1 shekel of silver = 1 *PA* of grain. The latter is of course the oldest and best known equivalency of the cuneiform civilizations of Mesopotamia. In the light of what has been said above, it might not be too rash to infer that it expressed the status relations of two potential currencies, namely, a currency of the prestige sphere of the ruling classes (silver) and one of the subsistence sphere of the common people (grain).

Indeed, it seems well possible that, similarly to the *prestige* function of treasure, which introduces the silver shekel into all records of *prestige* activities, the fact of *status* (another building stone of archaic society) may enter into broad sectors of economic life as a quantifying factor. In Aristotle's time—fifteen centuries later—it was still possible to argue the just price in terms of the producer's status. Some quantitative facts of the Alalakh economy bear traces of such a connection. That both deliveries and rations reflect status seems to us in the nature of things. So may some equivalencies reflect social stratification, in a customary way.

In conclusion we might suggest the notion of a cultural continuum of monetary uses ranging from the zero point of Mycenae to the near-saturation point of the Mesopotamian empires of the middle of the first millennium. Palace economies, big and small, Asiatic, Egyptian, and European, may be found to have possessed organizations that were distinguished mainly by the manner in which the various monetary uses were institutionalized.[16]

---

[15] *Ibid.* pp. 93 f., No. 324*b*.

[16] Thoughts developed on the operational character of submonetary devices owe much to conversations with my colleagues Harry W. Pearson, Bennington College, and Paul Bohannan, Princeton University.

The survey of money uses was prepared with the assistance of Mr. Emmett Mulvaney, B.A., University of Manitoba.

The Mycenaean and Alalakh data were compiled with the help of Mrs. Mary S. Winch, B.Sc. (Econ.) , London, England, as Research Assistant.

The preparatory study underlying this essay was done partly with the support of the Wenner-Gren Foundation, New York, the Social Science Research Council, New York, and the American Philosophical Society, Philadelphia, Pa.

VI

Structures and Changes in the History of Religion

By MIRCEA ELIADE

Translated from French by KATHRYN K. ATWATER

The religious life appears complex even at the most archaic stages of culture. Among the peoples still in the stage of food-gathering and hunting small animals (Australians, Pygmies, Fuegians, etc.), the belief in a Supreme Being or "Lord of the Animals" is intermingled with beliefs in culture-heroes and mythical ancestors; prayers and offerings to the gods coexist with totemic practices, the cult of the dead, and hunting and fertility magic. The morphology of religious experience is also of a surprising richness. One has only to consider the experiences set in motion by the puberty initiation or by various seasonal ceremonies and especially the experiences of medicine men and shamans. The latter constitute the religious and cultural elite of any primitive society; phenomenologically their experiences may be likened to those of the mystics of more advanced cultures—a comparison which alone is enough to destroy any hypothesis of simplicity and homogeneity in primitive religious life.

The mythologies of archaic peoples are less dramatic than those of people belonging to superior cultures, but the religious and social function of myths is the same. Myths reveal how the world, life, men, institutions, etc. came into being. In other words, they recount the different aspects of the creative activity of divine and supernatural beings. Consequently, the myth is believed to express an "absolute truth," since it tells a sacred history, an event which took place at the beginning of time. The myth assures the sacredness and also the reality of all the creations of the supernatural beings and at the same time sets the exemplary model for human behavior and activity. In brief, even in the archaic stages of culture we are dealing not only with an astonishingly rich and complex religious life but also with a unified and systematic world view, that is, with an "ideology" which explains and justifies the actual human situation as well as man's relations with the world and with supernatural beings.

When "primitive" peoples began to be studied scientifically, they were far from being peoples "without a history." All of them had, to a greater or a lesser extent, been subjected to the influences of culturally superior peoples. In certain cases these influences had drastically modified the original cultural configuration. Thus we do not have at our disposal any documents concerning an ultimate "first phase" of the religious life of primitives. Up to a point we can distinguish cultural elements which are relatively recent. For example, it is not difficult to identify the Melanesian elements in the Australian Kunapipi cult[1] nor the influence of a superior culture on the male secret society of the Selk'nam.[2]

But it would be naïve to think that we could ever isolate and describe the primordial kernel of the religious life of primitive or prehistoric peoples. For the complexity of that life is not uniquely the result of outside influences. The variety of religious experience is in a way coexistent with the human condition. Every religious experience is susceptible of transformation, revalorization, or perversion. On the other hand, the mystical experiences of the medicine man, the shaman, and the ecstatic are continually integrated into the religious traditions of primitive societies. Images, symbols, divine or demonic figures, dramatic scenarios, cultural values, and so forth engendered by the experiences of these few "specialists in the sacred" lead, for the most part, to an eventual enrichment of the religious heritage of the community as a whole.

It is no less true, however, that we can sort out several major lines of development in the religious history of ancient mankind. For, while the religious life has, from the beginning, manifested itself as rich, complex, and varied, its configuration changes conjointly with the changes effected on the cultural horizon. The dominant characteristics of religious life vary from one historical age to another and from one culture to another. It is a matter not only of stylistic variations but frequently of a radical modification of structures. We are

[1] See A. P. Elkin's preface to R. M. Berndt, *Kunapipi* (Melbourne, 1951) p. xxii; Wilhelm Schmidt, "Mythologie und religion in Nord-Australien," *Anthropos* XLVIII (1953) 898–924.

[2] See Josef Haekel, "Jungendweihe und Männerfest auf Feuerland: Ein Beitrag zu ihrer kulturhistorischen Stellung," *Mitteilungen der Österreichische Gesellschaft für Anthropologie, Ethnologie und Prähistorie* LXXIII–LXXVII (Wien, 1947) 84–114, esp. pp. 106 ff.

thus concerned on the one hand with profound changes in religious concepts and behavior, even with the substitution of one religious view for another, and on the other hand with changes in the expressions of a religious belief without any structural modification. We shall try (pp. 361 ff.) to analyze the different expressions of one universally attested form of behavior, the religious valorization of the world, that is to say, the manner in which man assumes his own role in a world conceived to be the work of supernatural beings. We shall then be ready to specify the sense in which one can speak of constants in religious experience and the measure in which these constants can be recognized in their innumerable variations of expression.

The fact that religious structures are susceptible to radical changes does not imply an absence of "invariables" in the religious life of man. The dichotomy of sacred and profane is the invariable par excellence. For, while the sacred is manifested in an infinity of forms and objects, there is always a difference of an ontological order between sacred objects and those which are not. But there are also other constants in religious history—for example, the belief that human actions and institutions (work, eating, sexuality, the family, society, culture, etc.) are founded or revealed at the beginning of time (i.e., in mythical time) by gods or supernatural beings. Even though this fundamental conception remains almost unchanged up to the eve of Christianity, the idea that is formed of divine beings and the place that they occupy in the religious life changes appreciably in the course of history. And it is precisely these modifications of perspective which are significant for the historian of religions.

Actually, the development of the religious life especially concerns the function and destiny of divine beings. In examining the religious configurations of the most archaic societies (i.e., those in the phase of food-gathering and hunting small animals) and laying them alongside those of more highly evolved societies (totemistic hunters, paleocultivators, pastoral nomads) we notice two distinct but interrelated facts. (1) The belief in a Supreme Being of a celestial structure, a creator and an all-powerful god, while attested in the most archaic stages of culture, does not play a central role in the religious life, and in several cases this belief is in the process of disappearing. (2) At the more advanced stages of culture, the Supreme Being has been almost completely forgotten; his place is taken by divine figures of various kinds—mythical ancestors, cultural heroes, great mothers and goddesses of fertility, solar and atmospheric gods, etc. All of these divine figures present one common feature: in a direct and efficacious manner they govern the forces of life and procreation.

We need to make it clear that the primitive belief in a Supreme Being who is creator and all-powerful does not necessarily imply the existence of an *Urmonotheismus* in the sense which the Vienna school of historical ethnology has ascribed to this term.[3] It is beyond doubt that "monotheistic" ideas exist, or have existed, among numerous primitive populations. This fact is important; it proves that the categories of religious experience and the structure of intelligence of primitive man are not fundamentally different from those of historical man. But it is not sufficient grounds for postulating the existence of a primordial monotheism. For, on the one hand, we lack much information concerning the most ancient phases of culture (the first prehistorical religious documents date only from the late paleolithic, and the oldest cultures known by ethnologists are quite advanced) and, on the other hand, as already mentioned, the belief in a Supreme Being does not exclude adherence to other religious forms. This is to be explained by the variety of religious experience and differences in temperament[4] and also by the cultural inequality between the sexes or even between the specialists or the initiated (medicine men, shamans, ecstatics, secret societies) and the rest of the tribe.

In pointing out, then, the disappearance of the cult of a Supreme Being and the substitution of other divine figures we do not have in mind a process of progressive deterioration which finally vitiates a primordial monotheism. Historically, things happen in another perspective: certain original divine figures are transformed, disappear, and are replaced by others. This process is not to be explained by changes which have taken place in the economy, the social organization, or the cultural configuration. It indicates modifications in man's existential situation. In other words, it is part and parcel of the

[3] The bibliography is considerable. The documentation and history of the controversy will be found in the *opus magnum* of Father Wilhelm Schmidt, *Ursprung der Gottesidee* I–XII (Münster i. W, 1912–1954) esp. Vols. I, II, and IV. Cf. W. Koppers, *Der Urmensch und sein Weltbild* (1949) = *Primitive Man and His World Picture* (London–New York, 1952); W. E. Mühlmann, "Das Problem des Urmonotheismus," *Theologische Literaturzeitung*, 1953, pp. 705–18; P. Schebesta, "Das Problem des Urmonotheismus: Kritik einen Kritik," *Anthropos* XLIX (1954) 690–97. See also Paul Radin, *Monotheism among Primitive Peoples* (1924; reprinted in Basel, 1954); R. Pettazoni, *Dio* I (Roma, 1922); "La formation du monothéisme, *Revue de l'histoire des religions* LXXXVIII (1923) 193–229; *L'Onniscienza di Dio* (Torino, 1955) = *The All-knowing God* (London, 1956).

[4] Paul Radin has insisted on this point in several instances; cf. Radin, *op. cit.* pp. 24 ff.

discoveries which man has been led to make about himself and his world. These discoveries are of a religious nature. The task of the historian of religions is to show how they are articulated in the total process of history.

The supreme gods of the primitives are almost completely without a cult. According to the myths they created the world, life, and man, and a short time afterward they abandoned the earth and withdrew into the sky. In their place they left their sons or emissaries or other divinities who are subordinate to them and who continue in some way to be concerned with the creation, to perfect it or sustain it. When he withdrew into the sky, Ndyambi, the supreme god of the Herero, abandoned mankind to inferior divinities. "Why should we offer him sacrifices?" reasons one native, "we have nothing to fear from him, for, quite unlike our dead (*okakurus*), he does us no harm." The Supreme Being of the Tumbukas is too great "to be concerned with the affairs of men." The detachment and indifference of the Supreme Being are admirably expressed in a chant of the Fang people of equatorial Africa:

> God (Nzama) is on high, man is below.
> God is God, man is man.
> Each is at home, each in his house.[5]

It is useless to multiply the examples. Everywhere in primitive societies, the celestial Supreme Being has lost his religious actuality. He has removed himself from men; he has become a *deus otiosus*. He is nevertheless remembered and implored as a last resort, when all the steps taken toward the other gods and goddesses, the demons, and the ancestors have failed. Dzingbe ("the Universal Father"), the Supreme Being of the Ewe, is invoked during a drought: "O sky, to whom we owe our thanks, great is the drought. Let it rain, so the earth may be refreshed and the fields may prosper!" The Selk'nam of Tierra del Fuego call their Supreme Being "Inhabitant of the Sky" or the "One in the Sky." He has neither images nor priest. But they pray to him in case of sickness: "Thou, from on high, do not take away my child; he is still too little!" When the aid of other gods and goddesses has proven deceptive, the Oraon turn to their Supreme Being: "We have tried everything, but we still have thee to help us!" And they sacrifice

[5] See Mircea Eliade, *Patterns in Comparative Religion*, translated by Rosemary Sheed (New York, 1928) pp. 47, 49. (This work was first published in Paris [1949] as *Traité d'histoire des religions*.)

a white cock to him, crying: "O God! Thou art our creator. Have mercy on us!"[6]

This attitude is not exclusive to primitive populations. Let us recall what happened with the ancient Hebrews. Whenever they were living in a time of relative peace and economic prosperity, they abandoned Jahweh and drew near to the Baᶜals and the Ashtartes of their neighbors. It took some historic catastrophe or crisis to force them to look back to the true God. They cried to the Eternal and said: "Lo, we have sinned, for we have abandoned the Eternal and have served the Baᶜals and Ashtartes; but now deliver us from the hands of our enemies, and we shall serve Thee" (I Samuel 12:10).

The Hebrews turned toward Jahweh following historical catastrophes and in the face of imminent annihilation by one of the great military empires. The primitives remember the Supreme Being in cases of cosmic crises such as drought, storms, and epidemics. But the meaning of this return to the Supreme Being is the same among the one group as among the other. In an extremely critical situation, in a border situation where the very existence of the collective group is at stake, the divinities who assure and exalt life in normal times are abandoned, and the Supreme Being is invoked.

Let us add that this momentary religious reactualization of the Supreme Being in times of existential crisis is not too frequent a phenomenon, nor could it be so. But we have nevertheless mentioned it because it has to do with a generally human type of behavior. It is even found among monotheistic peoples in our own times. For a Christian of the twentieth century, the place of the Baᶜals and Ashtartes is taken by other "idols" such as the preoccupation with and passion for economic activity or for social, political, and cultural affairs. With rare exceptions, a Christian turns toward his God sincerely, totally, and exclusively only when some catastrophe is imminent.

In analyzing the reasons why these celestial supreme beings have disappeared from the cult, we shall uncover at the same time the great lines of development in the religious history of mankind. For, as we shall quickly see, a similar process can be discerned among historical peoples. The very structure of celestial supreme beings predisposes, one might say, their "religious inactuality." In fact, to understand the ejection of the supreme gods, we must take into considera-

6 See references *ibid.* pp. 47, 49, 132, etc.

tion these factors: (1) the passivity of celestial gods, explainable by the sky's impassibility and its infinite remoteness (even though the infinite height may be religiously valorized; cf., for example, the clairvoyance and omniscience of ouranian gods); (2) the inactivity of the creator, his *otiositas,* after he finished the creation; (3) his "far-off," distant, and estranged character in the sense that he is not like human beings and does not take part in their drama; (4) the absence of any tragic elements in his existence (contrasted, for example, with the gods of vegetation), the paucity of myths concerning him (in comparison with the mythologies of fertility gods or cultural heroes). In a word, one could say that the disappearance of supreme beings from the cult indicates man's desire to enjoy a religious experience which is "stronger," more "dramatic," and, though it is often aberrant, more "human."

In the religions of the ancient Near East and in Indo-European religions, as well as in primitive religions, the old gods of the sky have been displaced by more dynamic gods: solar gods, gods of procreation or of the storm.[7] The old Indo-Aryan celestial deity Dyaus appears very rarely in the Vedas; in a remote age his place had already been taken over by Varuṇa and Parjanya, the god of the tempest. In turn, Parjanya was eclipsed by Indra, who became the most popular of the Vedic gods, for he unites in his person all power and all fertility. Indra incarnates the exuberance of life and of cosmic and biological energy. From a certain point of view he may be likened to the powerful and procreative gods of the ancient Near East, of the type of Bel. These are divinities of fertility, of opulence and vital plenitude, who exalt and amplify life, cosmic life—vegetation, agriculture, animal life—as well as human life. The "powerful" and "procreative" god becomes the husband of a great goddess, of an agrarian Magna Mater. He is no longer autonomous and all-powerful, like the old ouranian gods, but is reduced to the situation of one member of a divine pair. The cosmogony—essential attribute of the old celestial gods—is now replaced by the hierogamy. The procreative god does not *create* the world; he is content merely to *fertilize* it. And in certain cultures, the male god, the procreator, is reduced to quite a modest role; it is the Great Goddess alone who assures the fertility of the world; in time, her husband gives up his place to her son, who is also his mother's lover. These are the well-known gods of

[7] For all that follows, see *ibid.* pp. 82 ff.

vegetation, of the type of Tammuz, Attis, and Adonis, most of them characterized by their periodic death and resurrection.

Certain gods have succeeded in conserving—or recovering—their religious actuality by revealing themselves as *sovereign gods.* In other words, they have reinforced their power with magico-religious titles of a different order; in fact, sovereignty constitutes a source of sacred power capable of holding absolute supremacy in a pantheon. Such is the case with Zeus, Jupiter, Anu, Varuṇa, T'ien, and the god of the Mongols. The idea of sovereignty is also present in Ahura Mazda, beneficiary of the Zarathustrian revolution which elevated him above all the other gods. Jahweh, too, carries elements of a sovereign god of celestial structure, though his figure is much more complex. The monotheistic, prophetic, and messianic revolution of the Israelites (as also that of Muḥammad) is brought about against the Baʿals and the Belits, against the gods of tempest and procreation, the great male gods and the great goddesses. Unlike the Baʿals and the Belits, Jahweh does not possess numerous and various myths; his cult is neither complicated nor orgiastic; he abhors bloody and repeated sacrifices. He asks on the part of the believer a totally different type of behavior from that required by the cult of the Baʿals and Ashtartes.

The cult of the Baʿals and Ashtartes constitutes a type of religion which is extremely widespread. One could call it a cosmic and anthropocosmic religion, understanding by these terms every type of religious experience set in motion by the religious valorizations of the cosmos, of life, and of human existence. The most familiar form is the one which emerged after the discovery of agriculture, but this religious form is neither the only one nor is it the first. Very probably, the sacredness of the world and of life was taken for granted from the earliest appearance of *homo religiosus.* But in societies of paleocultivators, something more happens. On the one hand, sacredness is concentrated almost exclusively in the epiphanies of blood, sexuality, and reproduction; on the other hand, man assumes a direct responsibility in the mystery represented by the source and diffusion of this biocosmic sacrality.

On the horizon of the history of religions, the appearance of protoagriculture represents a considerable innovation. This does not mean that the essential elements of the agricultural religions—the mystical solidarity of the fecundity of the earth with the "mysteries" of woman and of sexuality, bloody sacrifices, periodic renewal through rites of death and resurrection, etc.—appear now for the first time. Sexual rites and symbolism are not absent in prehistory nor in pre-agricultural societies. Statuettes of a female divinity are found as early as the paleolithic era. Rites of fertility and of game increase, as well as the belief in a periodic renewal of animal life (the notion, for example, that skeletons will be covered with new flesh), play a capital role in the religious life of hunters, and this was probably true also in paleolithic times.[8]

But with the discovery of agriculture these ideas were charged with new values, articulated in a new pattern, and projected into a most vivid religious actuality. Let us add, however, that the revolutionary changes brought about in the economic realm and in social organization as a result of the development from the phase of food-gathering and hunting to that of proto-agriculture did condition the new religious valorizations of the world, but they did not "cause" them in the deterministic sense of the term. It is not the natural phenomenon of vegetation which is responsible for the appearance of mythico-religious systems of agrarian structure but rather the religious experience occasioned by the discovery of a mystical solidarity between man and plant life.

Indeed, according to the myths of early horticulturalists of the tropical regions, the edible plant is not *given* in nature; it is the product of a primordial sacrifice. In mythical times, a semidivine being is sacrificed in order that tubers and fruit trees may grow out of his or her body. The paleocultivator assumes the responsibility for assuring the life of nutritive plants, that is to say, the necessity to sacrifice human victims and domestic animals and to perform sexual and orgiastic rites. Head-hunting and human sacrifice for the sake of the harvest find their justification in this new religious ideology.[9] With the development of grain-growing in the Near East, numerous rites and myths became articulated around the idea of the periodic renewal of cosmic sacrality, that is, the ritual scenario of the death and resurrection of the gods of vegetation.

All these new religious forms, which came to light after the rise of paleo-agriculture and the organization of settled societies (villages, market places, towns), are generally characterized by a dramatic in-

8 Cf. Franz Hančar, "Zum Problem der Venusstatuetten im eurasiatischen Jungpaläolithikum," *Prähistorische Zeitschrift* XXX–XXXI (1939–40) 106–21; Johannes Maringer, *Vorgeschichtliche Religion* (Zürich-Köln, 1956) esp. pp. 86 ff., 193 ff.; Karl J. Narr in *Abriss der Vorgeschichte* (München, 1957) pp. 16 ff.

9 Cf. E. Volhardt, *Kannibalismus* (Stuttgart, 1939); Ad. E. Jensen, *Das religiöse Weltbild einer frühen Kultur* (Stuttgart, 1948).

tensity of the religious experience, by increased ritual antagonism between the sexes (matched by a reciprocal attraction), and by the importance ascribed to sexuality and especially to bisexuality and androgeneity, mythical and ritual expressions of "totality" as well as of divine perfection. Traces of divine androgeny are met with even in paleolithic times and among certain primitives in the phase of food-gathering and hunting, but it is primarily in agrarian cultures that these ideas form a religious system, integrating, moreover, the mythico-ritual complex of the *heiros gamos*.[10] We could cite other examples of the revalorization, in agrarian cultures, of such archaic forms of religious behavior. One of the most instructive of these is the cult of the dead. Attested as early as the paleolithic, it gains considerable importance especially in megalithic religions.[11]

In brief, the development of the religious life has since been dominated by the consequences of the discovery of the mystic solidarity between man and plant life, by the prime importance accorded to the epiphanies of life (blood, sexuality, fecundity), and by the religious valorization of tension, suffering, and pain. The gods enjoy popularity because of the drama which they have undergone and not because of what they are or what they have created. The most popular gods are not the creators but those possessing mythologies rich in dramatic episodes; they have had adventures without number, they have known suffering and sometimes death and resurrection. All of this makes them more "alive" and more "human." Supernatural beings of this type are already attested at the earliest stages of culture. Mythical ancestors, culture-heroes, and legendary founders of secert societies have a more dramatic existence than do the supreme gods and creators. But it is in agricultural societies that the interest in this type of divinity becomes general and dominant. The sovereign or warrior gods, as well as the gods of vegetation and death or the goddesses of fertility and of destiny, possess pathetic and extravagant mythologies. But these fantastic exploits, involving cosmic forces and powerful magic, stir the imagination of men. These myths reveal what took place in the world, after the Creation; they exalt action, force, and skillfulness, telling not only of combat and adventure but also of the wonders and trials of descents to the underworld, encounters with

10 Cf. Hermann Baumann, *Das doppelte Geschlecht* (Berlin, 1955).

11 Cf. Paul Wernert, "Le culte des crânes à l'époque paléolithique," *Histoire générale des religions*, ed. M. Gorce and R. Mortimer (1948) I 53–72; H. Kirchner, *Die Menhire in Mitteleuropa und der Menhirgedauken* (Wiesbaden, 1955).

death, and the quest for immortality. It is in this religious climate that there takes shape the figure of a divine being who meets a tragic end and who later will become the center of mystery cults. The process of "humanization" which the gods undergo, implying their progressive separation from the sources of cosmic sacrality, is attested almost everywhere in the Near East and the Mediterranean regions, but it comes to a close in classical Greece. In certain cases the withdrawal of the gods from cosmic sacrality ends by draining them of religious values.

Among pastoral peoples (Indo-Europeans, Turco-Mongols, etc.) the celestial god retains or regains his primacy.[12] As we have already said, the god of the atmosphere continued to play a primary role among agricultural peoples, especially in his capacity as husband of the Earth-Mother. What needs to be added here is that the eviction of the celestial High God does not imply the complete disappearance of prestige connected with the sacredness of the sky. Innumerable myths and rites of ascension continue to be popular for a long time after the disappearance of the sky gods from the cult.[13]

We must now show in what sense the expressions of religious behavior change during the course of history without, however, involving a modification of structure. Let us take as an example a fundamental and universally attested religious idea—that the world is the work of the gods. The problem is highly important for the history of religions as well as for religious anthropology. It reveals both the conception which the primitives have of the world and the meaning which they ascribe to human existence. For the religious men of archaic and paleo-Oriental societies, the "world" is the familiar space in which they live; it is "their world." This microcosm has a religious structure. Not only is it the work of supernatural beings, but it is impregnated with their presence, it is in communication with heaven or the underworld, where these supernatural beings retired after having created, fashioned, or organized the world. This conception ranks among the very oldest religious ideas. It is found even among nomads who live by the gathering of wild plants and the hunting of small animals. They suppose that the lands over which they wander have been formed by supernatural beings. In some cases the cosmogonic myth serves as a model for a ritual by which unknown territory is

[12] Cf. Eliade, *Patterns in Comparative Religion*, pp. 61 ff.

[13] Cf. Eliade, *Mythes, rêves et mystères* (Paris, 1957) pp. 133 ff.

"cosmicized," that is to say, transformed into a habitable world. The necessity for "cosmicizing" the world where one goes to live permanently (as among sedentary peoples) or temporarily (as among nomads) reveals a form of religious behavior which is attested universally. The few examples given below will permit us to grasp, on the one hand, the meaning of this behavior and, on the other, the structural unity of its numerous expressions.

According to the myth of the Achilpa, an Australian tribe, a divine being called Numbakula "cosmicized" their territory, created their ancestor, and founded their institutions. Numbakula fashioned a sacred pole out of the trunk of a gum tree and, after anointing it with blood, climbed up to the sky on it and disappeared. This pole represents the cosmic axis, for it is around it that the land becomes habitable and is transformed into a "world." For this reason the ritual role of the sacred pole is a considerable one; the Achilpa carry it with them in their wanderings and decide which direction to take according to the way it leans. This allows them, in spite of their continual moving about, always to find themselves in "their world" and at the same time to remain in communication with the heaven into which Numbakula has vanished. If the pole is broken, it is a catastrophe; in a way, it is the "end of the world" and a regression into chaos. Spencer and Gillen relate a legend in which the sacred pole was broken and the entire tribe fell prey to anguish. The people wandered haphazardly for a time and finally sat down on the ground and allowed themselves to perish.[14] This is an excellent illustration of the necessity for "cosmicizing" the land which is to be lived in. The "world," for the Achilpa, becomes "their world" only to the degree in which it reproduces the cosmos organized and sanctified by Numbakula. They cannot live without this vertical axis which assures an "opening" toward the transcendent and at the same time makes possible their orientation in space. In other words, one cannot live in a "chaos." Once this contact with the transcendent is broken off and the system of orientation disrupted, existence in the world is no longer possible—and so the Achilpa let themselves die.

A similar type of behavior with regard to unknown territory is found even among peoples who are considerably more advanced.

14 B. Spencer and F. J. Gillen, *The Arunta* (London, 1926) I 374 ff., 386. Cf. also E. de Martino, "Angoscia territoriale e riscatto culturale nel mito Achilpa delle origini," *Studi e materiali di storia delle religioni* XXIII (1951–52) 51–66.

We have given several examples in a previous work.[15] Let us recall some of them. When the Scandinavian colonists took possession of Iceland and cleared it for settling, they looked upon this as the repetition of a primordial act—the transformation of the chaos into a cosmos by the divine act of creation. And in Vedic India, a new territory was legally taken into possession by the erection of an altar of fire dedicated to Agni. The construction of such an altar was simply the imitation of the Creation on a microcosmic scale. In this manner, the land which was going to be lived in passed from a chaotic state into an organized state; it was "cosmicized."

Some fundamental religious ideas emerge from all these facts. (1) There is need for living in a "cosmos," that is, in a territory which resembles the paradigmatic "world" created by the supernatural beings. (2) The cosmogony, accomplished by the gods in mythical times, serves as a model for man and can be ritually reiterated an infinite number of times. (3) To "cosmicize" a place means at the same time to consecrate it, to sanctify it; this is so because, on the one hand, every "form" is an imitation of the paradigmatic "form," the world, and, on the other hand, by the symbolic repetition of the cosmogony the supernatural beings are rendered present. (4) A place is truly consecrated when it makes possible communication with the world of the gods, that is to say, when it involves in its very structure a sort of "rupture" which leaves it open toward the sky (cf. the pole of the Achilpa).

These religious conceptions may be deciphered in the cosmological imagery, the symbolism of habitation, and the rites of orientation and construction of a great number of peoples belonging to different cultural levels. But, though the world always proves itself to be a sacred world and one which is the work of gods, its images are always changing. The "world" of the Achilpa is the territory of a temporary camping ground, the space circumscribing the ritual pole (replica of the mythical pole of Numbakula). Other Australian tribes know as their world that which lies within the confines marked by a certain number of objects, distributed sometimes over a considerable area. These objects represent the remains left by the supernatural beings as they went along from place to place "cosmicizing" the land, before their disappearance into the sky or underworld. This "world" of the Australians has a religious structure, since it is "open" toward the

[15] Eliade, *The Myth of the Eternal Return*, translated by W. R. Trask (New York, 1954) pp. 10 ff. (This work was first published in Paris [1949] as *Le mythe de l'éternel retour.*)

sky or toward the nether regions. In many Australian tribes the young boys, accompanied by their guides, retrace the steps of the supernatural beings by visiting these remains during the period of their initiation. The discovery of the true picture of the world takes place along with the things revealed at the time of initiation, notably the names and myths of the supreme beings, religious traditions of the tribe, origin and religious significance of human actions and institutions, etc. The revelation of the mythical exploits of the supernatural beings is accompanied by the awareness of the shape or configuration of the "world." The revelations concerning sacred time go hand in hand with revelations about the structure of sacred space.

Among sedentary peoples—farmers or villagers—the situation proves more complex. We are dealing with a multiplicity of images of the world, whose structural solidarity is not always immediately evident. But all these images illustrate the symbolism of the "center"; consequently, they present a world which is "open" to celestial and subterranean regions. Having studied the symbolism of the "center of the world" in several previous works,[16] we need not pursue it here. It is enough to recall that the "center" always refers to what we call "our world," to the place where we live and which is familiar to us. It follows, then, that a village, a city, or a nation is considered to be in the center of the universe. When a people comes to imagine the whole of its national territory, it sees it both as situated at the "center of the world" and as the starting place of the Creation. This is so, for example, of the Israelites and the Iranians.[17] On the other hand, the capital, the temple, or the royal palace, but also the village or the dwelling, represents more or less clearly an *imago mundi*.[18] This means that the religious man feels the necessity to live in a consecrated space, whose structure may be likened to that of the cosmos, the divine work par excellence. In Bali, as well as in certain regions of Asia, in preparing to build a new village, the people look for a natural crossing where two roads are cut perpendicularly to each other. In the middle of the village a space is often left vacant; this is for the

16 *Ibid.* pp. 12 ff.; *Images et symboles* (Paris, 1952) pp. 52 ff.; "Centre du monde, temple, maison," *Le symbolisme cosmique des monuments religieux* (Roma, 1957) pp. 57–82.

17 *The Myth of the Eternal Return*, pp. 12 ff.; Lars-Ivar Ringborn, *Graltempel und Paradies: Beziehungen zwischen Iran und Europa im Mittelalter* (Stockholm, 1951) pp. 280 ff., 294 ff., 327, etc.

18 For examples, see works cited in n. 16.

construction at some later time of the cultic house, whose roof symbolizes the sky.[19]

The necessity to live in a consecrated microcosm is expressed very clearly in the habitation symbolism of subarctic peoples of North America and northern Asia. The central post is symbolically identified with the "pillar of the world" and thus has an important ritual role. Among the pastoralists of central Asia, where the type of dwelling with a conical roof and central pillar is replaced by the yurt, the mythico-ritual function of the pillar has been passed on to the overhead opening for the evacuation of smoke.[20] An analogous symbolism is attached to the smoke hole of archaic Chinese houses.[21]

Since the cosmicized territory, the sanctuary, and the human dwelling are replicas both of the cosmos and of the divine dwelling, the way remains open for further associations of the world, the house (or temple), and the human body. In fact, such similarities are found in all of the higher cultures of Asia, but they are also reported on the archaic cultural levels. This goes back to saying that in placing himself in an exemplary situation man "cosmicizes" himself; he reproduces on the human scale the system of reciprocal conditioning and rhythms which characterize and constitute a "world." One fact is important to emphasize: each of these equivalent images—cosmos, house, human body—presents in itself or is susceptible of receiving an "opening" which allows passage into another world. To the "hole" in the sky through which the *axis mundi* passes corresponds the opening for smoke or the "eye" of the dome and, in Indian speculations, the "opening" situated at the top of the head (*brahmarandhra*) and through which the soul escapes at the moment of death. To express the passage from a conditioned existence to an unconditioned mode of being (*nirvāna, asamskṛta, samādhi,* etc.), the Buddhist texts utilize a double image, that of breaking through the roof and flying through the air. Arhats shatter the roofs of their houses (*brahmarandhra*) and fly up into the sky.[22] This means that the transcending of the human condition is figuratively expressed by the

19 Cf. C. Tg. Bertling, *Vierzahl, Kreuz und Maṇḍala in Asien* (Amsterdam, 1954) p. 11. For analogous conceptions in ancient Italy and among the ancient Germans, cf. Werner Müller, *Kreis und Kreuz* (Berlin, 1938) pp. 60 ff.

20 Cf. Eliade, "Centre du monde, temple, maison," p. 73.

21 Cf. Rolf Stein, "L'Habitat, le monde et le corps humain en Extrême Orient et en Haute Asie," *Journal asiatique,* 1957, pp. 37–74.

22 Eliade, "Centre du monde, temple, maison," pp. 78 ff.

imagery of the destruction of the "house," that is to say, of the personal cosmos which has been chosen for a home. Every "stable dwelling" wherein one is "installed" is equivalent for Indian thought to an existential situation which one assumes. The image of breaking through the roof means that one has now abolished every "situation" and has chosen not installation in the world but the absolute freedom which, for India, implies the annihilation of every conditioned world.

The Buddhist image of "breaking through the roof" brings an end to the archaic idea that man can live only in a cosmos (i.e., territory, city, village, body), that is to say, in a "world" which is sacred because it is patterned after the divine paradigm. In studying the different cultural expressions of this religious idea, we have at the same time touched upon another problem—the function of religion in the cultural process and the changes which this function has undergone in the course of history. The examples which we have just cited admirably illustrate the principal function of religion, that of maintaining an "opening" toward a world which is superhuman, the world of axiomatic spiritual values. These values are "transcendent" in the sense that they are considered revealed by divine beings or mythical ancestors. They therefore constitute absolute values, paradigms for all human activity. The function of religion is to awaken and sustain the consciousness of another world, of a "beyond," whether it be the divine world or the world of the mythical ancestors. This other world represents a superhuman "transcendent" plane, that of absolute realities. It is this experience of the sacred, that is, the meeting with a transhuman reality, that generates the idea of something which *really* exists and, in consequence, the notion that there are absolute, intangible values which confer a meaning upon human existence. It is thus through the experience of the sacred that the ideas of *reality, truth,* and *meaning* come to light, ideas which will later be elaborated and articulated in metaphysical speculations and will ultimately be the basis of scientific knowledge.

VII

Man's Day of Fate: The Influence of Homer on Later Greek Literature

By DAVID GRENE

"So then neither can God, since he is good, be the cause of everything as the many say, but for man he is the cause of a few things but of many he is not the cause. For good things are far fewer with us than evil and it is God and no one else that we must take to be the cause of the good, but for the evil we must find some other cause, but not God." So Plato in the *Republic,* written in the first quarter of the fourth century B.C. He is illustrating the fundamental difference he recognizes between the thought of Homer and the tragic poets, the material of popular education in his day, and that which he wished to inculcate in the citizens of his model state. It is unimportant here to enter into discussion of the exactness of the prescription for education in the ideal state, or the place of the ideal state in the argument of the *Republic.* What is significant is that Plato felt that Homer *and* the tragedians had created an image of a world in which God (or some nonhuman agency) was the cause of all things good and bad and that he wished for the expression of a different philosophy according to which God alone is responsible for what is good and something else or some combination of other things the author of what is undeniably bad. The first view, that of Homer, conveys the notion of an inexplicable world, since what man calls good and what bad cannot be harmonized in a vision of an understandably good government of the universe. The latter may introduce original sin or man's responsibility or whatever agent is most plausible as the author of the evil; it can leave God as the author of good and therefore permit the world to have a humanly explicable end and purpose.

This is perhaps Plato's most striking statement of his philosophical difference from the popular religious notions of his time. Since he is discussing the influence of literature on popular belief, he can lump together Homer and the tragedians. In a way he is perfectly right. The tragic spirit of the *Iliad* and the *Odyssey is* very largely that of the Greek tragedy in the fifth century. And, in comparison with the religious ideas which he wished to spread, there is little difference between the epic poems of the ninth century and the plays of the fifth. On one side of a great divide belong the two great schools of Greek poetry, the epic and the dramatic, on the other, Plato and his many successors in the same line of thought. But to us the differences in the emphasis placed by Homer and by the tragic poets are almost as interesting as the similarity in acceptance of the idea itself—that is, of the universal responsibility of the Divine (nonhuman) agent, the consequent meaninglessness of the world for human beings and therefore the formation of a human ethic and human tragedy independent in themselves and when in touch with the Divine in touch only with what is unknown and unknowable. These differences are certainly to be related to the audience to which the literary works were adressed, but such deductions as can be drawn from the material must be very cautiously made. True, it is easier to argue from this epic and dramatic material to the society they were addressed to than is often the case, for in Greek both are popular art forms—that is, both were addressed to relatively large bodies of people who can be looked upon as representative of their time and place. But it is hard always to be sure of how the poet, even the popular poet, stands vis-à-vis his own time. True, he must, at least in externals, conform to the expectations of his public. He must in a deeper way satisfy or provoke them. But further than that it is difficult to be precise as to the nature of the society from which he springs and to which he speaks. Is he leader and teacher or exponent of what is half in the mind of them he speaks to, or is he only expressing what is already accepted—who can say, particularly when one can clearly distinguish elements which are both new and traditional in the work of both Homer and the tragedians? Still, the main line of the reception we can undoubtedly trace, and in this development from the audience of the epic poet to the crowds at the Greater Dionysia there is something to be learned of the shifts in belief and understanding of the Greek society. And to study the continuity of the Homeric pattern of thought and its ramifications in tragedy to the moment of the great challenge issued by Plato is one of the ways to understand the break between the Greek and the Christian world, even if the moment of the Christian expression of the second vision is many centuries delayed.

Plato continues his treatment of the appropriate tales about Gods and men in the part of the book following the passages quoted. God, he says, is perfect; he uses "a God," but it is not false to Plato's meaning to translate the word by "God" rather than "*a* god" or "*the* gods," for he certainly does not accept literally the diverse characters in the Olympian hierarchy. As a consequence of God's perfection he not only cannot be the cause of what is bad, and therefore imperfect, but he cannot at any time show himself as other than he is, since by such transformation or disguise he becomes just that much short of his natural perfection, which is impossible. Another very important element of the Divine character is here expressed—his perfection and uniformity—which bears the strongest contrast with the Gods in Homer. And it is not only the Gods who according to Plato are uniform and stable in their manifestation and should be so presented, but one must strive also for an ideal of man in which there are no violent alterations of mood, from laughter to tears or from happiness to despair. Especially the notion that death is an evil and the afterworld a place of doubtful or painful possibilities must never be entertained, otherwise courage disappears and with it the resolution of heroism.

Plato has set his face entirely against a long theological and ethical tradition stretching from Homer to the tragic poets. Of course the passages just quoted are carefully framed with an eye to *how* Homer and the tragic poets had written and what effect they had on Greek education and in a broader sense on Greek culture. We can be reasonably sure that what Plato criticizes about the poets—Homer, Aeschylus, Sophocles, and Euripides—is what the people of the fifth century have come to accept from them and to believe in. When Plato emphasizes certainty of belief and constancy of character and conduct, it is sure that what the people have got from the poets is a conception of uncertainty in the government of the world and of violent alternations of mood and belief on the part of even the greatest heroes.

If an unprejudiced reader who had never looked at Homer before were to take up the *Iliad* after reading Plato's criticism of the poet, his first impression would probably be amazement. For to speak of God as being the cause of everything in Homer, both good and bad, seems to miss the point completely. The *Iliad* is a poem in which the issue of the events seems less important than the mood in which the participants engage or the relationships which exist between them. Plato's criticism is, indeed, a philosophical analysis of a work the philosophy of which is buried so deep that almost everything overlaid on it seems more important than the philosophy itself. The expression of this is very apt in Helen's conversation with her brother-in-law Hector (*Il.* vi. 341 f.): "Brother-in-law of me that am an evil designing and destructive bitch, I would that on the day that my mother bore me some fell blast of tempest had carried me away to a mountain or into the waves of the surging sea, where the wave would have washed me away, before all these things happened. But since the Gods have created these evils for a testimony, would at least that I had been the mate of a better man who knew the occasions of indignation and the many things that cause shame among men." This is the essence of the Homeric view of life. God, or something other than ourselves, has caused everything to be as it is, and this we cannot help, nor does it make sense to repine. Our vivid sentiments are reserved for indignation or joy at the particular human associations which the events involve. The causes of events the Homeric man does not know, and he cannot guess their outcome. But what he feels in experiencing them and how he is drawn to or repelled by others in the same situation are his only sure sensations. There is no certainty that a man may know in Homer except death, and there is no certainty in the government of the world, for either men or Gods, except destiny, which is impersonal, inexplicable, and, from the view of either Gods or men, incomprehensible. Thus, with very few exceptions, which will be discussed later, virtue in man or what is recognized as such does not necessarily make for success in this life, or even peace at the last, since there is no clear picture of the next world or how it is related to this. Perhaps more important—even success, glory, riches in this life are largely unavailing, since they cannot defend man against death or even old age. The role of the Gods, seen from one angle, only serves to emphasize the universal pessimism, for they are released from the necessity of death and yet are still balked of completeness of satisfaction, for they cannot save those they love from destiny. Death and destiny, death being the supreme expression of man's destiny, rule the world, and yet it can hardly be said they rule it, since they give it no comprehensible direction nor discernible pattern. But death and destiny lie across the path of men and Gods and are the only ultimately significant forces with which all beings human and divine have to reckon.

There is an ascending scale of importance as the personality of the force concerned diminishes. What man can feel for man or do for him is in Homer very personal indeed. Squabbles, resentment, friendship are motivating forces everywhere on the human side. But not much that is decisive results from them because there are the Gods as the complicating factor in the developing situation. It is the quarrel between Agamemnon and Achilles which precipitates the events of the *Iliad;* but it is Athena's intervention which prevents Achilles' killing of Agamemnon, it is Athena's temptation of Pandarus to shoot Menelaus which causes the disruption of the truce, it is the evil dream sent by Zeus which leads Agamemnon to the famous trial of Book ii, it is the struggle among the Gods which causes the sending of Patroclus into the battle and his death, it is the intervention of Thetis which brings about Achilles' re-entry into the war, and last of all it is the successful deception of Hector by Athena which makes him take his stand against Achilles. The gods, too, are personal in the *Iliad,* yet not so personal as the men, perhaps because they lack the sobering necessity of facing death. They are somewhat light-weight interventionists, whimsical and rather theatrical in character, but the fact is we do not believe in their existence nearly so completely as in that of Achilles and Odysseus, Hector, Helen and Paris. They are mere figures of particular passions and are less complete people. Yet they undoubtedly cause more decisive things to happen than the heroes themselves. But at the top level of all Zeus himself is powerless to ensure the result that he wishes. Here is Zeus speaking as he looks at his son, Sarpedon, on his last day of battle: "And the son of crooked devising Kronos looked at them and pitied them and spoke to Hera his sister and his wife. 'Alas, since fate is on me that Sarpedon whom I loved most among men must be subdued by Patroclus son of Menoetius! As I reflect on it my heart is bent two ways in my breast, whether I shall snatch him alive from this fight full of tears and place him in the rich land of Lycia or here and now subdue him beneath the hands of the son of Menoetius.' Him then answered the ox-eyed Lady Hera: 'Most dread son of Kronos, what a word have you spoken! A mortal man, *long since condemned to fate,* will you release him from chill death? Do so—but all we other Gods will not praise you.' " The same formula is used in a conversation between Zeus and Athena on the outcome of the fight between

Achilles and Hector (*Il.* xxii. 168 ff.), and it concludes with the following figure: "And when for the fourth time they came to the Springs, then the Father set in weight the balance and into it cast the two fates of unspeakable death, that of Achilles and that of Hector the horsebreaker, and he took the balance and held it in the middle and Hector's day of fate sank down; down, down it went into the House of Hades, and Phoebus Apollo left him." The remarkable thing is, of course, what meaning is to be given each time to the resentful remark of the goddesses, Hera and Athena: "Do so, but we the other Gods will not praise you." It *looks* as though the will of Zeus were in fact omnipotent and, if he would, he might save Sarpedon and Hector. And yet there is evidence enough that, as the Gods are presented in Homer and later in Herodotus, this is not so. One of the most telling passages is *Od.* i. 31. Zeus again is speaking: "Alas, how mortal men blame the Gods. For they say that evils come from us but it is they themselves have sufferings through their heedless folly beyond their fate. So now Aegisthus married the wedded wife of Atreides *beyond fate* and killed the man himself on his homecoming, though he knew of his own sheer destruction, for we told him of it in advance, sending Hermes the messenger that he should neither kill Agamemnon nor marry his wife. 'For vengeance will come from Orestes when he grows up and comes to desire his own land.' So spoke Hermes but he did not persuade the mind of Aegisthus for all his good intent. So now he has paid for it all." The puzzling part of this passage is "beyond fate." It signifies apparently that in some sense doom is an elastic conception responsive to one's own action or to God's pleasure. It is in this sense that Apollo manages to postpone the ruin of Croesus for ten years (in Herodotus i). But we must notice each time that the elasticity of destiny, if it may be so expressed, is only relatively small and that, however the Divine pleasure may be theoretically capable of thwarting or adapting fate, the God never, even when he wishes it most, actually sets his will against fate. It is this strange concept of the dual authority of Zeus and fate which is to engross Aeschylus in his two greatest dramas, the *Prometheus* trilogy and the *Oresteia*.

We can see, therefore, to revert to Plato's criticism, that in Homer men say everything comes from God, including the ill things, and yet Homer has managed to insinuate that the Gods, in so far as they are intelligible, are not solely or finally responsible for the ruin of their worshipers or the death of their friends. But some order of the universe, in which they and an impersonal force, not entirely the will, called variously fate, doom, destiny (πότμος μοῖρα τὸ πεπρώμενον), both play a part, is the last and final sanction of everything that happens in the world, good and bad.

I think that the Homeric Gods, as they are presented in the *Iliad* and the *Odyssey*, though perhaps particularly in the *Iliad*, have the peculiar degree of personalization to convey the delicate degrees of man's comprehension of what happens to him. First there are his dealings with his fellow men, where one can understand motives and their issue. And then there are Gods, who traditionally have alliances, friendships, and enmities. And within the limits of report and story these, too, are comprehensible. But over all and above all is the ultimate sanction of death and the moment of its coming as it cuts a life crucially, and for it there can be no understanding and no justification or explanation in human or divine terms. I am not saying, of course, that Homer invents the Gods to explain action at certain levels. The Gods are part of the belief of the men of his time and are believed in as possessed of caprice, whimsicality, or faithfulness as fairies, witches, familiar spirits have been believed in at other periods of the world. But Homer has used the image of the Gods in a certain way in the *Iliad* to convey our second level of dim sight into the meaning of our lives and has shown that both we and the Gods will still be checked by some power, impersonal as opposed to any concept of personality, whose meaning and purpose is inscrutable and entirely inhuman.

There is in the *Iliad* a disjunction between the causes of events in the world and any reasonable human ethic. The good man in Homer, who is usually the brave man, the generous host, the good father, may benefit not at all from his goodness. He may incur the anger of the Gods accidentally or unconsciously or on grounds not comprehensible in human terms and may consequently incur suffering and failure. There is therefore in Homer pessimism as concerns the issue of events. There is no tendency to identify your own course with justice and therefore with the God's favor. You hope for God's favor; but when the Gods are against you, you put up with it without complaining. The causes and issues of events are theologically incomprehensible and are not tied in with any reasonable ethical system. Furthermore, in the punishment for offenses involving strong social sanctions, such as violence to fathers or suppliants or violence to oaths (perjury), the actual administrators of punishment are the Furies, and the Olympian Gods, when they intervene at all, do so as up-holders of a law outside themselves. The Furies were also concerned where some fundamental natural law was broken. For instance, they intervene to prevent Achilles' horses from speaking. There is, of course, in the *Iliad* and the *Odyssey* a certain difference in the under-standing of causation by Gods and men. Homer in his capacity as narrator tells us that Zeus does not wish the death of Sarpedon and Hector but has to yield to fate. To Hector it must certainly have seemed that his deception by Athena was the ultimate cause of his destruction. Agamemnon declares his belief that the Olympian Gods will punish the breaking of the treaty by the Trojans. He is unaware that Athena has tempted Pandarus to his act. It seems, indeed, that at times the Gods, aware of fate, tempt mortals to their doom. But in every instance when the Gods either tempt man toward or warn him against his fate, it is something outside the Gods' control. Of this man is not always aware. He is conscious of fate as such, but he may think of it as synonymous with the Gods' will—which it is not. "For well I know that there shall come a day when Troy will fall" (Hector in *Il.* vi). The total impression of the *Iliad* is that men and women live without certainty, belief, or faith in any universal sanction for moral-ity, without, that is, believing that the just or righteous man has any special reason to anticipate good fortune in this world or the next, and draw all their deepest ethical sentiments from their human soli-darity. The commonness of death and old age, of slavery for captives taken in war, of savage and cold-hearted treatment of women and children at the capture of an enemy town—these are the bonds which unite all men. These are the circumstances that call forth the senti-ments and virtues they admire. They demand a very special sort of courage and pride in a man and devotion in a woman.

If the Homeric hero faces the future with so little to hope for with certainty and with no conviction of rewards after death, it is natural that his mood is not always one of devoted courage. And so in Achilles' famous speech to the Embassy in Book ix. 401 we can see why Plato regarded Homer as a possible corrupter of the courage of his soldiers in the ideal state:

> For in my eyes they are all not worth a life—not all the storied wealth of Ilium in the days before the sons of the Achaeans came nor all the treasures contained in the stone threshold of Phoebus Apollo in rocky Pytho. You can carry off cattle and fat sheep; you can win tripods and golden-maned horses. But a man's life, that it may come again once it has slipped the barrier of his teeth, that one cannot

take nor gain by prayers. For my mother the Goddess, Thetis Silver Foot, said that twin fates were carrying me to the end of death. If I remain here and fight around Troy's city, gone is my home-return but my fame will be deathless. But if I go home to my own native land, gone is my good renown but my life will be long and not quickly will the end of death get hold of me.

To sum up, the Homeric hero has no certainty about the government of the world or his own destiny in this or any other life. The Gods themselves are presented as not being in control of the universe, which ultimately holds on its course at the dictates of an impersonal force called fate or destiny. Ethical beliefs and practices are mostly entirely human in origin and sanction; and when this is not true—as in matters affecting parents, suppliants, the dead, or the keeping of oaths—what is involved is some force other than the Olympian Gods, such as the Furies, and if the Olympian Gods act, they do so only as upholders of a law of the universe outside their own will.

Fifth-century Athens accepted all of this position, ethically. It ought to surprise us that in the lapse of nearly four centuries and in the shift to a very different order of society things did not change more. And yet we are certainly right in concluding that in fundamentals, down to 432 at least, the position was unaltered. Listen to Pericles in the Funeral Speech, written during the first years of the Peloponnesian War: "We live our daily life with one another privately, without offence, and for our public conduct we live lawfully, out of fear chiefly, through obedience to those who may happen to be in authority and to the laws, and particularly to those laws that are laid down for the advantage of men unjustly treated and such as, though unwritten, carry the burden of a generally admitted shame." Are we far from Helen's cry: "Since the gods have contrived these ills to be a testimony, would at least that I had been the mate of a better man who knew the occasion of indignation and the many shames among men." The human sanction springing from man's community in victimization to chance torture, murder, and certain old age and death, the inexplicable sanction of destiny unknown and unknowable, the whimsies of the irresponsible Gods—these are the elements of the morality of the Homeric hero, and in essentials there they are again in fifth-century Athens.

But with an important difference which itself perhaps constitutes the bridge to the new position which Plato is trying to establish in the *Republic*. The fifth-century Athenian was preoccupied with *justice* as the Homeric hero, or the Homeric commoner, never was.

Justice is hardly a concept in currency in the *Iliad* and the *Odyssey*. True, there is a proper and a fit way to do things. Odysseus, we are told in the *Odyssey*, was a kind and good master and for these qualities his wife and his household were devoted to him. There is a proper way for a son or a father to behave. Such conduct is characterized by the phrase "knowing θἑμις" or "the law." The Cyclopes, for instance, live each one, lonely to himself, and "know lawlessness." But such "law" is really almost restricted to the duties to fathers, suppliants, or oaths of which we spoke earlier. There is hardly any right as such that any man in the Homeric society from King Agamemnon down to the meanest servant can demand unquestioningly *as a person,* as his due before God and man. This is one of the most important features of Homeric society as it is presented in the two epic poems. It is a feudal and aristocratic society with no long tradition of security behind it and no hope of permanence ahead. This may be because Homer is really presenting the society of his own day, the ninth century, with only echoes of the Mycenaean past. This great Mycenaean past may indeed have been different. But the insecurity of Homeric society is obvious. Agamemnon makes a valiant claim for his primacy and sanctity as he swears by the scepter of the kings of Mycenae. But he is obviously afraid that his authority may be questioned at any time. Hence the "trial" of Book ii. Even for great princes, the future status of their wives and children is uncertain. Andromache anticipates slavery for herself and death for her child as a result of the fall of Troy. Over any man lesser than the very greatest princes hangs slavery as a likely lot when his side is beaten in war. The Homeric society in its normal operation is dominated by small or great princes or chiefs or what we should call "country gentlemen," each with his little domain where he administers a rough and ready law to his dependents but himself risks his life, his power, and his possessions in wars and forays against enemies near and far. There is almost no one in the Homeric world who can be sure of the position of his family in the next generation. Hence the tremendous power of common human appeal as between one hero and another. Priam appeals to Achilles to give him back his son and reminds him of the position of his own father, whom the neighbors likely harry and make miserable because there is no son to protect him, for Achilles sits in Troy destroying Priam and his kingdom.

There is no justice to be had from Gods or destiny and none to be found with certainty on earth. Mercy and pity are powerful emotions in Homer exactly because those to whom the pleas are directed may well need mercy and pity in their turn.

Security for the individual, in the sense of recognized rights to which he could appeal, was not attained in the Greek world of the fifth century either. The Homeric princes and their domains passed away and their place was taken by the city-states, but the wars went on, and the total involvement of the populations continued, and still over every man's head hung the threat of death and slavery. In the last half of the fifth century, filled with the savage episodes of the almost continuous Peloponnesian War, Greek literature shows the interest of all men in the philosophical analysis of justice. This interest seems to have developed largely out of the cruel interdependence of war and the slave market. The speech of Diodotus in Thucydides iii about the fate of the people of Mitylene, whom the state of Athens proposed to execute and sell their wives and children to slavery, is a classic piece of popular rhetoric on the significance of justice to the democratic society—or the importance of disregarding the concept. Euripides at the same time is asking the bigger question whether any man is *justly* a slave. Thus it is probably no exaggeration to say that the popular interest in justice was most dramatically stirred by the issue of war and slavery—the same issue which had characterized the Greek world from the Homeric epics on. But, proceeding from the practical and detailed question of the justice or injustice of the individual's lot in the society, the discussion widened to the theoretic questions whether the government of the world was just and whether there was any congruency between human concepts of justice and what men had been told of the conduct of the Gods. Such questions were certainly current as early as the Ionian philosophers of the seventh and sixth centuries, but they found their most powerful artistic expression in the popular tragic theater of the fifth century at Athens and the works of the three poets, Aeschylus, Sophocles, and Euripides.

Aristotle says that the Greek tragedians started by writing plays with all sorts of myths for their plots, almost as Shakespeare did with medieval stories, North's Plutarch, Froissart's Chronicles. The early Greek poets even made some plays openly on contemporary themes, and until late in the fifth century there was also an occasional purely "fictional" play, that is, one with no myth involved. But in most of the tragedies and in all of them that we possess, the subjects are mythical, and, furthermore, as Aristotle says, a very small number of

377

myths is used by the dramatists. It is not easy for us to understand the increasing restriction in the number and range of the myths. It seems possible that certain themes such as the Orestes story and that of Oedipus lay deep at the heart of the experience of the fifth-century Athenian. We would have to know much more detail than we do about their public and private lives to see exactly why. But it is easy to imagine that once such themes were employed by any poet, Aeschylus or Sophocles might well seize the opportunity to use them again, exactly because the facts of the story were well known, the novelty had worn off, and the audience was receptive to the deeper and more particular meaning the author had found in the story.

There is no reason to suppose that the tragic dramatist of Athens wrote his plays in a manner essentially different from that of Shakespeare or a modern playwright. No doubt the idea for the play came to him out of a scene in a street, a sentence in a story, or a public happening. But for his audience this must be enlarged and accommodated, archaized and still left contemporary, in the dress of a myth of altogether unhistorical times. The myth itself, certainly for the two elder dramatists and perhaps for Euripides also, is not only the dress, the disguise for a modern story. It is also the touchstone of the validity of the idea gained conceivably from another source. The three tragic poets must have had an inner acquaintance with the myths and a capacity to reconcile them and their personal ideas and impressions rather like the relation existing between the epic minstrel and his story. The minstrel told the story of Hector or Agamemnon or Achilles, but the sentences and the lines were age-old and formulaic and he had learned them as a boy from his father. When Sophocles wrote of Oedipus, the unconstitutional ruler of Thebes, challenged in his authority by the affliction of the plague on his people, he was not just writing of the contemporary Pericles in disguise. The manner in which the figure of Sophocles' Oedipus came into being was probably a union of that contemporary Pericles and the man of the legend. Certainly the manner in which the people at the theater understood Oedipus was a union of legend and the contemporary fact. At one end of the scale the myth, the given, the truth, perhaps even (especially for Aeschylus) the sacred truth, if you understood. At the other, the world of observed life—the political life of Greece, the wars, law courts, festivals. The play is the image of the relation between the two. At no other time in Europe has the tragic dramatist shared so completely with his audience the materials of his artistic creation, both the simple and profound story and the vividness of public and private contemporary life.

Few people would dispute that the *Oresteia* is the greatest work of Aeschylus which we possess. It is certainly the best evidence for the way in which Aeschylus handled his dramatic theme as far as its production is concerned, for only here do we have a complete trilogy and only here, therefore, can we see the way in which the three movements of the story are integrated. The play deals with the progress of justice from the single act of vengeance complicated by many personal factors to the abstract principle of justice as it exists in the political and social community. This latter is represented in the play by the foundation in Athens of the court of the Areopagus and its relation to the goddess Athena. Thus the concluding play of the *Oresteia* trilogy carries the meaning of the story into the actual creation of a still existent Athenian institution. This institution, the Areopagus, had been for the five years prior to the play's production a topic of political debate in Athens. It seems probable on the basis of the fragments of the *Prometheus* trilogy—we possess only a single play complete and a few fragments of the rest—that Aeschylus may have often adopted the same design, in which an individual situation is finally raised to a level of abstraction and then this abstraction considered as it is embodied in a political or legal or religious institution. The achievement of Aeschylus was enormous. It must have been appallingly difficult to present the philosophic meaning, which lies at the heart of his plays, to a very large audience without compromising its subtlety. The bulk of this audience, quite unselected as it was, must have been very simple people and many of them presumably illiterate.

Of the three dramatists, Aeschylus is the most explicit in his treatment of the theme of Justice. And, like Plato, he saw that in the Greek world Justice became a question whether there is a God who is responsible for everything, or only a multiplicity of causes. The Homeric dichotomy of the Gods and of Destiny is his starting point. It was probably Aeschylus' deepest concern, and it is fortunate for us that we possess the *Oresteia* trilogy complete and the first play of the *Prometheus* sequence, in which he dealt with it. These two, the *Prometheus* and the *Oresteia*, should be read in conjunction in order to obtain a clear picture of Aeschylus' ideas on the subject.

He solves the Homeric puzzle by imagining an evolutionary Justice, the final stage of which is a compromise between Zeus and Necessity, otherwise called Destiny. This evolution and final compromise is brilliantly linked with the historical process by which the old pre-Greek Gods were conquered by the new and in which the old Gods belong to the rule of Necessity. Prometheus and the Titans, Themis (Prometheus' mother), Earth and the Furies are all forces that at last are accommodated into a single rule of Justice. For Justice, says Aeschylus, is the rule of order by Gods. But there are (or were, for it is not clear whether Aeschylus thinks of the process in time) two Justices—that of the old Gods and that of the new. There is a struggle between the two. Human beings must find in their institutions the image of a Justice which is a compromise between that of the old Gods and that of the new and in which the rights of both are acknowledged. In the *Oresteia,* the conflict is institutionalized in the trial between the Furies and Apollo about the actions of Orestes. It is tried by a human court—the Areopagus—and ends in an equal verdict of the judges. The issue is settled by the deciding vote of Athena, the local god. She gives it for the new Gods on the grounds of her own preference based on her exclusively male ancestry. The anger of the defeated Furies is overcome by their installation in a new role as the overseeing deities of the city.

Thus, for Aeschylus, Justice becomes the life process between Necessity and the personality of the new Gods. Its image must be truly found and expressed in the life of cities and the free choice of the individual. The essence of Justice is the principle that for sin there is always payment, in either this world or the next. "Out of suffering comes forth wisdom." On both the levels—that of the Divine and that of the human—the rule of Justice works itself out over the generations. In a sense, Aeschylus is already in contradiction with the Homeric split authority of Zeus and Destiny. The end of the *Choephoroi* contains the line "now the will of Zeus and Necessity have come together."

But two things stand out for comment. Aeschylus' principle of justice and Aeschylus' divine government of the world are evolutionary. It is quite impossible to be clear about the timelessness of a process which in the drama must be presented as continuing in time. In the *Prometheus,* Zeus inflicts on Prometheus unjust punishment for many centuries till Prometheus' knowledge of the future dangers to Zeus forces the sovereign of the Gods to come to terms. In the *Agamemnon,* someone will unquestionably pay for the murder of Cassandra, but for the time being the injustice is real. It is possible that Aeschylus really believed that when finally the Greek Gods made terms with the pre-Greek gods the rule of unified law was instituted. But it is also possible that this conquest was for him the symbolic expression of a process perpetually occurring. So that Aeschylus would still be guilty of holding, as Plato says, that God is the author of all things, both good and ill, even though he would declare that in the long run they all turn to good. For those who are unlucky enough to exist before the final revelation and reconciliation of the opposites, God is the source, albeit temporary, of evil.

The second matter concerns the individual. In a Chorus of the *Agamemnon* (*Ag*. 743), the old men give the following version of their own beliefs and the more conventional religion:

There is an ancient saying on men's mouths of old that a man's prosperity when completed and grown to greatness breeds and does not die childless, but that from good fortune there grows in generation insatiate misery. But in this I have a mind different from others. For it is the wicked deed which breeds more, and like to its own kind, and the straight-dealing house has a fate always blessed in its children.

Surely in the very marked disassociation from popular belief the Chorus is voicing Aeschylus' own views. The gist of the *Oresteia* is that the individual acts of free will, even in the sequence of actions conditioned by the past. Thus, even if Agamemnon is driven hard by circumstances to the sacrifice of his daughter and even though the phrase of the Chorus describing it is "when he put upon him the yoke of necessity," it is not the necessity which compelled the death of Hector. Nor is it the necessity which leads Abraham to sacrifice Isaac. It is a necessity which amounts to an enormous preponderance in favor of one alternative (the destructive one) over the other. This is probably the illustration within the play of the Chorus' expressed principle. It would have been very hard for Agamemnon to resist the pressure of his fellow princes. It was not impossible. There is a somewhat perplexing factor in all such cases in Aeschylus. It would seem that the man who makes the decision is being tempted by Ate (*Ag*. 230): "When he had put on him the harness of necessity, breathing in his spirit a veering impious mood, he changed his mind to venture everything. For dreadful destruction of the wits [this is certainly Ate] gives daring to mortal men. She is the Evil Counselor, the Founder of Sorrows. So he set his heart to become the sacrificer of his daughter, to give help to a war waged to win back a woman, and a first offensive to win passage for the ships." However, it is probably wrong to see in this Ate the old divinity of Homer's world. Most likely it is a description of the sinner's state as he makes his deadly decision and does not imply the existence of any other power than Zeus.

Aeschylus made a tremendous effort to see the ethic of the developing democracy in the context of what was at least one version of the old religion. He accepted the Homeric split between destiny and the Gods and then explained it away by the concept of an evolutionary process in which a new Justice, the rule of the old Gods and the new, was established. Clearly the society for which he wrote, or perhaps which he led by his plays, was seeking for a statement of the harmonization of the order of Justice in the city-state with that of the powers outside the human world. The notion of evolution in Justice was probably acceptable to the fifth-century Athenian state. Thucydides' speeches of statesmen of the fifth century are full of references to the "advances" made by the democratic society. For instance, here are some remarkable sentences in the speech of the Corinthian delegates (Thuc. i. 71.3): "For, as in the case of craftmanship, the succeeding stages must always win out. If a city were to remain at rest, laws that may not be changed are best. But for those who are compelled to face many things there is need of *invention* too, and much of it." It may well be that for the Athenian of the mid-fifth century Aeschylus' dramatic story of the final reconciliation of the old Gods and the new, marked by certain typical Athenian institutions, the Areopagus (and a jury system) and the guardianship of the Furies, seemed a thing rooted in time and in almost historical time at that, as a point from which the new Athens started. When combined with Aeschylus' emphasis on the individual's free will, to sin or not to sin—though with proper weighting of the inclination to fall into error—it probably was a very acceptable religious view before the last Peloponnesian War.

It is an extraordinary change to turn from the work of Aeschylus to that of Sophocles. For Aeschylus the meaning of the myth must be wrested from it. It must all make sense—sense in a grand and imposing manner, but sense all the same, down to the institution of the jury system or the Argive alliance. The figures—Gods, demigods, or humans—are of enormous size, and they and the grotesque vocabulary and strange style are arranged to produce an image of majestic coherence. Sophocles wrote plays in which the superhuman sanctions which circumscribe and distort man's world are not only inexplicable but altogether cruel and humanly unreasonable. The dramatist, as well as his heroes, treats them as the given conditions of life. One cannot hope to understand them nor in any obvious way to fight them. On the other hand, all the nobility of man consists in maintaining stubbornly his own sense of integrity in defiance of them and, by whatever dim light he possesses, his own sense of innocence or guilt. So the Oedipus of both plays called after him, so Philoctetes and so Ajax. Ranged against the hero are the nonhuman forces who with seeming irony destroy or repair, mock or bless him at the unexpected moment. "When I am nothing any more, then has the God made me a power," says the old blind Oedipus as he learns that his grave will be a blessing to the land that contains it and a curse upon his enemies. But also against him are all the ordinary human beings who find it easy to change and turn to suit the circumstances and who with varying degrees of benevolence or the reverse treat the hero as something totally unlike themselves.

The heroic figure in Sophocles—and it is this heroic figure who is the dominating element in all his plays—is always lonely, the possessor of a power inevitably linked with mutilation. The stinking rotten foot of Philoctetes, the horror of incest and parricide which cling to Oedipus, the madness of Ajax, in a lesser degree but of the same kind the unreasoning devotion of Antigone, the twisted certainty of purpose of Electra—these are the marks of the lonely hero. These are what make him rejected by his fellows, who necessarily and sensibly choose an easier path. Notice that in Sophocles the lonely figures have their isolation thrust upon them. The bite of the serpent, the sardonic mockery of the oracle thrust Philoctetes and Oedipus into their loneliness. The compulsion of blood relationship and nothing else, as she so elaborately explains, forces Antigone to the act that separates her from the rest of Thebes. None of them seek their destiny. They are saddled with it, and, as it sets them apart from all their friends and all other human contact, their greatness is shown in the resolution with which they maintain their innocence—that in fact they had done nothing but what they had to do, and therefore that what they endure as punishment is cruel and unjust.

This is the figure Sophocles sets himself to bring to life for his audience. What he does is to make them feel *with* the hero in his loneliness and isolation. But, once their sympathy has been won, the dramatist makes no concessions to his audience but forces them to accept the whole of the character. The lonely hero is almost invariably possessed by hate and anger continuously. They have become the most potent passions of his life—see Ajax, Electra, Philoctetes, Oedipus. In no normal way can there be a reconciliation between him and any ordinary society or for that matter the ordinary processes of change in the world. Sometimes through death, as in the *Ajax,* sometimes at the very end of a lifetime of torture and rejection, as in the *Oedipus,* sometimes through surrender of all that he had made out of his loneliness, as in the *Philoctetes,* the hero is rehabilitated. But with the living human being branded through no will of his own to be the victim of God's displeasure and perhaps at last of God's grace, separated out by his conscious power of maintaining his own standards of innocence in spite of universal condemnation, wearing a changeless face and a changeless mood in a changing universe of men and things—with this living man there can be no terms.

The restoration to potency of the lonely hero is Sophocles' greatest mystery. It is not the Aeschylean doctrine that he who suffers will learn. The hero in Sophocles suffers, but he remains the same. It is much nearer the Christian doctrine that "he who endures to the end the same shall be saved," though what the Greek hero believes in is not God but himself.

It is impossible to be certain about the relation of Sophocles and his audience and time. He was tremendously popular—that we know from the number of first prizes he won. When Athens was in the process of changing from a democracy to an oligarchy in 412 B.C., Sophocles was put on the Board of Twelve Commissioners who were to act as an interim government. As he was at this time well over eighty, it is reasonable to guess that he was put there as a respectable figure whose reputation would help the board in its unpopular task and who could be trusted not to do much. His plays are full of a surface identification of democracy and the "proper" attitude to life— Theseus, for instance, the good king of the *Oedipus at Colonus,* is a strongly democratic monarch, and Antigone the rebel suffers for what we regard as democratic principles. But, on the other hand, the servants of authority like Odysseus in the *Ajax,* and again in the *Philoctetes,* are as readily servants of a democratic state as they are of this mythical version of the Mycenaean monarchy. And Sophocles is incessantly calling his audience to hate them as much as his heroes do. The great emphasis of his plays is on the loneliness of the great individual and the evocation of sympathy for him humanly and on the mystical value which from some source attends him in the end.

This is hardly a democratic attitude. For me the sentiment of Sophocles' tragedies has nothing much for or against the democracy. Man's fate is, for him, ineluctably tragic in its final senselessness. But grand also exactly in his humanity, in his boldness, as man, in facing the incomprehensible guilt and sin which attach to him. Sophocles has almost gone back to the ethic of the Homeric world, but his figures are far more twisted by their sufferings. Whether fate or Gods are responsible for the grim jokes played on Oedipus and Philoctetes neither we nor the heroes know. It couldn't matter less. For all that counts with us is at once the strangeness of the figure and yet his commonness with ourselves. He is a mysterious monster afflicted and blessed with equal incomprehensibility, yet in his sentiments and suffering exactly like us. The conjunction of greatness and defect, the madness, the lame foot, the incest, had undoubtedly some personal meaning for Sophocles. In transcending this he probably also arrived at some other significance that these stories had for his contemporary Athens. But it is little use guessing about this, though the figure of Alcibiades, both in Thucydides' history and in Plato, suggests tempting identifications with certain of the Sophoclean figures such as Philoctetes.

It is the humanization of all true standards of morality that is remarkable in Sophocles. The world of the myths—which is for all intents and purposes made into the world of fifth-century Athens—is an evil and cruel place. The rhythm of life is that of change. There are the people who accept this easily and gladly—for example, Odysseus and Creon—and they are contemptible. And there are those who in a mad nobility fight always for their personal, unimpairable identity—Ajax, Philoctetes, Oedipus. Their dominant passion is hate and anger for the wrongs they have suffered. The solution which is at once true and meaningful is a vindication of universal change, which is symbolized for us in the progress of the seasons. There is offense, though perhaps not guilt, and there are punishment and suffering for it. One day there is a solution, through infinite changes. There is nobility in constancy, even in hate, which fights against the order of the world. The mystery of why he that suffers and endures to the end will triumph, though not changing at all, is the mystery which Sophocles exploits for his peculiar version of the tragic passion. He never tries to solve it, only to give it life in the figure of his plays.

This emphasis on the humanity of all relevant standards must have been very strong in the late fifth century. The Funeral Speech of

Pericles delivered over the dead of the first two years of the Peloponnesian War contains hardly a reference to the Gods or religion of any sort. In one characteristic sentence it might almost be a summing-up of Sophocles' philosophy of tragedy: "What comes to us from outside of man we must endure perforce, what our enemies do to us we must resist."

In general, Euripides' treatment of the myth stands quite by itself. He assimilates the figures of the story to the fifth century more than either of the other dramatists, and he also uses the sharpness of reality so introduced into the characters to discredit the conventional meaning of the story as a whole. Sophocles, too, made fifth-century Greeks out of the heroic figures. But he did not try to place them in certain easily comprehensible fifth-century problem settings. Sophocles' Electra is a fifth-century Athenian all right but is chiefly a woman of any time or place, if one can say that of so strange and perverse a character. But Medea is a foreigner living in a Greek community and a wronged mistress, and in half a dozen speeches she is speaking directly to an audience who had a lot of experience of foreigners in their midst and who were also already discussing the rights of women and of slaves. I am not saying of Sophocles and Euripides that their realism ever approached what we would mean if we used the term of Hamlet. Greek tragedy is always skeletonic in its rendering of personality. But in Euripides the outlines are painted in with local colors. In Sophocles the injustice of the laws of the universe is a fact accepted by both the heroes and the audience, in so far as the dramatist can convince them. The injustice is itself mysterious and, in a way, uninteresting since we can neither understand it nor make it other than it is. Consequently the purely human ethic and the purely human tragic passion are all-important. But the nonhuman sanctions of life, which make the world a most unhappy place, are regarded by Sophocles as entirely true. Euripides does not really accept the notion of an unjust God, and his pessimism about the natural wrongness of things is tinged with a curious sort of sentimentality according to which love and friendship make everything worth while. Here is Heracles in the *Heracles Furens* (1341–46) summing up his feelings about the general meaning of the tragedy: "I do not think the Gods love unlawfully. I never could believe, nor will I, that they bind one another's hands in chains, nor that one of them is born to be master of another. For God if he is truly God is in need of nothing. These are the wretched tales of the minstrels." In the end of the play, the devotion of Heracles' human father (in marked distinction to Zeus) and his earthly friend Theseus not only convince him not to kill himself but set him on the road to a new life, leaving behind him the bodies of his murdered wife and children.

The injustice and unhappiness which Euripides everywhere detects in his version of the myths is, according to him, largely an injustice and unhappiness based on the wrong interpretation of the story. If these stories were true, he says, this is how the people in them would be—and then how odious, how untrue to our human sense of decency would be both the story and the Gods it describes! There is always the hint in Euripides that the story was not really like that, that the Gods are not really like that, that perhaps if we understood more, and accepted less, of such "wretched tales of minstrels," we could be happier and better. The humanity of such tragedies is weaker than that of Sophocles exactly because the latter, and his heroes who express his thoughts, could face the pessimistic truths they find in the myths, and, while accepting them as truth, still believe in the value of man or at least the individual and peculiar man. It is worth noticing that Euripides is the only one of the three tragedians who surrendered to the emotionalism of the propaganda play. The *Andromache* is a real "hate Sparta" venture, written from what was no doubt the standpoint of the average Athenian.

As we read the passage quoted from the *Heracles Furens*, it becomes clear that there is far less separating Euripides (if we assume he is speaking with the voice of Heracles) from Plato than is usually thought. Plato might object to the performances of Euripides' plays in his ideal commonwealth, on the ground that they show Gods doing a number of evil things which would be repudiated by men. But Euripides might answer that this was his way of indicating the untruth of such stories, by showing what such Gods would be like if the story were accepted as true. As far as the moral goes, even if Euripides does not assert that God is responsible for only the good of the world, he certainly declares that he is not responsible for the evil. Euripides' God, indeed, may be and probably is quite aloof from the concerns of humanity.

The Homeric concept with which we started was man's day of fate. That is just what the nonhuman dispensation means for Homer— the moment which cuts across man's life with all its hopes and promise of an unrealized future. Homer's heroes do not speculate on the justice or injustice with which the powers outside this control have treated them. Homer as narrator has given us some explanation in the friendship or enmity of the Gods who are, as has been said so often, a kind of group of super-heroes yet withal less full of life and importance than the men. But he has also reserved the final authority for the inexplicable element, Destiny or Fate. Thus, though the shades are drawn rather subtly, there is a God, or at least some nonhuman element, which is responsible for everything in the world and this power knows nothing of justice or morality in our terms. This image of life is probably only acceptable to the few in an aristocratic society who combine simplicity with individual courage and sophisticaton. I can magine that to them the stories of Achilles and Hector were eloquent. Probably the other country gentlemen enjoyed quite adequately the feats of arms, the genealogies, the half-humorous tales of the Gods, and the set pieces like the catalogue of the ships and the description of the Shield of Heracles.

All the tragedians accepted as a framework this Homeric view of life, with its dichotomy of man's ethics and the government of the Universe. But the sense of the equality and community of this society, reflected in the giant popular spectacles for which they prepared their plays and at which the play judges were chosen by lot, led them to the enormous task of interpreting this tragic philosophy anew for a whole people. For such a whole people, war is not an opportunity for glorious exploits. It is an occasion when thousands lose their lives for the whim of a prince or politician or the caprice of God. Hence, in the Attic tragedies, great store is laid on the relation of war and the community and the sufferings of the community, all themes utterly foreign to the legends belonging to the Homeric era. The question of justice or injustice, of the punishment of sin in a universal sense, is raised in the issues of the Trojan War by Aeschylus. And by blending this with the private story of Agamemnon and his son Orestes and finally raising the solution of the blood feud to the abstract notion of justice within the community and its institutions, Aeschylus really did, on a titanic scale, justify the ways of God to the state of Athens.

The ancient commentators said that Sophocles was closest to Homer and they were quite right. He accepted the Homeric notion of the inexplicability of the ultimate sanctions of the world, the cruelty of fate. But his sense of humanity is at least no less than Homer's, and his probing touches a depth in the isolation of the individual from his fellows that Homer could not have known, for it was only the radiant association of the fifth-century state which, once lost, taught Sophocles to express the essential loneliness of the great figures. The accent is on the certainty of the injustice of life, the certainty of final loneliness, the greatness of courage and endurance in the face of these facts.

Euripides did not, as many believe, finish off the city-state and its religion by his question-raising mockeries. He only protested against what he regarded as superstition and pointed somewhat vaguely but with great emphasis in other directions. The Gods of the Epicureans, removed from interference with man's lot, but existing quite certainly somewhere outside, and leaving questions of right and justice to be fixed rationally and intelligently by man, would have suited him very well. We are on the edge of the new view of the world, in the light of which Plato speaks, which will not let us think or say that the final sense of everything good or bad is inexplicable and its goodness or badness inexplicable and will not let us affirm the grandeur of spirit in which man can face his life and his death, alone, neither denying the existence of the incomprehensible forces which destroy him nor allowing them to deprive him of the only thing he truly owns, his truth to his own standards of innocence or guilt.

VIII

The Moral Order in the Expanding Society

By CLYDE KLUCKHOHN†

Human life is a moral life precisely because it is a social life and because in the case of the human species the minimum necessities for orderly and co-operative behavior are not provided by biologically inherited instincts. In other words, all moral orders are human artifacts, the products of the cultural process. Given the nature of a society (its size, economic base, presence or absence of writing, etc.) one could not hope to predict in all particulars its moral order, for factors of location, accessibility to currents of diffusion, and all the accidents of history make for variations. There are, however, broad recurrent regularities as well as differences. There are certain inescapable "givens" in the human situation, always and everywhere. Some arise from the fact that protohistoric man and historic man represent a single biological species with the same kind of anatomy, physiology, and neural nets. The species is bisexual. Multiple births are rare, and infants are helpless or dependent for a considerable period. In all populations there are significant differences between individuals as to their physical and mental endowments. Nutritional and body-temperature-control requirements for survival vary appreciably with environment, and yet there are features with respect to which it may be said that this kind of organism must make a minimum adjustment to a common environment. The life span of human beings has a distinctive range. There are likewise certain social universals. In all groups there must be a division of labor; differential status, power, and authority; established ways of instructing the young and otherwise transmitting skills and knowledge; expectable social reciprocities. Thus there are similarities as well as divergences in cultures. And, as Redfield (1953, pp. 152 f.) says:

... while the thought of Frazer's time rather simply conceived of man's inherent mental nature as the cause of the resemblances, the present-day view, while not denying that the psychological and biological nature of man provides part of the explanation, turns to *the similarities of the conditions of life,* as necessary for the persistence of men in groups, in attempting to develop explanations of the common human. [Italics mine.]

Moreover, the association of type of economy with a specific kind of social organization and of these and other aspects of culture with one sort of moral order as opposed to another is by no means altogether a random one. Hence one can anticipate that there will ordinarily be some determinable relationships between the size of social groups and characteristics of their value systems.[1] With this view many (I think almost all) anthropologists are presently in agreement (see e.g. Steward *et al.*, 1955). I shall quote only two (an archeologist and an ethnologist):

Not only in material things do the parallels hold. In the New World as well as in the Old, priesthoods grew, and, allying themselves with temporal powers, or becoming rulers in their own right, reared to their gods vast temples adorned with painting and sculpture. The priests and chiefs provided for themselves elaborate tombs richly stocked for the future life. In political history it is the same. In both hemispheres group joined with group . . . ; coalitions and conquests brought pre-eminence; empires grew and assumed the paraphernalia of glory. . . . In other words, we must consider that civilization is an inevitable response to laws governing the growth of culture and controlling the man-culture relationship [Kidder, 1940, pp. 534–35].

Extraordinary similarities are to be observed in the nature and order of appearance among widely separated peoples of certain social practices and religious observances [Kidder as quoted in Steward, 1950, p. 118].

The general sequence of social, religious, and military patterns ran a similar course in each center of civilization, and a generally valid formulation is possible [Steward, 1949, p. 18].

But the empirical task is not an easy one. For archeological evidence will permit only the most tenuous reconstruction of the moral order of food-gathering societies which evolved into food-producing. Indeed we cannot picture firmly the values of food-producing societies prior to a few centuries ago except in those cases where there is a written record. Redfield (1953, pp. 58 ff.) has attempted it for the Maya. During the period since 1500 we have documentation on what has happened to the moral order in societies which have expanded, which have become food-producers, and the like. But these data are not satisfactory for determining the consequences of the sheer process of increase in size of social units because the issues are confounded by such factors as colonialism, religious proselytization, and rapid communication on a global rather than a local or regional scale. It

---

[1] This is, of course, general tendency rather than literal fact. For example, Goldschmidt (1951) has demonstrated some surprising parallels between the "Protestant Ethic" and the ethical system of two small Indian groups in Northwest California (Yurok and Hupa).

would seem, therefore, that the best we can do is to contrast the moral order in tribal societies limited to a few thousand persons (at most) or small villages with that in (town or city) urban groups. I shall, somewhat arbitrarily, exclude from consideration the large tribes or nation-states of Negro Africa, on the ground that these peoples, before they were studied ethnologically, had had centuries of direct or indirect contact with Islamic civilization and, in some cases, perhaps millenniums of influence from the western Mediterranean basin (cf. Snowden, 1948) and Mesopotamia. I exclude these Negro peoples also on the ground that they were nonliterate, and I am convinced that, though the two factors are certainly correlated, the absence of a written language makes for at least as much difference in value systems as do population density and concentration.

Many peasant societies would be excluded from consideration on this criterion. All peasant societies will be excluded if we accept Redfield's (1953, p. 31) definition of the peasant as "a rural native whose long established order of life takes important account of the city." E. K. Francis, on the basis of a study of Hesiod's *Works and Days,* has outlined the moral order in peasant society in a manner that Redfield finds generally acceptable:

... a pattern of dominant attitudes emphasizing a practical and utilitarian attitude toward nature, yet with such a positive valuation of work as sees it not only materially productive but also a fulfillment of divine command; a de-emphasis of emotion; a concern with security rather than adventure; a high valuation of procreation and children; a desire for wealth; and the joining of social justice with work as basic ethical notions [Redfield, 1953, pp. 38–39; cf. also Redfield, 1956, pp. 106–7, 112 ff.].

Let us, however, restrict the inquiry to the direct consequences for the moral order of increases in the population of social groups to the point where basic interpersonal relations are no longer face-to-face relations nor predominantly those of kin groups. There are at least two fundamental kinds of social and cultural change (cf. Wittfogel, 1957, pp. 419–20). The one is diverse (externally conditioned); the other is developmental (internally conditioned). Let us limit ourselves to "development, the transformation effected essentially by internal forces" (e.g. expansion of population to the point where division of labor becomes complex and where the mechanisms of social control must become more abstract and more formalized). In concrete cases, to be sure, diversive and developmental changes can be disentangled only by abstraction. Nevertheless, we can bypass complications that cannot be treated adequately in a paper of this length if we exclude arbitrarily any treatment of, on the one hand, peasant societies influenced by cities and, on the other hand, tribal societies whose moral order has disintegrated under the impact of Western pressure or been revitalized by counteractive messianic movements.

Let us, then, proceed to generalize contrasts in the moral order between non-face-to-face societies and primary groups (even largish tribes are broken down into bands, lineages, or other segments so that in most contexts interaction is on a primary-group basis). Remember always that peasant societies and societies in process of detribalization are left out of account. I can add little to what others (and notably Redfield and Childe) have already said. Nevertheless an interpretative summary may be worth while. It seems to me that there are two primary variables: (1) the direct consequences of increase in size and (2) the indirect consequences such as those of cumulative growth of specialization in division of labor.

Direct Consequences of Expansion

"As towns get larger, it becomes physically impossible for everybody to interact daily with everyone individually. Therefore, as towns get larger the pair interactions may be expected to be proportional to a power of the population larger than the first power yet smaller than the second power or square" (Dodds, 1957, p. 135). In six American communities varying in size from 1,304 to 325,944 people, Dodds studied internal interaction. He found that "the relative interacting, whether physical or social, varied inversely with a power of the population" (*ibid.* p. 134). Students of social organization have shown that factors affecting the number of interactions (population size, occupation, residence, food supply, etc.) modify family and kinship systems. What does the increase in interactions (actual and potential) mean for the moral order?

Surely it means, inevitably, several things. If the minimum of social order and of the capacity of one individual to predict the behavior of his fellows in a group where many persons never encounter certain other persons at all and where numerous contacts that do occur are casual and transitory is to be maintained, the moral code must be relatively abstract. In "primitive" society, ethics is based upon acts more than upon words and upon concrete words more than abstract ones (cf. Radin, 1927, p. 72). While it is mythological to maintain that no abstract terms are found in "primitive" languages, no one would dispute that abstractions (and not least the large moral abstractions) are less prominent. Where all adults have had, to a first approximation, "the same" experiences the functional need for abstractions is appreciably less. Moreover, the moral order must be codified so that it is publicly accessible in standardized form rather than dependent upon the idiosyncratic version which a given priest or shaman or headman might give in a particular context. Finally, it cannot be enforced solely by the rather diffuse and often informal sanctions of the kin group. Enforcement, at least in principle, must be impersonal, that is, applied regardless of kin ties, personal acquaintance, status (with some exceptions for royal, priestly, or noble figures), and details of context other than those specified in law. Though it is also true that one of the characteristics of large societies is that various moral orders may coexist in different sectors of the group, there is only one official moral order. In this sense, as Redfield (1953) repeatedly says, the moral order in the expanded society is "more inclusive."

Another consequence of a social organization not structured primarily along kin lines and where the individual encounters some other persons only impersonally and ephemerally—or not at all—is the sharpening of the demarcation between self 'and not-self. In "primitive" groups the solidarity of brothers or sisters or of other relatives is such that the lines of completely separate individuality are not always distinct. Indeed in whole families the delimitation between "mine" and "our" may be a vague or shifting one. The same kind of thing was true in "Archaic" Jewish and Greek cultures (cf. Dodds, 1951, pp. 34, 53, and *passim*). For instance, Dodds remarks: ". . . the son's life was a prolongation of his father's, and he inherited his father's moral debts exactly as he inherited his commercial ones." In "primitive" thought the self may be merged[2] with a divine being, a totem, or a natural phenomenon. It is a commonplace among anthropologists that the conception of the self is not firm and clear. Thus Lee (1954, pp. 50, 52) says:

> In our own culture we are clear as to the boundaries of the self. In our commonly held unreflective view, the self is a distinct unit, something we can name and define. We know what is the self and what is not the self; and the distinction between the two is always the same. With the Wintu, the self has no strict bounds, is not named and is not, I believe, recognized as an entity. . . . A study of the

2 As Childe (1952, p. 19) says, "its distinctive peculiarity would be, not that mind and matter, subject and object were confused, but that they had never been finally torn apart."

grammatical expression of identity, relationship and otherness, shows that the Wintu conceive of the self not as strictly delimited or defined, but as a concentration, at most, which gradually fades and gives place to the other. Most of what is other for us, is for the Wintu completely or partially or upon occasion, identified with the self.

Dodds (1951) points out that the Homeric man has no unified concept of personality (p. 15), that only at the end of the Archaic Age did there appear "a new and revolutionary concept of the relation between body and soul" (p. 142), that "the liberation of the individual from the bonds of family and clan is one of the major achievements of Greek rationalism" (p. 34).

Marian Smith (1952, p. 400) adds another dimension:

This brief survey of four cultures reveals certain sharp contrasts in concepts of ego extension. The Western ego may extend infinitely into the future—at any rate it is importantly involved in future events; Hindu egos extend infinitely into both past and future—with a definite understanding of the beginning in the past and the eventual end of the individual soul; Chinese egos start their extensions not from remote time but from the present, flowing into both past and future, with individuality becoming more and more tenuous; and for the Coast Salish, ego extension is hardly temporal at all but carries the individual inevitably into relation with the world around him.

I suspect that the case of the Coast Salish is typical of "primitive" societies. I know of no case *where the possibility of contamination from the great "world religions" can be excluded* in which the culture postulates a clearly bounded self as continuing through all eternity and as responsible for specific deeds committed by the individual during earthly life.

The clear-cut demarcation of the self which develops in the larger societies I believe to be a precondition of the personal interiorization of the moral order which is also a characteristic of these societies. The smaller groups largely exteriorize moral sanctions. It is the gods or the implacable operations of external natural or supernatural forces or public opinion within the community which punish the individual. I think that Breasted (1934) has correctly designated what occurred in Egypt during the transition to urban and literate existence as "the dawn of conscience." That is, the self-aware individual comes to punish himself in accord with the standards of a more inclusive moral order. Dodds (1951) deals with the changes in Greek civilization as city life and literacy became fully established under the rubric "From Shame-Culture to Guilt-Culture." These may be the wrong or at least greatly oversimplified terms. At best, we can probably say that "guilt" is a more frequent and more powerful phenomenon in literate-urban cultures. The problems are, as Piers and Singer (1953) have shown, very complicated. Nevertheless, taking advantage of their analysis (see esp. pp. 36–37, 76–79), I think the following are valid statistical generalizations:

1. All cultures utilize both "shame" and "guilt" to ensure socialization of the individual.
2. But "primitive" cultures achieve social conformity with greater emphasis upon "shame" based on identification (in the technical psychoanalytic sense). Morality is dominantly centered in the family and in the face-to-face group.
3. Whereas literate-urban cultures give increased importance to internalized self-responsibility.
4. And these same cultures are associated with the delimitation and specialization of the person's sense of moral responsibility, with the emergence of an individual-centered moral order.

We can agree with Piers and Singer that there is both latent or unconscious shame as well as guilt. But we need not follow their definitions: shame "as the anxiety aroused by failure to internalize parental ideals under the unconscious threat of abandonment." There may well be something to the "threat of abandonment" in the small, kin-type society, but one of the main contrasts between tribal and urban peoples is that in the latter the moral order is derived far more exclusively from the parents, whereas in nonliterate groups (where the extended family often prevails) grandparents, older siblings, uncles, and other relatives may be crucial in "the incorporation of the superego." Piers and Singer define guilt as "the anxiety aroused by transgression of internalized prohibitions under the unconscious threat of mutilation." The final phrase is far too speculative, and by use of the word "prohibitions" they neglect the fact that guilt can also arise from failure to live up to positive injunctions.

Another direct consequence of expansion of population arises from contact with divergent moral orders, with contrasting perspectives. Expansion of population often brings with it a need for more territory. Or, if the food-producing economy permits not only feeding the increased population but also a surplus of food or other goods for exchange, trade and travel are initiated on an accelerated scale. Expansion leads to a turning-outward in various dimensions. In the small, isolated, self-contained society there is always change, but it takes place ordinarily at a slow pace. In all or most groups there are, as Radin (1927) and others have shown, at least a few individuals who reflect, speculate, and question. But moves into new territory for conquest or trade and subsequent acquaintance with ways of life that are appreciably different greatly heighten reflection or questioning. Reasons must be found to justify the existing moral order or it will be altered by negation, reshaping, or syncretism. The simple and unchallenged integrity of the code disappears. There is no longer one and only one standard of the right and the good. One must be defensive or one must change or both. The moral order becomes for the first time a genuine problem. Ideas take their place as forces in history.

Finally, expansion presumably gives a new form to an old human "value." The cruelty of man to man is most ancient. We may assume that raiding (for food, including other human beings in certain instances; for property, including slaves; for retaliation) goes back to the dawn of human history. However, the notions of conquest and permanent subjugation of a whole people and of religious conversion appear to be rather recent. Systematic armed warfare ("militarism") for these purposes seems no more than sporadic at most before Neolithic cultures. It was practiced, of course, by nonliterate tribal peoples but probably only by large societies which were organized considerably beyond the level of the band or village. The evidence is incomplete and complex (cf. Childe, 1941; Childe, 1951, pp. 111–12, 165, and elsewhere), but there is certainly a strong association between "expanded societies" and organized warfare (see also Steward, 1949, pp. 10, 11, 17, 20–22).

On the other hand, some case can also be made for a compensatory movement as stated by Muller (1958, p. 628):

> Until some 2500 years ago community loyalty was usually accompanied by a then healthy suspicion and even hostility toward other communities, especially those with different cultures, and often by a zeal in striving against them that matched and nourished the intragroup cohesion. But with the rise of the great empires that embraced many previously separate peoples, doctrines of brotherhood among all mankind began to gain increasing acceptance. Along with this there was a growing adherence to abstract conceptions that were supposed to embody universally higher values.

Indirect Consequences of Expansion

Naroll (1956) has argued that there is an allometric relationship between size of population and the number of craft specialties and ramifications. While I cannot accept fully either his data or his reasoning, I am convinced that there is something to this general line of attack. Food-production leads to population growth, and, other things being equal, nutritional stability and especially a food surplus are followed by some further specialization in the division of labor. Among other things this process gives the creative minority (or some portion of it) the opportunity of devoting their full skills in a cumulative way rather than dividing their energies among the part-time tasks of the tribesman or the villager. With the advent of literacy, this division of labor with many full-time specialists goes still farther. Before the advent of written language, knowledge can cumulate only by the flickering fire of tradition—roughly in a simple arithmetical series. With documents, accumulation becomes geometric and eventually, perhaps, according to some exponential series. This enormously increased corpus of knowledge requires both specialists to preserve it and specialists to acquire it.

Writing also, of course, facilitates control over larger numbers of men. Wide-scale bureaucratization is hardly conceivable without written records, though the Inca constitute a partial exception (only by means of the quipu) and some of the kingdoms of Negro Africa are exceptions. I think, however, Lévi-Strauss (1955, p. 318) goes too far when he writes:

... il faut admettre que la fonction primaire de la communication écrite est de faciliter l'asservissement. L'emploi de l'écriture à des fins désintéressées, en vue d'en tirer des satisfactions intellectuelles et esthétiques, est un résultat secondaire, si même il ne se réduit pas le plus souvent à un moyen pour renforcer, justifier eux dissimuler l'autre.

The consequences are manifold. For one thing, another facet of impersonality is added to the environment. One no longer learns entirely from persons; one learns from books, from individuals one has never seen and will never see and about whose personalities one may have no information—let alone a kin tie or some other personal relationship to them. This tendency toward impersonalization is projected into the nonhuman world. Nature and the cosmos are conceived in *less* humanized or personalized terms (Redfield, 1953, p. 9).

For another thing, literacy creates a new class of specialists: those who preserve, teach, enforce, and interpret the moral order. And "churches" arise. That is, no longer are religious practitioners, who have acquired their power through private revelation or through informal apprenticeship to relatives, free to vary myths and rituals within considerable limits. Documents make possible unchanging (or changing only slowly or by violent "revolution") standards of orthodoxy. For example:

Spinden thinks he has the evidence for a congress of astronomer-priests at Copan in the early centuries of the Christian era, when certain local differences as among Maya cities in the writing of certain calendrical corrections were ironed out and there was adopted a general plan to be followed by all communities represented in the conference [Redfield, 1953, p. 65].

On the other hand, cities, as has often been remarked, are fertile sources of innovating and divisive tendencies in the moral order. There is the development of what Toynbee has called the "external and internal proletariat." Slaves or serfs scattered among large estates or large households seldom can attain cohesion. But juxtaposition of a proletariat in one or more of the quarters of a city establishes common interest in creating class solidarity. Moreover, an urban proletariat is largely anonymous as far as a ruling group is concerned. The city has a tendency to widen the extremes of the social scale, if only temporarily. As Louis Wirth (1940, p. 752) has remarked:

The anomalous situation symbolic of urban life consists in the presence of close physical proximity coupled with vast social distances of men. This has profoundly altered the basis of human association and has subjected the traits of human nature as molded by simpler social organizations to severe strain.

In any case, freed from the daily, personal, and face-to-face scrutiny of the authority figures of the small society, city-dwellers can turn to heresies or to secularism. The official moral order can only to a limited extent be enforced in an intimate and informal way. Control can be maintained only by bureaucracies, whether priestly, legal, or military, and these bureaucracies must be guided at least in theory by the abstract rules of the "inclusive moral order." At the same time, heterogeneity,[3] as much as the inclusive moral order, remains an obvious property of the city.

Heterogeneity also makes for "alienation" vis-à-vis the moral order as well as in other respects. Man in "primitive" society "knows," even if he does not follow the dictates of, "what is right." Many fewer city-dwellers[4] can have the same unquestioning acceptance. They are aware of competing moral orders both within their community and among foreign peoples.

This observation leads to some points which Redfield (1953, pp.

[3] This raises the question of "Culture, genuine and spurious," discussed by Sapir in his famous paper of that title and in Tumin's (1945) "re-evaluation."

[4] Throughout this paper I have deliberately used such expressions as "city-dweller" and "urban" loosely to designate societies characterized by at least two of the following features: 1) towns of upward of, say, 5,000 inhabitants; 2) a written language; 3) monumental ceremonial centers.

23–25, 112–13, 119) has beautifully expounded. One can do no better than quote from him:

> In the folk society the moral order is great and the technical order is small. . . . In folk societies the moral order predominates over the technical order. It is not possible, however, to reverse this statement and declare that in civilizations the technical order predominates over the moral. . . . There are ways in civilization in which the moral order takes on new greatness. In civilization the relations between the two orders are varying and complex . . . the moral order begins as something pre-eminent but incapable of changing itself, and becomes perhaps less eminent but more independent. In folk society the moral rules bend, but men cannot make them afresh. In civilization the old moral orders suffer, but new states of mind are developed by which the moral order is, to some significant degree, taken in charge. The story of the moral order is attainment of some autonomy through much adversity. . . . In the folk societies men do not seek to make over their own natures. . . . Man later attempts to take control of this process and to direct it where he wills . . . the transformation of the folk society into civilization through the appearance and development of the idea of reform, of alteration of human existence, including the alteration of man himself, by deliberate intention and design . . . the moral order, though it is shaken by civilization, is also, in civilization, taken by reason into charge.

Redfield (*loc. cit.*) also summarizes ten features which Childe finds characteristic of life in the cities of Mesopotamia, the Indus Valley, and Middle America. Of these, three which are immediately relevant to the moral order have not been touched upon here or have been mentioned only obliquely: (1) value placed upon the central accumulation of capital (collected through tribute or taxation); (2) special privileges explicitly extended to the ruling class; (3) high value accorded to "the state" (i.e., "the organization of society on a basis of residence in place of, or on top of, a basis of kinship"). To these one may probably add (as rough inductions; cf. Steward, 1949) the rise of "national" religions with all or most of the following corollaries: priestly classes; god-rulers or god-priests or a combination of the two; ceremonial-bureaucratic centers.

Discussion

If we are to adhere to the limitations stated at the beginning of this paper, it seems to me that the foregoing two sections contain about all that can be said on the basis of present knowledge about those consequences of the expanding social order which appear to be nearly universal. There are other phenomena which are exceedingly common among food-producing societies but about as frequent among nonliterate tribal peoples as among city-dwellers. One thinks of the religious beliefs and practices about which Frazer (cf. Redfield, 1957, p. 152) wrote: the spirit of the harvest as incorporated in certain men or women; the sacrifice of god-kings; the safeguarding of crops through honoring the mother-spirit of the corn; scapegoat figures by which peoples cleanse themselves of evil. Similarly, it is well known that "shamans" are *more* characteristic of small societies, "priests" *more* characteristic of the larger ones. There are likewise still more restricted features of the moral order such as the prizing of individual achievement and looking to the future (sometimes including the notion of "progress") which are found in many but by no means the majority of the expanded societies.

I should like to note explicitly my awareness that I have bypassed certain complications which would require extended treatment in a comprehensive consideration of the moral order in expanding societies. For example, I have made no systematic attempt to distinguish towns, proto-cities, and cities; cities of the literati, of entrepreneurs, of the bureaucracy; primary and secondary urbanization. The additional issues and qualifications attendant upon the introduction of such important refinements are admirably illuminated by Redfield and Singer (1954). Here I must limit myself to calling attention to only a few of their points.

Some types of cities mainly carry forward "into systematic and reflective dimensions" (p. 58) an old culture. This process has, to be sure, consequences for the moral order but of a different sort than in the kinds of cities that create "original modes of thought that have authority beyond or in conflict with old cultures and civilizations" (*ibid.*). Cities of the first class are those of "orthogenetic transformation" and of the moral order, the second class those of "heterogenetic transformation" and of the technical order. The one set of phenomena characterizes mainly the phase of primary urbanization, the other that of secondary urbanization.

I have sometimes spoken as though particular institutions (e.g. the market) inevitably contributed to the diversification of the moral order and as though social inventions, including those relating to the moral order, always spread from the city to the country. Such generalizations, as Redfield and Singer convincingly show, oversimplify complex matters. The market may either reinforce traditional norms or simply have no appreciable effect upon the moral order in any way. When the student enlarges his time span and also wishes his generalizations to refer to all types of cities ". . . the processes of cultural innovation and 'flow' are far too complex to be handled by simple mechanical laws concerning the direction, rate, and 'flow' of cultural diffusion between 'city' and 'country' " (p. 71).

Summary

The following features appear in a general way to be relative to the emergent expanded societies:

1. The moral order becomes more explicit and self-conscious,[5] more abstract, more codified, more rationalized.
2. The moral order is more internalized.
3. It is more projected into the life after death.
4. The moral order is less unquestionable and more heterogeneous but at the same time more inclusive.
5. External enforcement of the moral order is more impersonal and more bureaucratic. A full-time priesthood develops.
6. Nature and the cosmos are *somewhat* less personalized or humanized.
7. A moral order is used to impose the dictates of a ruling class upon a large subordinate majority.
8. "Militarism" develops.
9. Values are placed upon the central accumulation of capital and upon "the state."
10. Conditions for heterodoxy and for revolutionary changes in the moral order are created.
11. ". . . 'advanced' cultures are differently integrated than 'simple' cultures . . ." (Steward, 1955, p. 51; cf. pp. 51–63).
12. There arises a necessary (but not a sufficient) condition for the conception of a universal moral order that will embrace the most diverse people.

WORKS CITED

Breasted, J. H. 1934. The dawn of conscience. New York.

Childe, V. Gordon. 1941. War in prehistoric societies. Sociological review XXXIII 126–38.

———. 1951. Social evolution. London.

———. 1952. Social worlds of knowledge. *In* Hobhouse Memorial Lectures 1941–1950. Oxford.

Dodds, E. R. 1951. The Greeks and the irrational. Los Angeles.

Dodds, S. C. 1957. A power of town size predicts an internal interacting. Social forces XXXVI 132–37.

Goldschmidt, W. 1951. Ethics and the structure of society: An ethnological contribution to the sociology of knowledge. Amercian anthropologist LIII 506–24.

Kidder, A. V. 1940. Looking backward. American Philosophical Society. Proceedings LXXXIII 527–37.

[5] Cf. Redfield (1953; p. 15): "Each pre-civilized society was held together by largely undeclared but continually realized ethical conceptions."

Lee, D. 1954. Notes on the conception of the self among the Wintu Indians. Explorations III 49–58.

Lévi-Strauss, C. 1955. Tristes tropiques. Paris.

Muller, H. J. 1958. Human values in relation to evolution. Science CXXVII 625–29.

Naroll, R. 1956. A preliminary index of social development. American anthropologist LVIII 687–715.

Piers, Gerhart, and Singer, Milton. 1953. Shame and guilt. Springfield, Illinois.

Radin, Paul. 1927. Primitive man as philosopher. New York.

Redfield, Robert. 1953. The primitive world and its transformations. Ithaca, New York.

———. 1956. Peasant society and culture. Chicago.

———. 1957. The universally human and the culturally variable. Journal of general education X 150–60.

Redfield, Robert, and Singer, Milton. 1954. The cultural role of cities. Economic development and cultural change III 53–73.

Smith, Marian W. 1952. Different cultural concepts of past, present, and future. Psychiatry XV 395–400.

Snowden, F. M., Jr. 1948. The Negro in ancient Greece. American anthropologist L 31–44.

Steward, J. H. 1949. Cultural causality and law: A trial formulation of the development of early civilizations. American anthropologist LI 1–27.

———. 1950. Area research: Theory and practice. Social Science Research Council. Bulletin No. 63. New York.

———. 1955. Theory of culture change. Urbana, Illinois.

Steward, J. H., *et al.* 1955. Irrigation civilizations: A comparative study. Pan American Union. Social science monographs I. Washington, D.C.

Tumin, Melvin M. 1945. Culture, genuine and spurious: A re-evaluation. American sociological review X 199–207.

Wirth, Louis. 1940. The urban society and civilization. American journal of sociology XLV 743–55.

Wittfogel, K. A. 1957. Oriental despotism: A comparative study of total power. New Haven.

IX

Process and Change in the Cultural Spectrum Coincident with Expansion: Government and Law

By MAX RHEINSTEIN

The title of this paper contains the word "law," a word which can be used with a great many different meanings. The laws of Kepler, the law of supply and demand, the law of the New Covenant, the law of the United States of America, the traffic laws of Illinois—these phrases illustrate just some of the meanings with which the word "law" can be used. When in the present paper we speak of law and government, we mean by law neither some observed or postulated regularity of nature or social conduct, nor the ordainment of the deity, nor a command of ethics or social convention, but that body of norms of social conduct which have their sanction in some action of government.

Law, as used here, thus refers to a phenomenon which, like a poem, a symphony, or a philosophical system, has its existence as a content of the minds of a not inconsiderably small number of human beings, such as the idea that in the relations to other human beings one ought to behave in a certain way, or else! This "or else" is the expectation that against the violator of the norm some special officer of the government will go into action. Law, as understood here, and government are thus inseparably tied together. By very definition there can be no law without a government. Our problem is thus that of tracing the origin and development of government and of the law which is maintained and enforced by it.

In modern society we think of government as necessarily being the government of the state, and it is an essential characteristic of the state that it has the monopoly of both lawmaking and law enforcement. All other groups having lawmaking powers are regarded as having received such powers from the state. The ordinances of a city, the statutes of a club, the bylaws of a corporation, the collective agreement between a labor union and an employer are binding because, and in so far as, lawmaking power has been delegated by the state. A gang may have actual power to impose its rules upon its members or victims, but these rules are not law because no lawmaking power has been delegated to the gang by the state.

A rule of conduct, in order to be enforced as law, must originate either with one of the lawmaking organs of the state or with some group to which the state has delegated some limited lawmaking powers. What the lawmaking organs of the state are is determined by its constitution. Under the Constitution of the United States, for instance, the lawmaking organs are the Congress in co-operation with the President and those organs which the—necessarily—republican states may designate as their lawmaking organs in their constitutions. By virtue of unwritten constitutional law, limited lawmaking power also pertains to the courts, especially the Supreme Court of the United States and the supreme courts of the several states.

A constitution in this sense must be had by every state, even one of absolute despotism; there the constitution may consist of the one single rule that the will of the ruler is the law, provided that it has been pronounced in a certain way. However, the essential function of a constitution is that of making clear what norms of social conduct are law and are to be enforced as such.

In modern society the state holds the monopoly not only of lawmaking but also of law enforcement and of the legitimate use of violence. No one is allowed to take the law into his own hands and to enforce it by way of self-help. If the buyer does not pay the ten dollars which he owes the seller for goods bought and delivered, the latter is not allowed to hold up his debtor and take the money forcibly away from him. He must resort to the services of an officer of the government, the sheriff, who will not go into action, however, until he has been authorized to do so by a court. But if he meets resistance in his effort to enforce the court's judgment, the sheriff can call out a posse; on his request the governor will send the state militia, and upon the governor's request, the President will send into action the armed forces of the United States, all to enforce the ten-dollar claim which the creditor is not allowed to enforce by himself.

It is thus characteristic of modern society that (1) all law emanates from the state; (2) the law is enforced by the enforcement officers of the state; (3) the enforcement officers of the state will not go into action unless they have been authorized to do so by the state's adjudication officers; (4) the state's adjudication officers will not order an enforcement officer to go into action against an individual unless such action is authorized in the situation by the law; and (5) self-help is forbidden; the monopoly of the legitimate use of violence belongs to the government.

This state of affairs has not been of long standing. As a matter of fact, it constitutes a recent phase in the history of mankind. We have been assigned the task of tracing how it has come about. That task is so vast and complicated, however, that we can do no more than try to sketch some of the main lines of the earlier stages. If in this context we speak of development or growth, it ought to be understood that we are not thinking of a unilinear course of universal history but rather of a series of different "ideal types" of social structures as they can be found to have been connected with certain types of human association.

To that one end of the social scale at which we find the modern state as just defined we can contrast that other type in which there exists no state, no government, and no law. Nineteenth-century anarchists have held the belief that such a paradise might again be achieved by modern man, and Friedrich Engels hoped that in a communistic society the state would wither away. In historic reality, anarchy in the sense of an orderly society has existed only in small groups living in conditions of comparative isolation and showing no or little social stratification. It has not been limited, however, to such extremely primitive peoples as the Bushmen of Africa or to peoples living in such small isolated groups as the Eskimos. Primitive in the sense of being orderly without having a government or law have been societies not only of food-gatherers, hunters, or herdsmen but even of agricultural groups in which division of labor and social stratification have been developed to a certain extent. Examples are presented by the Trobriand Islanders, where a fairly well-functioning system of exchange exists between the fishermen of the coast and the tapioca-growers of the interior, or the rice-growing Ifugaos and Kalingas of Luzon, where a refined system of property in both land and chattels has been maintained without law and government even in the face of considerable differences of individual wealth. But in such societies peace and order are precarious. They constitute rare limiting examples of a type of social organization which has generally not survived the stage of comparatively unstratified, simple, and isolated small group existence; an additional condition of such primitive anarchy is the absence of conditions requiring rapid change. Society can dispense with government and law as long as continuity of conduct patterns is guaranteed by habit and tradition, based upon or strengthened by tabu notions of a magical-religious character. Primitive man is certainly not the blind slave of unchanging habituation as he was imagined to be by Lévy-Bruhl. Malinowski is right in maintaining that primitive man, too, is tempted to break the customary patterns but is kept in line by the comparative rareness of such temptations, by the recognition of his self-interest in observing the patterns, especially where they result in mutually beneficial "relations of reciprocity," by the effective sanction of unorganized but effectively dispersed disapproval as well as by the fear of supernatural sanctions.

These forces can suffice to hold a society together for a long time, but they are insufficient when a society finds itself confronted with major tasks which require the long-term, disciplined, and organized co-operation of large groups. Such tasks are typically induced by war, especially where it results in conquest and the desire to establish a lasting domination of the conquering group over the conquered. The view that all government has universally and exclusively had its root in war and conquest probably constitutes an exaggeration. Perhaps government has also arisen out of conditions requiring such large-scale common enterprises as flood control, irrigation, or organized worship and ritual. It certainly has occasionally had its origin in necessities of defense; situations of the latter kind have actually been observed. As to the rest, we are limited to speculation and conjecture.

We should not assume, however, that where government arose, it originated all at once and as a fully grown institution. In history and ethnology numerous cases have been observed in which some rudimentary form of government operates for limited periods and disappears with the termination of the need. We are told by Tacitus of the *dux* to whose rule a Germanic tribe would submit for the duration of a war but not in times of peace. Analogy is furnished by certain tribes of Plains Indians, such as the Cheyennes and the Commanche, where the clubs of the young men, the so-called "soldiers' societies," exercised certain "official" police functions to maintain the discipline of the buffalo hunt, the success of which would be endangered by the untimely action of some single hunter. Intermittent government could also be found among Central Asiatic tribes, who submitted to the rule of elders when the herds were in the winter pasture but not when they were in the summer pastures.

To speak of government, even rudimentary, makes little sense unless the social unit in question is larger than a single kinship group. Within the kinship group there is always some authority by which order is maintained. The problem of government does not arise until several kinship groups live together in that major unit for which the term "tribe" is customary.

No organized government is needed to deal with those dangers which arise to the social group through the antisocial acts of individual group members. Against such acts the group members react spontaneously and personally rather than through a specially organized staff. The dangerous or obnoxious individual is beaten up, ridiculed, ostracized, banished, or killed. The reaction of the group may be entirely spontaneous and unorganized, or it may be formalized and carried out as a solemn rite, secular, magic, or religious. However, the scope of acts to which the group thus reacts as a group is limited. It typically comprises acts which, by provoking the wrath of the deity or the working of other supernatural forces, endanger the existence of the group, such as sorcery, sacrilege, or breach of tabus, especially of important sex tabus. Other acts to which the group reacts as a group are treason and cowardice. Finally, the group may try to rid itself of an individual who endangers its existence through a permanent conduct of general obnoxiousness. Group reaction seems hardly ever to occur at this stage in the case of what may be called private wrong, that is, injury inflicted upon an individual, his honor, his property, his body, his health, or his life. Not even murder appears as an affair in which the community as such is interested. Revenge for personal injury is left to the individual and his kinship group. Of course, where a wrong is inflicted upon a person by another member of his own kinship group, some group reaction is likely to take place. But where a wrong is wrought upon a member of one kinship group by a member of another, the major unit, usually called the tribe, does not react as such. The injured himself or, almost universally, his kinship group takes on the task of avenging the wrong on the wrongdoer or some other member of his kinship group. Private wrong thus becomes the source of a feud between two "sibs," in which the first act of revenge provokes counterrevenge, and so on in a theoretically interminable sequence. Although the very existence of the larger unit, the tribe, may be endangered by such feuds within its midst, the elimination of the feud and the substitution of a peaceful system of adjudication has been a process of painfully long duration, even when government has arisen and grown beyond its first rudimentary stage.

The "taming" of the feud has occurred along two main lines. Ethnology knows of many instances of formalization and ritualization of quarrel and feud. The combat may be concentrated upon the original parties or their champions, who may be limited to certain weapons to be used in certain strictly limited ways; or the combat of arms may be replaced by some form of ordeal or of formalized verbal encounter, as, for instance, among the Eskimos, whose harsh environment does not allow to man the luxury of a fight for life.

The other, historically more important, line is that of the slow elimination of the feud and its replacement by governmental adjudication. The main stages in this complicated development appear, as ideal types, to be voluntary agreement, mediation, arbitration, compulsion to submit to adjudication, and adjudication by default proceedings.

The possibility of a feud being terminated, or perhaps even nipped in the bud, by agreement between the two groups concerned appears to have been as universal as the feud itself, and equally universal seems to have been the possibility that revenge can be prevented or terminated through the payment of a typically determined sum of money or money's worth, the "wergild." Not everywhere have the wergild schedules been so detailed and elaborate as in the folk laws of the Germanic tribes, but some form of wergild schedule can be found in civilizations as remote from one another as those of the Celtic tribes of Ireland, the Kalingas of Luzon, the African Bantus, the American Indians, and the Slavs of the Russkaya Pravda. Typically the amount of the wergild varies with the social standing of the person murdered or injured, typically it is paid not just by the wrongdoer but by his kinship group and received not by the person injured but by his kinship group, and typically the contributions of each member of the payor group and the share of each member of the payee group are determined by fixed scales. Typically, although not universally, we find that the payment of wergild may be averted by *noxae datio,* that is, the physical surrender of the wrongdoer. The tenacity with which social institutions may survive long beyond the periods in which they fulfill an actual need is evidenced by the fact that *noxae datio* remained an institution of Roman law not only through all stages of the Roman Empire but even into the modern Roman-Dutch law of Ceylon.

Where no government has as yet emerged, the community's interest in preventing or terminating a feud through such a treaty of compensation cannot be made effective except through the mediation of a go-between or, as a next step, by inducing the contestants to submit to the arbitration of elders, priests, or other persons enjoying personal or charismatic authority. Such a state of affairs has been widely regarded to be depicted in the famous "court" scene of the shield of Achilles; it seems to have existed in prehistoric Rome, and it played a vast role in the Dark Ages of Europe. In the primitive form of the institutionalized go-between it survived into the twentieth century even among a people of an agricultural economy so well developed as that of certain rice-growing tribes in the Philippines.

Roman law of the early republic illustrates a stage of development which seems to have existed in early Greece also and which may be typical of government which has grown to sufficient strength to suppress the feud but has not yet developed the technical means effectively to enforce the law on behalf of the individual citizen. At this stage it is still left to the person injured, or, more precisely, to the head of the house of the person injured, to seize the debtor or adversary and to take vengeance on him or, at a somewhat later time, to seek to obtain payment through the sale of the debtor into slavery or, still later, by the seizure of his property. But, before he is allowed to take such measures, the creditor must obtain the permission of the community as represented, in Rome, by the praetor and judex. It is equally characteristic of this stage of the so-called procedure *per legis actionem* that, in order to obtain such adjudication, the plaintiff must personally seize the defendant without being aided by any public official. Our scanty knowledge of this early phase of Roman procedure seems to indicate that at one stage the public official had not to be invoked unless, after the alleged debtor's seizure, official proceedings for his liberation were set into motion by some relative or friend and that it was only at a second stage that the captor had under all circumstances to justify the arrest before the praetor. Of the causes of this fateful emergence of governmental control of self-help we have no direct knowledge. If it is correct that Rome and other city-states of antiquity grew up by way of συνοικισμός of several kinship or neighborhood groups (gentes, tribes), the procedure *per legis actionem* appears as the product of a situation in which, perhaps under the pressure of needs of defense, it was necessary for the "federal" authority to assert its pacifying power over the member groups. In the sequence of Roman procedure from *legis actio,* through the "formulary procedure" of the late Republic and the classical age and the *cognito extraordinaria* of the dominate, to the bureaucratic procedure of the Byzantine state we can follow step by step the development from government-controlled self-help to the fully grown monopoly of law enforcement through a government enjoying the full monopoly of the legitimate use of violence. Clearly this development is connected with the expansion of the Roman state, the needs of its economy, the growing power and centralism of its government, and the development by it of the necessary technical machinery; but, strangely enough, no systematic effort has so far been made to investigate these relationships in detail.

In Mesopotamia the stage of development which Rome took so many centuries to complete seems to have been reached much earlier. Governmental adjudication of disputes and governmental prosecution of crime seem to have existed as early as the period of the city-states. Of a murder trial by public authority we have evidence from the eighteenth century b.c. Perhaps this fact finds its explanation in some peculiar circumstance of the case, such as the possible connection of the murder with the violation of a sex tabu. But if murder as such was tried by a public tribunal, the comparative material from other civilizations indicates that there must already have been a long procedural development which can have taken place only in a fairly complex civilization.

In the Roman world, the full development of the Empire signified not only the absence of war between its several parts but also the presence of a well-functioning administration of justice. Crimes of all kinds were prosecuted and punished by the state. In civil litigation it was no longer necessary for the plaintiff to seize the defendant and drag him into court. Following a stage in which the defendant was compelled to appear by the threat of governmental seizure of his property, there was at long last invented that most effective as well as simple method of proceeding against a recalcitrant or absent defendant, viz., that of accepting as true the allegations of the plaintiff and rendering judgment by default against the nonappearing defendant. That it took such a long time before this simple invention was made, so that no proceedings were possible without the co-operation of the defendant, is widely regarded as a survival from that earlier stage in which the nonviolent settlement of a dispute had been possible only through "voluntary" agreement of composition or submission to arbitration.

At least in the West, the fully developed system of adjudication collapsed together with the collapse of the Roman Empire. For the vigorous prosecution of crime and the enforcement of private rights the governments of the Germanic states were both too weak and too inefficient. They had neither the power nor the technical means necessary for an effective administration of justice. Under such strong rulers as Charlemagne, public safety and governmental protection of private rights improved temporarily, but the general state of affairs is characterized by Bishop Hincmar's letter to Charles the Bald in which he complains that the king not only would do nothing to stop private violence but also declared that he regarded such efforts as lying outside the sphere of regal duty. Government had withdrawn to the selfish enjoyment of whatever emoluments weak power might yield. In order to be protected against crime and the depredations of the Norsemen and other organized bands of pirates and robbers, the humble man had to "commend" himself and his land to the protection of some local potentate, secular or ecclesiastical, and for the settlement of the disputes arising among these potentates resort had to be had to the feud, which again became a recognized institution.

Efforts to eliminate the feud and again to substitute for it methods of nonviolent settlement occurred all through the Middle Ages and strikingly resembled the efforts of our age to replace war by nonviolent methods of settling international disputes. The efforts moved along three different paths: the truce of God, the nonaggression pact, and the king's peace. Under the patronage of the Church, efforts were made to stop fighting at least on the Lord's day and in the Lord's house. Extension of the truce was gradually sought as to both time and place; feuds were to cease from Friday morning to Monday night, during the Easter and Christmas seasons, in the Church yard, and in the vicinity of shrines and were to spare priests, ecclesiastics, pilgrims or even, more generally, orphans, widows, and other persons supposed to be protected by the Church. These attempts to limit the feud and its results were to some extent effective as long as they originated in locally limited compacts or resolutions of local ecclesiastical councils. When it was sought to expand the command of the truce of God into a general command of the Papacy, it remained a dead letter. A thirteenth-century glossator of the *Corpus Juris Canonici* tells us, almost in the fashion of a modern sociologist, that that truce was ineffective because "it was not in accordance with the mores of those to which it was meant to apply."[1]

Of no lasting effect either were the numerous nonaggression and arbitration pacts which were concluded among local princes and communities, especially in Germany. Only two of them were of such duration that they ultimately matured, after many vicissitudes, into modern states with fully developed governmental administration of justice: the Swiss Confederacy and the United Netherlands. Generally, however, the elimination of private self-help and the feud and the consequent establishment of a permanent regime of law and order were in each nation the work of the king, who, by imposing his peace, compelled his subjects, including the great of his realm, to seek justice in the orderly peaceful ways of the royal court. That process, too, was long and tortuous, however. It began with modest claims of the king that there be preserved the peace of his palace and his men; it was extended to the king's highway and the peace of those whom the king, for good and valuable consideration, placed under his protection, for instance Jews. That even the general peace of the king long remained to be regarded as an exception rather than the normal state of affairs is shown by the fact that even in England, where, through the conquest, the kings succeeded earliest in their pacifying efforts, the king's peace died with every king's death and was not revived until it had been specially proclaimed again by the new ruler. It was not until 1272 that the king's peace became so institutionalized that it was recognized to obtain even during the interval between the old king's death and the new king's coronation. Generally it can be said that in no nation did even the king's government fully succeed in substituting the rule of law for that of self-help and violence until there had been established within such nation not only functioning systems of criminal and civil justice but also machinery to bring about the peaceful change of existing rights through legislation and, above all, the possibility of peacefully changing existing positions of economic power through the interplay of competition and the free market.

The attempt of our present age in the international sphere to replace the rule of force by that of law resembles in many respects the

1 *Glossa ord. in decret. Greg.* IX 1 I, tit. 34: "Sed quod dicit hic hodie non tenet; et episcopi non servant hanc constitutionem, non discuntur transgressus, quia non fuit moribus intentium approbata huius modi treuga" (Bernhard of Parma).

attempts to replace, within each nation, the violence of the feud by the orderly processes of law. At present we have hardly reached beyond the stage of voluntary submission to arbitration, and of inducing the "voluntary" abandonment of power positions tending to become obsolete, by more or less gracefully yielding to the diffuse pressure of public opinion or the fear of force. International law still is law not in the full sense in which it has been defined above but in the sense of that mixture of tradition, morals, diffuse public pressure, and rudimentary government which has been characteristic of the transition from primitive society to the archaic state.

How difficult it is to establish a system of complete and exclusive governmental enforcement of law can be observed in those new nations which have recently been emancipated from colonial rule. Not all of them have so far been able to maintain by their own means those efficient and incorruptible systems of administration of justice which had been established by the former colonial masters. The maintenance of the Pax Britannica, Batavica, etc. requires tradition, skills, and political conditions which have not yet been fully developed in all of the new nations.

Even in modern society not all norms of social behavior need or can be enforced as norms of law. We have to decide not only what human activities shall be left free in the sense of being completely unregulated by any social norms, but among those which are felt to require regulation a choice has to be made between those which shall be regulated by the norm systems of religion, ethics, and social convention and those in which the sanction of these norm systems shall be supplemented or fortified by that of the law, that is, governmental coercion. One kind of norms is by its very nature excluded from the possibility of legal enforcement, viz., those which are to regulate the very activities of the highest law-enforcement officers of the community. The institutionalized safeguards of a system of constitutional checks and balances may greatly help to "watch the watchmen," but the ultimate guarantee of law observance can be found only in the restraining forces of tradition, ethics, and religion. For the rest no sphere of human activity is by nature excluded from legal regulation. Even man's thoughts are "free" only in so far as they find no outward expression. What spheres are actually made the subject matter of legal regulation depends upon both the ideals and the technical enforcement devices of any given society and, consequently, upon its size and its state of culture. The mass nations of the machine age obviously must and can subject to legal regulation more areas of human activity than the small groups of a primitive society or a large empire of antiquity. The need for regulation through law also increases in the measure in which the pressures of family, neighborhood, peer group, or religion decrease. The loosening of the hold of religion, which was concomitant with the rise of religious toleration in the Roman Empire as well as in the modern world, would not have been possible without the simultaneous growth of the scope and intensity of governmental regulation. The latter development in turn had to intensify a problem which was bound to arise with the very first advent of government, viz., that of taming the leviathan into which government had to grow in order to fulfill its task of eliminating private violence and enforcing peace and order among the subjects. Abuse of governmental power by a despotic monarch or ruling group was horrible enough even when it was mitigated by inefficiency or escapable by emigration. With the growth of the size of the nations and the increase of governmental efficiency, abuse of the law has come to be insufferable. Doctrines of fundamental rights and institutional safeguards for their protecion against government had thus to be elaborated, but the ultimate guarantee cannot lie in the law itself.

With the growing expansion of the groups in which human existence takes place and the growing complexity and intensity of social life, the scope of legal regulation had thus to expand. However, this expansion of law and government has not always been felt by the individual. As a matter of fact, the direct relation between the national government and the individual, which was postulated by the French Revolution, has long been the exception rather than the rule. In the empires of antiquity as well as in western Europe far into our own days, not to speak of the Orient, the individual has lived in his "little community," whose life has been intensely regulated by custom, convention, and religion and into which the government and its law have intruded only in exceptional situations. Normally, the government has concerned itself only with the affairs of the great of the realm. With the expansion and growing complexity of modern life, the sphere of immediate contacts between the government and the little man had to expand. The measures in which the government has succeeded in directing toward itself the emotional ties between the individual and his little community have to a large extent been decisive for the greater or lesser success of democratic government in a nation.

The fact that an ever growing complex of human activity has had to be subjected to regulation by law, that is, governmental compulsion, by no means implies that all law is also the creation of government. The social norm to the enforcement of which the government lends its power may have its source in custom, in religious beliefs, or in ethical conviction. The notion that new norms of social conduct might be created by governmental command has not appeared until government has achieved a position of overwhelming importance. In the Orient, both ancient and more recent, as well as in medieval Europe, the government, where it attempted at all to issue norms of its own, had mostly to disguise them as revelations of the deity, or as restatement of ancient custom, or as the compact of those affected. The notion that valid norms of conduct might be established by way of legislation was peculiar to later stages of Greek and Roman history; in western Europe it was dormant until the rediscovery of Roman law and the rise of the absolute monarchy. The proposition that all law is the command of the sovereign is a postulate engendered by the democratic ideology of the French Revolution that all law had to emanate from the duly elected representatives of the people. It is not, however, a true description of reality, least of all in the countries of the Anglo-American Common Law. But it is true, on the other hand, that in the expanding and complex society of modern nations, many more of the government-enforced norms of social conduct are also government-created than in any earlier, smaller, and less complex society.

In accordance with the theme of the symposium, this paper has been concerned with the interrelations between the numerical and spatial expansion of societies on the one side and the growth and development of law on the other. But more important in relation to the need for law and its development may be a factor other than mere societal expansion, viz., societal diversification. Culture consists in the harmonic interaction of modes ("categories"; cf. Gehlen, *Urmensch und Spaetkultur*) of human existence. In a society of just one mode of existence, integration is achieved without law. The need for law arises with the need of correlating in one society different modes of human existence, and that need grows with growing complexity. Where there is acceptable just one mode of human attitude

417

toward the supernatural, law is less needed than in a society where there is an attempt to achieve the coexistence of several such modes. In isolated South Sea societies, such as that of Samoa, law seems to have arisen in connection with mere internal diversification and without expansion. In so far as expansion of a society has influenced the rise and growth of law, it seems to have done so more indirectly through the concomitant need to correlate diverse modes of existence than through the sheer growth of number and space.

BIBLIOGRAPHY

Barton, R. F. Ifugao law. 1914.

———. The Kalingas. 1944.

Gehlen, Arnold. Urmensch und Spaetkultur. 1956.

Hoebel, E. Adamson. The law of primitive man. 1954.

Kluckhohn, August. Geschichte des Gottesfriedens. 1857.

Llewellyn, Karl N., and Hoebel, E. Adamson. The Cheyenne way. 1941.

Lowie, R. H. The origin of the state. 1927.

Malinowski, Bronislaw. Crime and custom in savage society. 1926.

Mims, Helen. The master artifice. Unpublished manuscript.

Quidde, Ludwig. Histoire de la paix publique en Allemagne au moyen âge. Recueil des cours de l'Académie de droit international XXVIII 449. 1929.

Radcliffe-Brown, A. R. Law, primitive. Encyclopaedia of the social sciences IX 202. 1933.

Redfield, Robert. Primitive law. Unpublished manuscript.

Seagle, William. The history of law. 1946.

Thurnwald, Richard. Die menschliche Gesellschaft. IV. Werden, Wandel und Gestaltung von Staat und Kultur. V. Werden, Wandel und Gestaltung des Rechts. 1935 *and* 1934.

Weber, Max. Law in economy and society. Translated by Rheinstein and Shils. 1954.

Wenger, Leopold. Institutes of the Roman law of civil procedure. Translated by Fisk. 1940.

X

Culture and Art

By OTTO G. VON SIMSON

The following inquiry into the interaction between culture and art is limited to Western civilization—classical, medieval, and modern.

Art, Style, Culture, World View

It will be useful at the outset to define the key terms used in this paper. *Culture* is taken to mean the total life pattern of a community, this pattern being understood (by the community itself as by the outside observer) as the significant expression of distinct beliefs or ideas. A work of *art* we shall call an artifact the form of which is not primarily determined by considerations of usefulness or efficiency. A utensil may be beautiful. If we study the evolution of a hammer or a bathtub over a period of time (as Gideon has done) we may discover a development toward maximum efficiency, and we may consider the end product of such "streamlining" beautiful. But such beauty does not make a hammer or a bathtub a work of art any more than a work of art ceases to be a work of art by not being beautiful.

The hallmark of a work of art is that it possesses *style*. Style is the shape that an artist imposes on his handiwork under the guidance of a compelling inner experience. The shape of a utensil is determined by the outside world, with the laws of which it will have to cope. But the shape of an art work—its style—subjects the outside world to man's inner vision. (Of course an artifact may be both a utensil and a work of art, and its maker may be both craftsman and artist. We shall identify and appraise such a work according as the esthetic or the functional aspects prevail. A purely "functional art work," however, is a contradiction in terms.)

But our definition of style is as yet incomplete. Neither style nor the inner vision which shapes it is the exclusive property of one creative individual. "All art is a collaboration." Style transcends personality; it is to a large extent anonymous and collective. Even the Sistine ceiling, by so marked an artistic personality as Michelangelo, is "early sixteenth century"; Phidias' Parthenon pediments are "about 440 B.C." These dates convey not chronological accidents of origin but significant characteristics of the cultures that produced them. We are increasingly accustomed to use the same term to identify an artistic style and an entire culture.

The reason for this remarkable fact is that in esthetically comprehending the style of an art work we also grasp intuitively the character or spirit of the culture that produced it. Herein lies again a profound difference between the works of the craftsman and the artist. True, the work of the first, inasmuch as it is the product of the skills, tools, and materials employed by its maker, may tell us much about his knowledge and the material circumstances of his life. But the work of art is not primarily a product of these factors. "Art," Lethaby wrote, "is man's thought expressed in his handiwork." Hence art is transparent as regards the realm of ideas, whereas the tool is opaque. We may call even a door hinge "Gothic" and a goblet "baroque" when we sense that they are works of art, because their styles reflect, like monadic mirrors, the essence or spirit or *world view* of Gothic or baroque culture. None of these terms is very useful. The alternative for "world view" proposed by Heidegger, "man's attitude in the midst of the existent," would be preferable were it less unwieldy. The vagueness of terminology reflects inadequacy of knowledge. We know neither the exact nature nor the origin of world views or existential attitudes, nor their relationship to the different aspects of a given culture. But we can say this much: as form, in scholastic terminology, is real only when individuated in matter, so world view can be grasped only when manifested in any aspect of culture. World view, moreover, is a universal in the sense that it comprehends all these aspects, enabling us to grasp the common character of which everyone of them partakes.

World view and style are intimately related. Style, too, may be called a universal. It has no existence apart from the art works in which it appears, but it does provide the ordering principle and common pattern for artistic creations of every conceivable variety and enables us to recognize them as cultural blood brothers. Style is linked to world view not by such an analogy only; it is the expression or, shorter still, an image of the world. There can be no style without a world view, but there is perhaps also no world view without its visual image in the style of art. At least we would probably be unable to identify world views were it not for the great artistic styles that are the clearest and in many instances the only timelessly meaningful and immediately understandable expression that a culture may leave behind. Nevertheless, the importance and function of art within a given culture will vary widely according to the basic character of the world view.

The Poetic Instinct and the Importance and Function of Art

If we seek to understand the function of art within a given culture, we must first of all consider the role of the poetic instinct within that culture. The poetic instinct interprets physical as well as metaphysical reality by lending them the sentiments and motivations of man, not unlike a child that approaches even inanimate objects as if they were living persons. The poetic instinct is probably present in all cultures and in all individuals, but in neither of them is it always equally powerful. In the so-called primitive cultures the poetic instinct colors all thought processes and decisively shapes the world view itself. Vico was the first to suggest that in the "childlike" early cultures all men were "poets by nature" and that such cultures possessed not only a "poetic" theology and metaphysics, but a "poetic" jurisprudence, a "poetic" economy, a "poetic" politics, etc., because in those cultures all institutions and customs were defined in terms of poetic imagery.

The poetic world view not only lends itself with particular ease to expression in art but it requires such expression. It will allow no work produced by human hands to remain untouched by the poetic instinct. Even utensils will tend to be works of art, and the anthropomorphic and zoömorphic shapes given to tools or architectural details in such cultures should probably be understood less as ornaments than as interpretations of what to us are abstract physical laws as animated and straining forces.

In cultures of this type art will naturally be of the greatest public importance. The answers to man's ultimate questions being defined in terms of image and symbol, theology itself will require art to convey its insights. In this sense it is quite right to say that the temple is the cradle of art. In the early "poetic" cultures, moreover, the state itself left to art the definition of the meaning, source, and functioning of political authority. Significant vestiges of this survived for a long time. In the Roman Empire the most curious example, perhaps, was the juridical significance of the emperor's portrait. The emperor was the source of all law. No legal act was valid without his authority. To implement this fact Roman statute required that the image of the emperor be placed wherever the law was administered because, as one contemporary put it, the emperor cannot be present in all his cities at the same time. In other words, because the abstract legal concept was, as it were, unable to exist apart from its human embodiment, the emperor's portrait was required to give it reality. Far more than a mere symbol of authority, the emperor's portrait derived its significance from the primitive identification of a living person with its image.

The public function of art is limited to cultures with an essentially poetic world view. And such a world view does not survive the gradual increase of empirical knowledge and reason. As soon as it is realized that the poetic image, the myth, is not reality and cannot convey it, the character and function of art will undergo a profound change. As theologians and metaphysicians insist that art is a lie if measured against reality, art will either be banished altogether from the realm of supreme truth (as Plato postulated and Jews, Muslims, Iconoclasts carried into effect) or tolerated only as a means of visual instruction, a kind of pictorial primer for unilluminated minds. This was the situation during the Western Middle Ages. While it allowed much scope for the arts, it also accounts for the illustrative rather than expressive character of so much medieval art, for the often crude, repetitious, uninspired storytelling (which the great masterpieces of the period must not make us overlook), and, on the other hand, for a play of decorative fancy that often runs wild, as if unhinged from the meaning of the events told. We do not encounter this disparity between the sacred event and the mode of its representation in Byzantine art when Iconoclasm had been defeated.

Farther still along the road of enlightenment, the "discovery of the world" of the Renaissance led to the "discovery of man" by making him aware of the mind's power to recreate God's creation. This experience assigned to art a task hardly less exalted than its earlier one; instead of the supernatural world it now conveyed the natural one. And the central perspective (Panofsky has shown its symbolic significance) recreated God's Universe as the vision of one individual upon whose "point of view" the whole picture depended. Although objective truth and subjective experience still converge in Renaissance art, we are never made to forget that its creations are the products of one individual mind and vision. In subsequent centuries the increasing knowledge of the empirical world bred an increasing skepticism with regard to man's ability to know truth. "The new philosophy calls all in doubt," as it seemed to Donne, while Calderon described life as a dream. The emerging world view was immediately mirrored in art. The art of the seventeenth and eighteenth centuries is an art of illusion, just as is the art of the other skeptical age, that of Lucretius. The robust empiricism with which the baroque still life, landscape, or portrait renders optical phenomena creates illusions of sensuous reality, while the theatrical handling of religious themes in the baroque altarpiece treats all sensuous reality as illusion. But in Rembrandt, the greatest painter of the time, the supernatural seems to be entirely absorbed into the inner experience of man; art begins to be personal confession.

Within our own contemporary culture the place and function of art are defined by three remarkable facts, all unprecedented in the history of civilization: the simultaneous presence before our eyes and minds of the artistic creations of all cultures and epochs, the institution of the museum, and the trend of contemporary art toward the "abstract" or "nonobjective."

The three facts are closely connected. Their common denominator is the emergence into our awareness of the "esthetic" as an independent category of experience. The philosophic discipline of "esthetics" that defined this experience and isolated it from others was established only toward the end of the eighteenth century, at the very time when the first museums in the modern sense were founded. The coincidence is significant, for in these museums we confront sculptures and paintings cut off from the cultural, symbolic, and social context within which and for which they were originally created; and only in their new isolation, as museum pieces, have these works become objects of esthetic appreciation. Only a strange metamorphosis deeply significant for our time and brilliantly described by André Malraux has transformed the statue of a Greek god into a sculpture or made a medieval virgin reveal pictorial *valeurs* of which its painter was as unconscious as Molière's *Bourgeois Gentilhomme* was of his ability to talk prose.

Not that these esthetic values do not exist or that they are unimportant. But those who created the statue or image were concerned with values other than esthetic. So were those who contemplated these works. Their languages did not even know the terms "artist" or "work of art." Worshiping in a Gothic cathedral or paying homage to the statue of a god, medieval or ancient man would have been un-

423

able to distinguish religious and esthetic experience. Even such high-ly formalized works as an Archaic Kouros or a Byzantine mosaic are described by contemporary sources as though they were alike. Today, when assessing a work of art, the connoisseur tends to ignore its sub-ject matter. When we contrast this attitude with that of the earlier civilizations we become aware of something that is very characteristic for our own cultural situation.

What this is becomes apparent when we look at contemporary art. We notice, first of all, the restriction of its scope. The poetic world view left its imprint on nearly every artifact, even upon the tool and utensil. There was hardly a distinction between artist and craftsman. Jörg Syrlin, the master of the prophets and sibyls of the stalls of Ulm Cathedral, was not only a great sculptor but also a great cabinet-maker. In our own civilization we observe the opposite process: the sphere of art contracts while the world of the tool—as I have defined it above—seems to encroach upon the realm of art. The designs of applied art follow the same functional principles as do those of the worker's utensil. Few of us have much use for, or understanding of, the decorative. We prefer the design of our furniture or table silver to bespeak that adaptation to the laws of maximum efficiency that we admire in the design of an engine. Le Corbusier demanded at one time that even the house be considered a "machine for living."

Art, on the other hand, appears isolated and idle. Its domain is no longer in the center of civic life—temple or palace. Commercial art and the pictorial propaganda of the totalitarian regimes only prove how difficult it has become for art to speak a common idiom without losing its true character. The proper dwelling place of contemporary art is the museum or private collection, sanctuaries remote from our daily preoccupations. Artistic insight is experienced as unrelated to, or meaningless in, other realms of existence. That is the meaning of *l'art pour l'art.*

In its new idleness and isolation art has become self-conscious. That, I think, is the explanation for the general trend toward the "abstract" or "nonobjective." The creative process represented in paintings or sculptures of this kind has deliberately distilled from objects only values that are specifically painterly or sculpturesque—values, it is hardly necessary to add, that reveal themselves to esthetic experience only.

How are the isolation, the idleness, the self-consciousness of contemporary art related to our civilization and world view? Meyer Schapiro has recently suggested that contemporary art may have to be understood as a revolt against the mechanical and scientific view of the universe and that the fancies and extravagances of modern sculpture and painting (that contrast so sharply with the prevailing "functionalism" of architecture and industrial design) may be a last, unquenchable stirring of poetic freedom in a world increasingly dominated by mechanical rule and predictability. I think it is an even deeper conflict that is mirrored in contemporary art.

The poetic and the modern world views are opposites. Poetic insight that determines the first cannot be harmonized with the mathematical definition of truth that, under the impact of science, we have come to demand in nearly all realms of knowledge. Yet science can never explain the meaning of human existence nor silence the poetic instinct. As a result, a chasm has opened between two spheres of our experience that is as keenly felt by the artist as it is by the scientist. The artistic situation of our time is the result and reflection of this chasm. Nietzsche's polemical answer to the positivists that facts are precisely what we do *not* know, that all is interpretation, not only coincides with the artistic revolt against naturalism but heralds the endeavor of art to the present day.

This interpretation, however, which the artist and poet give of reality, knows itself to be unverifiable, valid only within its own restricted realm—a lie (to quote Nietzsche once more). How significant that art has relinquished the representation of the natural world after relinquishing that of the supernatural one. A modern landscape, a still life, and even a portrait are not primarily likenesses of their models; these have been used merely as raw materials from which the artist has shaped his peculiar vision. One is reminded of Schiller's demand that the true artist "annihilate" his subject matter. If modern art is "unintelligible," that is precisely its message and meaning. The "abstract" painting brings us up hard against the fact that the umbilical cord has been severed between what we acknowledge as objective truth and what we perceive by subjective experience. To sum up: The subject of contemporary art, the cause of its isolation, idleness, and self-consciousness, is the chasm that in our world view has come to divide the universe around us from the universe within.

Single Aspects of Culture in Their Impact
  upon the Shaping of Styles

That I have so far focused attention upon the interaction between world views and styles hardly requires explanation. Style is the most significant aspect of a work of art, for the student of cultures no less than for the student of art. Style is also, as we have seen, the sensitive response to cultural changes that occur in the realm of ideas. We must, on the other hand, understand the world view if we seek to appraise any of the distinct aspects of culture—such as art or legal institutions or science—because the world view is their common foil or their common framework. As I have said, we do not know how world views come into existence; we cannot even know whether it is the world view that conditions or shapes the specific structure of the law or the political thought or the literature of a given culture or whether, conversely, it is the sum of these aspects that produces the world view. As we have seen, no doubt appears possible so far as the causal impact of world view upon artistic style is concerned. But this may not be equally true for other aspects of culture. However, we can probably agree to the propositions that different facets of a cultural prism appear related to one another by morphological affinity and that it is precisely this affinity that enables us to comprehend the otherwise exceedingly complex patterns of social life as wholes, as *gestalten*, in short, as cultures. The question as to what causes these affinities lies beyond the scope of a paper dealing with one single aspect of culture.

Here, the concept of world view has to be introduced once more, but merely as the "universal," according to our earlier definition, of which the separate manifestations of a culture partake. So understood, the term is useful and even indispensable as we set out to consider the impact of single aspects of culture upon the shaping of styles. The assumption of world views will help explain the cohesiveness, the close interdependence of the different elements within a cultural pattern, a cohesiveness which precludes the true understanding of any individual element if it is neatly isolated from the others. The notion of the world view moreover will guard us against any rash attempt to identify one cultural aspect as the cause of another. For we can rarely be sure whether connections observed between any two aspects disclose a relationship of cause and effect or whether such connections do not result merely from the fact that both aspects partake of the same ideational climate that we call world view.

Let us consider one example, Byzantine art. Today no one will seriously doubt that it cannot be fully understood by an approach that considers the development of art forms unrelated to the historical life of Byzantium. It is equally clear that we cannot understand Byzantine art as the product of one single aspect of Byzantine culture. The sociological approach will point to the rigid state-imposed organization of artists and artisans in the Byzantine Empire as a likely cause of the curious uniformity characteristic of Byzantine art. But this interpretation is incomplete. Were not both the style and the regimentation of those producing it called into existence by the public function of Byzantine art? That art was autocratic in message and purely intellectual in inspiration. Its concern was to formulate the esoteric insights of religious doctrine with the precision required by the political significance of orthodoxy in the Byzantine Empire and with the clarity demanded by the desire to make that doctrine intelligible to everyone. Obviously, such subjects have to be carefully fixed by theologians and their artistic execution must be commandeered by the organs of administrative power, a mode of production that allows very little room for the creative impulse of the individual artist. But even this explanation seems insufficient. We might step back even farther, taking a more comprehensive view, and argue that all aspects of Byzantine culture reflect upon one another since behind them all stands the theocentric Byzantine world view.

None of the following examples of the influence exerted by individual aspects of culture upon the style of art—nor, I think, any other examples that could be adduced—will adequately explain how artistic styles come into existence. In fact, my examples might have been chosen to prove just the opposite. But taken together they attest the rich complexity of influences which all the aspects of culture exert upon one another, in this case upon art.

The Impact of Ideas

We must be careful to distinguish ideas from world views or existential attitudes. Ideas are more precise and more rational, though they may often be so closely connected with world views that it is difficult to tell them apart. In such cases ideas are definitions of world views, just as myths are poetic expressions of world views.

427

No doubt, ideas have consequences for the life of art. They may decisively affect the evolution of styles; they may be the most plausible cause of sudden stylistic change. Consider, for example, the astonishing artistic revolution which occurred at the end of the classical age. Until two or three generations ago, it was customary, in the wake of Gibbon's *Decline and Fall,* for us to write this revolution off as the "barbarization" of Greco-Roman art without worrying too much about either the exact cause and nature of the phenomenon observed or the usefulness and historical validity of the criteria used for its description. Subsequently (and under the influence of such contemporary art movements as impressionism and expressionism) art historians arrived at a much more positive evaluation of subantique art. Again, the criteria used were esthetically rather than historically meaningful. Today scholarship inclines toward viewing that artistic revolution as closely tied up with a profound transformation principally in the sphere of history and political ideology.

The development that changed the Roman emperor from a first magistrate into a god and from a god into the godlike protector of the Christian Church has been traced, by Alfoeldi and others, in the sphere of imperial ceremonial and attire and in connection with the gradual adaptation of these to Christian symbolism. It would be surprising if the same change were not reflected in the style of imperial art inasmuch as that art was deliberately used for purposes of ideological propaganda. The so-called decadence of classical art is in fact the destruction of the Hellenistic canons of representation by the older, antinaturalistic mode of pictorial expression. Earlier Roman art was realistic and descriptive, consistent with its themes and purposes which, in the public realm, called for visual documentation of historical events and for illusionism satisfying the demands of luxury in the private sphere. After the third century this artistic tradition was discarded. Art adopted frontality and symmetry; it arranged human figures and differentiated their sizes, not in order to record physical fact but in order to convey metaphysical values and distinctions of hierarchical rank. The emperor appears no more as a *primus inter pares* in these compositions than he does in the political thought of the period. He has become the awesome embodiment of superhuman authority. And the entire art of the period imparts a curiously dualistic way of viewing things; natural appearance is distorted by an abstract interpretation of symbolic significance.

This profound change, though its roots can be traced back farther, conquers the art of the Empire under Constantine the Great. Now we might explain this stylistic metamorphosis as rhetoric in view of the public purpose of the political and religious monuments erected by Constantine. The strident, oversimplified, and overexplicit language they speak is the idiom of the political speech, slogan, and poster. Political rhetoric always leads to abstraction and distortion, to the highly emotional interpretation of facts rather than to their accurate description. However, political purpose alone does not create a new style, to wit the abortive attempts in this direction undertaken by the totalitarian dictatorships. It is the message Constantine meant to convey that accounts for the new style.

It is significant that the emotions Constantinian art evokes are emotions that really belong not in the political but in the religious sphere—emotions of awe and reverence, a feeling of the observer's insignificance compared to the majesty of the person or symbol depicted, a sense of the mystical source of power. An appeal to these emotions would have been out of tune with the sober, matter-of-fact spirit of the earlier phases of the Empire. But it conveys admirably the Empire's gradual transformation into a religious institution. The change appears, most surprisingly perhaps, in architecture. The Christian basilica almost certainly owes its origin to Constantine's directives. Its likeliest model is the throne-basilica which existed in nearly every imperial palace. Constantine chose this model deliberately. He wanted to convey in the symbolic language of architecture the full meaning of his momentous decision to transfer his power over the Eternal City to the Christian Church or, as he saw it, to Christ. That, put in oversimplified terms, is how the Christian basilica came into existence. But the traditional structure of the Roman civil basilica, as its purpose ceased to be secular and became esoteric, gradually underwent a complete change of style. It could be shown that the same dualistic and symbolizing world view that is reflected in a Constantinian sculpture or mosaic also transformed the style of the Roman basilica until even the last architectural detail of the Christian edifice became the mysterious, seemingly disembodied, symbol of supernatural reality.

What is quite clear, then, is that the artistic revolution of the fourth century was caused not by political motivations but by a profound transformation of outlook that Constantine the Great recognized, utilized, and satisfied with uncanny ability in the political realm and to which his architects, sculptors, and painters gave expression in the field of art.

This impression is confirmed by yet another interpretation of the end of classical art. In an essay on "Plotinus and the sources of medievil art," A. Grabar has argued, with a great deal of plausibility, that many, if not all, decisive elements that we identify with medieval art—the elimination of space and volume, the frontality and shadowless luminosity of figures—have curious parallels in the metaphysics of Plotinus. In his system pure form is comprehended if depth and volume are discarded as belonging to matter and if the distortions wrought by perspective, distance, and the shading of an object are seen as belonging to the category of the contingent. Of course, Grabar does not suggest that after the third century artists found in Plotinus the metaphysical inspiration for their style. Styles can only rarely be linked with specific philosophical systems (the art of Michelangelo being a case in point). It would be more correct to say that the dualism, the preoccupation with transcendental reality that we meet in Plotinus' thought pervaded the entire age, and it is this insight into the ideological situation that actually helps us to see also the political and artistic events of the time in their proper perspective.

Sociological and Economic Factors

The role of the first of these has already been discussed in the case of Byzantine art. An even better example is furnished by Roman architecture. Designed for the easy assembly rather than the artful execution of individual parts, it demanded much physical strength but little skill on the part of the workers. It would not be altogether false to call Roman architecture an architecture of forced labor. Just the opposite is true for Gothic. The exquisite precision of its vaults attests a level of skilled workmanship unsurpassed in the history of architecture. It is not surprising to find the medieval mason esteemed and fairly prosperous, trained for a profession that required not only craftsmanship but also knowledge and artistic talent to an extent that rendered it possible for him eventually to rise to the position of architect. However, the development of the medieval mason's skill and hence of his social position may also have been influenced by economic factors. In the architectural budget of the Middle Ages the cost of transporting building materials was the largest item. This made the saving of building material wherever possible a necessity, a fact that is hardly unrelated to the magnificent economy of material in the

Gothic architectural system and to the extraordinarily high standard of workmanship without which that system could not have been effected.

The Artist's Materials

The importance of this factor need not be stressed. The geological deposits of the Île de France yielded a limestone at once light and resilient, qualities that rendered possible the reduction of architecture to the structural skeleton so typical of French Gothic. In near-by England, where the French model was eagerly received, the continued use of rubble construction made English Gothic into something very different from its French parent.

Yet, we must not exaggerate the influence of materials upon the development of styles. In our time the invention and use of new building materials, especially steel, have certainly brought about an architectural revolution. But the new materials can hardly be considered the only cause of this revolution. At any rate, the curious fact remains that traditional architecture in stone had exhausted its creative potentialities long before the new architecture came into existence. A radically new departure was demanded by architects and critics, and it was this esthetic demand that was satisfied by means of metal construction.

Technical Knowledge

It seems very doubtful whether either the limitations or the possibilities of technical knowledge have had much influence upon the vitality of art. Our own unlimited power over the materials at our disposal seems to stifle rather than inspire artistic productivity, while during the truly creative periods of art crudeness of tools never prevented man from realizing his vision. We cannot even say that technical changes have ever been causes of a new style, since no artist conceives his artistic vision other than in terms of the materials and techniques that happen to be at his disposal. Where we can trace the parallel development of an art and of the technical knowledge required for its execution, technical knowledge appears as the instrument not the cause of stylistic development. Thus the science of statics developed not before but after the Gothic cathedrals, though the architects' needs and insights may have helped develop it. Again, the stained-glass windows of the twelfth and thirteenth centuries exhibit a relatively simple straightforward design that one may well connect with the crude method of cutting glass by means of the red-hot iron then in use. After the diamond came into use as a cutting tool in the fourteenth century, design became more subtle and contours described flowing, often complicated, lines. But we would not speak of progress. The vigorous designs of the older windows are perfectly attuned to the Romanesque style of the period and express perfectly the experience which the artist wanted to convey. The later windows tell us something entirely different, something no one would claim is more important, more moving, or more beautiful than the message of their predecessors. And no one would claim that the possibilities offered by the new tool were responsible for the new style, since the new style appeared at the same time in all the other artistic mediums of "flamboyant" Gothic. To our own eyes the early glass appears even more beautiful than that produced in subsequent epochs, and we even know that this superiority is due to the perfection of a coloring technique—the "marbling" of colored into white materials. But this technical accomplishment was discarded or gradually forgotten in later periods as though it had outserved its function along with the artistic style that had seized upon it as its means of expression.

Tradition

The four factors mentioned in the preceding paragraphs are all modified and controlled by tradition. In the life of cultures, as in the life of art, tradition exerts at once a retardatory and a fertilizing influence. We have noted the impact of available building materials upon the divergent developments of French and English architecture. Perhaps even more important was the national tradition which in England preserved certain constant architectural features from Saxon times to the end of the Middle Ages and beyond and thus prevented a complete adaptation of French Gothic. Or, take another example. Michelangelo's exact contemporary in Germany was Riemenschneider, in his own way nearly as great a sculptor as the Florentine. The immense difference between their two styles is to a considerable extent due to the difference in the materials used—marble in one case, wood in the other. Yet this is not the primary reason for the difference in style. The respective styles of the two sculptors grew out of traditions that called for mediums of expression as different as marble and wood. Woelfflin has described the difference between Mediterranean and North European art. The southern artist is basically a sculptor. Even when he paints, he seeks to convey the volume of clearly defined bodies. The northern artist, even if he is a sculptor, thinks basically in terms of line and linear rhythm; his preferred medium is the drawing. If he turns to wood, it is not only because other material is less readily available but also because the grain of wood enables him to be a "draftsman" even as a sculptor, guiding his hand to produce forms that seem to be all movement and growth in the playful restlessness of lines. The Italian sculptor, on the other hand, would find his vision impeded rather than served by wood; he of necessity turns to marble.

Traditions such as these are deep rooted and long lived. They may be regional or national; a recent book by N. Pevsner seeks to uncover the "Englishness of English art." And such traditions can obstruct all other influences. During the sixteenth century German art used many classical features imported from Italy. But it remained emphatically and unmistakably German and is in essence more closely akin to German works of the eighth or the eighteenth century than it is to sixteenth-century Italian art. Tradition, we might say, is the matrix in which all other cultural influences are gathered, appropriated, and recast. And who can tell whether even the great artistic innovations are possible without tradition? To cite Gothic once again: Its grand theme, luminosity, is one of the most original inventions in the history of art; it is moreover an invention responding directly to the metaphysics of "illumination" that stirred the minds of theologians in twelfth-century France. Yet ideas alone could not have provoked the "discovery" of the art of the stained-glass window. What mattered was that this art was traditionally French, having been cherished in France for centuries before the birth of Gothic—an artistic potential preserved by tradition until the propitious moment that allowed all the esthetic possibilities of stained glass to unfold.

Art within the Cultural Climate

I have indicated some, out of a great variety, of the influences upon which the existence of art and the physiognomy of style depend. These forces in their totality constitute what may be called the "cultural climate," and we may ask which kind of climate artistic growth requires. The answer can at best be only tentative.

As regards political structure, monarchies or aristocracies appear at first sight most favorable to the arts. As one looks at the European past, one might recall Walt Whitman's view that not one among the great art works received from the ages is anything but "a denial and insult to democracy." The advantages of the monarchy are obvious in this regard; great artistic projects require the accumulated wealth and effort—sometimes over a span of generations—that autocratic regimes can most easily muster. Also, the monarchical institution is rooted in the "poetic" world view that, as we have seen, nourishes art. Yet, the prodigious artistic achievements of the ancient and the Renaissance city, of the medieval commune, of Dutch bourgeois culture during the seventeenth century should guard us against one-sided conclusions. And the rigidity, the academic flavor of court art have often proved stifling to talent and taste where conditions of political freedom have not. Perhaps the happiest political constellation, also so far as the arts are concerned, is the *governo misto,* that blend of authority and freedom that seems throughout the ages to have coincided with the classical moments of art.

What is true for politics is equally true for the realm of ideas. Where myth or theology dominates the arts, the rigidity of the icon results. At the opposite extreme, where freedom is based only upon agnosticism, stands the deterioration into the merely whimsical.

The most important prerequisite for a significant development of the arts seems to be the city. Village cultures, peasants, nomads, hunters, and seafaring peoples have hardly ever produced more than marginal art, adornments—often of extraordinarily high quality—of utensils, tools, weapons. This is true also for the world described by Homer. Even early Irish book illumination, though the work of monks, drew its formal repertoire from Celtic ornament and belongs in the artistic category here described. The city, on the other hand, offers tradition, social stability, and cultural cohesion and homogeneity yet at the same time the free exchange of ideas, techniques, and tastes.

Art seems to require all of these. The hereditary stability of wealth and, resting on this material basis, a similar continuity of social distinctions create the demands of luxury, taste, and ostentation—demands that, when steady in quantity and fairly predictable (conservative) in quality, call into existence a highly skilled class of craftsmen, artisans, and artists. The more widely distributed, sociologically speaking, such demand for art, the better for all. During the periods of artistic efflorescence the arts were appreciated by almost everyone, not by a small elite only. Neither the ancient nor the modern metropolis—Imperial Rome no more than New York or perhaps even contemporary Paris—fits the foregoing description. The popu-

lation—cosmopolitan, rapidly changing, and without any community of tradition—lacks precisely that homogeneity of cultural tradition so characteristic of the ancient as of the medieval city. In the
metropolis strangely hybrid art forms develop under the impact of
contrasting influences, to say nothing of the vulgarity of industrialized art production at low cost thrown on the market in modern
Milan and Chicago as in ancient Alexandria.

Prosperity and security do not seem to vouchsafe a vigorous artistic life. Burckhardt's radical skepticism in this regard is hard to re-
fute. While the opulence and peace of the Roman Empire and of
the reign of Victoria produced little more than uninspired medioc-
rity, the grandeur of Greek art followed upon the national peril and
material exhaustion of the Persian wars and the golden age of Byzantine art mellowed in the midst of Justinian's "Gothic war."

The Evaluation of the Arts and the Cultural Process

One question seems to remain unsolved. In the first two sections I
tried to show the connection between world views—as the foci of cultures—and styles and hence the close parallel between the cultural
process and the general evolution of the arts. But in the third and
fourth sections it was suggested that styles are created by the complex
interplay of material and intellectual factors. Does not that variety
of forces which—in that peculiar configuration at least—exists only at
a given historical moment render impossible that steady, consistent
process of evolution that we noticed in the sequences of world views
and styles?

The contradiction does not exist in fact. World views represent the
boundaries within which cultural and artistic processes unfold, but
within these boundaries a rich variety of patterns is possible. One
may certainly study the evolution of art or the structure of styles
without reference to the cultural framework. Woelfflin's categories
are a case in point. One may even maintain that there are stylistic
cycles within each culture and that the arts always pass from a "renaissance" to a "baroque" phase and so on; this theory, however, does
not invalidate the significance of world views as the encompassing
panorama to which stylistic change is attuned and without which
such change would remain incomprehensible.

Constantinian art may once more serve as an example. To students
of this art it seemed at first as though the long, steady evolution of
antique art had suddenly been cut off, that unpredictable political

and ideological schemes, to some extent even the will of a single individual, had created a new style. But upon close inspection it was
realized that the single and singular events of Constantine's reign
have themselves to be seen as parts of a much wider landscape. The
arts, the statecraft, the metaphysical thought of the age all blended
into one universal pattern. Constantine, though he considered himself the playwright of the drama, was really only its principal actor
and skillful stage manager. What was it that rendered the stylistic
change in the fine arts so radical, so unexpected that we may rightly
speak of a stylistic revolution?

The answer is that the whole culture and world view of the epoch
underwent a turning-back, a revolution in the true sense. It was
again Vico who first described the end of antiquity as a retrogression,
a return, as he saw it, to a "poetic" culture. And this interpretation
—whatever one may think of the general theory of cultural cycles—
seems to be the only one to do justice to the new primitivism to
which art returned at the dawn of the Middle Ages.

What renders the example so interesting—one might say, a test case
of the view proposed here—is that it shows with particular clarity
how a given style (in this case that of the early 4th century of our
era) is being created out of an interplay of innumerable and seemingly purely accidental forces; yet, as we watch these forces at play,
their movements turn out to be neither free nor haphazard but
blending into the powerful pattern of a profound cultural transformation. The resulting style is the physiognomy of that transformation.

XI

Islam: Its Inherent Power of Expansion and Adaptation

By G. E. VON GRUNEBAUM

The spectacular success of the Arab Muslims in establishing an empire by means of a small number of campaigns against the great powers of the day has never ceased to stimulate the wonderment and the admiration of the Muslim world and Western scholarship. The survival of Arab-Muslim dominance, in fact its solidification after the first three or four generations had passed, does not seem to have impressed the observers as requiring an explanation. It is the causes of the political decay of the caliphate that have attracted attention. And yet, when the history of the Muslim state is compared with that of other empires which before or after the coming of Islam controlled the Middle East, it is the persistence of the Muslim political community and the growth of a Muslim civilizational area expanding in the face of political fragmentation that emerge as phenomena peculiar to the Islamic development and as such call for consideration.

The survival of the Muslim state after the explosive *élan* of the origins had spent itself, confronted as the state was by unsympathetic neighbors, supported by nothing more than a militant minority within its borders, and engaged in a constant struggle against the weaknesses and inefficiencies of its obsolescent organization, cannot be attributed to the scientific or technological superiority of the rulers. What scientific and technological superiority they came to possess was acquired slowly and painfully after the great battles had been won and the community had demonstrated its staying power. It is open to question whether the Muslims ever actually did surpass the military technology of their permanent enemies, the Byzantines.

The argument could be proposed that the power constellation of the decisive centuries during which the Muslim community took root throughout the Middle East was such that the caliphate was never seriously endangered by an outside government bent on conquest or reconquest. This argument may well be sustained and yet ruled inadequate to account for the stabilization of Muslim unity. For it was not, to point to an obvious contrasting instance, an outside force that shattered the two Mongol empires of the thirteenth/ fourteenth and fourteenth/fifteenth centuries; they fell apart for lack of numbers, yes, but mostly for want of a cohesiveness that would have been strong enough to outweigh the disintegrative effect on them of the higher civilization, the more complex ideologies of their subjects. The Arab Muslims, on the other hand, used the superior achievements of the conquered to debarbarize and amalgamate the alien culture under their leadership.

With more justice it could be claimed that the Muslim victors did not in fact have to contend with an ideology of an appeal comparable to that of their own message. Zoroastrianism had passed its missionary phase; though it was the official religion of the Sasanians to the end, it had had to fight formidable opposition in its homeland and was besides too intimately identified with a specific culture area to offer effective resistance to the potential universalism of Islam. Judaism, then as later, seemed to its followers and to the outside world restricted to social groups whose stability, not to speak of their history, would lead to their being considered not merely a community but a people apart. Manicheanism proved attractive to an urban intelligentsia that was irritated by the comparative crudeness of Arab-Muslim thinking and resented the assumption of Arab superiority on which much of the contemporary social and political life was based. But, as in an earlier battle in which dualism had succumbed to monism, Islam pushed Manicheanism aside even more decisively than the Christians had defeated the Gnostic separatists and the Manicheans themselves.

Christianity itself, separated from its intellectual centers by political and, increasingly, by linguistic and cultural boundaries, divided into competing denominations reflecting competing ethnic and cultural aspirations, was in a sense discredited by the subordinate position of the Christian communities in relation to the Muslim rulers. Though retaining recognition as the theologically strongest and, as a matter of fact, the sole dangerous adversary of the Muslim faith, it had been marked by the Koranic revelation as obsolete while the heart-pieces of its doctrine and the concept of man which this doctrine presupposed had been branded in the Koran as errors and fictions far removed from the message and intentions of Jesus. The

shunting-off of Christianity into the ghettos of denominational isolation effectively prevented any specifically Christian intellectual
movement from taking the lead in the spiritual debates of the Muslim world and gradually imposed on the Christian communities, in
the sphere of cultural creativeness, an unmistakable aura of parochial
irrelevancy.

The survival and consolidation of the rule imposed on vast and
highly heterogeneous territories by comparatively small Arab armies
are inseparable from the fact that those armies were serving a distinctive ideology. It has often been pointed out, and correctly so, that the
overwhelming majority of the conquerors were not primarily actu-
ated by religious zeal or that at least the bulk of the Arab soldiery
had a very poor idea of the nature of the ideology whose paramountcy
they were striving to establish. However, their lack of commitment to
Islam does not invalidate the fact that this ideology constituted the
raison d'être of the organization they fought to make powerful, just
as indifference and even hostility to the communist ideology on the
part of Chinese or Viet-Minh soldiers prevent them, by the very fact
that they bear arms in its service, from upholding a government
whose *raison d'être* is the communist ideology. It is true, too, that
the conquerors tended to look on Islam as an Arab affair and a justification of Arab privilege; but, while the Arabs have maintained a
"special position" within Islam, it is no less true—and perhaps one of
the decisive factors when it comes to accounting for the enduring
character of the structure—that there was nothing in the fundamentals of the new religion that militated against its interpretation as a
universally valid message which could be accepted by all mankind.
An ideology provides the hard shell without which no social body
can survive for long; the more complex the social body, the greater
the political strains to which it is exposed, the more clearly the function of the ideology as a primary means of cohesiveness, as the fountainhead of any practical measures to insure it, emerges. An ideology
—articulated as creed, law, rules of social conduct—often outlives the
political organization that carried it forward, developed and imposed
it. To mention but one example, the customary law, codified as the
Yasā, long survived the Mongol empire that put it into practice beyond the area of its origin.

The Muslim elite was, in many respects, distinguished by its openness to foreign cultural influences. In matters of administration and
legal practice the following of foreign, that is to say non-Arab and

"non-Muslim" models, was unavoidable, their adjustment to the maturing pride and clarified self-vision of the ruling community a gradual process. In many cases assimilation by means of Arabization of Byzantine or Sasanian governmental procedures and integration in the Muslim system by superimposition of an Islamic emblem or motto on the traditional techniques (as in the early development of caliphal coinage) were found a sufficient method of appropriation. The omnipresence, in the minds of the spokesmen of the community, of the fundamentals of the ideology and, stronger still, of the need to relate the total institutional framework within which the community was to live to this ideology resulted early in that peculiar "Islamic" patina which any cultural element, however "un-Islamic" its origin, received upon acceptance into the way of life of the *umma Muḥammadiyya.*

Acceptability of an ideology to diverse groups beyond the circle of adherents as a response to whose existential needs it came into being has an intellectual as well as a sociological aspect. The new system must prove itself attractive through the intellectual solutions it proposes and through the social order which it seems to presuppose or to demand. (It hardly needs to be stressed that what is here called the intellectual appeal of an ideology is inextricably commingled with its appeal to the emotions.) The fundamentals of the Islamic ideology, as they became accessible to non-Arab peoples, demonstrated precisely this double appeal. The nature of this appeal and therewith the causes of its effectiveness are in large measure open to analysis.

The Islamic message has been characterized by A. L. Kroeber as a reduction and a simplification of the religious concepts of the contemporary faiths, particularly of Christianity. This judgment has its merits when one adopts an ecumenical approach; viewed from the Arabian standpoint, the preaching of Muḥammad marked unmistakably a step forward toward religious maturity and intellectual sophistication. Yet it remains true that the Koranic revelation concentrates on relatively few motifs, all of them clearly of intense concern to the Middle Eastern populations of the seventh century, both inside and outside the Arabian Peninsula. There is Revelation through the Chosen Spokesman—in operational terms, the assurance of unimpeachable authority and the security of direct divine guidance of the community; there are monotheism and the Book—concepts whose acknowledgment brought the Arabs onto the level of religious thinking that their future subjects had reached many a century before and without which there would not have existed as much as the possibility of discourse nor the enjoyment of intellectual respectability by the conquerors. (It must be realized as well that reliance on revelation and a Book tends everywhere to establish the same methods of argumentation, the same criteria of acceptability and, incidentally, to say the least, similar theological or epistemological problems—one more factor in creating a climate in which shared assumptions can advance a new message.) A Day of Judgment on which sinners would be relegated to the Fire and the pious admitted to Paradise coupled with the apprehension of the impending end of the world had long formed a cluster of motifs of unusual emotional effectiveness.

The discarding of the intricacies of trinitarianism, the harkingback to docetism that had, among Christian sectarians, often been the recourse of a certain primitive rationalism, the elimination of the idea of original sin and the burden of an inevitable inherited corruption that was yet the faithful's personal responsibility, the more optimistic outlook on human nature as needful of guidance rather than redemption and hence the discouragement of the more extreme forms of asceticism (which has, however, been overstated by interpreters, both Muslim and Western[1])—in short, Islam's more realistic but also more vulgar adjustment to the world as it is—assisted in presenting the untutored with a system of beliefs that satisfied his primary religious concerns and relieved him of the typically Christian paradox of being in, but not of, the world and, equally comfortingly, of involvement with doctrinal subtleties that he had only too often come to know through the political consequences of their adoption or rejection. With the different concept of man's condition and of his contractual status relation (*ḥukm*) to the Majesty of the Lord, the mysteries of man's redemption by a suffering God-man, God's son and yet not a second deity, mysteries whose articulation had led astray so many, lost their vital significance; the absoluteness of the divine will—for the Islamic God is first and foremost will, apprehensible through the experience of His Majesty—made obedience the gate to rescue, a gate not too difficult to unlock.

The absence of a clerical hierarchy gave the believer relief from fiscal oppression and a certain social discrimination. Whether or not

[1] Cf. the interesting discussion by René Brunel, *Le monachisme errant dans l'Islam: Sīdi Heddi et les Heddāwa* (Paris, 1955) pp. 7–15.

the Islamic message would have been as attractive without its prestige as the faith of the ruling group is an idle question, for without the military victories of the Arabs the message would hardly have had an opportunity to compete in a sufficiently wide area with the existing religious organizations. In any event, what must be stressed is the fact that the Islamic message did contain an overwhelming proportion of those religious motifs that appealed to the religious consciousness of the conquered.

Islam's attitude toward conversion must be considered attractive to the outsider on both the ideological and the sociological plane. Ideologically, Islam discourages compulsory conversion. The appeal it hopes to exercise consists, one might say, in its existence, in the availability of ultimate truth made visible through the life of the community in which it is embodied, and of course—and here the sociological aspect comes to the fore—in the possibility that conversion presents of full participation in the activities of the politically and socially leading group. Islam requires control of the body politic for the Muslims; it does not require bringing every subject of the caliph, every human soul, into the fold and thus eschews the ambiguous successes of persecution. Conversion is desirable from the religious, but not necessarily from a governmental, point of view. In any case, however, it is made easy. There is no period of preparation through which the candidate to community membership must go, no examination which he must pass. His unilateral testimonial to the truth of the basic verities of monotheism and revelation through the historical person of Muḥammad ibn ʿAbdallāh of Mecca, the last and the most perfect of the prophets, suffices as credential. This commitment once made in due form is binding on the declarant and, in contradistinction for instance to Christian sentiment, on the receiving community as well. Contact with the Holy Book and systematic instruction in the faith are to follow rather than to precede that commitment to the community. Affiliation with the community is expressed primarily in action—in the common performance of the prescribed practices and in the adoption of a way of life. It is orthopraxy that matters most of all, not orthodoxy.[2] The comparative indifference to purity of doctrine and even to accurate conformance with standard practice has made possible, with relatively little strain, the identification with the community of very disparate social bod-

---

[2] To borrow the terminology of W. C. Smith, *Islam in Present History* (Princeton, 1957) p. 20.

ies. The acceptance into Islam of an individual or a group on the basis of declared intention to belong constitutes the premise of Islamic inclusiveness and hence its amazing cross-cultural absorptiveness. "The abstractness of the identification renders possible a sense of belonging together among peoples that in their actual mentality and way of life have very little in common, and that, on the strictly cultural plane, may regard each other with contempt or incomprehension; it has, in later times, also kept alive a sense of super-national values and obligations which national loyalties are apt to obliterate."[3]

The simplest and most effective mechanism for sociological integration into the community was, in the early period, the institution of clientship, *walā'*. To attain full status, not as a believer before God but as an affiliate of the Muslim community, the convert had to win acceptance as client by an Arab tribe or clan. The *maulà* suffered certain social disabilities, but he retained sufficient freedom of action to feel elevated above his earlier status as a protected outsider. While the system seemed devised to perpetuate Arab supremacy in the religious community, it proved to non-Arabs that admittance into the community was possible—an admittance the more complete the more the *maulà* steered clear of political ambitions and was satisfied with influence on a more specifically religious level. In retrospect, it is easy to see that the system had to break down when the numbers of converts increased sharply with the consolidation of Muslim power and especially when whole groups transferred their allegiance to the new religion, aiming more or less consciously at eliminating the racism of the social structure of the *umma.*

The success of the non-Arab converts in winning equality or near-equality with the Arabs—symbolized by the shift from the "Arab" empire of the Umayyads to the "Persian" empire of the 'Abbasids (A.D. 750)—was to set the precedent and the pattern for the absorption of additional populations into the Muslim fold. This divorce from Arab ethnocentrism represented one decisive step in the direction of the implementation of the implied universalism of the Islamic revelation; divorcing the Muslim institution from the tutelage of the Muslim state or states was the next step. It is not that the community ever relinquished the concept of the identity of the religious and the secular; but, under the leadership of the guardians of

[3] This writer's "Reflections on the community aspect of the Muslim identification," in *Proceedings of the International Islamic Colloquium at Lahore, Pakistan, December 28, 1957, to January 8, 1958.*

religious tradition and the exponents of Canon Law, the *umma* established a purely religious and later also a cultural identity which made its spiritual development, internal continuity, and sense of cohesion very nearly independent of the transitory territorial states under whose rule the sectional communities were to find themselves. Not infrequently, a state advanced the domain of Islam into as yet unbelieving lands; but conversion, although often achieved initially by military pressure, meant affiliation with the timeless far-flung *umma*, of which the particular body politic whose subjects the converts were to become was nothing but an accidentally delimited segment whose existence per se was relevant for the community at large only in so far as it enabled the faithful under its sway to lead the correct life, to safeguard and perhaps to expand the boundaries of the autonomous *umma*.

With the development in the tenth to twelfth centuries of Persian as the second culture language, the community's catholicity was further strengthened, even though Arabic—the language of revelation and later of its exposition and its unfolding into law and theology—maintained not only a position of prestige but also fulfilled the function of a link, a means of communication, a repository of the traditions and the memories which the community accepted as their shared past. So it could truly be said that "knowledge of Arabic is religion,"[4] and it becomes understandable that a certain uneasiness persisted as to whether a non-Arab *dhimmī* should be taught the holy language and whether a *dhimmī* born to Arabic should be permitted to teach his mother tongue.

The gradual drifting-away of Canon Law from operational effectiveness, its character as a moral code, a *Pflichtenlehre* (rather than a regulatory code of community relations), called forth by and calling forth the growing encroachment of local custom and governmental decree as directives in most areas of practical living, again fortified the catholicity of the Muslim institution. It did so in two comple-

---

[4] Cf. e.g. A. S. Tritton, *Materials on Muslim Education in the Middle Ages* (London, 1957) p. 131, n. 2. As in a nutshell the increasing credulity and the craving for the miraculous, together with the not too effective resistance of the theologians, can be perceived in the *fatwà* in which Ibn Taimiyyah (d. 1328) rejects the wondrous deeds which the pious ascribed to ʿAlī as inventions; *Majmūʿat fatāwī* (Cairo, 1326/1907–1329/1910) I 310–11, No. 227. The competition between different Muslim lands in regard to their religious rank and the function of the *ʿālim* in stressing the basic equality of the community everywhere is reflected in *fatwà* No. 228 (*ibid.* Vol. I 331) in which Ibn Taimiyyah tries to dispel the notion of his Syrian questioners that divine blessing, *baraka*, consists of seventy-one parts of which but one has been placed in Iraq and the remaining seventy in Syria.

mentary ways. On the one hand, it facilitated the integration into the community of as yet alien communities by allowing them to carry over into their existence as Muslims much of their traditional way of life; on the other hand, it provided the community with a norm that was all the more readily acceptable because there was to a large extent no insistence on full compliance. So the Canon Law became one of the strongest cementing factors among disparate communities that continued much of their customary law. At the same time, however, the sense of unity that permeated the *umma* and that was sufficiently intense to submerge vast ethnic and cultural differences on the level of the ideal and that was thus an indispensable basis of expansion required a certain disregard of the realities of life, psychologically speaking an existence on two levels, an existence in a tension which was never completely to be relieved and which is still an important element in the inner unrest besetting the crucial parts of the Muslim world.

The ability to absorb alien communities into the *umma* without loss of identity is but the counterpart, as it were, of the ability of functional adaptation of religious belief to changing existential needs within the *umma*. This ability, which alone enables a widespread and both ethnically and socially heterogeneous community to outlast historical change, Islam and especially Sunnite Islam has shown to a remarkable degree. That some of the modifications appear not only to the outside observer but to many a learned believer as an abandonment, perhaps even a betrayal, of the blessed origins and the genuine message is only natural. The decisive factor in successful adaptation is, however, not the accuracy in objective and so to speak scholarly terms with which an attempted reinterpretation renders the meaning of founder and sacred text but the conviction it is able to generate in the minds and hearts of the contemporary believers that it answers to their needs as would the founder's words were he still in their midst. The maintenance of a sense of community continuity and of undisturbed relatedness to the same authority *in spiritualibus* is in itself a powerful remedy of collective psychological disturbance, for it offers perspective and precedent and through them the guidance of an explanation and direction regardless of the distortion which the memory of the group may wreak on its past.

The principal means of adapting the changing existential needs to which Islam, as other faiths, has resorted is the integration into "orthodox" belief of religious motifs that the original message had rejected or left to one side. Shīʿism (which became definitely sectarian only in some of its more "extremist" versions and precisely because of "exaggerated" recourse to the motif) almost immediately reactivated the motif of the God-man, of the leader from the Prophet's line who differed in substance from the rest of mankind and continued that direct contact with Divinity that orthodoxy asserted had ended with Muḥammad's death. The Islamic message was most anxious to reserve creativeness and mastery over nature to God alone; where miracles did occur, they were done by permission or at the behest of the Lord in order to advance His plans for mankind. But no man, however pious and however great, had of himself the power to work miracles; and the reverencing of human beings, which could only too easily shade off into worship of the creature, was both blasphemous and absurd. The Prophet himself was careful to insist on his humanity. But the traditions and needs of the converts throughout the Middle East demanded otherwise. And after a prolonged theological battle, in which the principal issue would seem to have been to preserve the superiority of the prophetic office over that of the saint and the secondary the avoidance of an imitation of non-Islamic custom, the consensus of the learned yielded to the yearnings of the untaught. Not only was sainthood admitted into Islam, but much thought came to be given to its characteristics and the modality of its operation through a hierarchy of elect. Not only was the extra-human uniqueness of the Prophet accepted, but he was allowed to become the emotional center of worship.

The only time perhaps when Sunnite Islam was faced with a serious threat of disintegration from within (in conjunction with the political threat of Shiʿite domination of the *umma Muḥammadiyya*) was during the eleventh century when not only was Sunnite theology put on the defensive, but indifference and a certain disillusionment with Sunnite religiosity was spreading among the masses. It is quite possible that, without the political support extended to the Sunnite caliphate by the Seljuq Turks, internal reform would have had no chance to succeed. At any rate, the orthodox leadership was ready to accept a far-reaching reorientation which secured to mystical piety an increasingly dominant place in the religious life of the community and laid the groundwork for the growth of those religious brotherhoods which were to become the true center and repository of the "living" faith throughout the domain of Islam. To accept the piety of the people and its antirational premises and expectations meant, in the long run, a lowering of the theological level and a withdrawal from those philosophical and scientific pursuits that had been one of the glories of the community. The retrenchment of "official learning" to essentially Koran, Tradition, and the Law represents another concession to the needs of the times that may be interpreted as complementary to the emotional surrender to the more popular currents of piety. It was also in tune with the sentiment that people and times inevitably decline, a process to be reversed only at the onset of the "end time."[5]

Acceptance of a mystical religiosity did not mean removal of conflicts between the representatives of Islam as a religion of legal and theological learning and the representatives of Islam as a means for guiding souls toward the unitary experience, between the *ʿulamāʾ* and the *mashāʾikh* of the *ṭarīqāt*. Nor did it bridge the chasm between the religious ideas and the mores of rustic and peripheral groups and the norms upheld by the learned who obtained their education overwhelmingly in urban centers. The problem of the admissibility of the untutored marginal populations (that were, as in the case of the Berbers of southern Morocco, both numerous and politically of great moment) to full Islamic status, so to speak, was common to most parts of the Islamic world, as was the function of saints and brotherhoods in mediating between the conflicting concepts of what constitutes Islam and hence in safeguarding the catholicity of Sunnism. One may perhaps go so far as to say that the ubiquitousness of the contrasts between the Islam of the common man and the Islam of the elite constituted a unifying link between the several Muslim communities, since it created comparable conditions and a kindred outlook among the recognized spokesmen of the *umma* in widely separated lands.

The Law itself, however, contains what in theory at least must be considered the most potent means of self-adaptation, by recognizing the consensus of the competent as one of its foundations. This *ijmāʿ* of the local learned is neither postulative nor normative; it is merely verifying, taking note that an agreement on a certain point actually does exist and by doing so making the material content of the agree-

---

5 Cf. Ibn al-ʿImād, *Shadharāt al-dhahab* (Cairo, 1350/1931–1351/1932) V 144; Tritton, *op. cit.* pp. 114 and 188. The outlook is typified in the remark of ʿUmar ibn Khalda, judge in Medina (82–87/701–6): "I still knew people who acted and did not talk while nowadays people talk and do not act"; cf. Wakīʿ (d. 918), *Akhbār al-Quḍāt*, ed. ʿA. M. al-Marāghī (Cairo, 1366/1947) I 132.

ment binding on the community. It is true that the *ijmāᶜ* has assumed a self-limiting character in that the creative initiative of the jurisprudent has increasingly been viewed as restricted by the previously accepted opinions of the leading authority of the school or *madhhab* with which he is identified. Yet to make the *ijmāᶜ* an active instrument of adjustment or even a tool of planned change, nothing is needed but a shift in public opinion sufficiently marked to compel its formal recognition by the learned in terms of a restatement of the nature of the consensus (which, were it to come, would unquestionably be experienced and presented as the discovery of its true and original character).

A community's law is, in the last analysis, precisely as elastic and adaptive as the community would have it, its criteria of admission as catholic or exclusivistic as its identification implies. In Sunnite Islam, the community at large has, for many a century, been more cautious in putting the dissenter (who in the Muslim environment is often more significantly recognized by his practice than by his creed) outside the pale than the lawyer-theologians who act as its spokesmen and, in a sense, its executives. In the general consciousness, the intention to be and remain a Muslim counts for more than the failings that are observable in its implementation. The concern for the grandeur of Islam, which is inseparable from its unity, overrides the concern for uniformity in detail of practice and doctrine. The adaptability of Islam to changing and especially to "moral" conditions has become a prominent element in the believers' outlook on their faith and a painful problem to those Muslims who are troubled by the actual history of their community since the high Middle Ages. To some extent it can be held that the belief in its adaptability guarantees this adaptability even though the "natural" tendency in a community as tradition-conscious as the Islamic is toward limiting the actual adjustment to the ineluctable minimum. Here, as everywhere in societal life, the primacy of the collective aspiration must be realized and with it the superiority of a religious culture to a merely ethnic or political affiliation as the foundation of a social structure which is capable of expansion and continued existence in history.

PRINTED IN U.S.A.